Annual Editions: Anthropology, 42/e

Elvio Angeloni

http://create.mheducation.com

ISBN-10: 126018031X ISBN-13: 9781260180312

1 2 3 4 5 6 QVS 22 21 20 19 18

Contents

Detailed Table of Contents

Unit 3: The Organization of Society and Culture

Unit 4: Other Families, Other Ways

Unit 5: Gender and Status

Dethroning Miss America, Roxane Gay, *Smithsonian*, 2018
The Miss America pageant has never been a progressive event, but in 1968, it sparked a feminist revolt. Today, women and their allies are marching in the nation's capital and in cities around the world "to reaffirm women's rights, and the rights of all marginalized people as human rights. And, for the first time, men are facing real consequences for their predation. The connective tissue between 1968 and now is stronger than ever, vibrantly alive."

Me Too Anthropology, Elizabeth Beckmann, *Culture and Capitalism: A Sussex University Anthropology Blog*, 2017
As an anthropologist considers her reluctance to disclose her own experiences of sexual abuse, she reflects on the fact that she has elicited the same kinds of stories from informants while doing fieldwork. Even as she realizes that keeping traumatic events to oneself is an absolutely valid coping mechanism, she also has come to understand that anthropology and anthropologists can share the weight of such a burden and give voice to those that still feel unable to do this for themselves.

What About *The Breakfast Club*? Molly Ringwald, *The New Yorker*, 2018
How can revisiting a coming of age film from the eighties spark thoughtful conversations in the age of #MeToo?

Unit 6: Religion, Belief, and Ritual

Thoughtlessly Thoughtless, Graham Lawton, *New Scientist*, 2017
The human tendency to engage in cognitive shortcuts results in the belief in "folk theories," such as the notion that the sun moves across the sky or that rocks are there for animals to scratch themselves. Even though such theories get knocked back by education, they never go away because scientific thinking is hard-won—a matter of overcoming first impressions, snap judgments and our tendency to favor the status quo. In other words, we dislike ambiguity, cognitive complexity, and the burden of thinking analytically.

The Adaptive Value of Religious Ritual, Richard Sosis, *American Scientist,* 2004
Rituals promote group cohesion by requiring members to engage in behavior that is too costly to fake. Groups that do so are more likely to attain their collective goals than the groups whose members are less committed.

Understanding Islam, Kenneth Jost, *CQ Researcher,* 2005
As the world's second largest religion after Christianity, Islam teaches piety, virtue, and tolerance. Yet, with the emphasis of some Islamist's on a strong relationship between religion and state, and with an increasing number of Islamic militants calling for violence against the West, communication and mutual understanding are becoming more important than ever.

We Were Different, Julia G. Young, *Commonweal,* 2018
Today's immigrants are not the same as those that came from Southern and Eastern Europe 100 years ago and earlier. Even the Catholics coming to America in more recent times are different from those who came before. And, yet, differences in language, culture and economic circumstances continue to account for recurring themes of exclusion and marginalization that echo the past.

Reputation Is Everything: Unearthing Honour Culture in America, Emma Young, *New Scientist*, 2016
Anthropologists have found "honor cultures" to be characterized by a deep concern for reputation and a sense of being duty-bound to retaliate against anything perceived as a slight. In contrast with "dignity cultures," such societies tend to be misogynistic, violent and retaliatory. In parts of the United States, particularly in the South, such traits are expressed in the objectification of women, lax gun laws, and higher rates of school shooting. As might be expected, "honor cultures develop where there is some degree of economic insecurity and lawlessness.

Losing Our Religion, Graham Lawton, *New Scientist,* 2014
The world is becoming less religious in the formal sense, a trend that seems to be related to prosperity, security, and democracy. Yet, most of those who no longer affiliate with a particular religious institution still subscribe to some form of spiritual belief in a continuing effort to seek the comfort that organized religion provides.

Unit 7: Sociocultural Change

Coming to America, Ann Morse, *State Legislatures*, 2017
Given the persistent focus on illegal immigration in the public dialogue, the author answers such questions as who is coming to America, how do they impact our economy and how are lawmakers responding?

Population Seven Billion, Robert Kunzig, *National Geographic,* 2011
With the world's population rising by several billion from the current seven billion, inevitable questions arise as to how this will impact the quality of life as well as the condition of Planet Earth.

Preface

This edition of *Annual Editions: Anthropology* contains a variety of articles on contemporary issues in social and cultural anthropology. In contrast to the broad range of topics with minimum depth that is typical of standard textbooks, this anthology provides an opportunity to read first-hand accounts by anthropologists of their own research. In allowing scholars to speak for themselves about the issues in which they are experts, we are better able to understand the kinds of questions anthropologists ask, the ways in which they ask them, and how they go about searching for answers. Indeed, where there is disagreement among anthropologists, this format allows the readers to draw their own conclusions. Given the very broad scope of anthropology—in time, space, and subject matter—the present collection of highly readable articles has been selected according to a certain criteria. The articles have been chosen from both professional and nonprofessional publications for the purpose of supplementing standard textbooks that are used in introductory courses. Some of the articles are considered classics in the field, while others have been selected for their timely relevance.

Finally, it should be pointed out that an *Author's Note* is available for some of the classic articles that have been in this book since they were originally published. These updates consist of fresh perspectives on important issues, written by the authors themselves exclusively for this book.

Included in this volume are a number of features that are designed to make it useful for students, researchers, and professionals in the field of anthropology. Each unit is preceded by an overview, which provides a background for informed reading of the articles and emphasizes critical issues. *Learning Outcomes* accompany each article and outline the key concepts that students should focus on as they are reading the material. *Critical Thinking* questions, found at the end of each article, allow students to test their understanding of the key points of the article. The *Internet References* section can be used to further explore the topics online.

Those involved in producing this volume wish to make the next one as useful and effective as possible. Your criticism and advice are always welcome. Any anthology can be improved. This continues to be—annually.

Editor

Elvio Angeloni received his BA from UCLA in 1963, MA in anthropology from UCLA in 1965, and MA in communication arts from Loyola Marymount University in 1976. He has produced several films, including *Little Warrior,* winner of the Cinemedia VI Best Bicentennial Theme, and *Broken Bottles,* shown on PBS. He served as an academic adviser on the instructional television series *Faces of Culture.* He received the Pasadena City College Outstanding Teacher Award in 2006 and has since retired from teaching. He is also the academic editor of *Annual Editions: Physical Anthropology* and co-editor of *Annual Editions: Archaeology.* His primary area of interest has been indigenous peoples of the American Southwest. Contact: evangeloni@gmail.com

Academic Advisory Board

Members of the Academic Advisory Board are instrumental in the final selection of articles for the *Annual Editions* series. Their review of the articles for content, level, and appropriateness provides critical direction to the editor(s) and staff. We think that you will find their careful consideration reflected in this book.

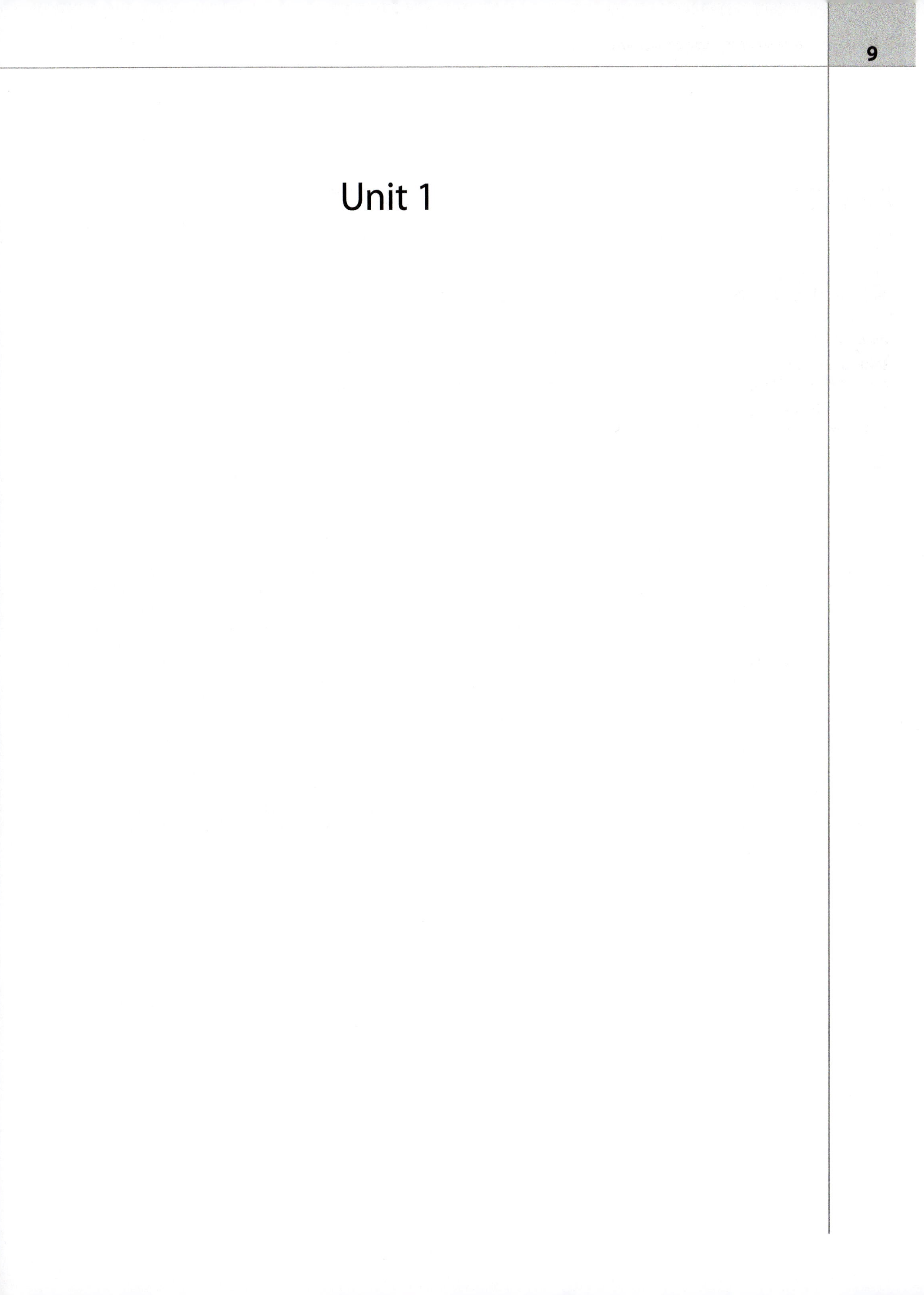

Unit 1

UNIT

Prepared by: Elvio Angeloni

Anthropological Perspectives

For at least a century, the goals of anthropology have been to describe societies and cultures throughout the world and to compare and contrast the differences and similarities among them. Anthropologists study in a variety of settings and situations, ranging from small hamlets and villages to neighborhoods and corporate offices of major urban centers throughout the world. They study hunters and gatherers, peasants, farmers, labor leaders, politicians, and bureaucrats. They examine religious life in Latin America as well as revolutionary movements.

Wherever practicable, anthropologists take on the role of "participant observer." Through active involvement in the life ways of people, they hope to gain an insider's perspective without sacrificing the objectivity of the trained scientist. Sometimes the conditions for achieving such a goal seem to form an almost insurmountable barrier, but anthropologists call on persistence, adaptability, and imagination to overcome the odds against them.

The diversity of focus in anthropology means that it is earmarked less by its particular subject matter than by its perspective. Although the discipline relates to both the biological and social sciences, anthropologists know that the boundaries drawn between disciplines are highly artificial. For example, while in theory it is possible to examine only the social organization of a family unit or the organization of political power in a nation-state, in reality it is impossible to separate the biological from the social, from the economic, from the political. The importance of the cultural aspects of our being can be stated very simply in the anthropology axiom: Biology is not destiny.

One might get the impression while reading about some of the anthropological field experience that the field has had primarily to do with the exotic and the unusual and, therefore, is not particularly relevant to the larger world in which most of us live. On the contrary, much is at stake in our attempts to achieve a more objective understanding of the diversity of peoples' ways. The more we understand why others do as they do, the more we come to appreciate why we are as we are and vice versa. After all, the purpose of anthropology is not only to describe and explain, but also to develop a special vision of the world in which cultural alternatives (past, present, and future) can be measured against one another and used as guides for human action.

Article

Prepared by: Elvio Angeloni

How PTSD Became a Problem Far Beyond the Battlefield

Though only 10 percent of American forces see combat, the U.S. military now has the highest rate of post-traumatic stress disorder in its history.

SEBASTIAN JUNGER

Learning Outcomes

After reading this article, you will be able to:

- Explain, from an evolutionary perspective, why PTSD is exactly the response you want to have when your life is in danger.
- Explain why some people fail to overcome trauma.
- Discuss the biological and social root causes of PTSD and what that implies for a solution.

The first time I experienced what I now understand to be post-traumatic stress disorder, I was in a subway station in New York City, where I live. It was almost a year before the attacks of 9/11, and I'd just come back from two months in Afghanistan with Ahmad Shah Massoud, the leader of the Northern Alliance. I was on assignment to write a profile of Massoud, who fought a desperate resistance against the Taliban until they assassinated him two days before 9/11. At one point during my trip we were on a frontline position that his forces had just taken over from the Taliban, and the inevitable counterattack started with an hour-long rocket barrage. All we could do was curl up in the trenches and hope. I felt deranged for days afterward, as if I'd lived through the end of the world.

By the time I got home, though, I wasn't thinking about that or any of the other horrific things we'd seen; I mentally buried all of it until one day, a few months later, when I went into the subway at rush hour to catch the C train downtown. Suddenly I found myself backed up against a metal support column, absolutely convinced I was going to die. There were too many people on the platform, the trains were coming into the station too fast, the lights were too bright, the world was too loud. I couldn't quite explain what was wrong, but I was far more scared than I'd ever been in Afghanistan.

I stood there with my back to the column until I couldn't take it anymore, and then I sprinted for the exit and walked home. I had no idea that what I'd just experienced had anything to do with combat; I just thought I was going crazy. For the next several months I kept having panic attacks whenever I was in a small place with too many people—airplanes, ski gondolas, crowded bars. Gradually the incidents stopped, and I didn't think about them again until I found myself talking to a woman at a picnic who worked as a psychotherapist. She asked whether I'd been affected by my war experiences, and I said no, I didn't think so. But for some reason I described my puzzling panic attack in the subway. "That's called post-traumatic stress disorder," she said. "You'll be hearing a lot more about that in the next few years."

I had classic short-term (acute) PTSD. From an evolutionary perspective, it's exactly the response you want to have when your life is in danger: you want to be vigilant, you want to react to strange noises, you want to sleep lightly and wake easily, you want to have flashbacks that remind you of the danger, and you want to be, by turns, anxious and depressed. Anxiety keeps you ready to fight, and depression keeps you from being too active and putting yourself at greater risk. This is a universal human adaptation to danger that is common to other mammals as well. It may be unpleasant, but it's preferable to getting eaten. (Because PTSD is so adaptive, many have begun leaving the word "disorder" out of the term to avoid stigmatizing a basically healthy reaction.)

Because PTSD is a natural response to danger, it's almost unavoidable in the short term and mostly self-correcting in the long term. Only about 20 percent of people exposed to trauma react with long-term (chronic) PTSD. Rape is one of the most psychologically devastating things that can happen to a person, for example—far more traumatizing than most military deployments—and, according to a 1992 study published in the *Journal of Traumatic Stress,* 94 percent of rape survivors exhibit signs of extreme trauma immediately afterward. And yet, nine months later 47 percent of rape survivors have recovered enough to resume living normal lives.

Combat is generally less traumatic than rape but harder to recover from. The reason, strangely, is that the trauma of combat is interwoven with other, positive experiences that become difficult to separate from the harm. "Treating combat veterans is different from treating rape victims, because rape victims don't have this idea that some aspects of their experience are worth retaining," says Dr. Rachel Yehuda, a professor of psychiatry and neuroscience and director of traumatic-stress studies at Mount Sinai Hospital in New York. Yehuda has studied PTSD in a wide range of people, including combat veterans and Holocaust survivors. "For most people in combat, their experiences range from the best to the worst of times," Yehuda adds. "It's the most important thing someone has ever done—especially since these people are so young when they go in—and it's probably the first time they're ever free, completely, of their societal constraints. They're going to miss being entrenched in this very important and defining world."

Oddly, one of the most traumatic events for soldiers is witnessing harm to other people—even to the enemy. In a survey done after the first Gulf War by David Marlowe, an expert in stress-related disorders working with the Department of Defense, combat veterans reported that killing an enemy soldier—or even witnessing one getting killed—was more distressing than being wounded oneself. But the very worst experience, by a significant margin, was having a friend die. In war after war, army after army, losing a buddy is considered to be the most distressing thing that can possibly happen. It serves as a trigger for psychological breakdown on the battlefield and readjustment difficulties after the soldier has returned home.

Terrible as such experiences are, however, roughly 80 percent of people exposed to them eventually recover, according to a 2008 study in the *Journal of Behavioral Medicine.* If one considers the extreme hardship and violence of our prehistory, it makes sense that humans are able to sustain enormous psychic damage and continue functioning; otherwise our species would have died out long ago. "It is possible that our common generalized anxiety disorders are the evolutionary legacy of a world in which mild recurring fear was adaptive," writes anthropologist and neuroscientist Melvin Konner, in a collection called *Understanding Trauma.* "Stress is the essence of evolution by natural selection and close to the essence of life itself."

A 2007 analysis from the Institute of Medicine and the National Research Council found that, statistically, people who fail to overcome trauma tend to be people who are already burdened by psychological issues—either because they inherited them or because they suffered trauma or abuse as children. According to a 2003 study on high-risk twins and combat-related PTSD, if you fought in Vietnam and your twin brother did not—but suffers from psychiatric disorders—you are more likely to get PTSD after your deployment. If you experienced the death of a loved one, or even weren't held enough as a child, you are up to seven times more likely to develop the kinds of anxiety disorders that can contribute to PTSD, according to a 1989 study in the *British Journal of Psychiatry.* And according to statistics published in the *Journal of Consulting and Clinical Psychology* in 2000, if you have an educational deficit, if you are female, if you have a low IQ, or if you were abused as a child, you are at an elevated risk of developing PTSD. These factors are nearly as predictive of PTSD as the severity of the trauma itself.

Suicide by combat veterans is often seen as an extreme expression of PTSD, but currently there is no statistical relationship between suicide and combat, according to a study published in April in the *Journal of the American Medical Association Psychiatry.* Combat veterans are no more likely to kill themselves than veterans who were never under fire. The much-discussed estimated figure of 22 vets a day committing suicide is deceptive: it was only in 2008, for the first time in decades, that the U.S. Army veteran suicide rate, though enormously tragic, surpassed the civilian rate in America. And even so, the majority of veterans who kill themselves are over the age of 50. Generally speaking, the more time that passes after a trauma, the less likely a suicide is to have anything to do with it, according to many studies. Among younger vets, deployment to Iraq or Afghanistan *lowers* the incidence of suicide because soldiers with obvious mental-health issues are less likely to be deployed with their units, according to an analysis published in *Annals of Epidemiology* in 2015. The most accurate predictor of postdeployment suicide, as it turns out, isn't combat or repeated deployments or losing a buddy but suicide attempts *before* deployment. The single most effective action the U.S. military could take to reduce veteran suicide would be to screen for preexisting mental disorders.

It seems intuitively obvious that combat is connected to psychological trauma, but the relationship is a complicated one. Many soldiers go through horrific experiences but fare better than others who experienced danger only briefly, or not at all.

Unmanned-drone pilots, for instance—who watch their missiles kill human beings by remote camera—have been calculated as having the same PTSD rates as pilots who fly actual combat missions in war zones, according to a 2013 analysis published in the *Medical Surveillance Monthly Report.* And even among regular infantry, danger and psychological breakdown during combat are not necessarily connected. During the 1973 Yom Kippur War, when Israel was invaded simultaneously by Egypt and Syria, rear-base troops in the Israeli military had psychological breakdowns at three times the rate of elite frontline troops, relative to their casualties. And during the air campaign of the first Gulf War, more than 80 percent of psychiatric casualties in the U.S. Army's VII Corps came from support units that took almost no incoming fire, according to a 1992 study on Army stress casualties.

Conversely, American airborne and other highly trained units in World War II had some of the lowest rates of psychiatric casualties of the entire military, relative to their number of wounded. A sense of helplessness is deeply traumatic to people, but high levels of training seem to counteract that so effectively that elite soldiers are psychologically insulated from even extreme risk. Part of the reason, it has been found, is that elite soldiers have higher-than-average levels of an amino acid called neuropeptide-Y, which acts as a chemical buffer against hormones that are secreted by the endocrine system during times of high stress. In one 1968 study, published in the *Archive of General Psychiatry,* Special Forces soldiers in Vietnam had levels of the stress hormone cortisol go down before an anticipated attack, while less experienced combatants saw their levels go up.

Shell Shock

All this is new science, however. For most of the nation's history, psychological effects of combat trauma have been variously attributed to neuroses, shell shock, or simple cowardice. When men have failed to obey orders due to trauma they have been beaten, imprisoned, "treated" with electroshock therapy, or simply shot as a warning to others. (For British troops, cowardice was a capital crime until 1930.) It was not until after the Vietnam War that the American Psychiatric Association listed combat trauma as an official diagnosis. Tens of thousands of vets were struggling with "Post-Vietnam Syndrome"—nightmares, insomnia, addiction, paranoia—and their struggle could no longer be written off to weakness or personal failings. Obviously, these problems could also affect war reporters, cops, firefighters, or anyone else subjected to trauma. In 1980, the APA finally included post-traumatic stress disorder in the third edition of the *Diagnostic and Statistical Manual of Mental Disorders.*

Thirty-five years after acknowledging the problem in its current form, the American military now has the highest PTSD rate in its history—and probably in the world. Horrific experiences are unfortunately universal, but long-term impairment from them is not, and despite billions of dollars spent on treatment, half of our Iraq and Afghanistan veterans have applied for permanent disability. Of those veterans treated, roughly a third have been diagnosed with PTSD. Since only about 10 percent of our armed forces actually see combat, the majority of vets claiming to suffer from PTSD seem to have been affected by something other than direct exposure to danger.

This is not a new phenomenon: decade after decade and war after war, American combat deaths have dropped steadily while trauma and disability claims have continued to rise. They are in an almost inverse relationship with each other. Soldiers in Vietnam suffered roughly one-quarter the casualty rate of troops in World War II, for example, but filed for disability at a rate that was nearly 50 percent higher, according to a 2013 report in the *Journal of Anxiety Disorders.* It's tempting to attribute this disparity to the toxic reception they had at home, but that doesn't seem to be the case. Today's vets claim three times the number of disabilities that Vietnam vets did despite a generally warm reception back home and a casualty rate that, thank God, is roughly one-third what it was in Vietnam. Today, most disability claims are for hearing loss, tinnitus, and PTSD—the latter two of which can be exaggerated or faked. Even the first Gulf War—which lasted only a hundred hours—produced nearly twice the disability rates of World War II. Clearly, there is a feedback loop of disability claims, compensation, and more disability claims that cannot go on forever.

Part of the problem is bureaucratic: in an effort to speed up access to benefits, in 2010 the Veterans Administration declared that soldiers no longer have to cite a specific incident—a firefight, a roadside bomb—in order to be eligible for disability compensation. He or she simply has to report being impaired in daily life. As a result, PTSD claims have reportedly risen 60 percent to 150,000 a year. Clearly, this has produced a system that is vulnerable to abuse and bureaucratic error. A recent investigation by the VA's Office of Inspector General found that the higher a veteran's PTSD disability rating, the more treatment he or she tends to seek until achieving a rating of 100 percent, at which point treatment visits drop by 82 percent and many vets quit completely. In theory, the most traumatized people should be seeking more help, not less. It's hard to avoid the conclusion that some vets are getting treatment simply to raise their disability rating.

In addition to being an enormous waste of taxpayer money, such fraud, intentional or not, does real harm to the vets who truly need help. One Veterans Administration counselor I spoke with described having to physically protect someone in a PTSD support group because some other vets wanted to beat him up for faking his trauma. This counselor, who asked to remain anonymous, said that many combat veterans actively avoid the VA because they worry about losing their temper around patients who are milking the system. "It's the real deals—the guys who have seen the most—that this tends to bother," this counselor told me.

The majority of traumatized vets are *not* faking their symptoms, however. They return from wars that are safer than those their fathers and grandfathers fought, and yet far greater numbers of them wind up alienated and depressed. This is true even for people who didn't experience combat. In other words, the problem doesn't seem to be trauma on the battlefield so much as re-entry into society. Anthropological research from around the world shows that recovery from war is heavily influenced by the society one returns to, and there are societies that make that process relatively easy. Ethnographic studies on hunter-gatherer societies rarely turn up evidence of chronic PTSD among their warriors, for example, and oral histories of Native American warfare consistently fail to mention psychological trauma. Anthropologists and oral historians weren't expressly looking for PTSD, but the high frequency of warfare in these groups makes the scarcity of any mention of it revealing. Even the Israeli military—with mandatory national service and two generations of intermittent warfare—has by some measures a PTSD rate as low as 1 percent.

If we weed out the malingerers on the one hand and the deeply traumatized on the other, we are still left with enormous numbers of veterans who had utterly ordinary wartime experiences and yet feel dangerously alienated back home. Clinically speaking, such alienation is not the same thing as PTSD, but both seem to result from military service abroad, so it's understandable that vets and even clinicians are prone to conflating them. Either way, it makes one wonder exactly what it is about modern society that is so mortally dispiriting to come home to.

Soldier's Creed

Any discussion of PTSD and its associated sense of alienation in society must address the fact that many soldiers find themselves missing the war after it's over. That troubling fact can be found in written accounts from war after war, country after country, century after century. Awkward as it is to say, part of the trauma of war seems to be giving it up. There are ancient human behaviors in war—loyalty, inter-reliance, cooperation—that typify good soldiering and can't be easily found in modern society. This can produce a kind of nostalgia for the hard times that even civilians are susceptible to: after World War II, many Londoners claimed to miss the communal underground living that characterized life during the Blitz (despite the fact that more than 40,000 civilians lost their lives). And the war that is missed doesn't even have to be a shooting war: "I am a survivor of the AIDS epidemic," a man wrote on the comment board of an online talk I gave about war. "Now that AIDS is no longer a death sentence, I must admit that I miss those days of extreme brotherhood . . . which led to deep emotions and understandings that are above anything I have felt since the plague years."

What all these people seem to miss isn't danger or loss, per se, but the closeness and cooperation that danger and loss often engender. Humans evolved to survive in extremely harsh environments, and our capacity for cooperation and sharing clearly helped us do that. Structurally, a band of hunter-gatherers and a platoon in combat are almost exactly the same: in each case, the group numbers between 30 and 50 individuals, they sleep in a common area, they conduct patrols, they are completely reliant on one another for support, comfort, and defense, and they share a group identity that most would risk their lives for. Personal interest is subsumed into group interest because personal survival is not possible without group survival. From an evolutionary perspective, it's not at all surprising that many soldiers respond to combat in positive ways and miss it when it's gone.

There are obvious psychological stresses on a person in a group, but there may be even greater stresses on a person in isolation. Most higher primates, including humans, are intensely social, and there are few examples of individuals surviving outside of a group. A modern soldier returning from combat goes from the kind of close-knit situation that humans evolved for into a society where most people work outside the home, children are educated by strangers, families are isolated from wider communities, personal gain almost completely eclipses collective good, and people sleep alone or with a partner. Even if he or she is in a family, that is not the same as belonging to a large, self-sufficient group that shares and experiences almost everything collectively. Whatever the technological advances of modern society—and they're nearly miraculous—the individual lifestyles that those technologies spawn may be deeply brutalizing to the human spirit.

"You'll have to be prepared to say that we are not a good society—that we are an *anti-human* society," anthropologist Sharon Abramowitz warned when I tried this theory out on her. Abramowitz was in Ivory Coast during the start of the civil war there in 2002 and experienced, firsthand, the extremely close bonds created by hardship and danger. "We are not good to each other. Our tribalism is about an extremely narrow group of people: our children, our spouse, maybe our parents. Our society is alienating, technical, cold, and mystifying. Our fundamental desire, as human beings, is to be close to others, and our society does not allow for that."

This is an old problem, and today's vets are not the first Americans to balk at coming home. A source of continual embarrassment along the American frontier—from the late 1600s until the end of the Indian Wars, in the 1890s—was a phenomenon known as "the White Indians." The term referred to white settlers who were kidnapped by Indians—or simply ran off to them—and became so enamored of that life that they refused to leave. According to many writers of the time, including Benjamin Franklin, the reverse never happened: Indians never ran off to join white society. And if a peace treaty required that a tribe give up their adopted members, these members would often have to be put under guard and returned home by force. Inevitably, many would escape to rejoin their Indian families. "Thousands of Europeans are Indians, and we have no examples of even one of those aborigines having from choice become European," wrote a French-born writer in America named Michel-Guillaume-Saint-Jean de Crèvecoeur in an essay published in 1782.

One could say that combat vets are the White Indians of today, and that they miss the war because it was, finally, an experience of human closeness that they can't easily find back home. Not the closeness of family, which is rare enough, but the closeness of community and tribe. The kind of closeness that gets endlessly venerated in Hollywood movies but only actually shows up in contemporary society when something goes wrong—when tornados obliterate towns or planes are flown into skyscrapers. Those events briefly give us a reason to act communally, and most of us do. "There is something to be said for using risk to forge social bonds," Abramowitz pointed out. "Having something to fight for, and fight through, is a good and important thing."

Certainly, the society we have created is hard on us by virtually every metric that we use to measure human happiness. This problem may disproportionately affect people, like soldiers, who are making a radical transition back home.

It is incredibly hard to measure and quantify the human experience, but some studies have found that many people in certain modern societies self-report high levels of happiness. And yet, numerous cross-cultural studies show that as affluence and urbanization rise in a given society, so do rates of depression, suicide, and schizophrenia (along with health issues such as obesity and diabetes). People in wealthy countries suffer unipolar depression at more than double the rate that they do in poor countries, according to a study by the World Health Organization, and people in countries with large income disparities—like the United States—run a much higher risk of developing mood disorders at some point in their lives. A 2006 cross-cultural study of women focusing on depression and modernization compared depression rates in rural and urban Nigeria and rural and urban North America, and found that women in rural areas of both countries were far less likely to get depressed than urban women. And urban American women—the most affluent demographic of the study—were the *most* likely to succumb to depression.

In America, the more assimilated a person is into contemporary society, the more likely he or she is to develop depression in his or her lifetime. According to a 2004 study in *The Journal of Nervous and Mental Disease,* Mexicans born in the United States are highly assimilated into American culture and have much higher rates of depression than Mexicans born in Mexico. By contrast, Amish communities have an exceedingly low rate of reported depression because, in part, it is theorized, they have completely resisted modernization. They won't even drive cars. "The economic and marketing forces of modern society have engineered an environment promoting decisions that maximize consumption at the long-term cost of well-being," one survey of these studies, from the *Journal of Affective Disorders* in 2012, concluded. "In effect, humans have dragged a body with a long hominid history into an overfed, malnourished, sedentary, sunlight-deficient, sleep-deprived, competitive, inequitable and socially-isolating environment with dire consequences."

For more than half a million years, our recent hominid ancestors lived nomadic lives of extreme duress on the plains of East Africa, but the advent of agriculture changed that about 10,000 years ago. That is only 400 generations—not enough to adapt, genetically, to the changes in diet and society that ensued. Privately worked land and the accumulation of capital made humans less oriented toward group welfare, and the Industrial Revolution pushed society further in that direction. No one knows how the so-called Information Age will affect us, but there's a good chance that home technology and the Internet will only intensify our drift toward solipsism and alienation.

Meanwhile, many of the behaviors that had high survival value in our evolutionary past, like problem-solving, cooperation, and intergroup competition, are still rewarded by bumps of dopamine and other hormones into our system. Those hormones serve to reinforce whatever behavior it was that produced those hormones in the first place. Group affiliation and cooperation were clearly adaptive because in many animals, including humans, they trigger a surge in levels of a neuropeptide called oxytocin. Not only does oxytocin create a glow of well-being in people, it promotes greater levels of trust and bonding, which unite them further still. Hominids that were rewarded with oxytocin for cooperating with one another must have out-fought, out-hunted, and out-bred the ones that didn't. Those are the hominids that modern humans are descended from.

According to one study published in *Science* in June 2010, this feedback loop of oxytocin and group loyalty creates an expectation that members will "self-sacrifice to contribute to in-group welfare." There may be no better description of a soldier's ethos than that sentence. One of the most noticeable things about life in the military is that you are virtually never alone: day after day, month after month, you are close enough to speak to, if not touch, a dozen or more people. You eat together, sleep together, laugh together, suffer together. That level of intimacy duplicates our evolutionary past very closely and must create a nearly continual oxytocin reward system.

Hero's Welcome

When soldiers return to modern society, they must go through—among other adjustments—a terrific oxytocin withdrawal. The chronic isolation of modern society begins in childhood and continues our entire lives. Infants in hunter-gatherer societies are carried by their mothers as much as 50 to 90 percent of the time, often in wraps that keep them strapped to the mother's back so that her hands are free. That roughly corresponds to carrying rates among other primates, according to primatologist and psychologist Harriet J. Smith. One can get an idea of how desperately important touch is to primates from a landmark experiment conducted in the 1950s by a psychologist and primatologist named Harry Harlow. Baby rhesus monkeys were separated from their mothers and presented with the choice of two kinds of surrogates: a cuddly mother made out of terry cloth or an uninviting mother made out of wire mesh. The wire-mesh mother, however, had a nipple that would dispense warm milk. The babies invariably took their nourishment quickly in order to rush back and cling to the terry-cloth mother, which had enough softness to provide the illusion of affection. But even that isn't enough for psychological health: in a separate experiment, more than 75 percent of female baby rhesus monkeys raised with terry-cloth mothers—as opposed to real ones—grew up to be abusive and neglectful to their own young.

In the 1970s, American mothers maintained skin-to-skin contact with their nine-month-old babies as little as 16 percent of the time, which is a level of contact that traditional societies would probably consider a form of child abuse. Also unthinkable would be the common practice of making young children sleep by themselves in their own room. In two American studies of middle-class families during the 1980s, 85 percent of young children slept alone—a figure that rose to 95 percent among families considered "well-educated." Northern European societies, including America, are the only ones in history to make very young children sleep alone in such numbers. The isolation is thought to trigger fears that make many children bond intensely with stuffed animals for reassurance. Only in Northern European societies do children go through the well-known developmental stage of bonding with stuffed animals; elsewhere, children get their sense of safety from the adults sleeping near them.

More broadly, in most human societies, almost nobody sleeps alone. Sleeping in family groups of one sort or another has been the norm throughout human history and is still commonplace in most of the world. Again, Northern European societies are among the few where people sleep alone or with a partner in a private room. When I was with American soldiers at a remote outpost in Afghanistan, we slept in narrow plywood huts where I could reach out and touch three other men from where I slept. They snored, they talked, they got up in the middle of the night to use the piss tubes, but we felt safe because we were in a group. The Taliban attacked the position regularly, and the most determined attacks often came at dawn. Another unit in a nearby valley was almost overrun and took 50 percent casualties in just such an attack. And yet I slept better surrounded by those noisy, snoring men than I ever did camping alone in the woods of New England.

Many soldiers will tell you that one of the hardest things about coming home is learning to sleep without the security of a group of heavily armed men around them. In that sense, being in a war zone with your platoon feels safer than being in an American suburb by yourself. I know a vet who felt so threatened at home that he would get up in the middle of the night to build fighting positions out of the living-room furniture. This is a radically different experience from what warriors in other societies go through, such as the Yanomami, of the Orinoco and Amazon Basins, who go to war with their entire age cohort and return to face, together, whatever the psychological consequences may be. As one anthropologist pointed out to me, trauma is usually a group experience, so trauma recovery should be a group experience as well. But in our society it's not.

"Our whole approach to mental health has been hijacked by pharmaceutical logic," I was told by Gary Barker, an anthropologist whose group, Promundo, is dedicated to understanding and preventing violence. "PTSD is a crisis of connection and disruption, not an illness that you carry within you."

This individualizing of mental health is not just an American problem, or a veteran problem; it affects everybody. A British anthropologist named Bill West told me that the extreme poverty of the 1930s and the collective trauma of the Blitz served to unify an entire generation of English people. "I link the experience of the Blitz to voting in the Labour Party in 1945, and the establishing of the National Health Service and a strong welfare state," he said. "Those policies were supported well into the 60s by all political parties. That kind of cultural cohesiveness, along with Christianity, was very helpful after the war. It's an open question whether people's problems are located in the individual. If enough people in society are sick, you have to wonder whether it isn't actually society that's sick."

Ideally, we would compare hunter-gatherer society to post-industrial society to see which one copes better with PTSD. When the Sioux, Cheyenne, and Arapaho fighters returned to their camps after annihilating Custer and his regiment at Little

Bighorn, for example, were they traumatized and alienated by the experience—or did they fit right back into society? There is no way to know for sure, but less direct comparisons can still illuminate how cohesiveness affects trauma. In experiments with lab rats, for example, a subject that is traumatized—but not injured—after an attack by a larger rat usually recovers within 48 hours *unless it is kept in isolation,* according to data published in 2005 in *Neuroscience & Biobehavioral Reviews.* The ones that are kept apart from other rats are the only ones that develop long-term traumatic symptoms. And a study of risk factors for PTSD in humans closely mirrored those results. In a 2000 study in the *Journal of Consulting and Clinical Psychology,* "lack of social support" was found to be around two times more reliable at predicting who got PTSD and who didn't than the severity of the trauma itself. You could be mildly traumatized, in other words—on a par with, say, an ordinary rear-base deployment to Afghanistan—and experience long-term PTSD simply because of a lack of social support back home.

Anthropologist and psychiatrist Brandon Kohrt found a similar phenomenon in the villages of southern Nepal, where a civil war has been rumbling for years. Kohrt explained to me that there are two kinds of villages there: exclusively Hindu ones, which are extremely stratified, and mixed Buddhist/Hindu ones, which are far more open and cohesive. He said that child soldiers, both male and female, who go back to Hindu villages can remain traumatized for years, while those from mixed-religion villages tended to recover very quickly. "PTSD is a disorder of recovery, and if treatment only focuses on identifying symptoms, it pathologizes and alienates vets," according to Kohrt. "But if the focus is on family and community, it puts them in a situation of collective healing."

Israel is arguably the only modern country that retains a sufficient sense of community to mitigate the effects of combat on a mass scale. Despite decades of intermittent war, the Israel Defense Forces have a PTSD rate as low as 1 percent. Two of the foremost reasons have to do with national military service and the proximity of the combat—the war is virtually on their doorstep. "Being in the military is something that most people have done," I was told by Dr. Arieh Shalev, who has devoted the last 20 years to studying PTSD. "Those who come back from combat are re-integrated into a society where those experiences are very well understood. We did a study of 17-year-olds who had lost their father in the military, compared to those who had lost their fathers to accidents. The ones whose fathers died in combat did much better than those whose fathers hadn't."

According to Shalev, the closer the public is to the actual combat, the better the war will be understood and the less difficulty soldiers will have when they come home. The Israelis are benefiting from what could be called the shared public meaning of a war. Such public meaning—which would often occur in more communal, tribal societies—seems to help soldiers even in a fully modern society such as Israel. It is probably not generated by empty, reflexive phrases—such as "Thank you for your service"—that many Americans feel compelled to offer soldiers and vets. If anything, those comments only serve to underline the enormous chasm between military and civilian society in this country.

Another Israeli researcher, Reuven Gal, found that the perceived legitimacy of a war was more important to soldiers' general morale than was the combat readiness of the unit they were in. And that legitimacy, in turn, was a function of the war's physical distance from the homeland: "The Israeli soldiers who were abruptly mobilized and thrown into dreadful battles in the middle of Yom Kippur Day in 1973 had no doubts about the legitimacy of the war," Gal wrote in the *Journal of Applied Psychology* in 1986. "Many of those soldiers who were fighting in the Golan Heights against the flood of Syrian tanks needed only to look behind their shoulders to see their homes and remind themselves that they were fighting for their very survival."

In that sense, the Israelis are far more like the Sioux, Cheyenne, and Arapaho at Little Bighorn than they are like us. America's distance from her enemies means that her wars have generally been fought far away from her population centers, and as a result those wars have been harder to explain and justify than Israel's have been. The people who will bear the psychic cost of that ambiguity will, of course, be the soldiers.

A Bright Shining Lie

"I talked to my mom only one time from Mars," a Vietnam vet named Gregory Gomez told me about the physical and spiritual distance between his home and the war zone. Gomez is a pure-blooded Apache who grew up in West Texas. He says his grandfather was arrested and executed by Texas Rangers in 1915 because they wanted his land; they strung him from a tree limb, cut off his genitals, and stuffed them in his mouth. Consequently, Gomez felt no allegiance to the U.S. government, but he volunteered for service in Vietnam anyway. "Most of us Indian guys who went to Vietnam went because we were warriors," Gomez told me. "I did not fight for this country. I fought for Mother Earth. I wanted to experience combat. I wanted to know how I'd do."

Gomez was in a Marine Corps Force Recon unit, one of the most elite designations in the U.S. military. He was part of a four-man team that would insert by helicopter into enemy territory north of the DMZ and stay for two weeks at a time. They had no medic and no backup and didn't even dare eat C rations, because, Gomez said, they were afraid their body odor would give them away. They ate Vietnamese food and watched enemy soldiers pass just yards away in the dense jungle. "Everyone who has lived through something like that has lived through trauma, and you can never go back," he told me. "You are 17 or 18 or 19 and you just hit that wall. You become very old men."

American Indians, proportionally, have provided more soldiers to America's wars than almost any other ethnic group in this country. They are also the product of an ancient and vibrant warring culture that takes great pains to protect the warrior from society, and vice versa. Although those traditions have obviously broken down since the end of the Indian Wars, there may be something to be learned from the principles upon which they stand. When Gomez came home he essentially isolated himself for more than a decade. He didn't drink, and he lived a normal life except that occasionally he'd go to the corner store to get a soda and would wind up in Oklahoma or East Texas without any idea how he got there.

He finally started seeing a therapist at the VA as well as undergoing traditional Indian rituals. It was a combination that seemed to work. In the 1980s, he underwent an extremely painful ceremony called the Sun Dance. At the start of the ceremony, the dancers have wooden skewers driven through the skin of their chests. Leather thongs are tied to the skewers and then attached to the top of a tall pole at the center of the dance ground. To a steady drumbeat, the dancers move in a circle while leaning back on the leather thongs until, after many hours, the skewers finally tear free. "I dance back and I throw my arms and yell and I can see the ropes and the piercing sticks like in slow motion, flying from my chest towards the grandfather's tree," Gomez told me about the experience. "And I had this incredible feeling of euphoria and strength, like I could do anything. That's when the healing takes place. That's when life changes take place."

America is a largely de-ritualized society that obviously can't just borrow from another society to heal its psychic wounds. But the spirit of community healing and empowerment that forms the basis of these ceremonies is certainly one that might be converted to a secular modern society. The shocking disconnect for veterans isn't so much that civilians don't know what they went through—it's unrealistic to expect anyone to fully understand another person's experience—but that what they went through doesn't seem relevant back home. Given the profound alienation that afflicts modern society, when combat vets say that they want to go back to war, they may be having an entirely healthy response to the perceived emptiness of modern life.

One way to change this dynamic might be to emulate the Israelis and mandate national service (with a military or combat option). We could also emulate the Nepalese and try to have communities better integrate people of different ethnic and religious groups. Finally, we could emulate many tribal societies—including the Apache—by getting rid of parades and replacing them with some form of homecoming ceremony. An almost universal component of these ceremonies is the dramatic retelling of combat experiences to the warrior's community. We could achieve that on Veterans Day by making every town and city hall in the country available to veterans who want to speak publicly about the war. The vapid phrase "I support the troops" would then mean actually showing up at your town hall every Veterans Day to hear these people out. Some vets will be angry, some will be proud, and some will be crying so hard they can't speak. But a community ceremony like that would finally return the experience of war to our entire nation, rather than just leaving it to the people who fought.

It might also begin to re-assemble a society that has been spiritually cannibalizing itself for generations. We keep wondering how to save the vets, but the real question is how to save ourselves. If we do that, the vets will be fine. If we don't, it won't matter anyway.

Critical Thinking

1. In what ways has the national discussion about violence in the United States been a matter of talk without actually doing anything about it?
2. How does the Pistorius case illustrate the origins of white fear and how it has shaped the justice system's treatment of blacks in in South Africa as well in the United States?

Internet References

Harvard University Center on the Developing Child

http://developingchild.harvard.edu/resources/inbrief-early-childhood-mental-health/

National Institute of Mental Health

https://www.nimh.nih.gov/health/topics/post-traumatic-stress-disorder-ptsd/index.shtml

U.S. Department of Veterans Affairs

https://www.ptsd.va.gov/public/ptsd-overview/basics/what-is-ptsd.asp

World Psychiatry

http://onlinelibrary.wiley.com/

Article

Prepared by: Elvio Angeloni

Eating Christmas in the Kalahari

RICHARD BORSHAY LEE

Learning Outcomes

After reading this article, you will be able to:

- Describe some of the unique research strategies of anthropological fieldwork.
- Explain how anthropologists who become personally involved with a community through participant observation maintain their objectivity as scientists.
- Explain the ways in which the results of fieldwork depend on the kinds of questions asked.

The !Kung Bushmen's knowledge of Christmas is third-hand. The London Missionary Society brought the holiday to the southern Tswana tribes in the early nineteenth century. Later, native catechists spread the idea far and wide among the Bantu-speaking pastoralists, even in the remotest corners of the Kalahari Desert. The Bushmen's idea of the Christmas story, stripped to its essentials, is "praise the birth of white man's god-chief"; what keeps their interest in the holiday high is the Tswana-Herero custom of slaughtering an ox for his Bushmen neighbors as an annual goodwill gesture. Since the 1930s, part of the Bushmen's annual round of activities has included a December congregation at the cattle posts for trading, marriage brokering, and several days of trance-dance feasting at which the local Tswana headman is host.

As a social anthropologist working with !Kung Bushmen, I found that the Christmas ox custom suited my purposes. I had come to the Kalahari to study the hunting and gathering subsistence economy of the !Kung, and to accomplish this it was essential not to provide them with food, share my own food, or interfere in any way with their food-gathering activities. While liberal handouts of tobacco and medical supplies were appreciated, they were scarcely adequate to erase the glaring disparity in wealth between the anthropologist, who maintained a two-month inventory of canned goods, and the Bushmen, who rarely had a day's supply of food on hand. My approach, while paying off in terms of data, left me open to frequent accusations of stinginess and hard-heartedness. By their lights, I was a miser.

The Christmas ox was to be my way of saying thank you for the cooperation of the past year; and since it was to be our last Christmas in the field, I determined to slaughter the largest, meatiest ox that money could buy, insuring that the feast and trance-dance would be a success.

Through December I kept my eyes open at the wells as the cattle were brought down for watering. Several animals were offered, but none had quite the grossness that I had in mind. Then, ten days before the holiday, a Herero friend led an ox of astonishing size and mass up to our camp. It was solid black, stood five feet high at the shoulder, had a five-foot span of horns, and must have weighed 1,200 pounds on the hoof. Food consumption calculations are my specialty, and I quickly figured that bones and viscera aside, there was enough meat—at least four pounds—for every man, woman, and child of the 150 Bushmen in the vicinity of /ai/ai who were expected at the feast.

Having found the right animal at last, I paid the Herero £20 ($56) and asked him to keep the beast with his herd until Christmas day. The next morning word spread among the people that the big solid black one was the ox chosen by /ontah (my Bushman name; it means, roughly, "whitey") for the Christmas feast. That afternoon I received the first delegation. Ben!a, an outspoken sixty-year-old mother of five, came to the point slowly.

"Where were you planning to eat Christmas?"

"Right here at /ai/ai," I replied.

"Alone or with others?"

"I expect to invite all the people to eat Christmas with me."

"Eat what?"

"I have purchased Yehave's black ox, and I am going to slaughter and cook it."

"That's what we were told at the well but refused to believe it until we heard it from yourself."

"Well, it's the black one," I replied expansively, although wondering what she was driving at.

"Oh, no!" Ben!a groaned, turning to her group. "They were right." Turning back to me she asked, "Do you expect us to eat that bag of bones?"

"Bag of bones! It's the biggest ox at /ai/ai."

"Big, yes, but old. And thin. Everybody knows there's no meat on that old ox. What did you expect us to eat off it, the horns?"

Everybody chuckled at Ben!a's one-liner as they walked away, but all I could manage was a weak grin.

That evening it was the turn of the young men. They came to sit at our evening fire. /gaugo, about my age, spoke to me man-to-man.

"/ontah, you have always been square with us," he lied. "What has happened to change your heart? That sack of guts and bones of Yehave's will hardly feed one camp, let alone all the Bushmen around ai/ai." And he proceeded to enumerate the seven camps in the /ai/ai vicinity, family by family. "Perhaps you have forgotten that we are not few, but many. Or are you too blind to tell the difference between a proper cow and an old wreck? That ox is thin to the point of death."

"Look, you guys," I retorted, "that is a beautiful animal, and I'm sure you will eat it with pleasure at Christmas."

"Of course we will eat it; it's food. But it won't fill us up to the point where we will have enough strength to dance. We will eat and go home to bed with stomachs rumbling."

That night as we turned in, I asked my wife, Nancy: "What did you think of the black ox?"

"It looked enormous to me. Why?"

"Well, about eight different people have told me I got gypped; that the ox is nothing but bones."

"What's the angle?" Nancy asked. "Did they have a better one to sell?"

"No, they just said that it was going to be a grim Christmas because there won't be enough meat to go around. Maybe I'll get an independent judge to look at the beast in the morning."

Bright and early, Halingisi, a Tswana cattle owner, appeared at our camp. But before I could ask him to give me his opinion on Yehave's black ox, he gave me the eye signal that indicated a confidential chat. We left the camp and sat down.

"/ontah, I'm surprised at you: you've lived here for three years and still haven't learned anything about cattle."

"But what else can a person do but choose the biggest, strongest animal one can find?" I retorted.

"Look, just because an animal is big doesn't mean that it has plenty of meat on it. The black one was a beauty when it was younger, but now it is thin to the point of death."

"Well I've already bought it. What can I do at this stage?"

"Bought it already? I thought you were just considering it. Well, you'll have to kill it and serve it, I suppose. But don't expect much of a dance to follow."

My spirits dropped rapidly. I could believe that Ben!a and /gaugo just might be putting me on about the black ox, but Halingisi seemed to be an impartial critic. I went around that day feeling as though I had bought a lemon of a used car.

In the afternoon it was Tomazo's turn. Tomazo is a fine hunter, a top trance performer . . . and one of my most reliable informants. He approached the subject of the Christmas cow as part of my continuing Bushman education.

"My friend, the way it is with us Bushmen," he began, "is that we love meat. And even more than that, we love fat. When we hunt we always search for the fat ones, the ones dripping with layers of white fat: fat that turns into a clear, thick oil in the cooking pot, fat that slides down your gullet, fills your stomach and gives you a roaring diarrhea," he rhapsodized.

"So, feeling as we do," he continued, "it gives us pain to be served such a scrawny thing as Yehave's black ox. It is big, yes, and no doubt its giant bones are good for soup, but fat is what we really crave and so we will eat Christmas this year with a heavy heart."

The prospect of a gloomy Christmas now had me worried, so I asked Tomazo what I could do about it.

"Look for a fat one, a young one . . . smaller, but fat. Fat enough to make us *//gom* ('evacuate the bowels'), then we will be happy."

My suspicions were aroused when Tomazo said that he happened to know of a young, fat, barren cow that the owner was willing to part with. Was Tomazo working on commission, I wondered? But I dispelled this unworthy thought when we approached the Herero owner of the cow in question and found that he had decided not to sell.

The scrawny wreck of a Christmas ox now became the talk of the /ai/ai water hole and was the first news told to the outlying groups as they began to come in from the bush for the feast. What finally convinced me that real trouble might be brewing was the visit from u!au, an old conservative with a reputation for fierceness. His nickname meant spear and referred to an incident thirty years ago in which he had speared a man to death. He had an intense manner; fixing me with his eyes, he said in clipped tones:

"I have only just heard about the black ox today, or else I would have come here earlier. /ontah, do you honestly think you can serve meat like that to people and avoid a fight?" He paused, letting the implications sink in. "I don't mean fight you, /ontah; you are a white man. I mean a fight between Bushmen. There are many fierce ones here, and with such a small quantity of meat to distribute, how can you give everybody a fair share? Someone is sure to accuse another of taking too much or hogging all the choice pieces. Then you will see what happens when some go hungry while others eat."

The possibility of at least a serious argument struck me as all too real. I had witnessed the tension that surrounds the distribution of meat from a kudu or gemsbok kill, and had documented many arguments that sprang up from a real or imagined slight in meat distribution. The owners of a kill may spend up to two hours arranging and rearranging the piles of meat under the gaze of a circle of recipients before handing them out. And I also knew that the Christmas feast at /ai/ai would be bringing together groups that had feuded in the past.

Convinced now of the gravity of the situation, I went in earnest to search for a second cow; but all my inquiries failed to turn one up.

The Christmas feast was evidently going to be a disaster, and the incessant complaints about the meagerness of the ox had already taken the fun out of it for me. Moreover, I was getting bored with the wisecracks, and after losing my temper a few times, I resolved to serve the beast anyway. If the meat fell short, the hell with it. In the Bushmen idiom, I announced to all who would listen:

"I am a poor man and blind. If I have chosen one that is too old and too thin, we will eat it anyway and see if there is enough meat there to quiet the rumbling of our stomachs."

On hearing this speech, Ben!a offered me a rare word of comfort. "It's thin," she said philosophically, "but the bones will make a good soup."

At dawn Christmas morning, instinct told me to turn over the butchering and cooking to a friend and take off with Nancy to spend Christmas alone in the bush. But curiosity kept me from retreating. I wanted to see what such a scrawny ox looked like on butchering and if there *was* going to be a fight, I wanted to catch every word of it. Anthropologists are incurable that way.

The great beast was driven up to our dancing ground, and a shot in the forehead dropped it in its tracks. Then, freshly cut branches were heaped around the fallen carcass to receive the meat. Ten men volunteered to help with the cutting. I asked /gaugo to make the breast bone cut. This cut, which begins the butchering process for most large game, offers easy access for removal of the viscera. But it also allows the hunter to spot-check the amount of fat on the animal. A fat game animal carries a white layer up to an inch thick on the chest, while in a thin one, the knife will quickly cut to bone. All eyes fixed on his hand as /gaugo, dwarfed by the great carcass, knelt to the breast. The first cut opened a pool of solid white in the black skin. The second and third cut widened and deepened the creamy white. Still no bone. It was pure fat; it must have been two inches thick.

"Hey /gau," I burst out, "that ox is loaded with fat. What's this about the ox being too thin to bother eating? Are you out of your mind?"

"Fat?" /gau shot back, "You call that fat? This wreck is thin, sick, dead!" And he broke out laughing. So did everyone else. They rolled on the ground, paralyzed with laughter. Everybody laughed except me; I was thinking.

I ran back to the tent and burst in just as Nancy was getting up. "Hey, the black ox. It's fat as hell! They were kidding about it being too thin to eat. It was a joke or something. A put-on. Everyone is really delighted with it!"

"Some joke," my wife replied. "It was so funny that you were ready to pack up and leave /ai/ai."

If it had indeed been a joke, it had been an extraordinarily convincing one, and tinged, I thought, with more than a touch of malice as many jokes are. Nevertheless, that it was a joke lifted my spirits considerably, and I returned to the butchering site where the shape of the ox was rapidly disappearing under the axes and knives of the butchers. The atmosphere had become festive. Grinning broadly, their arms covered with blood well past the elbow, men packed chunks of meat into the big cast-iron cooking pots, fifty pounds to the load, and muttered and chuckled all the while about the thinness and worthlessness of the animal and /ontah's poor judgment.

We danced and ate that ox two days and two nights; we cooked and distributed fourteen potfuls of meat and no one went home hungry and no fights broke out.

But the "joke" stayed in my mind. I had a growing feeling that something important had happened in my relationship with the Bushmen and that the clue lay in the meaning of the joke. Several days later, when most of the people had dispersed back to the bush camps, I raised the question with Hakekgose, a Tswana man who had grown up among the !Kung, married a !Kung girl, and who probably knew their culture better than any other non-Bushman.

"With us whites," I began, "Christmas is supposed to be the day of friendship and brotherly love. What I can't figure out is why the Bushmen went to such lengths to criticize and belittle the ox I had bought for the feast. The animal was perfectly good and their jokes and wisecracks practically ruined the holiday for me."

"So it really did bother you," said Hakekgose. "Well, that's the way they always talk. When I take my rifle and go hunting with them, if I miss, they laugh at me for the rest of the day. But even if I hit and bring one down, it's no better. To them, the kill is always too small or too old or too thin; and as we sit down on the kill site to cook and eat the liver, they keep grumbling, even with their mouths full of meat. They say things like, 'Oh this is awful! What a worthless animal! Whatever made me think that this Tswana rascal could hunt!' "

"Is this the way outsiders are treated?" I asked.

"No, it is their custom; they talk that way to each other too. Go and ask them."

/gaugo had been one of the most enthusiastic in making me feel bad about the merit of the Christmas ox. I sought him out first.

"Why did you tell me the black ox was worthless, when you could see that it was loaded with fat and meat?"

"It is our way," he said smiling. "We always like to fool people about that. Say there is a Bushman who has been hunting. He must not come home and announce like a braggard, 'I have killed a big one in the bush!' He must first sit down in silence until I or someone else comes up to his fire and asks, 'What did you see today?' He replies quietly, 'Ah, I'm no good for hunting. I saw nothing at all [pause] just a little tiny one.' Then I smile to myself," /gaugo continued, "because I know he has killed something big."

"In the morning we make up a party of four or five people to cut up and carry the meat back to the camp. When we arrive at the kill we examine it and cry out, 'You mean to say you have dragged us all the way out here in order to make us cart home your pile of bones? Oh, if I had known it was this thin I wouldn't have come.' Another one pipes up, 'People, to think I gave up a nice day in the shade for this. At home we may be hungry but at least we have nice cool water to drink.' If the horns are big, someone says, 'Did you think that somehow you were going to boil down the horns for soup?'

"To all this you must respond in kind. 'I agree,' you say, 'this one is not worth the effort; let's just cook the liver for strength and leave the rest for the hyenas. It is not too late to hunt today and even a duiker or a steenbok would be better than this mess.'

"Then you set to work nevertheless; butcher the animal, carry the meat back to the camp and everyone eats," /gaugo concluded.

Things were beginning to make sense. Next, I went to Tomazo. He corroborated /gaugo's story of the obligatory insults over a kill and added a few details of his own.

"But," I asked, "why insult a man after he has gone to all that trouble to track and kill an animal and when he is going to share the meat with you so that your children will have something to eat?"

"Arrogance," was his cryptic answer.

"Arrogance?"

"Yes, when a young man kills much meat he comes to think of himself as a chief or a big man, and he thinks of the rest of us as his servants or inferiors. We can't accept this. We refuse one who boasts, for someday his pride will make him kill somebody. So we always speak of his meat as worthless. This way we cool his heart and make him gentle."

"But why didn't you tell me this before?" I asked Tomazo with some heat.

"Because you never asked me," said Tomazo, echoing the refrain that has come to haunt every field ethnographer.

The pieces now fell into place. I had known for a long time that in situations of social conflict with Bushmen I held all the cards. I was the only source of tobacco in a thousand square miles, and I was not incapable of cutting an individual off for non-cooperation. Though my boycott never lasted longer than a few days, it was an indication of my strength. People resented my presence at the water hole, yet simultaneously dreaded my leaving. In short I was a perfect target for the charge of arrogance and for the Bushmen tactic of enforcing humility.

I had been taught an object lesson by the Bushmen; it had come from an unexpected corner and had hurt me in a vulnerable area. For the big black ox was to be the one totally generous, unstinting act of my year at /ai/ai, and I was quite unprepared for the reaction I received.

As I read it, their message was this: There are no totally generous acts. All "acts" have an element of calculation. One black ox slaughtered at Christmas does not wipe out a year of careful manipulation of gifts given to serve your own ends. After all, to kill an animal and share the meat with people is really no more than Bushmen do for each other every day and with far less fanfare.

In the end, I had to admire how the Bushmen had played out the farce—collectively straight-faced to the end. Curiously, the episode reminded me of the *Good Soldier Schweik* and his marvelous encounters with authority. Like Schweik, the Bushmen had retained a thorough-going skepticism of good intentions. Was it this independence of spirit, I wondered, that had kept them culturally viable in the face of generations of contact with more powerful societies, both black and white? The thought that the Bushmen were alive and well in the Kalahari was strangely comforting. Perhaps, armed with that independence and with their superb knowledge of their environment, they might yet survive the future.

Critical Thinking

1. To what extent do the Bushmen typically celebrate Christmas?
2. Why did Lee wish to slaughter an ox for the Bushmen?
3. What was it about the Bushman ways of life and Lee's role as an anthropologist that led to their reactions to his generosity?
4. Why was the Bushman reaction "strangely comforting" to Lee in the final analysis?

Internet References

Anthropology Links
http://anthropology.gmu.edu

Archaeology and Anthropology Computing and Study Skills
www.isca.ox.ac.uk/index.html

Introduction to Fieldwork and Ethnography
http://web.mit.edu/dumit/www/syl-anth.html

The Institute for Intercultural Studies
www.interculturalstudies.org/main.html

Richard Borshay Lee is a full professor of anthropology at the University of Toronto. He has done extensive fieldwork in southern Africa, is coeditor of *Man the Hunter* (1968) and *Kalahari Hunter-Gatherers* (1976), and author of *The !Kung San: Men, Women, and Work in a Foraging Society.*

Article

Prepared by: Elvio Angeloni

Tricking and Tripping

Fieldwork on Prostitution in the Era of AIDS

CLAIRE E. STERK

Learning Outcomes

After reading this article, you will be able to:

- Explain how anthropologists who become personally involved with a community through participant observation maintain their objectivity as scientists.
- Give examples of the kind of ethical obligations fieldworkers have toward their informants.

Students often think of anthropological fieldwork as requiring travel to exotic tropical locations, but that is not necessarily the case. This reading is based on fieldwork in the United States—on the streets in New York City as well as Atlanta. Claire Sterk is an anthropologist who works in a school of public health and is primarily interested in issues of women's health, particularly as it relates to sexual behavior. In this selection, an introduction to a recent book by the same title, she describes the basic fieldwork methods she used to study these women and their communities. Like most cultural anthropologists, Sterk's primary goal was to describe "the life" of prostitution from the women's own point of view. To do this, she had to be patient, brave, sympathetic, trustworthy, curious, and nonjudgmental. You will notice these characteristics in this selection; for example, Sterk begins her book with a poem written by one of her informants. Fieldwork is a slow process, because it takes time to win people's confidence and to learn their language and way of seeing the world. In this regard, there are probably few differences between the work of a qualitative sociologist and that of a cultural anthropologist (although anthropologists would not use the term "deviant" to describe another society or a segment of their own society).

Throughout the world, HIV/AIDS is fast becoming a disease found particularly in poor women. Sex workers or prostitutes have often been blamed for AIDS, and they have been further stigmatized because of their profession. In reality, however, entry into prostitution is not a career choice; rather, these women and girls are themselves most often victims of circumstances such as violence and poverty. Public health officials want to know why sex workers do not always protect their health by making men wear condoms. To answer such questions, we must know more about the daily life of these women. The way to do that, the cultural anthropologist would say, is to ask and to listen.

As you read this selection, ask yourself the following questions:

- What happens when Sterk says, "I'm sorry for you" to one of her informants? Why?
- Why do you think fieldwork might be a difficult job?
- Do you think that the fact that Sterk grew up in Amsterdam, where prostitution is legal, affected her research?
- Which of the six themes of this work, described at the end of the article, do you think is most important?

One night in March of 1987 business was slow. I was hanging out on a stroll with a group of street prostitutes. After a few hours in a nearby diner/coffee shop, we were kicked out. The waitress felt bad, but she needed our table for some new customers. Four of us decided to sit in my car until the rain stopped. While three of us chatted about life, Piper wrote this poem. As soon as she read it to us, the conversation shifted to more serious topics—pimps, customers, cops, the many hassles of being a prostitute, to name a few. We decided that if I ever finished a book about prostitution, the book would start with her poem.

This book is about the women who work in the lower echelons of the prostitution world. They worked in the streets and other public settings as well as crack houses. Some of these women viewed themselves primarily as prostitutes, and a number of them used drugs to cope with the pressures of the life. Others identified themselves more as drug users, and their main reason for having sex for money or other goods was to support their own drug use and often the habit of their male partner. A small group of women interviewed for this book had left prostitution, and most of them were still struggling to integrate their past experiences as prostitutes in their current lives.

The stories told by the women who participated in this project revealed how pimps, customers, and others such as police officers and social and health service providers treated them as "fallen" women. However, their accounts also showed their strengths and the many strategies they developed to challenge these others. Circumstances, including their drug use, often forced them to sell sex, but they all resisted the notion that they might be selling themselves. Because they engaged in an illegal profession, these women had little status: their working conditions were poor, and their work was physically and mentally exhausting. Nevertheless, many women described the ways in which they gained a sense of control over their lives. For instance, they learned how to manipulate pimps, how to control the types of services and length of time bought by their customers, and how to select customers. While none of these schemes explicitly enhanced their working conditions, they did make the women feel stronger and better about themselves.

In this book, I present prostitution from the point of view of the women themselves. To understand their current lives, it was necessary to learn how they got started in the life, the various processes involved in their continued prostitution careers, the link between prostitution and drug use, the women's interactions with their pimps and customers, and the impact of the AIDS epidemic and increasing violence on their experiences. I also examined the implications for women. Although my goal was to present the women's thoughts, feelings, and actions in their own words, the final text is a sociological monograph compiled by me as the researcher. Some women are quoted more than others because I developed a closer relationship with them, because they were more able to verbalize and capture their circumstances, or simply because they were more outspoken.

The Sample

The data for this book are qualitative. The research was conducted during the last ten years in the New York City and Atlanta metropolitan areas. One main data source was participant observation on streets, in hotels and other settings known for prostitution activity, and in drug-use settings, especially those that allowed sex-for-drug exchanges. Another data source was in-depth, life-history interviews with 180 women ranging in age from 18 to 59 years, with an average age of 34. One in two women was African-American and one in three white; the remaining women were Latina. Three in four had completed high school, and among them almost two-thirds had one or more years of additional educational training. Thirty women had graduated from college.

Forty women worked as street prostitutes and did not use drugs. On average, they had been prostitutes for 11 years. Forty women began using drugs an average of three years after they began working as prostitutes, and the average time they had worked as prostitutes was nine years. Forty women used drugs an average of five years before they became prostitutes, and on the average they had worked as prostitutes for eight years. Another forty women began smoking crack and exchanging sex for crack almost simultaneously, with an average of four years in the life. Twenty women who were interviewed were ex-prostitutes.

Comments on Methodology

When I tell people about my research, the most frequent question I am asked is how I gained access to the women rather than what I learned from the research. For many, prostitution is an unusual topic of conversation, and many people have expressed surprise that I, as a woman, conducted the research. During my research some customers indeed thought I was a working woman, a fact that almost always amuses those who hear about my work. However, few people want to hear stories about the women's struggles and sadness. Sometimes they ask questions about the reasons why women become prostitutes. Most of the time, they are surprised when I tell them that the prostitutes as well as their customers represent all layers of society. Before presenting the findings, it seems important to discuss the research process, including gaining access to the women, developing relationships, interviewing, and then leaving the field.[1]

Locating Prostitutes and Gaining Entree

One of the first challenges I faced was to identify locations where street prostitution took place. Many of these women worked on strolls, streets where prostitution activity is concentrated, or in hotels known for prostitution activity. Others, such as the crack prostitutes, worked in less public settings such as a crack house that might be someone's apartment.

I often learned of well-known public places from professional experts, such as law enforcement officials and health care providers at emergency rooms and sexually transmitted disease clinics. I gained other insights from lay experts, including taxi drivers, bartenders, and community representatives such as members of neighborhood associations. The contacts universally mentioned some strolls as the places where many women worked, where the local police focused attention, or where residents had organized protests against prostitution in their neighborhoods.

As I began visiting various locales, I continued to learn about new settings. In one sense, I was developing ethnographic maps of street prostitution. After several visits to a specific area, I also was able to expand these maps by adding information about the general atmosphere on the stroll, general characteristics of the various people present, the ways in which the women and customers connected, and the overall flow of action. In addition, my visits allowed the regular actors to notice me.

I soon learned that being an unknown woman in an area known for prostitution may cause many people to notice you, even stare at you, but it fails to yield many verbal interactions. Most of the time when I tried to make eye contact with one of the women, she quickly averted her eyes. Pimps, on the other hand, would stare at me straight on and I ended up being the one to look away. Customers would stop, blow their horn, or wave me over, frequently yelling obscenities when I ignored them. I realized that gaining entree into the prostitution world was not going to be as easy as I imagined it. Although I lacked such training in any of my qualitative methods classes, I decided to move slowly and not force any interaction. The most I said during the initial weeks in a new area was limited to "how are you" or "hi." This strategy paid off during my first visits to one of the strolls in Brooklyn, New York. After several appearances, one of the women walked up to me and sarcastically asked if I was looking for something. She caught me off guard, and all the answers I had practiced did not seem to make sense. I mumbled something about just wanting to walk around. She did not like my answer, but she did like my accent. We ended up talking about the latter and she was especially excited when I told her I came from Amsterdam. One of her friends had gone to Europe with her boyfriend, who was in the military. She understood from her that prostitution and drugs were legal in the Netherlands. While explaining to her that some of her friend's impressions were incorrect, I was able to show off some of my knowledge about prostitution. I mentioned that I was interested in prostitution and wanted to write a book about it.

Despite the fascination with my background and intentions, the prostitute immediately put me through a Streetwalker 101 test, and apparently I passed. She told me to make sure to come back. By the time I left, I not only had my first conversation but also my first connection to the scene. Variations of this entry process occurred on the other strolls. The main lesson I learned in these early efforts was the importance of having some knowledge of the lives of the people I wanted to study, while at the same time refraining from presenting myself as an expert.

Qualitative researchers often refer to their initial connections as gatekeepers and key respondents. Throughout my fieldwork I learned that some key respondents are important in providing initial access, but they become less central as the research evolves. For example, one of the women who introduced me to her lover, who was also her pimp, was arrested and disappeared for months. Another entered drug treatment soon after she facilitated my access. Other key respondents provided access to only a segment of the players on a scene. For example, if a woman worked for a pimp, [she] was unlikely . . . to introduce me to women working for another pimp. On one stroll my initial contact was with a pimp whom nobody liked. By associating with him, I almost lost the opportunity to meet other pimps. Some key respondents were less connected than promised—for example, some of the women who worked the street to support their drug habit. Often their connections were more frequently with drug users and less so with prostitutes.

Key respondents tend to be individuals central to the local scene, such as, in this case, pimps and the more senior prostitutes. Their function as gatekeepers often is to protect the scene and to screen outsiders. Many times I had to prove that I was not an undercover police officer or a woman with ambitions to become a streetwalker. While I thought I had gained entree, I quickly learned that many insiders subsequently wondered about my motives and approached me with suspicion and distrust.

Another lesson involved the need to proceed cautiously with self-nominated key respondents. For example, one of the women presented herself as knowing everyone on the stroll. While she did know everyone, she was not a central figure. On the contrary, the other prostitutes viewed her as a failed streetwalker whose drug use caused her to act unprofessionally. By associating with me, she hoped to regain some of her status. For me, however, it meant limited access to the other women because I affiliated myself with a woman who was marginal to the scene. On another occasion, my main key respondent was a man who claimed to own three crack houses in the neighborhood. However, he had a negative reputation, and people accused him of cheating on others. My initial alliance with him delayed, and almost blocked, my access to others in the neighborhood. He intentionally tried to keep me from others on the scene, not because he would gain something from that transaction but because it made him feel powerful. When I told him I was going to hang out with some of the other people, he threatened me until one of the other dealers stepped in and told him to stay away. The two of them argued back and forth, and finally I was free to go. Fortunately, the dealer who had spoken up for me was much more central and positively associated with the local scene. Finally, I am unsure if I would have had success in gaining entrance to the scene had I not been a woman.

Developing Relationships and Trust

The processes involved in developing relationships in research situations amplify those involved in developing relationships in general. Both parties need to get to know each other, become aware and accepting of each other's roles, and engage in a reciprocal relationship. Being supportive and providing practical assistance were the most visible and direct ways for me as the researcher to develop a relationship. Throughout the years, I have given countless rides, provided child care on numerous occasions, bought groceries, and listened for hours to stories that were unrelated to my initial research questions. Gradually, my role allowed me to become part of these women's lives and to build rapport with many of them.

Over time, many women also realized that I was uninterested in being a prostitute and that I genuinely was interested in learning as much as possible about their lives. Many felt flattered that someone wanted to learn from them and that they had knowledge to offer. Allowing women to tell their stories and engaging in a dialogue with them probably were the single most important techniques that allowed me to develop relationships with them. Had I only wanted to focus on the questions I had in mind, developing such relationships might have been more difficult.

At times, I was able to get to know a woman only after her pimp endorsed our contact. One of my scariest experiences occurred before I knew to work through the pimps, and one such man had some of his friends follow me on my way home one night. I will never know what plans they had in mind for me because I fortunately was able to escape with only a few bruises. Over a year later, the woman acknowledged that her pimp had gotten upset and told her he was going to teach me a lesson.

On other occasions, I first needed to be screened by owners and managers of crack houses before the research could continue. Interestingly, screenings always were done by a man even if the person who vouched for me was a man himself. While the women also were cautious, the ways in which they checked me out tended to be much more subtle. For example, one of them would tell me a story, indicating that it was a secret about another person on the stroll. Although I failed to realize this at the time, my field notes revealed that frequently after such a conversation, others would ask me questions about related topics. One woman later acknowledged that putting out such stories was a test to see if I would keep information confidential.

Learning more about the women and gaining a better understanding of their lives also raised many ethical questions. No textbook told me how to handle situations in which a pimp abused a woman, a customer forced a woman to engage in unwanted sex acts, a customer requested unprotected sex from a woman who knew she was HIV infected, or a boyfriend had realistic expectations regarding a woman's earnings to support his drug habit. I failed to know the proper response when asked to engage in illegal activities such as holding drugs or money a woman had stolen from a customer. In general, my response was to explain that I was there as a researcher. During those occasions when pressures became too severe, I decided to leave a scene. For example, I never returned to certain crack houses because pimps there continued to ask me to consider working for them.

Over time, I was fortunate to develop relationships with people who "watched my back." One pimp in particular intervened if he perceived other pimps, customers, or passersby harassing me. He also was the one who gave me my street name: Whitie (indicating my racial background) or Ms. Whitie for those who disrespected me. While this was my first street name, I subsequently had others. Being given a street name was a symbolic gesture of acceptance. Gradually, I developed an identity that allowed me to be both an insider and an outsider. While hanging out on the strolls and other gathering places, including crack houses, I had to deal with some of the same uncomfortable conditions as the prostitutes, such as cold or warm weather, lack of access to a rest room, refusals from owners for me to patronize a restaurant, and of course, harassment by customers and the police.

I participated in many informal conversations. Unless pushed to do so, I seldom divulged my opinions. I was more open with my feelings about situations and showed empathy. I learned quickly that providing an opinion can backfire. I agreed that one of the women was struggling a lot and stated that I felt sorry for her. While I meant to indicate my "genuine concern for her, she heard that I felt sorry for her because she was a failure. When she finally, after several weeks, talked with me again, I was able to explain to her that I was not judging her, but rather felt concerned for her. She remained cynical and many times asked me for favors to make up for my mistake. It took me months before I felt comfortable telling her that I felt I had done enough and that it was time to let go. However, if she was not ready, she needed to know that I would no longer go along. This was one of many occasions when I learned that although I wanted to facilitate my work as a researcher, that I wanted people to like and trust me, I also needed to set boundaries.

Rainy and slow nights often provided good opportunities for me to participate in conversations with groups of women. Popular topics included how to work safely, what to do about condom use, how to make more money. I often served as a health educator and a supplier of condoms, gels, vaginal douches, and other feminine products. Many women were very worried about the AIDS epidemic. However, they also were worried about how to use a condom when a customer refused to do so. They worried particularly about condom use when they needed money badly and, consequently, did not want to propose that the customer use one for fear of rejection. While some women became experts at "making" their customers use a condom—for example, "by hiding it in their mouth prior to beginning oral sex—others would carry condoms to please me but never pull one out. If a woman was HIV positive and I knew she failed to use a condom, I faced the ethical dilemma of challenging her or staying out of it.

Developing trusting relationships with crack prostitutes was more difficult. Crack houses were not the right environment for informal conversations. Typically, the atmosphere was tense and everyone was suspicious of each other. The best times to talk with these women were when we bought groceries together, when I helped them clean their homes, or when we shared a meal. Often the women were very different when they were not high than they were when they were high or craving crack. In my conversations with them, I learned that while I might have observed their actions the night before, they themselves might not remember them. Once I realized this, I would be very careful to omit any detail unless I knew that the woman herself did remember the event.

In-Depth Interviews

All interviews were conducted in a private setting, including women's residences, my car or my office, a restaurant of the women's choice, or any other setting the women selected. I did not begin conducting official interviews until I developed relationships with the women. Acquiring written informed consent prior to the interview was problematic. It made me feel awkward. Here I was asking the women to sign a form after they had begun to trust me. However, often I felt more upset about this technicality than the women themselves. As soon as they realized that the form was something the university required, they seemed to understand. Often they laughed about the official statements, and some asked if I was sure the form was to protect them and not the school.[2] None of the women refused to sign the consent form, although some refused to sign it right away and asked to be interviewed later.

In some instances the consent procedures caused the women to expect a formal interview. Some of them were disappointed when they saw I only had a few structured questions about demographic characteristics, followed by a long list of open-ended questions. When this disappointment occurred, I reminded the women that I wanted to learn from them and that the best way to do so was by engaging in a dialogue rather than interrogating them. Only by letting the women identify their salient issues and the topics they wanted to address was I able to gain an insider's perspective. By being a careful listener and probing for additional information and explanation, I as the interviewer, together with the women, was able to uncover the complexities of their lives. In addition, the nature of the interview allowed me to ask questions about contradictions in a woman's story. For example, sometimes a woman would say that she always used a condom. However, later on in the conversation she would indicate that if she needed drugs she would never use one. By asking her to elaborate on this, I was able to begin developing insights into condom use by type of partner, type of sex acts, and social context.

The interviewer becomes much more a part of the interview when the conversations are in-depth than when a structured questionnaire is used. Because I was so integral to the process, the way the women viewed me may have biased their answers. On the one hand, this bias might be reduced because of the extent to which both parties already knew each other; on the other, a woman might fail to give her true opinion and reveal her actions if she knew that these went against the interviewer's opinion. I suspected that some women played down the ways in which their pimps manipulated them once they knew that I was not too fond of these men. However, some might have taken more time to explain the relationship with their pimp in order to "correct" my image.

My background, so different from that of these women, most likely affected the nature of the interviews. I occupied a higher socioeconomic status. I had a place to live and a job. In contrast to the nonwhite women, I came from a different racial background. While I don't know to what extent these differences played a role, I acknowledge that they must have had some effect on this research.

Leaving the Field

Leaving the field was not something that occurred after completion of the fieldwork, but an event that took place daily. Although I sometimes stayed on the strolls all night or hung out for several days, I always had a home to return to. I had a house with electricity, a warm shower, a comfortable bed, and a kitchen. My house sat on a street where I had no fear of being shot on my way there and where I did not find condoms or syringes on my doorstep.

During several stages of the study, I had access to a car, which I used to give the women rides or to run errands together. However, I will never forget the cold night when everyone on the street was freezing, and I left to go home. I turned up the heat in my car, and tears streamed down my cheeks. I appreciated the heat, but I felt more guilty about that luxury than ever before. I truly felt like an outsider, or maybe even more appropriate, a betrayer.

Throughout the years of fieldwork, there were a number of times when I left the scene temporarily. For example, when so many people were dying from AIDS, I was unable to ignore the devastating impact of this disease. I needed an emotional break.

Physically removing myself from the scene was common when I experienced difficulty remaining objective. Once I became too involved in a woman's life and almost adopted her and her family. Another time I felt a true hatred for a crack house owner and was unable to adhere to the rules of courteous interactions. Still another time, I got angry with a woman whose steady partner was HIV positive when she failed to ask him to use a condom when they had sex.

I also took temporary breaks from a particular scene by shifting settings and neighborhoods. For example, I would invest most of my time in women from a particular crack house for several weeks. Then I would shift to spending more time on one of the strolls, while making shorter and less frequent visits to the crack house. By shifting scenes, I was able to tell people why I was leaving and to remind all of us of my researcher role.

While I focused on leaving the field, I became interested in women who had left the life. It seemed important to have an understanding of their past and current circumstances. I knew some of them from the days when they were working, but identifying others was a challenge. There was no gathering place for ex-prostitutes. Informal networking, advertisements in local newspapers, and local clinics and community settings allowed me to reach twenty of these women. Conducting interviews with them later in the data collection process prepared me to ask specific questions. I realized that I had learned enough about the life to know what to ask. Interviewing ex-prostitutes also prepared me for moving from the fieldwork to writing.

It is hard to determine exactly when I left the field. It seems like a process that never ends. Although I was more physically removed from the scene, I continued to be involved while analyzing the data and writing this book. I also created opportunities to go back, for example, by asking women to give me feedback on parts of the manuscript or at times when I experienced writer's block and my car seemed to automatically steer itself to one of the strolls. I also have developed other research projects in some of the same communities. For example, both a project on intergenerational drug use and a gender-specific intervention project to help women remain HIV negative have brought me back to the same population. Some of the women have become key respondents in these new projects, while others now are members of a research team. For example, Beth, one of the women who has left prostitution, works as an outreach worker on another project.

Six Themes in the Ethnography of Prostitution

The main intention of my work is to provide the reader with a perspective on street prostitution from the point of view of the women themselves. There are six fundamental aspects of the women's lives as prostitutes that must be considered. The first concerns the women's own explanations for their involvement in prostitution and their descriptions of the various circumstances that led them to become prostitutes. Their stories include justifications such as traumatic past experiences, especially sexual abuse, the lack of love they experienced as children, pressures by friends and pimps, the need for drugs, and most prominently, the economic forces that pushed them into the life. A number of women describe these justifications as excuses, as reflective explanations they have developed after becoming a prostitute.

The women describe the nature of their initial experiences, which often involved alienation from those outside the life. They also show the differences in the processes between women who work as prostitutes and use drugs and women who do not use drugs.

Although all these women work either on the street or in drug-use settings, their lives do differ. My second theme is a typology that captures these differences, looking at the women's prostitution versus drug-use identities. The typology distinguishes among (a) streetwalkers, women who work strolls and who do not use drugs; (b) hooked prostitutes, women who identify themselves mainly as prostitutes but who upon their entrance into the life also began using drugs; (c) prostituting addicts, women who view themselves mainly as drug users and who became prostitutes to support their drug habit; and (d) crack prostitutes, women who trade sex for crack.

This typology explains the differences in the women's strategies for soliciting customers, their screening of customers, pricing of sex acts, and bargaining for services. For example, the streetwalkers have the most bargaining power, while such power appears to be lacking among the crack prostitutes.

Few prostitutes work in a vacuum. The third theme is the role of pimps, a label that most women dislike and for which they prefer to substitute "old man" or "boyfriend." Among the pimps, one finds entrepreneur lovers, men who mainly employ streetwalkers and hooked prostitutes and sometimes prostituting addicts. Entrepreneur lovers engage in the life for business reasons. They treat the women as their employees or their property and view them primarily as an economic commodity. The more successful a woman is in earning them money, the more difficult it is for that woman to leave her entrepreneur pimp.

Most prostituting addicts and some hooked prostitutes work for a lover pimp, a man who is their steady partner but who also lives off their earnings. Typically, such pimps employ only one woman. The dynamics in the relationship between a prostitute and her lover pimp become more complex when both partners use drugs. Drugs often become the glue of the relationship.

For many crack prostitutes, their crack addiction serves as a pimp. Few plan to exchange sex for crack when they first begin using; often several weeks or months pass before a woman who barters sex for crack realizes that she is a prostitute.

Historically, society has blamed prostitutes for introducing sexually transmitted diseases into the general population. Similarly, it makes them scapegoats for the spread of HIV/AIDS. Yet their pimps and customers are not held accountable. The fourth theme in the anthropological study of prostitution is the impact of the AIDS epidemic on the women's lives. Although most are knowledgeable about HIV risk behaviors and the ways to reduce their risk, many misconceptions exist. The women describe the complexities of condom use, especially with steady partners but also with paying customers. Many women have mixed feelings about HIV testing, wondering how to cope with a positive test result while no cure is available. A few of the women already knew their HIV-infected status, and the discussion touches on their dilemmas as well.

The fifth theme is the violence and abuse that make common appearances in the women's lives. An ethnography of prostitution must allow the women to describe violence in their neighborhoods as well as violence in prostitution and drug-use settings. The most common violence they encounter is from customers. These men often assume that because they pay for sex they buy a woman. Apparently, casual customers pose more of a danger than those who are regulars. The types of abuse the women encounter are emotional, physical, and sexual. In addition to customers, pimps and boyfriends abuse the women. Finally, the women discuss harassment by law enforcement officers.

When I talked with the women, it often seemed that there were no opportunities to escape from the life. Yet the sixth and final theme must be the escape from prostitution. Women who have left prostitution can describe the process of their exit from prostitution. As ex-prostitutes they struggle with the stigma of their past, the challenges of developing a new identity, and the impact of their past on current intimate relationships. Those who were also drug users often view themselves as ex-prostitutes and recovering addicts, a perspective that seems to create a role conflict. Overall, most ex-prostitutes find that their past follows them like a bad hangover.

Notes

1. For more information about qualitative research methods, see, for example, Patricia Adler and Peter Adler, *Membership Roles in Field Research* (Newbury Park: Sage, 1987); Michael Agar, *The Professional Stranger* (New York: Academic Press, 1980) and *Speaking of Ethnography* (Beverly Hills: Sage, 1986); Howard Becker and Blanche Geer, "Participant Observation and Interviewing: A Comparison," *Human Organization* 16 (1957): 28–32; Norman Denzin, *Sociological Methods: A Sourcebook* (Chicago: Aldine, 1970); Barney Glaser and Anselm Strauss, *The Discovery of Grounded Theory: Strategies for Qualitative Research* (Chicago: Aldine, 1967); Y. Lincoln and E. Guba, *Naturalistic Inquiry* (Beverly Hills: Sage, 1985); John Lofland, "Analytic Ethnography: Features, Failings, and Futures," *Journal of Contemporary Ethnography* 24 (1996): 30–67; and James Spradley, *The Ethnographic Interview* (New York: Holt, Rinehart and Winston, 1979) and *Participant Observation* (New York: Holt, Rinehart and Winston, 1980).
2. For a more extensive discussion of informed consent procedures and related ethical issues, see Bruce L. Berg, *Qualitative Research Methods for the Social Sciences,* 3rd edition, Chapter 3: "Ethical Issues" (Boston: Allyn and Bacon, 1998).

Critical Thinking

1. How do prostitutes gain a sense of control over their lives?
2. How does the author describe the women in her study?
3. How does the author describe people's reactions when she tells them what her research is about?
4. How and where did she find places of prostitution?
5. What was the main lesson she learned in her early efforts?
6. How does she describe "key respondents"?
7. How did she manage to develop relationships with prostitutes? What was the single most important technique?
8. How did the author handle situations involving ethical questions?
9. Describe the author's interview techniques and the rationale behind them.
10. How did the author feel about being able to "leave the field" daily?
11. Under what circumstances would she leave a scene temporarily?
12. What explanations do the women themselves give for their involvement in prostitution?
13. What is the author's typology regarding prostitutes? What kinds of strategies are thereby explained? Which has the most bargaining power? Which has the least?
14. How does the author describe the different kinds of pimps?
15. Who is historically held responsible for the spread of HIV/AIDS? Who is not held responsible?
16. How does the author describe the violence and abuse suffered by prostitutes and who is likely to inflict it?
17. With what do ex-prostitutes come to struggle?

Internet References

Anthropology Links
http://anthropology.gmu.edu

Archaeology and Anthropology Computing and Study Skills
www.isca.ox.ac.uk/index.html

Introduction to Anthropological Fieldwork and Ethnography
http://web.mit.edu/dumit/www/syl-anth.html

Women Watch
www.un.org/womenwatch/about

Article

Prepared by: Elvio Angeloni

The House Gun

White Writing, White Fears, and Black Justice

To comprehend the background to the Pistorius case, in this article Nancy Scheper-Hughes reflects on the seeds of violence and self-destruction among whites living in South Africa as well as in other divided societies, such as the United States and Israel. Ed.

NANCY SCHEPER-HUGHES

Learning Outcomes

After reading this article, you will be able to:

- Discuss the seeds of violence that have become so pervasive among whites living in South Africa as well as in other divided societies such as the United States and Israel.
- Draw the connections between structural and everyday violence in the homes, streets, and schools in the United States.
- Discuss the origins of white fear and how it has shaped the justice system's treatment of blacks in both the United States as well as in South Africa.

On the day that the death of Nobel Prize laureate Nadine Gordimer was announced, I set up an altar over my Berkeley fireplace featuring a selection of my favourite of her books; not the more celebrated ones, but her anthology of short stories, *Jump and other stories* (1992), and her less admired post-apartheid novels, *The pickup* (2001) and *The house gun* (1998). Like her white South African literary contemporaries (J.M. Coetzee, André Brink, and Breyten Breytenbach) Gordimer was a literary captive of the apartheid regime. Some would say that apartheid was her *only* topic and she herself confided that apartheid had forced her to adopt a genre of critical realism so as to 'describe a situation so truthfully ... that the reader could no longer evade it' (Gordimer 1988: 298).

South American novelists, like Gabriel García Márquez and the Czech novelist Michal Ajvaz, also writing under adverse political conditions, deployed the subterfuge of 'magical realism' to expose and mock the absurdity of the state. One could hardly imagine a magical realist genre emerging under the yoke of apartheid, which produced other genres; one I might call literary brutalism. On receiving the Jerusalem Prize, J.M. Coetzee said that the apartheid state had 'so deformed and stunted human beings and their inner lives that South African literature [was] a literature of bondage ... a less than fully human literature, the kind of literature you would expect people to write from prison' (*The New York Times*, 11 April 1987). In his painfully confessional memoirs (*Boyhood* and *Youth*) Coetzee addressed the unbearable 'whiteness' of being a white Afrikaner in South Africa. In his post-apartheid novel, *Disgrace*, he questioned the Afrikaner settler descendants' right to exist in the country except as eviscerated and passive penitents.

As an anthropologist sometimes working in South Africa I found Gordimer's books better to *think with*, while finding the emotional force of Coetzee's oeuvre better to *feel with*. Here I want to honour Gordimer's anticipatory imagination, her ability to predict the twisted legacies of apartheid, not only for black South Africans but also for white South Africans. I refer to the seeds of violence and self-destruction that can be found among whites living in South Africa as well as in other racially deformed societies, such as the United States and Israel.

The Enemy Within

We have met the enemy and he is us.
(Walt Kelly's (1913–1973) *Pogo* comic strip)

Some years ago, as I was about to deliver a lecture on violence in war and in peace at a large public university in the United

States, the event was interrupted by a bomb threat. The lecture was rescheduled and moved to the home of the university's dean who lived in a gated community that had grown up around his lovely modernist home. He assured me that I could enter the gated community without inspection by the private security guards. He had refused to support the excessive monitoring of residents and their guests, as an absurd performance. The threat was not from outsiders, the residents of low-income neighborhoods, but rather from within the gated community itself. One day his son had come home with a story of 'cops and robbers', boasting of real guns owned by the neighboring children's parents. Complaints were lodged, apologies delivered, and the guns moved to a locked cabinet. Meanwhile, the dean and his family remained trapped inside a pistol-packing gated community, a good enough metaphor of white fright.

This was not the first time I participated in a lecture that was interrupted by the threat of violence. At the University of Cape Town (UCT) in 1994, just before the election of Nelson Mandela, a deadly period of political anarchy resulted in a spate of massacres in pubs, schools, worker hostels, churches, and petrol stations (Scheper-Hughes 1994). The UCT faculty knew how to 'duck-and-hide' during academic lockdowns, which occurred with frequency. One lockdown accompanied a guest lecture by a British literary scholar who I was charged to introduce. While I reassured the scholar that the call-and-response between police and black student protesters was performative, being *locked down* in the Arts Block building and surrounded by *toyi-toyi* high-stepping dance crowds waving sticks to approximate traditional weapons felt as weirdly crazy as being locked down in that suburban gated community.

Then, in 2001, just as I was to give a lecture on organ trafficking at the Hebrew University in Jerusalem, a bomb exploded outside the entrance to the Mount Scopus campus. The damage was minor, no one was hurt, and I delivered the lecture on time. Everyone in the lecture hall was relaxed except for me. After the talk, an Israeli colleague confided that people were so accustomed to daily violence that they missed it when nothing happened for a stretch. I was told, 'It is as if our bodies are wired or primed for the violence and we become bored during the quiet periods'.

These vignettes illustrate the militarization of everyday life in countries accustomed to war. Philippe Bourgois and I (2004) have referred to a 'continuum of violence' in which war crimes gradually seep into civilian life: armed and dangerous gated communities, racial profiling, stop-and-frisk laws, and the performance of heightened security in airports. Each time I pass through TSA (Transportation Security Administration) screening in US airports, I think of Aaron Alexis, the 34-year-old Navy reservist who opened fire at a US naval base in Washington, DC in September 2013, killing 12 people and wounding several others before dying in a shootout with police. Later, he was found to have been arrested in previous shooting incidents, despite which he passed security clearance as a contract worker for the US Navy Yard. After that 'incident' I refused to take off my shoes.

How to Talk About Violence without Doing Anything About It

On the second anniversary of the Arizona mall shoot-out, Gabrielle Giffords (2014) spoke frankly about her uphill battle to regain speech and the use of her right arm and leg after having been shot in the head by a disgruntled shooter. While expressing her disappointment that the US Congress failed to approve a modest bill to increase the use of background checks on gun owners, she made it clear that she and her husband were political moderates and 'proud gun owners' themselves, a position carefully worded so that it would not offend members of the hypervigilant gun lobby.

Following the Columbine High School shooting in 1999, President Clinton gave an impassioned speech in the White House Rose Garden during which he announced a 'National Campaign against Youth Violence' to mobilize businesses, volunteer organizations, the media, and advertising agencies to develop violence reduction programmes.[1] The campaign sought to encourage city officials, churches, schools, mental health services, and families across a racially and class divided United States to find ways to unite against youth violence. Wall Street advertising executives recruited youth leaders from inner cities to interrupt *flare-ups* in schoolyards and street corners using gang slang (*'squash it'*) and hand signs to *cool it*! A 'Just Say No to Violence' campaign enlisted schoolchildren to cover city walls with black paint handprints to memorialize those who died in gang wars and street violence. School counsellors introduced techniques of *behavioural self-management* through meditation and mindfulness to sensitize *at-risk youth* (i.e. poor black and Latino urban youth) to 'the tragedy of senseless homicides, drugs, and racist rap music'.

During meetings of President Clinton's Academic Advisory Board on Youth Violence (of which I was a member), headed by critical anthropologist John Devine, our committee of urban violence scholars identified key variables missed by the national campaign. We differentiated mass shootings in suburban schools from the broader context of youth homicides in poor communities, including police homicides. The latter are not counted in government statistics on 'violence' which justify self-defence by police.[2] We questioned criminological labels such as 'death by cop', or 'suicide by cop', which attributed to the victims of police violence a desire to die by provoking police to shoot them. We explained the 'code of the street'

(Anderson 2000) and the 'search for respect' (Bourgois 2003) that led to the deaths of minority youth. We linked the hypersensitivity and overreaction to imagined racial insults to a culture of shame, defeat and self-hatred honed by the US prison system as a black and Latino gulag (Gilligan 1997). We described the lethal association of male honour with physical force and primitive right to shoot laws, like today's 'Stand your Ground' legislation, which states that an individual has no duty to retreat from any place they have lawful right to be and may use lethal force if they face immediate threat of serious bodily harm. We drew connections between structural and everyday violence in the homes, streets, and schools of the United States. Finally, we linked the so-called epidemic of youth violence to the militarization of US society as the relentless wars waged abroad come home to roost in homelessness, drug addiction, PTSD (post-traumatic stress disorder), and domestic violence among war veterans.

We delivered a report to the President's office that went against the grain. Passages dealing with the dangers of weapons in US homes and proposals to buy back weapons from gang leaders were deleted. Censorship and self-censorship ruled the day. In the end, the report delivered to President Clinton and his staff was shelved. Today, one can barely find it online, hidden in digitized government archives. Our findings were effectively *disappeared.*

The Spectre of Violence

The youth violence campaign directed the national spotlight on the inner city and black youth despite the fact that the Columbine shooters were white and middle class. Youth violence itself is color-coded. White children are not *youth*, but *adolescents* or *teenagers*. Greenberg and Schneider (1994) nailed the problem in the title of their article 'Violence in American cities: Young black males is the answer, but what was the question?' in which they compared crime in three disintegrating cities in New Jersey—Camden, Trenton, and Newark. They found that assaults, rapes and homicides (discounting police homicides) were equally distributed among poor blacks, whites, and Latinos. They attributed the causes of urban violence to deindustrialization, unemployment, urban deserts, poor land use, and the social abandonment of poor and working class people of all backgrounds. However, the target of violent crimes is not equally distributed: black men are four times more likely to be victims of homicide than white men.[3]

The unidentified risk factor at the center of this analysis is the gated community in affluent suburban neighborhoods with their citadel mentality, xenophobia, and exaggerated fears of 'intruders' invading exclusive enclaves in Pretoria, in picturesque New England towns, and in upscale shopping malls. Mass shootings are largely contained to suburbs and affluent communities, not to inner cities and poor suburbs.[4] No other mature democratic nation allows private citizens to assemble military arsenals in their homes, as does the United States, a practice that endangers the lives and freedom of all citizens.

In my seminar on 'Violence and human rights in war and peace' at the University of California's Washington DC Center in the fall of 2013, my students expressed blasé attitudes following the Navy Yard shooting which had taken place not far from our building on 16 September that year. Invited to talk about their thoughts and feelings regarding the shooting, their concerns were that the impending government shutdown would interrupt their university internships. The public response to the Navy Yard incident focused on the crumbling mental health system in the United States. The figure of the mentally ill sociopath replaced that of the black young man as the prime suspect when, in fact, there are robust statistics funded by the National Institute of Mental Health showing that there is no correlation between mental illness and violent crime except that the mentally ill are at greater risk of being the victims of violence at the hands of family members and police (Hiday et al. 1999; Stuart 2003).

The suburban response to a perceived state of siege is the neighborhood watch group whose members sometimes blur into vigilantes. The murder of Trayvon Martin in a gated community in Sanford, Florida is a case in point. The 17-year-old African American student was shot in February 2012 by neighborhood watch captain, George Zimmerman, who feared that the black teenager, face obscured by a hoodie, must be a dangerous intruder and that the object (a mobile phone) in his hand might be a weapon.[5] Although Zimmerman's defence team did not use Florida's controversial 'Stand your Ground' law, the judge instructed the jurors that the defendant had a legal right to use 'deadly force' if he had reason to believe that his life was in danger, *even if that was not the case.*[6] The jury exonerated Zimmerman of second degree murder charges and even manslaughter. They could empathize with the fear that a black teenager out of place might be a murderous intruder.

Then came the murder of 17-year-old Michael Brown in Ferguson, Missouri, by a white police officer, Darren Wilson, who shot and killed the young man who fell to the ground after being shot six times with his hands raised in surrender. Based on released and contested autopsy reports, there is debate as to whether there was a closeup struggle for the officer's gun and whether one of the head wounds occurred when Brown was charging the officer (according to the officer's statement) or whether it happened when the victim was kneeling with his head down (as some witnesses claim). Immediately following the murder protesters and demonstrators gathered, raising their hands in what has since become a universal symbol of police injustice in the United States. Meanwhile, Wilson is on paid leave while a Saint Louis grand jury has until January 2015 to decide if the officer will be criminally charged for the death of the unarmed black teenager.

White Fears, Black Justice: The Oscar Pistorius Trial in South Africa

While often compared to the O.J. Simpson trial, the case of Oscar Pistorius is more closely analogous to those of the killers of Trayvon Martin and Michael Brown in which armed white men attributed violent intent to black strangers. Tried for the murder of his live-in girlfriend in South Africa, 27-year-old Oscar Pistorius was an Olympic paraplegic athlete and sprinter known as the 'Blade Runner' (Sokolove 2012), who raced on J-shaped carbon-fibre prostheses in Olympic competitions against able-bodied runners. South Africans adored him until Pistorius turned himself into the police after killing his girlfriend, Reeva Steenkamp in the early hours of Valentine's Day, 14 February 2013.

Pistorius admitted to shooting Reeva four times in the head through the locked door of a small bathroom cubicle, but claimed that it was a mistake. Awakened by strange sounds inside the house, he feared an intruder. He jumped from his bed, grabbed his pistol and ran to investigate without taking the time to put on his prosthetic legs. Hearing a noise that resembled heavy wood being moved or dragged, Pistorius claims that he shot through the door not knowing that his girlfriend was hiding there. He realized what he had done after returning to his bed and finding it empty at which point he called the police. The prosecution argued that Pistorius had shot his girlfriend in a jealous rage after an argument.

Pistorious' emotional outbreaks, sobbing and retching in the courtroom, resulted in a month-long psychiatric examination to determine if he was competent to stand trial. Witnesses described the defendant as over-reactive to perceived threats to his physical security, a trauma attributed to the amputation of his legs below his knees when he was a toddler. The psychiatric report confirmed symptoms of anxiety and PTSD, to be expected, but no evidence of mental incompetence. Declared sane on 16 June 2014, Pistorius' fate rested in the hands of the judge and her two assessors. Judge Thokozile Matilda Masipa, a former social worker and crime reporter who became a lawyer and subsequently a high court judge, was born in Soweto in 1947. She is extremely knowledgeable about violent crimes, assaults, break-ins, homicides and rapes in South Africa.

South Africa is one of the most violent nations in the world.[7] The defendant's unusual behaviour in the courtroom, his retching, vomiting and strangulated begging at the feet of the judge, was televised publicly. His calls for mercy from 'My Lady' had little effect on the stone-faced judge except to clear the room and shut off the cameras until Pistorius could compose himself. His credibility was further weakened by the media release of the defence team's video of Pistorius running on his stumps to reenact the scene of the shooting. The athlete's claim that he was unsteady and vulnerable without his prostheses was proven false by his own video.[8]

The verdict, announced on 12 September 2014, was controversial. The state was unable to prove beyond reasonable doubt that Oscar was guilty of *premeditated* murder. The state could not disprove Pistorius' claim that he was terrified and confused when he jumped out of bed to kill a suspected intruder who might have entered the bathroom via a ladder left by the window by careless construction workers. Masipa judged the defendant guilty of culpable homicide having 'failed to take any steps to avoid the death' and having 'acted hastily' in using excessive force. Moreover, he was also found guilty of 'reckless endangerment' in his illegal possession of ammunition.

The small extended family of Oscar Pistorius owned 55 firearms, including automatic weapons.[9] However, the silver 9-mm pistol that Pistorius used to kill his girlfriend is a common accessory in white middle class South African households. In this, the Pistorius trial bears an uncanny resemblance to Gordimer's novel, *The house gun*, about a homicide in a white suburban community.

The House Gun

> The gun is in court. It has become Exhibit 1.
>
> The fingerprints of the accused's left hand, the
>
> Prosecutor says, were discovered upon it by forensic
>
> tests . . .
>
> -You know this handgun? –
>
> -Yes.–
>
> - Do you own it? –
>
> -No.–
>
> -Who does? –
>
> -I don't know in whose name it was licensed. It was the gun kept in the house so that if someone was attacked, intruders broke in; so whoever it was could defend himself. –
>
> (Gordimer, *The house gun*, 1998)

The protagonist of the *The house gun* is a young white architect, Duncan Lindgard, who is charged with the murder of his live-in lover, Natalie, a rudderless drifter of 27. Duncan's parents, Claudia, a public health doctor, and Harald, an insurance executive, are from backgrounds similar to the Pistorius family, although less affluent. Like Oscar, Duncan grows up in a white South African suburb that isolates him from the larger society, which is black and poor. Both sets of parents (Lindgard and Pistorius) see themselves as moderately progressive though disengaged from the social and political realities of democratic South Africa. Duncan is now living in a middle class professional community in Pretoria. There is a house with three young gay men and a cottage across a small garden where Duncan and his current girlfriend, Natalie, live. Times have changed enough so that one of the young men is a gay black journalist living with another gay couple, but their sexual identities and relations are fluid, bisexual. There are also other intimacies that unite these five young people into a communal post-apartheid cocoon.

One evening Duncan finds Natalie in *flagrante delicto* with his friend and former male lover, Carl Jespersen, in the communal house across from the cottage. Natalie and Carl cannot stop the culmination of their sexual act although they can see Duncan observing them. Duncan leaves to brood in his cottage like a festering Hamlet. When he returns to confront Jespersen, Natalie has already left the house and Jespersen, casually exposing his long, naked legs on the couch, makes light of the incident, and invites Duncan to have a drink with him. Natalie is just a 'bird', after all, he says, it meant nothing to him. But Duncan, in something akin to a trance state, picks up the house gun that is sitting on the end table next to the sofa where Carl is relaxing and where he had made love with Natalie a few hours earlier. He shoots his rival point-blank in the head. When the police are called, they find the victim 'lying half-on, half-off the sofa, as if he had been taken by surprise when shot and had tried to rise' (p. 15). One of Jespersen's flip-flops dangles off his foot. Beneath his silk dressing gown, he is naked. The description put me in mind of Jacques-Louis David's painting 'Death of Marat'.

In short order, Duncan is arrested, charged with murder, and he admits the crime. There is to be a trial and there is a lawyer. Duncan does not want to speak with his parents who feel as if they are suddenly thrown into another country. Inside the public courtroom filled with black faces, Claudia and Harald Lindgard are confused, shaken to the roots. Like Henke Pistorius, Duncan's parents are forced to appear in a public world that is totally unfamiliar to them and to confront the turbulent life of a son who is a stranger to them. Duncan's lawyer, Hamilton Motsamai, spends a few minutes before the black judge who denies bail to the accused as if he were a public threat or likely to flee the country.

Where would her son go Claudia wonders, before excusing herself to use a dirty, public restroom where she vomits, just as Oscar Pistorius retched in the Pretoria courtroom. Motsamai squeezes Duncan's shoulder as he swings his briefcase and rushes out of the courtroom. Claudia and Harald cannot imagine that their son is at the mercy of a black lawyer and a black judge. Harald wonders if the lawyer is 'competent'. Although proud, skilled and confident, Motsamai is anathema to Duncan's parents. He taxes their patience with his roundabout way of speaking. Here Gordimer is exposing the post-apartheid situation of white South Africans who are forced to confront their fall from power and grace simultaneously. The parents are concerned that the death penalty, the legacy of apartheid, is still on the books.

The white South Africans in this book appear like sleepwalkers in a society that has recently replaced a violent, racist, militarized state with an imperfect democratic one. Duncan is indifferent to his fate. Whether he is free on bail or left to rot in a cell awaiting trial doesn't seem to matter to him. Natalie also suffers from a kind of lethal passivity, indifferent to her life and the life of the infant she is now carrying. She had once tried to commit suicide and was furious that Duncan rescued her. She doesn't know or care who fathered her foetus. She had sex with both Jespersen and Duncan on the same fateful day.

The centre doesn't hold. Violence is a constant. It is in the air they breathe. It circles their heads like cigarette smoke. But they are surrounded by the smoky, smouldering townships, about which they know nothing, but which they fear constantly. Whites are now strangers in uncharted land, living in constant fear of random acts of violence by intruders from the *de facto* segregated South African townships. They barricade themselves in gated communities and arm themselves with a gun in every room.

Like J.M. Coetzee, Nadine Gordimer, has often been described as 'the conscience of white South Africans', a white liberal who chronicled the lives of ordinary South Africans, most of them whites, from the distance of her elegant home in an upscale Johannesburg neighbourhood. Gordimer was accused of losing her authorial voice and literary power after the end of apartheid. Both Gordimer and J. M. Coetzee were viewed with suspicion by whites—Afrikaner and Anglo, Christian, and Jew—and by black South Africans because they told painful secrets about often unlovely people, and were brutally honest and unpredictable. In her essay 'How shall we look at each other then?' Gordimer (1999: 140) predicted the legacy of apartheid for post-apartheid South Africa: 'Just as there are people physically maimed by the struggle between white power and black liberation, there is psychological, behavioral damage that all of us in South Africa have been subject to in some degree, whether we know it or not, whether we are whites who have shut eyes and locked electronically controlled gates on what was happening to blacks, or whether we are blacks who have been transported and dumped wherever the government wished, teargassed and shot, detained, forced into exile, or have left to join the liberation army which came into being when no other choice remained'. In the end, she writes, 'Violence became the South African way of life'.

Gordimer's anti-apartheid books were banned by the apartheid regime and one of her most famous novels, *July's people*, irritated the democratic public education system in Gauteng so much that it threatened to remove the book from the school curriculum in 2001. Set in a future apocalyptic South Africa where unsettled racial conflicts erupt into civil war, *July's people* struck the post-apartheid educators as too removed from current social realities. Both J. M. Coetzee's *Disgrace* and Gordimer's *The house gun* nailed rather than hailed the reconstruction and reconciliation involved in building a democratic new South Africa.

Those unfamiliar with South African social and political realities might find it difficult to believe that Pistorius—that tall, handsome, internationally beloved demigod—could possibly fear an intruder in the bathroom of his high security suburb. Pistorius' fortress-like home inside the exclusive Silver Woods Estate in Pretoria was protected by an 8-foot-high electrified fence, walls, razor wire, motion sensors and armed guards. The gated security estate is the 21st-century South African *laager*, the 19th-century Afrikaner settlers' strategy against the ever-present black threat, circling their wagons to create a blockade against the natives (Perry 2013). Despite the intense security, Pistorius' defence was that he was a poor sleeper and was awakened by strange sounds in the bathroom that he attributed to an *intruder*, a code for black *intruder*. Described by character witnesses as hypervigilant, anxious and short-tempered, Pistorius admitted shooting through the door without much forethought. The gun was handy and he ran shooting at it like a cowboy.

The state could not disprove this argument. The neighbours who reported screams were deemed unreliable witnesses. Judge Masipa knew better than most that both violence and fear are a way of life in South Africa. All South Africans, white, black and coloured, live every day anticipating ghosts past and fears of retribution to be sure, but also ghosts present; the realities of a continuing, smouldering and woefully incomplete revolution that still burns in the forgotten 'lost generation' of black anti-apartheid youth. Today in their 40s, they sacrificed everything (education, families, lovers) to create a society based not only on political democracy but on the foundation of a viable and fair economy. Perhaps Judge Masipa knows that whites have reason to fear violence. A great many South Africans sleep uneasily with nightmares of razor fences, ferocious dogs, rape, assault, and homicide. South Africa is a land of terrible beauty and of terrible crime, the statistics so far surpassing those in the United States as to make our private security apparatuses and neighbourhood night watchmen seem like a collective mass hysteria, a hallucination.

In South Africa today, the political tables have turned but the economic tables have not. People's expectations were dashed and everyday violence has become the new norm. *The house gun* describes a situation in which 'a daily tally of deaths was as routine as a weather report; elsewhere, taxi drivers shot one another in rivalry over who would choose to ride with them, quarrels in discotheques were settled by the final curse-word of guns. State violence under the old, past regime had habituated its victims to it. People had forgotten there was any other way' (1998: 48–49).

The Pistorius case cracked open the code of the gated community based on the technical manipulation of white fears. Oscar Pistorius' expressed sense of personal threat, his rapid mobilization for self-defence, his mistaking the sound of the washing machine for a break-in by an intruder, was not implausible in the South African context. The ubiquitous house gun appears as a transitional object; the comforting pacifier, the ruby blanket, the house cat, like the house gun, are things that every white household needs.

Gordimer wrote *The house gun* amidst political debates in South Africa about ending the death penalty and about gun control during an alarming increase in violence against middle class white homes that were once protected by the apartheid machine. Today, whites in South Africa are forced to rely on private resources, their private guards, razor wire, and electronic security systems, and in the last instance, their pistols. In her short story, *Once upon a time*, Nadine Gordimer (1992) describes how she balked at an invitation to contribute to an anthology of stories for children. What kind of fairy tale could she write in the midst of the apartheid struggle? One that was the kind of bedtime story that only a sadistic parent would tell their children, a fairy tale equal to Hans Christian Andersen or the Brothers Grimm? Gordimer told the story of a house in a suburb, where the parents 'loved each other very much'. They had a son, a little boy who they also loved very much as well as a cat and a dog, a car and a caravan, and a swimming pool that their son and his playmates enjoyed and which they protected with a fence. While the parents could not protect their child from the storm of riots by people of colour who lived outside, they could install burglar alarms and build a high security barricade of razor wire to prevent intruders from entering their blessed estate.

One night the parents put their son to sleep and were awakened by the sound of their burglar alarm and the screams of their trusted itinerant gardener who tore his hands trying to remove the bloodied body of their son who was caught in the wire. The house cat survived . . . but not the houseboy, nor their son.

Epilogue: White Fears, Black Justice

Judge Masipa sentenced Oscar Pistorius to a maximum of five years in Pretoria's state prison. He could be released to house arrest and parole in two years. The sentence did not please many ordinary South Africans, but especially white women who wanted Pistorius to get the full treatment for having killed his girlfriend in cold blood, and black men who imagined that under similar circumstances they would be unlikely to get away with murder so easily. Anticipating these criticisms the judge said that she was not accountable to the clamour of the crowds outside the courtroom 'who might not even know the difference between punishment and vengeance'. She evoked the language of the South African Truth and Reconciliation Commission (TRC) in trying to achieve balance based on proportionality: 'A long sentence would lack mercy, while a more lenient one would send the wrong message to the community'.

Turning to the grieving parents of Reeva Steenkamp, Judge Masipa used words similar to the TRC testimony of Ntobeko Peni, one of the young militants convicted of the politically incited murder of American student, Amy Biehl in 1994. Peni said: 'It does not matter how I feel about what happened. My feelings cannot bring her back'. Similarly, Masipa spoke of a loss that could never be undone.

Addressing the parents, Judge Masipa said apologetically: 'Nothing I do or say today can reverse what happened to the deceased. Hopefully this sentence shall provide some sort of closure'.

While both parents gracefully accepted the judgment, Reeva's mother, June, said that there would never be closure unless someone could 'magic' her daughter back. Meanwhile, the public and legal debates will continue if the prosecution's petition for an appeal is upheld by the court. The prosecution contends that Judge Masipa should have convicted Pistorius of murder, based on a legal principal of *dolus eventualis*, meaning that intent can be attributed to a person who can foresee the possibility that his actions might cause death and yet he or she persists regardless of the consequences. Unlike the US, Canada, or Brazil, where one can defend killing a person by mistake in self-defence in one's home, there is no comparable 'stand your ground' defence in South Africa. Thus the prosecutors argue that the judge was too concerned about who was behind the door—Reeva or an intruder—when this should not have mattered in the first place. When [Pistorius] pulled the trigger he had to have foreseen the possibility that the person hiding in the cubicle would in all likelihood die and that is sufficient, under South African law, to convict a person of murder.

However this plays out in the future, an ugly domestic crime committed by a favourite white son of South Africa, a crime that may or may not have been intentional, was decided by a black woman judge with reason and justice tempered by mercy and compassion. Under the apartheid regime Pistorius might well have ended up on the gallows. Perhaps the case will allow white South Africans to realize how lucky they are to be living under the new ANC democracy. And perhaps it will inspire Americans to contemplate how white fears of black men have turned American homes into arsenals, militarized the police force, and turned the US correctional system into a 21st-century version of the penal colony.

References

I wish to thank the AT anonymous reviewers of this article and Justice Albie Sachs, South African Constitutional Court Judge (Emeritus); Captain Louis Helberg, Serious Commercial Crimes, SAPS, Durban.

Tony Platt, Center for Law & Society, UC Berkeley; Loic Wacquant, Professor of Sociology, UC Berkeley, and the members of my graduate anthropology workshops, especially, Martha Stroud, Nicole Rosner for their helpful critiques and comments. Brad Erikson, independent consultant and engaged anthropologist, helped editing the piece and clarifying the ideological semantics of 'suicide by cop'.

1. http://www.adweek.com/news/advertising/fcb-wins-feds-anti-violencegig-43841.
2. http://anthropoliteia. net/2014/08/21/blue-on-black-violence-and-originalcrime-a-view-from-oaklandcalifornia/.
3. http://www.vpc.org/studies/blackhomicide14.pdf.
4. http://www.cnn.com/2013/09/16/us/20-deadliest-mass-shootings-inu-s-history-fast-facts/.
5. http://www.motherjones.com/politics/2012/03/what-happened-trayvon-martin-explained.
6. http://www.miamiherald.com/news/state/florida/trayvon-martin/article1953286.html.
7. http://www.unodc.org/documents/data-and-analysis/Crime-statistics/International_Statistics_on_Crime_and_ Justice.pdf.
8. http://www.mirror.co.uk/news/world-news/oscar-pistorius-trial-bladerunner-3829646.
9. http://www.theglobeandmail.com/news/world/the-unmakingof-oscar-pistorius/article10585576/?page=all.

Anderson, E. 2000. *Code of the street: Decency, violence, and the moral life of the inner city*. New York: W.W. Norton & Company.

Bourgois, P. 2003. *In search of respect: Selling crack in El Barrio*. Cambridge: Cambridge UP.

Brink, A. 2000. Free thoughts. *The Guardian*, 13 February http://www.theguardian.com/world/2000/feb/13/nelsonmandela.theobserver.

Coetzee, J.M. 1997. *Boyhood*. London: Secker & Warburg.

Coetzee, J.M. 1998. *White writing: On the culture of letters in South Africa*. New Haven, CT: Yale University Press.

Coetzee, J.M. 2000. *Disgrace*. New York: Penguin.

Erikson, B. 2014. Blue on Black violence and original crime: A view from Oakland California. 21 August, http://anthropoliteia.net/tag/braderikson/.

Giffords, G. 2014. The lessons of physical therapy. *The New York Times*, 7 January. http://www.nytimes.com/2014/01/08/opinion/gabrielle-giffordss-callfor-persistence-on-gunreform.html.

Gilligan, J. 1997. *Violence: Reflections on a national epidemic.* New York: Vintage Books

Gordimer, N. 1974. *The conservationist*. New York: Viking Press.

Gordimer, N. 1979. *Burger's daughter*. New York: Viking Press.

Gordimer, N. 1981. *July's people*. New York: Viking Press.

Gordimer, N. 1992. Once upon a time. *In Jump and other stories.* Harmondsworth: Penguin.

Gordimer, N. 1998. *The house gun*. New York: Farra, Straus & Giroux.

Gordimer, N. 1999. *Living in hope and history: Notes from our century*. London: Bloomsbury Publishing.

Gordimer, N. 2001. *The pickup*. New York: Farrar, Straus & Giroux.

Greenberg, M & D Schneider 1994. Violence in American cities: Young black males is the answer, but what was the question? *Social Science & Medicine* 39(2): 179–87.

Hewson, K. 1988. Making the 'revolutionary gesture': Nadine Gordimer, J.M. Coetzee and some variations on the writer's responsibility. http://ariel.synergiesprairies.ca/ariel/index.php/ariel/article/viewFile/2145/2101.

Hiday, V.A. et al. 1999. Criminal victimization of persons with severe mental illness. *Psychiatric Services* 50: 62–68.

Perry, A. 2013. Pistorius and South Africa's culture of violence. *Time Magazine*, 11 March.

Scheper-Hughes, N. 1994. The last white Christmas: The Heidelberg pub massacre. *American Anthropologist* 96(4): 85–817.

Scheper-Hughes, N. 2013. No more magic bullets: Deadly lessons from the Sandy Hook massacre. *CounterPoint*, 6 February.

Scheper-Hughes, N. & P. Bourgois 2004. Introduction: Making sense of violence. In Bourgois, P. & N. Scheper-Hughes (eds). *Violence in war and peace: An anthology*. Oxford: Blackwell.

Sokolove, M. 2012. The fast life of Oscar Pistorius. *The New York Times*, 18 January. http://www.nytimes.com/2012/01/22/magazine/oscar-pistorius.html?pagewanted=all&_r=0.

Stuart, H. 2003. Violence and mental illness: An overview. *World Psychiatry* 2(2): 121–124.

Critical Thinking

1. In what ways has the national discussion about violence in the United States been a matter of talk without actually doing anything about it?
2. How does the Pistorius case illustrate the origins of white fear and how it has shaped the justice system's treatment of blacks in in South Africa as well in the United States.

Internet References

National Institute of Justice
https://www.usa.gov/federal-agencies/national-institute-of-justice

The South African Civil Society Information Service
http://sacsis.org.za/site/article/186.1

World Psychiatry
http://onlinelibrary.wiley.com/

Nancy Scheper-Hughes is a professor of anthropology at the University of California, Berkeley, where she directs the doctoral program in Medical Anthropology. She is the founding director of Organs Watch, a documentation and medical human rights project. Her many writings are based on her long-term ethnographic research engagements in Brazil, Israel, South Africa, and the United States.

Article

Prepared by: Elvio Angeloni

Gun Owners, Ethics, and the Problem of Evil

A Response to the Las Vegas Shooting

JOE ANDERSON

Learning Outcomes

After reading this article, you will be able to:

- Describe and explain the ethical system employed by many gun owners in their response to instances of mass gun violence.
- Discuss the analogy of "sheep, sheepdogs, and wolves" as a justification for gun ownership.
- Describe the "five stages of mental awareness" as a guide for how some gun users fell while armed.

Following the tragic Las Vegas shooting on October 1, 2017, the American news media were left asking a series of familiar questions: how could this have happened here? What could we have done? News personalities and pundits frame the American public as split into two camps, one that favors stricter gun control and another that wants unfettered access to firearms. Analysts are recruited to argue one or another side of this dichotomy, moving public discourse no closer to a realistic solution to gun violence. Recently returned to the United Kingdom from San Diego, CA, where I was conducting an ethnographic study of a gun rights activist community, I am also left with a series of difficult questions: how could this have happened in such a familiar ethnographic setting? As an academic committed to understanding gun ownership in the United States from an analytical perspective, how can I also retain a genuine emotional connection to a tragedy on such a huge scale?

These questions inevitably circle around the ethical—not only what it means for anthropologists to engage with the ethical systems we study but also how our own ethics uncomfortably rub up against an almost compulsive (even therapeutic?) need to layer real-world events with analysis. Just as David Berliner (2016) argued in a previous Hau debate on contradictions, I found that fieldwork thrust various ethical challenges upon me as I came to know and like people whose ethical systems contrasted, but overlapped, with what I might have considered to be my own. This forced me into a unique state of awareness of a personal ethics that usually bubbles beneath the realm of conscious thought. The recent explosion of work in the anthropology of ethics suggests that I am not alone in these concerns. But, despite this growing focus, there is still an unwillingness to take seriously the ethical systems of those who we are often guilty of "othering" within the United States. This is particularly obvious when it comes to that remarkably mainstream American phenomenon—gun ownership.

There has been little ethnographic work done on this topic, and none that deals with the way in which the ethical permeates the practice and ideology of gun ownership. Over a period of four years, I have spent 15 months living with gun owners, attending gun rights activist meetings, and learning to shoot with informants. Throughout this time, I avoided looking too deeply into the topic of ethics, as I worried that any description that associated gun ownership with the pursuit of an ethical life might be seen as "dealing with the enemy." Instead, I followed others in focusing on the associations between gun ownership and nationalism (Cox, 2007; Springwood, 2007), gender (Kohn, 2004; Arjet, 2007; King, 2007), "whiteness" (Song, 2010), and embodiment (Springwood, 2014). However, as I listened to my informants talk about their need to defend their families and the wider public from threats and took part in a number of defensive shooting courses that explicitly discussed the ethical hurdles involved with carrying a gun, I started to pay attention to how a particular ethical system was being produced through gun use.

In this article, I use ethnographic data to show that owning a firearm brings with it an ethical system that makes the prospect of giving up guns in the aftermath of a mass shooting even less attractive to my informants. Through the relentless cultivation of what might be called a "gun-carrying habitus," my informants come to inhabit an ethical subjectivity that orders the world into "good guys" (gun owners and the people they protect) and "bad guys" (gang members, drug dealers, and mass shooters). Furthermore, the construction of that system of ethics relies upon a personification of the opposition between good and evil that ultimately defines who fits within the category of human and who is relegated to the inhuman, or monstrous, realm. This helps us to understand why advocates of gun ownership react to mass shootings by reaffirming their need to possess firearms. Because if inhuman monsters like the Las Vegas shooter roam the world, you sure as hell want to be able to protect yourself and your community from them.

Despite the federal funding ban on the social effects and the extent of America's gun violence problem, qualitative researchers, and anthropologists in particular, are well positioned to fly under the radar of government bureaucracy. I will argue that now is the time to talk about guns. But rather than lamenting the inefficacy of a political class beholden to corporate interests (the firearms industry) and powerful lobby groups (the National Rifle Association [NRA]), I call for innovative research on this topic that includes gun owners in the conversation about violence prevention, thereby moving beyond the stale bipartisan terms of the gun control debate.

Terminology and "Ordinary Ethics"

In my use of the term "ethics," I allude to the body of work by Michael Lambek and contributors in Ordinary Ethics (2010b) that seeks to relocate the domain of the ethical from its imprisonment within minds and written codes toward a more dynamic concept primarily found in action and practice. This allows anthropologists to observe how ethical systems permeate the everyday lives of social groups. Inspired by Foucault, James Faubion (2011, pp. 3–5) suggests that humans are not born ethical subjects but must creatively sculpt themselves within an environment of social and conventional ethical institutions. Gun owners engage in this practice daily as they move through the world, guarding public spaces with the knowledge that they might have to use deadly force if they encounter a "bad guy" like the Las Vegas shooter. This takes a great deal of reflexive ethical thinking but also involves sculpting one's physical capacities to respond effectively to threatening situations.

I also repeat challenges by Thomas Csordas (2013) and Steven Caton (2010) that the anthropology of ethics needs to deal more directly with what has been called, presumably ironically, the "problem of evil." Csordas argues that anthropologists have too often avoided using the term "evil" because of its association with Christian theology and urges the discipline to attend to the ways in which the concept is still relevant to the groups of people we study (2013, p. 526). Furthermore, following David Pocock (1985), I suggest that once evil has been located and defined, it can give a guide as to what constitutes the categories of human and inhuman. My informants engage in this kind of ordering, and it is obvious in a biblical metaphor often used to describe the distinction between two categories of human, and one inhuman, in the analogous "sheep, sheepdogs, and wolves." The sheep in society are willing to go on acting as if life isn't dangerous (a clear reference to advocates of gun control), but they require sheepdogs (gun owners) willing to live a hardier life to keep the wolves (mass shooters and other violent criminals) from taking weaker members of the herd. And so even political opponents are worth saving as long as they aren't the ultimate source of evil—"bad guys."

I will briefly look at responses to the Las Vegas shooting by gun rights activist groups in order to demonstrate how a particular ethical system is deployed in the aftermath of such events, before going on to show how the dichotomous construction of good versus evil is reaffirmed through the shaping of a "gun-carrying habitus." By understanding what evil looks like to gun owners, one can understand more fully why they respond the way they do when that evil rears its head in the form of mass shootings.

Responses to Las Vegas

Whenever a major mass shooting occurs, the inevitably sensational media coverage pushes the issue of gun control into public discourse, which is immediately followed by a response from gun rights organizations denying any need for a conversation. Just days after the Las Vegas shooting, the executive director of the gun rights association I was researching issued a statement in response to the tragedy.

> I am sickened and saddened by the horrific mass murder that happened Sunday night . . . in Las Vegas. Reading about it, hearing about it . . . put a lump in my throat all day yesterday . . . we are also seeing elected officials . . . [and] "journalists" . . . using this tragedy as an opportunity to advance their political agenda.

This was followed by a quote from a board member of the organization: "there is no legislation that will strip evil from an immoral man." A statement by Wayne LaPierre and Chris Cox from the NRA followed the next day echoing many of these themes: condemning the evil of the shooter, rebutting calls for a conversation about guns, and taking a tone of disgust that anyone should try to politicize this tragedy—while politicizing it.

In the aftermath of the evil and senseless attack in Las Vegas, the American people are looking for answers as to how future tragedies can be prevented. . . . Banning guns from law-abiding Americans based on the criminal act of a madman will do nothing to prevent future attacks. . . . The NRA remains focused on our mission: strengthening Americans' Second Amendment freedom to defend themselves, their families, and their communities (LaPierre and Cox, 2017).

"Senseless" is a key word here. An evil that is beyond explanation, or verbal analysis, literally absent of sense, locating the perpetrator in the realm of the inhuman. These responses may sound self-serving but contained within them are many of the themes that constitute the ethical system I describe below.

Ethical Subjectivity and a "Gun-carrying Habitus"

If, as Lambek (2010a, 2010c) suggests, the ethical is to be found in action and practice, how do gun owners make themselves into ethical subjects through gun use? In March 2017, the gun rights activist group I was researching organized their annual fundraiser for a national leukemia charity. This event took place at a firearms training institute outside of Las Vegas and revolved around a handgun course that teaches the intricacies of defensive shooting. I traveled there with an informant and main firearms instructor for the year, a 62-year-old woman called Patti. We became friends during my stay in San Diego, and she enthusiastically took on the task of teaching me how to shoot.

We arrived at the training facility at 6:30 a.m. on the first day of the course, and after learning the basics of gun safety and handling were ushered into a lecture called "The five stages of mental awareness." This theory of physiological and psychological states is popular among the firearms instructors I encountered who use it as a guide for how gun users are likely to feel while armed. It is an attempt to prepare gun owners for the kinds of automatic bodily responses that arise from situations of high threat. The lecture was given by a female instructor who explained how each color code in the hierarchy relates to carrying a gun.

"Condition white is characterized by a lack of awareness of your surroundings . . . we are an easy target, an easy victim." Next, condition yellow means being aware, checking the environment for threats but remaining relaxed. This is the condition in which the gun-carrying individual should be at all times. The instructor was adamant that this is not paranoia, simply awareness of "dangerous people on the streets." Condition orange involves acknowledging potentially suspicious activity and forming a tactical plan to respond to any emerging threats. Condition red is when a "specific threat has been perceived and it is real . . . set a mental trigger . . . if the bad guy turns toward you with a gun, you are ready to shoot." Finally, condition black is a combat mind-set and the instructor defined it as:

The ability to concentrate on the one thing you need to win, not just survive. You want to conquer, destroy. You've got to work on developing this mind-set. Realize the world is a violent place. Understand your opponent because they are not like you and me. They would cutoff your head for your jewelry. . . . Visualize. Create movies in your head about you and the bad guy. You have to see yourself winning.

While there are a number of themes to dissect here, victimhood immediately stands out as a stark opposition is drawn between the kind of people who aren't ready for attack (victims) and those who are (defined as those willing to carry a gun in public). In this orientation to the world, the nongun-wielding citizen is coded as irresponsible and weak both physically and morally. This hierarchy of mental states helps gun owners to define their experiences of arming, and I often observed my informants weighing up which condition to be in, deciding whether to bring their gun to particular events or places.

Utilizing tools like the five stages of mental awareness and their own experiences of carrying a gun in public, my informants convert their self-reported bodily perceptions of danger and responsibility into a morally charged guardianship of the spaces within which they move. Carrying a gun becomes a socially regulated way of attending to and with the body, forming particular "somatic modes of attention" (Csordas, 1993). The act of attending to the body in this way becomes ethically charged with the associations of victimhood (bad) and willingness to violently defend (good), as the perceptions that arise from carrying a gun produce the very conditions necessary for ethical action. This forms what one might call a "guncarrying habitus." This habitus is sculpted by the course in grueling 11-hour days of shooting drills that left rough calluses on my palms and my limbs aching. By day four, however, I was able to execute the drills with calm precision and the firearm I was using seemed to fit comfortably in my hand.

On day two, we attended a lecture titled "Moral and ethical decisions associated with the use of deadly force." The gruff, moustachioed instructor started by making a distinction between morals ("what you personally think is right and wrong") and ethics ("the morals of the community") and explained that:

you press the trigger based on your morals but are judged by the community's ethics . . . think carefully so that you know what you are prepared to do in the moment. If you press that trigger, that's gonna stay with you forever, but it's not the end of the world. You not coming home to your family is the end of the world.

The justifications for shooting people are nearly always framed in terms of the need to protect innocents (coded as female, i.e., granddaughter, daughter, wife) from other men, or "bad guys." The instructor went on to define more specifically who the "bad guys" are: "some scumbag is in your house, learn to sniff out bad guys, they probably stink. They probably live under the bridge in the bad part of town . . . they will kill you for the fried chicken in your refrigerator." He advised us to check around once we have dealt with the immediate threat during a gunfight because "rats travel in packs." Associating "bad guys" with rats reinforces this idea of a "senseless," uncaring evil that creates and dehumanizes an exemplary "other," which is characteristic of my informants' approach to imagined threats in society. The next two days reinforced these ideas in drills that aimed to commit lessons about ethical action and bodily states into muscle memory, making my informants capable of an automatic response should they encounter a bad guy "on the streets."

In many of our long conversations, Patti echoed these ideas as she thought reflexively about the ethical challenges that arise from carrying a gun in public:

Well you can force yourself into complacency, but it's not something you ever want to become complacent about. It's the decisions you have to make, like, what is the line that has to be crossed before I do something about something. Does it involve my people only, my family only? Does it involve anybody?. . . It's all about the training you've had and the decisions you have made. . . . A lot, a lot, of thought has to be involved.

When I asked what might justify shooting someone, a similar opposition between "good guys" and "bad guys" emerged:

The bad guy wants to impose their will on you; they'll find a way to do it because they are, by definition, a sociopath, they are going to find a baseball bat, their fists, their intimidation in size . . . The mark of a true psychopath is when they get their hands on a gun . . . and all of a sudden it makes them feel powerful. Whereas a nonpsychopath, or normal human being, when they receive that level of power or opportunity to be able to be equal, it humbles you. Because . . . you're saying, OK, now I have a lot more power than the other people around me, but I don't want to impose my will on people, I just want to make sure no-one imposes their will on me . . . and you understand that responsibility. And people on the bad side, don't get it that way, they say, wow, I can make somebody do what I want.

The very inability of a person to feel and accept the ethical responsibility of carrying a gun in public is evidence of their psychopathy and therefore proves that they are a "bad guy":

It's the same exact interaction for all gun owners because it has the ability to project power, but you want to project power in a reasonable, sane way. You're not one of the bad guys, you're trying to protect against the bad guys . . . you still don't want to sink to their level. You know, if the threat is over, if someone's running away, you don't want to shoot them in the back . . . when the guy drops his gun and puts his hand on his face, you're not going to shoot him in the head because you are not a psychopath.

Good guys know how to be compassionate even in threatening situations—they deploy their weapon and training in order to protect loved ones and the community. Bad guys, on the other hand, utilize the force-maximizing properties of a firearm to bend others to their will and wreak havoc because their perceptions of holding a gun are not accompanied by an ethically principled sense of personal responsibility.

Conclusion: Analysis as Ethics

Following Thomas Csordas (2013), I suggest that the anthropology of ethics requires a theory of evil in order to understand the "good" that people strive toward. Gun owners create a category of evil that constructs the very notion of what it is to be human, and they deploy these categories in an ethical system shaped by a "gun-carrying habitus." Five years prior to the attack in Las Vegas, in a response to the Sandy Hook school shooting that left 20 children dead, the NRA's executive vice president, Wayne LaPierre, claimed that "our society is populated by an unknown number of genuine monsters . . . the only thing that can stop a bad guy with a gun, is a good guy with a gun" (LaPierre, 2012). According to the NRA, our lecturers in Nevada, and the testaments of many of my informants, evil exists in the world in the form of "bad guys"—a category of inhuman monsters and psychopaths. Only well-trained and ethically prepared "good guys" can defend against the perpetrators of these evil acts. With monsters like the Las Vegas shooter walking the streets of America, why would gun owners be inclined to hand over what they see as the most effective tool for keeping the wolves at bay?

In trying to understand my own emotional connection to Las Vegas, I have found myself reaching for a familiar source of comfort in writing this article—the analytical gaze. In doing so, I have taken an approach that shows how ethical orientations emerge in the act of training with a firearm, which in turn produces particular responses to mass shootings. Extending this analysis to include my own response to Las Vegas, it is impossible not to see this article as an example of "ethics in action."

Writing represents a personal coping mechanism that not only helps me to process the pain of this event but also tries to deploy what expertise I have in order to help others understand America's complex relationship with guns and to hopefully move beyond the stale bipartisan debate about gun control.

References

Arjet, Robert. 2007. "'Man to man': Power and male relationships in the gunplay film." *In Open Fire: Understanding Global Gun Cultures*, edited by Charles Springwood, 125–37. Oxford: Oxford International Publishers Ltd.

Berliner, David. 2016. "Anthropology and the study of contradictions." *Hau: Journal of Ethnographic Theory* 6(1): 1–27.

Caton, Steven. 2010. "Abu Ghraib and the problem of evil." *In Ordinary Ethics: Anthropology, Language, and Action*, edited by Michael Lambek, 165–84. New York: Fordham University Press.

Cox, Amy. 2007. "Arming for manhood: The transformation of guns into objects of American masculinity." *In Open Fire: Understanding Global Gun Cultures*, edited by Charles Springwood, 141–52. Oxford, UK: Oxford International.

Csordas, Thomas. 1993. "Somatic modes of attention." *Cultural Anthropology* 8(2): 136–56.

Csordas, Thomas. 2013. "Morality as a cultural system?" *Current Anthropology* 54(5): 523–46.

Faubion, James. 2011. *An Anthropology of Ethics*. Cambridge, UK: Cambridge University Press.

King, C. Richard. 2007. "Arming desire: The sexual force of guns in the United States." *In Open Fire: Understanding Global Gun Cultures*, edited by Charles Springwood, 87–97. Oxford, UK: Oxford International Publishers Ltd.

Kohn, Abigail. 2004. *Shooters: Myths and Realities of America's Gun Cultures*. New York: Oxford University Press.

Lambek, Michael. 2010a. "Introduction." *In Ordinary Ethics: Anthropology, Language, and Action*, edited by Michael Lambek, 1–36. New York: Fordham University Press.

Lambek, Michael, ed. 2010b. *Ordinary Ethics: Anthropology, Language, and Action*. New York: Fordham University Press.

Lambek, Michael. 2010c. "Toward an ethics of the act." *In Ordinary Ethics: Anthropology, Language, and Action*, edited by Michael Lambek, 39–63. New York: Fordham University Press.

LaPierre, W. 2012. "NRA: Full statement by Wayne LaPierre in response to the Newton shootings." Guardian, December 21. https://www.theguardian.com/world/2012/dec/21/nra-full-statement-lapierre-newtown.

LaPierre, Wayne, and Chris Cox. 2017. "NRA's Wayne LaPierre and Chris Cox issue joint statement." NRA–ILA, May 10. http://cdn.nraila.org/articles/20171005/nras-wayne-lapierre-and-chris-cox-issue-joint-statement.

Los Angeles Times Staff. 2017. "Deadliest US mass shootings, 1984–2017." *Los Angeles Times*, February 10. http://timelines.latimes.com/deadliest-shooting-rampages/.

Pocock, David. 1985. "Unruly evil." *In The Anthropology of Evil*, edited by David Parkin, 42–56. Oxford, UK: Basil Blackwell.

Song, Hoon. 2010. *Pigeon Trouble; Bestiary Biopolitics in a Deindustrialized America*. Philadelphia, PA: University of Pennsylvania Press.

Springwood, Charles Fruehling, ed. 2007. *Open Fire: Understanding Global Gun Cultures*. Oxford, UK: Oxford International.

Springwood, Charles Fruehling. 2014. "Gun concealment, display and other magical habits of the body." *Critique of Anthropology* 34(4): 450–71.

Critical Thinking

1. What is the ethical system employed by many gun owners in their response to instances of mass gun violence?
2. What is the analogy of "sheep, sheepdogs, and wolves," and how is it used as a justification for gun ownership?
3. How and why do many gun owners make a distinction between "morals" and "ethics"?

Internet References

Arms with Ethics
www.armswithethics.org

Ethics from the Barrel of a Gun
www.catb.org/esr/guns/gun-etgusc.html

The Ethics of Owning a Gun
https://theethicsof.com/2013/11/21/the-ethics-of-owning-a-gun/

Joe Anderson is a social anthropology PhD candidate at the University of Edinburgh. His research focuses on the production of gender, embodied dispositions, and ethics among gun owners in San Diego, CA.

Article

Prepared by: Elvio Angeloni

Comment on "Gun Owners, Ethics, and the Problem of Evil"

HUGH GUSTERSON

Learning Outcomes

After reading this article, you will be able to:

- Discuss the possible drawbacks of an ethnography which presents only the subjective nativist point of view without a counterbalancing perspective.
- Examine the wisdom of arming "good" people with guns as a means for reducing gun violence.

Having written an ethnography of nuclear weapons scientists (Gusterson, 1996), I feel a certain kinship with Anderson's project in "Gun Owners, Ethics, and the Problem of Evil." This project involves making cultural sense of spaces in Western society inhabited by what Susan Harding (1991), writing about US Christian fundamentalists, refers to as anthropologists' "repugnant cultural other." Anthropologists, generally liberal, tend to avoid fieldwork with ideologically antipathetic populations in their own societies such as gun owners, weapons scientists, Tea Party activists, Chamber of Commerce lobbyists, antiabortion activists, and UKIP enthusiasts; when they do appear in our ethnographies, they are often subjects of cultural critique rather than relativist sensemaking.

Breaking the mold, Anderson—like the two other ethnographers of US gun culture I have read (Kohn, 2004; Doukas, 2010)—bends over backward to see the gun debate from his natives' point of view. Kohn and Doukas emphasize the aesthetic beauty of firearms, gun ownership as a rite of passage to manhood, and the belief that mass gun ownership offers a bulwark against government tyranny. Complementing their accounts, Anderson argues that gun ownership makes sense in the context of a Manichean worldview in which evil people will wreak havoc unless good people are armed to prevent this. He shows the reader how gun owners, in part through training courses like the one he took, come to perceive their mundane daily terrain of shopping malls, restaurants, and public buildings as a landscape of potential threat.

In an earlier discussion of Kohn's and Doukas' work, I wrote that "while such reports from behind ideological enemy lines are certainly useful and interesting . . . anthropology surely has more to contribute to the gun-control debate than a warmed-over rehash of NRA talking points legitimated by our discipline's historic legacy of cultural relativism" (Gusterson, 2013: p. 2). My point was that we risk naturalizing the ideology of gun owners if our explication of their worldview is not balanced either by critique or by the juxtaposition of a contrary community's viewpoint, and this argument applies as well to Anderson's article. While it is surely bad ethnographic form, lazily indulging our ideological reflexes, to simply condemn our human subjects, it is also problematic to just recite their worldview without pushing the conversation deeper, probing for friction between belief and reality. After all, Evans-Pritchard ([1937] 1976) did not just record a set of Azande statements about witchcraft; it was only by arguing with the Azande and recording their responses that he was able to show the full complexity of their belief system.

Thus, in reading Anderson's account of US gun owners, I was fascinated to read their earnest descriptions of their beliefs but frustrated that the conversation repeatedly ended where I wanted it to begin. They say that guns in the hands of "good" people can prevent bad people from running amok, but how does one know who is good and who is bad, and how does one prevent the bad people from getting guns (especially given the NRA's energetic lobbying against background checks for sales at gun shows)? How could armed citizens have prevented the recent Las Vegas massacre (with which Anderson's article opens), where Stephen Paddock mowed people down with a machine gun from a distant hotel window? And what do gun owners say when it is pointed out that 17,000 American gun owners a year commit suicide with their own guns, accounting for the majority of gun deaths (Gusterson, 2013)? Are they aware that so many gun owners die at their own hands? Do they see thousands of suicides a year as the sad price one has to pay for cherished Second Amendment rights (much as I see some traffic fatalities as the price we have to pay for the freedom to drink alcohol)? Do they favor more background checks to weed out "bad" people seeking guns? And would further questioning about those "bad" people confirm my sneaking suspicion that the categories "bad person" and "ethnic minority" overlap heavily?

Probing gun owners' beliefs with such questions would enable us to ascertain whether there are deeper levels of thoughtfulness to their beliefs (as I often found when interviewing nuclear weapons scientists) or whether the relationship of their beliefs to empirical reality is fundamentally one of "misrecognition" (Bourdieu, 1977). Knowing whether they have racialized their concept of the evil other would cast light on the broader political project of which gun ownership forms part. Responses to these questions would also help determine whether compromise measures to reduce gun violence might be politically feasible or whether gun owners are too dug in for compromise.

My own reflexive (and perhaps ill-informed) presumption is that the NRA is largely funded by the gun industry, which, like the tobacco industry, is willing to play a role in killing tens of thousands of Americans, especially the poor black Americans who are the main victims of gun violence, in order to make a profit; and that the NRA helps prevent politicians from interfering in this apparatus of death and profit by filling its supporters' heads with shallow, propagandistic narratives about crime on the street and liberal governments eager to take away Americans' constitutional rights (Brown and Abel, 2003; Gusterson, 2013; Hickey, 2013). Maybe my perception here is unfair to gun owners and to the NRA or maybe it is wrong to confuse gun-owners with the NRA. Unfortunately, this article, scrupulously generous to gun owners, has failed to persuade me otherwise precisely because of its asymmetrical generosity. Warmth always has a place in repatriated anthropology but so does critique.

References

Bourdieu, Pierre. 1977. *Outline of a Theory of Practice*. Translated by Richard Nice. Cambridge, UK: Cambridge University Press.

Brown, Peter Harry, and Daniel Abel. 2003. *Outgunned: Up Against the NRA—the First Complete Insider Account of the Battle for Gun Control*. New York: Free Press.

Doukas, Dmitra. 2010. "Targeting the gun question: The 'culture war' in scope." *Anthropology Now* 2 (3): 19–30.

Evans-Pritchard, E. E. [1937] 1976. *Witchcraft, Oracles, and Magic Among the Azande*. Oxford, UK: Oxford University Press.

Gusterson, Hugh. 1996. *Nuclear Rites: A Weapons Laboratory at the End of the Cold War*. Berkeley, CA: University of California Press.

Gusterson, Hugh. 2013. "Making a killing." *Anthropology Today* 29 (1): 1–2.

Harding, Susan. 1991. "Representing fundamentalism: The problem of the repugnant cultural other." *Social Research* 58 (2): 373–93.

Hickey, Walter. 2013. "How the gun industry funnels tens of millions of dollars to the NRA." *Business Insider*, January 16. http://www.businessinsider.com/gun-industry-funds-nra-2013-1.

Kohn, Abigail. 2004. *Shooters: Myths and Realities of America's Gun Culture*. Oxford, UK: Oxford University Press.

Critical Thinking

1. If an ethnographer uncritically presents only the National Rifle Association perspective on gun ownership, is the truth being served?
2. What are some of the pitfalls of doing an ethnography that presents only the informants' points of view and explanations for why they do as they do?

Internet References

Arms with Ethics
www.armswithethics.org

Ethics from the Barrel of a Gun
www.catb.org/esr/guns/gun-etgusc.html

The Ethics of Owning a Gun
https://theethicsof.com/2013/11/21/the-ethics-of-owning-a-gun/

Hugh Gusterson is a professor of International Affairs and Anthropology at George Washington University.

Gusterson, Hugh, Comment on "Gun Owners, Ethics, and the Problem of Evil: A Response to The Las Vegas Shooting," *Journal of Ethnographic Theory*, vol. 7, no. 3, 2017, 39–48.

Article

Prepared by: Elvio Angeloni

The Science of Good and Evil

YUDHIJIT BHATTACHARJEE

Learning Outcomes

After reading this article, you will be able to:

- Discuss the human tendencies toward both altruism and psychopathy in terms of our evolutionary past.
- Discuss the evidence for biological predispositions for both empathy and an "active disregard for others."
- Discuss the ways in which psychopathic behavior can be prevented or, at least, treated.

What Makes People Especially Giving or Cruel? Researchers Say the Way Our Brains Are Wired Can Affect How Much Empathy We Feel for Others.

From the kitchen window of her mobile home in Auburn, IL, Ashley Aldridge had a clear view of the railroad crossing about a hundred yards away.

When the 19-year-old mother first saw the man in the wheelchair, she had just finished feeding lunch to her two children, aged one and three, and had moved on to washing dishes—one more in an endless string of chores. Looking up, Aldridge noticed that the wheelchair wasn't moving. It was stuck between the tracks. The man was yelling for help as a motorcycle and two cars went by without stopping.

Aldridge hurried out to ask a neighbor to watch her kids so she could go help. Then she heard the train horn and the clanging of the crossing gate as it came down, signaling that a train was on its way. She ran, barefoot, over a gravel path along the tracks. When she got to the man, the train was less than half a mile away, bearing down at about 80 miles an hour. Failing to dislodge the wheelchair, she wrapped her arms around the man's chest from behind and tried to lift him, but couldn't. As the train barreled toward them, she pulled with a mighty heave. She fell backward, yanking him out of the chair. Within seconds, the train smashed the wheelchair, carrying fragments of steel and plastic half a mile up the track.

The man Aldridge saved that afternoon in September 2015 was a complete stranger. Her unflinching determination to save him despite the threat to her own life sets her apart from many. Aldridge's heroic rescue is an example of what scientists call extreme altruism—selfless acts to help those unrelated to oneself at the risk of grave personal harm. Not surprisingly, many of these heroes—such as Roi Klein, an Israeli army major who jumped on a live grenade to save his men—work in professions in which endangering one's life to protect others is part of the job. But others are ordinary men and women—like Rick Best, Taliesin Namkai-Meche, and Micah Fletcher, who intervened to defend two young women, one wearing a hijab, from a man spewing anti-Muslim abuse at them on a commuter train in Portland, Oregon. All three were stabbed; only Fletcher survived.

Contrast these noble acts with the horrors that humans commit: murder, rape, kidnapping, torture. Consider the carnage perpetrated by the man who sprayed bullets from the 32nd floor of the Mandalay Bay hotel in Las Vegas, NV, in October at a country music festival. Three weeks later, officials put the casualty toll at 58 dead and 546 wounded. Or think about the chilling ruthlessness of a serial killer like Todd Kohlhepp, a real estate agent in South Carolina, who appears to have left clues about his murderous habit in bizarre online reviews for products, including a folding shovel: "keep in car for when you have to hide the bodies." In spite of how aberrant these horrors are, they occur often enough to remind us of a dark truth: humans are capable of unspeakable cruelty.

Extreme altruists and psychopaths exemplify our best and worst instincts. On one end of the moral spectrum, sacrifice, generosity, and other ennobling traits that we recognize as good and on the other end, selfishness, violence, and destructive impulses that we see as evil. At the root of both types of behaviors, researchers say, is our evolutionary past. They hypothesize that humans—and many other species, to a lesser degree—evolved the desire to help one another because cooperation within large social groups was essential to survival. But because groups had to compete for resources, the willingness to maim and possibly kill opponents was also crucial. "We are the most social species on Earth, and we are also the most violent species on Earth," says Jean Decety, a social neurologist at the University of Chicago. "We have two faces because these two faces were important to survival."

For centuries, the question of how good and evil originate and manifest in us was a matter of philosophical or religious debate. But in recent decades, researchers have made significant advances toward understanding the science of what drives good and evil. Both seem to be linked to a key emotional trait: empathy, which is an intrinsic ability of the brain to experience how another person is feeling. Researchers have found that empathy is the kindling that fires compassion in our hearts, impelling us to help others in distress. Studies also have traced violent, psychopathic, and antisocial behaviors to a lack of empathy, which appears to stem from impaired neural circuits. These new insights are laying the foundation for training regimens and treatment programs that aim to enhance the brain's empathic response.

Researchers once thought young children had no concern for the well-being of others—a logical conclusion if you've seen a toddler's tantrums. But recent findings show that babies feel empathy long before their first birthday. Maayan Davidov, a psychologist at Hebrew University of Jerusalem, and her colleagues have conducted some of these studies, analyzing the behavior of children as they witness somebody in distress—a crying child, an experimenter, or their own mother pretending to be hurt. Even before six months of age, many infants respond to such stimuli with facial expressions reflecting concern; some also exhibit caring gestures such as leaning forward and trying to communicate with the one in distress. In their first year, infants also show signs of trying to understand the suffering they're seeing. Eighteen-month-olds often translate their empathy into such positive social behavior as giving a hug or a toy to comfort a hurt child.

That's not true of all children, however. In a small minority, starting in the second year of life, researchers see what they call an "active disregard" of others. "When someone reported that someone had hurt themselves," says Carolyn Zahn-Waxler, a researcher at the University of Wisconsin–Madison, "these children would kind of laugh at them or even kind of swipe at them and say, 'You're not hurt,' or 'You should be more careful'—saying it in a tone of voice that was judgmental." Following these toddlers into adolescence, Zahn-Waxler and her colleague Soo Hyun Rhee, a psychologist at the University of Colorado Boulder, found they had a high likelihood of developing antisocial tendencies and getting into trouble.

Other studies have measured callousness and lack of emotional expression in adolescents using questions such as whether the subject feels remorseful upon doing something wrong. Those with high scores for "callous–unemotional" traits tend to have frequent and severe behavioral problems—showing extreme aggression in fights, for instance, or vandalizing property. Researchers have also found that some of these adolescents end up committing major crimes such as murder, rape, and violent robbery. Some are prone to becoming full-blown psychopaths as adults—individuals with cold, calculating hearts who wouldn't flinch while perpetrating the most horrific acts imaginable. (Most psychopaths are men.)

If the empathy deficit at the core of psychopathic behaviors can be traced all the way back to toddlerhood, does evil reside in the genes, coiled up like a serpent in the DNA, waiting to strike? The answer isn't a categorical yes or no. As it is with many illnesses, both nature and nurture have a hand. Studies of twins have established that callous–unemotional traits displayed by some young children and adolescents arise to a substantial degree from genes they inherit. Yet in a study of 561 children born to mothers with a history of antisocial behaviors, researchers found that those living with adoptive families that provided a warm and nurturing environment were far less likely to exhibit callous–unemotional traits than those with adoptive families that were not as nurturing.

Children born with genes making it more likely that they will have difficulty empathizing are often unable to get a break. "You can imagine that if you have a child who doesn't show affection in the same way as a typically developing child, doesn't show empathy, that child will evoke very different reactions in the people around them—the parents, the teachers, the peers—than a child who's more amenable, more empathetic," says Essi Viding, a research psychologist at University College London. "And many of these children, of course, reside within their biological families, so they often have this double whammy of having parents who are perhaps less well equipped for many of the parenting tasks, are less good at empathizing, less good at regulating their own emotions."

The firefighters tried desperately to save the six Philpott children from their burning house in Derby, England, in the early hours of May 11, 2012. But the heat and smoke were so intense that only one of the kids was alive when rescuers finally made their way upstairs where they had been sleeping. That boy, too, perished two days later in the hospital. The police suspected arson based on evidence that the fire had been started by pouring gasoline through the door's mail slot.

Derby residents raised money to help the children's parents—Mick and Mairead Philpott—pay for a funeral. At a news conference to thank the community, Philpott was sobbing and dabbing his eyes with a tissue that remained curiously dry. Leaving the event, he collapsed, but Derbyshire's assistant chief constable, walking behind, was struck by the unnaturalness of the behavior. Eighteen days later, the police arrested Philpott and his wife. Investigators determined that they had set fire to the house with an accomplice to frame Mick's mistress. A court found all three guilty of manslaughter.

Philpott's faking of grief and his lack of remorse are among the characteristics that define psychopaths, a category of individuals who have come to embody evil in the popular imagination. Psychopaths have utter disregard for the feelings of others, although they seem to learn to mimic emotions. "They really just have a complete inability to appreciate anything like empathy or guilt or remorse," says Kent Kiehl, a neuroscientist at the Mind Research Network and the University of New Mexico who was drawn to studying psychopathy in part because he grew up in a neighborhood that was once home to the serial killer Ted Bundy. These are people who are "just extremely different than the rest of us."

Kiehl has spent the past two decades exploring this difference by scanning the brains of prison inmates. (Nearly one in every five adult males in prison in the United States and Canada scores high in psychopathy, measured using a checklist of 20 criteria such as impulsivity and lack of remorse, compared with one of every 150 in the general male population.)

Using an MRI scanner installed inside a tractor trailer, Kiehl and his colleagues have imaged more than 4,000 prison inmates since 2007, measuring the activity in their brains as well as the size of different brain regions.

Psychopathic criminals show reduced activity in their brain's amygdala, a primary site of emotional processing, compared with nonpsychopathic inmates when recalling emotionally charged words they were shown moments earlier, such as "misery" and "frown." In a task designed to test moral decision-making, researchers ask inmates to rate the offensiveness of pictures flashed on a screen, such as a cross burning by the Ku Klux Klan or a face bloodied by a beating. Although the ratings by psychopathic offenders aren't that different from those by nonpsychopaths—they both recognize the moral violation in the pictures—psychopaths tend to show weaker activation in brain regions instrumental in moral reasoning.

Based on these and other, similar findings, Kiehl is convinced that psychopaths have impairments in a system of interconnected brain structures—including the amygdala and the orbitofrontal cortex—that help process emotions, make decisions, control impulses, and set goals. There is "basically about 5–7 percent less gray matter in those structures in individuals with high psychopathic traits compared to other inmates," Kiehl says. The psychopath appears to compensate for this deficiency by using other parts of the brain to cognitively simulate what really belongs in the realm of emotion. "That is, the psychopath must think about right and wrong while the rest of us feel it," Kiehl wrote in a paper he coauthored in 2011.

WHEN ABIGAIL MARSH, a psychologist at Georgetown University, was 19, her car skidded on a bridge after she swerved to avoid hitting a dog. The vehicle spun out of control and finally came to a stop in the fast lane, facing oncoming traffic. Marsh couldn't get the engine to start and was too afraid to get out, with cars and trucks rushing past the vehicle. A man pulled over, ran across the highway, and helped start the car. "He took an enormous risk running across the freeway. There's no possible explanation for it other than he just wanted to help," Marsh says. "How can anybody be moved to do something like that?"

Marsh kept turning that question over in her head. Not long after she began working at Georgetown, she wondered if the altruism shown by the driver on the bridge wasn't in some ways the polar opposite of psychopathy. She began looking for a group of exceptionally kind individuals to study and decided that altruistic kidney donors would make ideal subjects. These are people who've chosen to donate a kidney to a stranger, sometimes even incurring financial costs, yet receive no compensation in return.

Marsh and her colleagues brought 19 donors in from around the country for the study. The researchers showed each one a series of black-and-white photographs of facial expressions, some fearful, some angry, and others neutral, while their brains were scanned using an MRI machine to map both activity and structure.

When looking at fearful faces, donors showed a greater response in their right amygdala than a control group. Separately, the researchers found that their right amygdalas were, on average, 8 percent larger than those of the control group. Similar studies done previously on psychopathic subjects had found the opposite: the amygdalas in psychopathic brains are smaller and activated less than those in controls while reacting to frightened faces.

"Fearful expressions elicit concern and caring. If you're not responsive to that expression, you're unlikely to experience concern for other people," Marsh explains. "And altruistic kidney donors just seem to be very sensitive to other people's distress, with fear being the most acute kind of distress—maybe in part because their amygdalas are larger than average."

The majority of people in the world are neither extreme altruists nor psychopaths, and most individuals in any society do not ordinarily commit violent acts against one another. And yet, there are genocides—organized mass killings that require the complicity and passivity of large numbers of people. Time and again, social groups organized along ethnic, national, racial, and religious lines have savaged other groups. Nazi Germany's gas chambers extinguished millions of Jews, the Communist Khmer Rouge slaughtered fellow Cambodians in the killing fields, Hutu extremists in Rwanda wielding machetes slaughtered several hundred thousand Tutsis and moderate Hutus, and Islamic State terrorists massacred Iraq's Yazidis—virtually every part of the world appears to have suffered through a genocide. Events such as these provide ghastly evidence that evil can hold entire communities in its grip.

How the voice of conscience is rendered inconsequential to foot soldiers of a genocide can be partly understood through the prism of the well-known experiments conducted in the 1960s by the psychologist Stanley Milgram at Yale University. In those studies, subjects were asked to deliver electric shocks to a person in another room for failing to answer questions correctly, increasing the voltage with every wrong answer. At the prodding of a person in a lab coat who played the role of an experimenter, the subjects often dialed up the shocks to dangerously high voltage levels. The shocks weren't real, and the cries of pain heard by the subjects were prerecorded, but the subjects only found that out afterward. The studies demonstrated what Milgram described as "the extreme willingness of adults to go to almost any lengths on the command of an authority."

Gregory Stanton, a former U.S. State Department official and founder of Genocide Watch, a nonprofit that works to prevent mass murder, has identified the stages that can cause otherwise decent people to commit murder. It starts when demagogic leaders define a target group as "the other" and claim it is a threat to the interests of supporters. Discrimination follows, and soon the leaders characterize their targets as subhuman, eroding the in-group's empathy for "the other."

Next, society becomes polarized. "Those planning the genocide say, 'You are either with us or against us,'" says Stanton. This is followed by a phase of preparation, with the architects of the genocide drawing up death lists, stocking weapons, and planning how the rank and file are to execute the killings. Members of the out-group are sometimes forced to move into ghettos or concentration camps. Then the massacres begin.

Many of the perpetrators remain untouched by remorse, not because they are incapable of feeling it—as is the case with psychopathic killers—but because they find ways to rationalize the killings. James Waller, a genocide scholar at Keene State College in New Hampshire, says he got a glimpse of this "incredible capacity of the human mind to make sense of and to justify the worst of actions" when he interviewed dozens of Hutu men convicted or accused of committing atrocities during the Rwandan genocide. Some of them had hacked children, even those they personally knew, to death. Their rationale, according to Waller, was: "if I didn't do this, those children would have grown up to come back to kill me. This was something that was a necessity for my people to be safe, for my people to survive."

OUR CAPACITY TO EMPATHIZE and channel that into compassion may be innate, but it is not immutable. Neither is the tendency to develop psychopathic and antisocial personalities so fixed in childhood as to be unchangeable. In recent years, researchers have shown the feasibility of nipping evil in the bud as well as strengthening our positive social instincts.

The possibility of preventing violent teenage boys from hardening into lifelong criminals has been put to the test at the Mendota Juvenile Treatment Center in Wisconsin, a facility that houses serious offenders but is run more as a psychiatric unit than as a prison. The adolescents referred to the center come in with already long criminal histories—teenagers who are a threat to others. "These are folks who essentially have dropped out of the human race—they don't have any connection to anyone, and they are in a real antagonistic posture with everybody," says Michael Caldwell, a senior staff psychologist.

The center attempts to build a connection with the kids despite their aggressive and antisocial behaviors. Even when an inmate hurls feces or sprays urine at staff members—a common occurrence at many correctional institutions—the staff members keep treating the offender humanely. The kids are scored on a set of behavior rating scales every day. If they do well, they earn certain privileges the following day, such as a chance to play video games. If they score badly, say, by getting into a fight, they lose privileges. The focus is not on punishing bad behavior but on rewarding good conduct. That's different from most correctional institutions. Over time, the kids start to behave better, says Greg Van Rybroek, the center's director. Their callous–unemotional traits diminish. Their improved ability to manage their emotions and control their violent impulses seems to endure beyond the walls of Mendota. Adolescents treated in the program have committed far fewer and less violent offenses between two and six years after release than those treated elsewhere, the center's studies have found. "We don't have any magic," Van Rybroek says, "but we've actually created a system that considers the world from the youth's point of view and tries to break it down in a fair and consistent manner."

During the past decade, researchers have discovered that our social brain is plastic, even in adulthood, and that we can be trained to be more kind and generous. Tania Singer, a social neuroscientist at the Max Planck Institute for Human Cognitive and Brain Sciences in Leipzig, Germany, has pioneered studies demonstrating this.

Empathy and compassion use different networks in the brain, Singer and her colleagues found. Both can lead to positive social behavior, but the brain's empathic response to seeing another person suffer can sometimes lead to empathic distress—a negative reaction that makes the onlooker want to turn away from the sufferer to preserve his or her own sense of well-being.

To enhance compassion, which combines awareness of another's distress with the desire to alleviate it, Singer and her colleagues have tested the effects of various training exercises. A prominent exercise, derived from Buddhist traditions, involves having subjects meditate on a loved one—a parent or a child, for example—directing warmth and kindness toward that individual and gradually extending those same feelings toward acquaintances, strangers, and even enemies, in an ever widening circle of love. Singer's group has shown that subjects who trained in this form of loving-kindness meditation even for a few days had a more compassionate response—as measured by the activation of certain brain circuits—than untrained subjects, when watching short film clips of people suffering emotional distress.

In another study, Singer and her colleagues tested the effects of compassion training on helpfulness by using a computer game in which subjects guide a virtual character on a computer screen through a maze to a treasure chest, opening gates along the way. They can also choose to open gates for another character wandering about, looking for treasure. The researchers found that subjects who underwent compassion training were more helpful than those in a control group toward the other character—the equivalent of a stranger.

That we might be able to mold our brains to be more altruistic is an ennobling prospect for society. One way to bring that future closer, Singer believes, would be to include compassion training in schools. The result could be a more benevolent world, populated by people like Ashley Aldridge, in which reflexive kindness loses its extraordinariness and becomes a defining trait of humanity.

Critical Thinking

1. Why are people especially giving or cruel?
2. Is human behavior the result of biology, culture, or both? Explain.
3. What are the primary antidotes to bad behavior?

Internet References

Health Place

https://www.healthyplace.com/personality-disorders/psychopath/psychopathic-children-psychopathic-behavior-in-children

Self-Assessment on Psychopathy

https://www.counseling-office.com/surveys/test_psychopathy.phtml

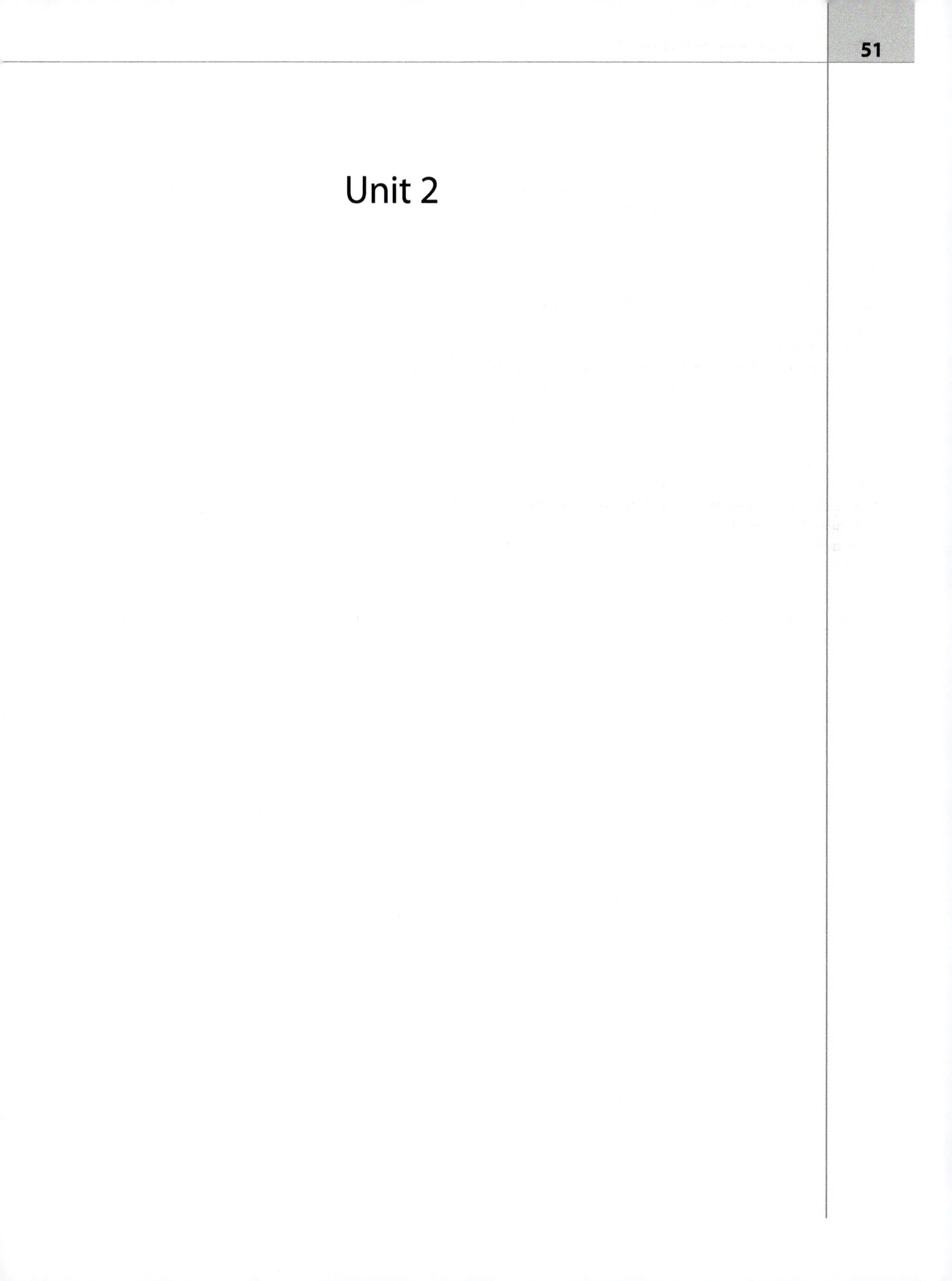

Unit 2

UNIT

Prepared by: Elvio Angeloni

Culture and Communication

Anthropologists are interested in all aspects of human behavior and how they interrelate. Language is a form of such behavior (albeit, primarily verbal behavior) and, therefore, worthy of study. Although it changes over time, language is culturally patterned and passed down from one generation to the next through learning, not instinct. In keeping with the idea that language is integral to human social interactions, it has long been recognized that human communication through language is, by its nature, different from the communication found among other animals. Central to this difference is the fact that humans communicate abstractly, with symbols that have meaning independent of the immediate sensory experiences of either the sender or the receiver of the message. Thus, for instance, humans are able to refer to the future and the past and not just the present.

Recent experiments have shown that anthropoid apes can be taught a small portion of Ameslan or American Sign Language. It must be remembered, however, that their very rudimentary ability has to be tapped by painstaking human effort and that the degree of difference between apes and humans serves only to emphasize the peculiar need of humans for, and development of, language.

Just as the abstract quality of symbols lifts our thoughts beyond our immediate sense perceptions, so also it inhibits our ability to think about and convey the full meaning of our personal experience. No categorical term can do justice to its referents—the variety of forms to which the term refers. The degree to which this is an obstacle to clarity of thought and communication relates to the degree of abstraction involved in the symbols. The word "chair," for instance, would not present much difficulty, as it has objective referents. However, consider the trouble we have in thinking and communicating with words whose referents are not tied to immediate sense perception—words such as "freedom," "democracy," and "justice." At best, the likely result is *symbolic confusion:* an inability to think or communicate in objectively definable symbols. At worst, language may be used to purposefully obfuscate.

A related issue has to do with the fact that languages differ as to what is relatively easy to express within the restrictions of their particular vocabularies and grammatical structure. Thus, although a given language may not have enough words to cope with a new situation or a new field of activity, the typical solution is to invent words or to borrow them. In this way, it has been claimed that any language can be used to say anything.

While we often become frustrated with the ways in which symbolic confusion cause misunderstandings between individuals or groups, we should also pause to admire the beauty and wonder inherent in this uniquely human form of communication—in all of its linguistic diversity—and the tremendous potential of recent research to enhance effective communication among all of us.

Article

Prepared by: Elvio Angeloni

Baby Talk

Every infant is a natural-born linguist capable of mastering any of the world's 7,000 languages like a native.

PATRICIA K. KUHL

Learning Outcomes

After reading this article, you will be able to:

- Discuss the important of "parentese" in babies' language acquisition.
- Discuss ways in which babies learn languages in general.
- Discuss the optimal circumstances for learning a second language.

An infant child possesses an amazing, and fleeting, Gift: the ability to master a language quickly. At six months, the child can learn the sounds that make up English words and, if also exposed to Quechua and Tagalog, he or she can pick up the unique acoustic properties of those languages, too. By age three, a toddler can converse with a parent, a playmate, or a stranger.

I still marvel, after four decades of studying child development, how a child can go from random babbling to speaking fully articulated words and sentences just a few years later—a mastery that occurs more quickly than any complex skill acquired during the course of a lifetime. Only in the past few years have neuroscientists begun to get a picture of what is happening in a baby's brain during this learning process that takes the child from gurgling newborn to a wonderfully engaging youngster.

At birth, the infant brain can perceive the full set of 800 or so sounds, called phonemes, that can be strung together to form all the words in every language of the world. During the second half of the first year, our research shows, a mysterious door opens in the child's brain. He or she enters a "sensitive period," as neuroscientists call it, during which the infant brain is ready to receive the first basic lessons in the magic of language.

The time when a youngster's brain is most open to learning the sounds of a native tongue begins at six months for vowels and at nine months for consonants. It appears that the sensitive period lasts for only a few months but is extended for children exposed to sounds of a second language. A child can still pick up a second language with a fair degree of fluency until age seven.

The built-in capacity for language is not by itself enough to get a baby past the first utterances of "Mama" and "Dada." Gaining mastery of the most important of all social skills is helped along by countless hours listening to parents speak the silly vernacular of "parentese." Its exaggerated inflections—"You're a preettee babbee"—serve the unfrivolous purpose of furnishing daily lessons in the intonations and cadences of the baby's native tongue. Our work puts to rest the age-old debates about whether genes or the environment prevails during early language development. They both play starring roles.

Knowledge of early language development has now reached a level of sophistication that is enabling psychologists and physicians to fashion new tools to help children with learning difficulties. Studies have begun to lay the groundwork for using recordings of brain waves to determine whether a child's language abilities are developing normally or whether an infant may be at risk for autism, attention deficit or other disorders. One day a routine visit to the pediatrician may involve a baby brain examination, along with vaccinations for measles, mumps and rubella.

The Statistics of Baby Talk

The reason we can contemplate a test for language development is that we have begun to understand how babies absorb language with seeming ease. My laboratory and others have shown that infants use two distinct learning mechanisms at the earliest stages of language acquisition: one that recognizes sound through mental computation and another that requires intense social immersion.

To learn to speak, infants have to know which phonemes make up the words they hear all around them. They need to discriminate which 40 or so, out of all 800, phonemes they need to learn to speak words in their own language. This task requires detecting subtle differences in spoken sound. A change in a single consonant can alter the meaning of a word—"bat" to "pat," for instance. And a simple vowel like "ah" varies widely when spoken by different people at different speaking rates and in different contexts—"Bach" versus "rock." Extreme variation in phonemes is why Apple's Siri still does not work flawlessly.

My work and that of Jessica Maye, then at Northwestern University, and her colleagues have shown that statistical patterns—the frequency with which sounds occur—play a critical role in helping infants learn which phonemes are most important. Children between eight and 10 months of age still do not understand spoken words. Yet they are highly sensitive to how often phonemes occur—what statisticians call distributional frequencies. The most important phonemes in a given language are the ones spoken most. In English, for example, the "r" and "l" sounds are quite frequent. They appear in words such as "rake" and "read" and "lake" and "lead." In Japan, the English-like "r" and "l" also occur but not as often. Instead the Japanese "r" sound is common but is rarely found in English. (The Japanese word "raamen" sounds like "laamen" to American ears because the Japanese "r" is midway between the American "r" and "l.")

The statistical frequency of particular sounds affects the infant brain. In one study of infants in Seattle and Stockholm, we monitored their perception of vowel sounds at six months and demonstrated that each group had already begun to focus in on the vowels spoken in their native language. The culture of the spoken word had already pervaded and affected how the baby's brain perceived sounds.

What exactly was going on here? Maye has shown that the brain at this age has the requisite plasticity to change how infants perceive sounds. A Japanese baby who hears sounds from English learns to distinguish the "r" and the "l" in the way they are used in the U.S. And a baby being raised among native English speakers could likewise pick up the characteristic sounds of Japanese. It appears that learning sounds in the second half of the first year establishes connections in the brain for one's native tongue but not for other languages, unless a child is exposed to multiple languages during that period. Later in childhood, and particularly as an adult, listening to a new language does not produce such dramatic results—a traveler to France or Japan can hear the statistical distributions of sounds from another language, but the brain is not altered by the experience. That is why it is so difficult to pick up a second language later on.

A second form of statistical learning lets infants recognize whole words. As adults, we can distinguish where one word ends and the next begins. But the ability to isolate words from the stream of speech requires complex mental processing. Spoken speech arrives at the ear as a continuous stream of sound that lacks the separations found between written words. Jenny Saffran, now at the University of Wisconsin-Madison, and her colleagues—Richard Aslin of the University of Rochester and Elissa Newport, now at Georgetown University—were the first to discover that a baby uses statistical learning to grasp the sounds of whole words. In the mid-1990s Saffran's group published evidence that eight-month-old infants can learn word-like units based on the probability that one syllable follows another. Take the phrase "pretty baby." The syllable "pre" is more likely to be heard with "ty" than to accompany another syllable like "ba."

In the experiment, Saffran had babies listen to streams of computer-synthesized nonsense words that contained syllables, some of which occurred together more often than others. The babies' ability to focus on syllables that coincide in the made-up language let them identify likely words.

The discovery of babies' statistical-learning abilities in the 1990s generated a great deal of excitement because it offered a theory of language learning beyond the prevailing idea that a child learns only because of parental conditioning and affirmations of whether a word is right or wrong. Infant learning occurs before parents realize that it is taking place. Further tests in my lab, however, produced a significant new finding that lends an important caveat to this story: the statistical-learning process does not require passive listening alone.

Baby Meet and Greet

In our work, we discovered that infants need to be more than just computational geniuses processing clever neural algorithms. In 2003 we published the results of experiments in which nine-month-old infants from Seattle were exposed to Mandarin Chinese. We wanted to know whether infants' statistical-learning abilities would allow them to learn Mandarin phonemes.

In groups of two or three, the nine-month-olds listened to Mandarin native speakers while their teachers played on the floor with them, using books and toys. Two additional groups were also exposed to Mandarin. But one watched a video of Mandarin being spoken. Another listened to an audio recording. A fourth group, run as a control, heard no Mandarin at all but instead listened to U.S. graduate students speaking English while playing with the children with the same books and toys. All of this happened during 12 sessions that took place over the course of a month.

Infants from all four groups returned to the lab for psychological tests and brain monitoring to gauge their ability to single out Mandarin phonemes. Only the group exposed to Chinese from live speakers learned to pick up the foreign phonemes. Their performance, in fact, was equivalent to infants in Taipei who had been listening to their parents for their first 11 months.

Infants who were exposed to Mandarin by television or audio did not learn at all. Their ability to discriminate phonemes matched infants in the control group, who, as expected, performed no better than before the experiment.

The study provided evidence that learning for the infant brain is not a passive process. It requires human interaction—a necessity that I call "social gating." This hypothesis can even be extended to explain the way many species learn to communicate. The experience of a young child learning to talk, in fact, resembles the way birds learn song.

I worked earlier with the late Allison Doupe of the University of California, San Francisco, to compare baby and bird learning. We found that for both children and zebra finches, social experience in the early months of life was essential. Both human and bird babies immerse themselves in listening to their elders, and they store memories of the sounds they hear. These recollections condition the brain's motor areas to produce sounds that match those heard frequently in the larger social community in which they were being raised.

Exactly how social context contributes to the learning of a language in humans is still an open question. I have suggested, though, that parents and other adults provide both motivation and necessary information to help babies learn. The motivational component is driven by the brain's reward systems—and, in particular, brain areas that use the neurotransmitter dopamine during social interaction. Work in my lab has already shown that babies learn better in the presence of other babies—we are currently engaged in studies that explain why this is the case.

Babies who gaze into their parents' eyes also receive key social cues that help to speed the next stage of language learning—the understanding of the meaning of actual words. Andrew Meltzoff of the University of Washington has shown that young children who follow the direction of an adult's gaze pick up more vocabulary in the first two years of life than children who do not track these eye movements. The connection between looking and talking makes perfect sense and provides some explanation of why simply watching an instructional video is not good enough.

In the group that received live lessons, infants could see when the Mandarin teacher glanced at an object while naming it, a subtle action that tied together the word with the object named. In a paper published in July, we also showed that as a Spanish tutor holds up new toys and talks about them, infants who look back and forth between the tutor and the toy, instead of just focusing on one or the other, learn the phonemes as well as words used during the study session. This example is an illustration of my theory that infants' social skills enable—or "gate"—language learning.

These ideas about the social component of early language learning may also explain some of the difficulties encountered by infants who go on to develop disorders such as autism. Children with autism lack basic interest in speaking. Instead they fixate on inanimate objects and fail to pay attention to social cues so essential in language learning.

Say, "Hiiiii!"

An infant's ability to learn to speak depends not only on being able to listen to adults but also on the manner in which grown-ups talk to the child. Whether in Dhaka, Paris, Riga or the Tulalip Indian Reservation near Seattle, researchers who listen to people talk to a child have learned one simple truth: an adult speaks to a child differently than to other adults. Cultural ethnographers and linguists have dubbed it "baby talk," and it turns up in most cultures. At first, it was unknown whether baby talk might hinder language learning. Numerous studies, however, have shown that motherese or parentese, the revisionist name for baby talk, actually helps an infant learn. Parentese, in fact, is not a modern invention: Varro (116 to 27 BC), an ancient Roman expert on syntax, noted that certain shortened words were used only when talking to babies and young children.

My lab—and those of Anne Fernald at Stanford University and Lila Gleitman at the University of Pennsylvania—has looked at the specific sounds of parentese that intrigue infants: the higher pitch, slower tempo, and exaggerated intonation. When given a choice, infants will choose to listen to short audio clips of parentese instead of recordings of the same mothers speaking to other adults. The high-pitched tone seems to act as an acoustic hook for infants that captures and holds their attention.

Parentese exaggerates differences between sounds—one phoneme can be easily discriminated from another. Our studies show that exaggerated speech most likely helps infants as they commit these sounds to memory. In a recent study by my group, Nairan Ramirez-Esparza, now at the University of Connecticut, had infants wear high-fidelity miniature tape recorders fitted into lightweight vests worn at home throughout the day. The recordings let us enter the children's auditory world and showed that if their parents spoke to them in parentese at that age, then one year later these infants had learned more than twice the number of words as those whose parents did not use the baby vernacular as frequently.

Signatures of Learning

Brain scientists who study child development are becoming excited about the possibility of using our growing knowledge of early development to identify signatures of brain activity, known as biomarkers, that provide clues that a child may be running into difficulty in learning language. In a recent study in my lab, two-year-old children with autism spectrum disorder listened to both known and unfamiliar words while we monitored their brain's electrical activity when they heard these words.

We found the degree to which a particular pattern of brain waves was present in response to known words predicted the child's future language and cognitive abilities, at ages four and six. These measurements assessed the child's success at learning from other people. They show that if a youngster has the ability to learn words socially, it bodes well for learning in general.

The prospect for being able to measure an infant or toddler's cognitive development is improving because of the availability of new tools to judge their ability to detect sounds. My research group has begun to use magnetoencephalography (MEG), a safe and noninvasive imaging technology, to demonstrate how the brain responds to speech. The machine contains 306 SQUID (superconducting quantum interference device) sensors placed within an apparatus that looks like a hair dryer. When the infant sits in it, the sensors measure tiny magnetic fields that indicate specific neurons firing in the baby's brain as the child listens to speech. We have already demonstrated with MEG that there is a critical time window in which babies seem to be going through mental rehearsals to prepare to speak their native language.

MEG is too expensive and difficult to use in a neighborhood medical clinic. But these studies pave the way by identifying biomarkers that will eventually be measured with portable and inexpensive sensors that can be used outside a university lab. If reliable biomarkers for language learning can be identified, they should help determine whether children are developing normally or at risk for early-life, language-related disabilities, including autism spectrum disorder, dyslexia, fragile X syndrome, and other disorders. By understanding the brain's uniquely human capacity for language—and when exactly it is possible to shape it—we may be able to administer therapies early enough to change the future course of a child's life.

Critical Thinking

1. How and why does "parentese" help babies learn to talk?
2. In what respects is language acquisition dependent upon both mental computation and intense social immersion?
3. What are the optimal circumstances for learning a second language and why?

Internet References

How Your Newborn Grows: Infant Development

http://www.webmd.com/parenting/baby/infant-development-9/baby-talk

The linguistic genius of babies

https://www.ted.com/talks/patricia_kuhl_the_linguistic_genius_of_babies?language=en

Pathways

https://pathways.org/

Article

Prepared by: Elvio Angeloni

The Eloquent Ape

Frogs croak, birds sing, and monkeys chatter. But no other species has our rich and infinitely adaptable language skills. Without them, trade, tribes, religions, and nations couldn't have existed, to say nothing of the Internet or the ink on this page.

To what do we owe our ability to share thoughts and influence others? How does it shape us, and how will it change?

Here's our guide to the nine biggest questions.

MARK PAGEL

Learning Outcomes

After reading this article, you will be able to:

- Discuss the importance of language as symbolic behavior.
- Discuss the ways in which learning a new language may help to rewire the brain and influence the way we think.
- Discuss the likely future of language in general.

Who Spoke the First Words?

Language is a powerful piece of social technology. It conveys your thoughts as coded puffs of air or dozens of drawn symbols, to be decoded by someone else. It can move information about the past, present, and future, formalise ideas, trigger action, persuade, cajole, and deceive.

Today, there are 7102 such codes spoken around the world. All human societies have language, and no language is "better" than any other: all can communicate the full range of human experience. To those of us who study human evolution, this incredible universality suggests that our species has had language right from when *Homo sapiens* arose in Africa between 200,000 and 160,000 years ago. A more recent origin could not explain how groups that stayed in Africa after *H. sapiens* migrated to the rest of the world 60,000 years ago also have language.

If *H. sapiens* has always had language, could other extinct human species have had it too? Some believe that Neanderthals did—which would imply we both inherited it from our common ancestor some 500,000 or more years ago. This theory is consistent with the discovery that FOXP2, a gene that is essential to speech, is identical at two key positions in humans and Neanderthals but different in chimpanzees. But a single gene is not enough to explain language. And recent genetic evidence shows that the Neanderthal brain regulated its version of FOXP2 differently.

What's more, language is inherently symbolic—sounds stand for words that stand for real objects and actions. But there is scant evidence that Neanderthals had art or other symbolic behaviour—a few pieces of pigment and some disputed etchings. By comparison, the humans who lived alongside them in Western Europe painted beautiful murals, made musical instruments, and had a wide variety of tools and weapons.

Suggestions that language evolved even earlier—for example in *Homo erectus*, an upright ape that walked on the African savannah two million years ago—are little more than idle speculation. It seems more likely, from the existing evidence at least, that our ability to bend each other's ears is indeed unique.

Why Did We Evolve Language?

Our language skills didn't come for free. Humans had to evolve complex brain circuits and sophisticated machinery in order to speak, and spend precious years teaching their children. Why pay that price?

Many people attribute our linguistic skills to our large brains, ability to make complex hand gestures, distinctive vocal tracts and to the gene FOXP2, which gives us the fine-tuned control of our facial muscles. But on their own, these traits do not explain why we evolved language. There are animals with larger brains, gesturing is widespread among primates and some bird species can imitate human speech without our descended larynx or our particular version of FOXP2.

Instead, the feature that most clearly separates us from other animals is the sophistication of our symbolic and cooperative social behaviour. Humans are the only species that routinely exchanges favours, goods and services with others outside their immediate family. We have an elaborate division of labour, we specialise at tasks and then trade our products with others. And we have learned to act in coordinated ways outside the family unit, such as when a nation goes to war or people combine their efforts to build a bridge.

We take the complexity of our social behaviour for granted, but all these actions rest on the ability to negotiate, bargain, reach agreements and hold people to them. This requires a conduit—like a modern USB cable—to carry complex information back and forth between individuals. Language is that conduit.

Some social insects—ants, bees, and wasps—have a level of cooperation without language. But they tend to belong to highly related family groups, genetically programmed to act largely for the good of the group. Human societies must police anyone who tries to take advantage. With words and symbols, we can expose them as cheats and tarnish their reputations. We can lavish praise on those worthy of it, whose reputations will be elevated even among those they have never met: words can travel further than a single action.

All these complicated social acts require more than the grunts, chirrups, odors, colors, and roars of the rest of the animal kingdom. They tell us why we and we alone have language: our particular brand of sociality could not exist without it.

What Were the First Words?

It's a fair guess that there was once an original mother tongue—the ancestor to all living and dead human languages. The evidence for this is that all human languages, unlike other forms of animal communication, string together words into sentences that have subjects, verbs and objects ("I kicked the ball"), and anyone can learn any language.

Comparative linguists search for sounds that come up again and again in languages from all over the world. They argue that if any relics of a mother tongue still exist today, they will be in those sounds. Merritt Ruhlen at Stanford University in California, for example, argues that sounds like tok, tik, dik, and tak are repeatedly used in different languages to signify a toe, a digit or the number one. Although studies by Ruhlen and others are contentious, the list of words they say are globally shared because they sound almost the same also includes who, what, two, and water.

Another approach is to look at words that change very slowly over long periods of time. My own team has used such statistical studies to show that words for the numbers 1 to 5 are some of the slowest evolving. Also on this list are words involved in social communication, like who, what, where, why, when, I, you, she, he, and it. This list fits with the expectation that language evolved because of its social role (see "Why did we evolve language?," page 28). It also has some overlap with Ruhlen's list.

More broadly, we can say with some confidence that the first words probably fitted into just a few categories. The first ones may have been simple names, like those used by some of our primate relatives. Vervet monkeys give distinct alarm calls for leopards, martial eagles and pythons, and young vervets must learn these. In humans, mama is a strong candidate for a very early noun, given how naturally the sound appears in babbling and how dependent babies are on their mothers. The sound "m" is also present in nearly all the world's languages.

Imperatives like look or listen are also likely to have appeared early on, perhaps alongside verbs like stab or trade that would have helped coordinate hunting or exchanges. Even this simple lexicon allows sentences like "look, wildebeest" or "trade arrows." Finally, simple social words like you, me and I, yes and no, were probably part of our early vocab. Amusingly, a recent study suggested that huh is universal, prompting headlines that it was among the first human words. Perhaps it was the second.

Can Learning a Language Rewire Your Brain?

As our species evolved parts of our brain expanded, resulting in more computing power for language. It's what makes us hardwired for communication. What is perhaps more surprising is how language can shape our brains throughout our lives.

Most of the evidence for this comes from studies of people who are bilingual. Brain scan studies show that switching between two languages triggers different patterns of brain activity compared with speaking in one language, particularly in the prefrontal cortex. That part of the brain, at the very front of our skulls, is involved in organizing and acting on information, including using working memory, reasoning and planning. Other studies show that bilinguals are faster at getting to grips with a new language.

Quadrilinguist Arturo Hernandez, director of the Laboratory for the Neural Bases of Bilingualism at the University of Houston in Texas, says these differences could reflect differences in the architecture of bilingual brains. In other words, learning another language could change how your brain is wired. "It would make sense, if you have had this very different linguistic experience, to see some sort of stable, long-lasting effect," Hernandez says.

It may also make the brain more resilient. Ellen Bialystok at York University in Toronto, Canada, has found that lifelong bilinguals tend to be diagnosed with dementia on average 4.5 years later than monolinguals, and have more white matter, including in their prefrontal cortex. White matter is made of nerve fibres that connect different brain regions, shuttling information back and forth between them. So boosting language skills appears to build more connected brains—although Bialystok cautions that this still needs to be confirmed.

More evidence for the benefits of second languages came last year from a study of 608 people who had had a stroke. Thomas Bak of the University of Edinburgh, UK, found that of the bilinguals among them, 40 per cent recovered full function, compared with only 20 per cent of monolinguals. Bak speculates that the mental gymnastics involved in speaking several languages could build extra connections that improve function and help cope with damage. "The idea is that if you have a lot of mental exercise, your brain is trained and can compensate better," says Bak.

Can Language Influence How You See the World?

Time flows from back to front for English speakers: we "cast our minds back" to the 1990s, and "hope for good times ahead." It's an example of a cultural concept encoded in language, but can language in turn influence how we think?

Maria Sera is a native Spanish-speaker who grew up believing all squirrels were female. The Spanish word for squirrel, ardilla, is feminine. As a linguist at the University of Minnesota, she has found some substance for her childhood belief. Studies of French and Spanish speakers, whose languages attribute genders to objects, suggest they associate those objects with masculine or feminine properties.

The idea that the language you speak could influence how you think dates back to 1940, when linguist Benjamin Lee Whorf proposed that people whose languages lack words for a concept would not understand it. It was relegated to fringe science until the early 2000s, when a few people began probing a related but more nuanced idea: that language can influence perception.

Greek, for instance, has two words for blue—ghalazio for light blue and ble for a darker shade. A study found that Greek speakers could discriminate shades of blue faster and better than native English speakers.

Language even seems to affect our sense of space and time. Some peoples, like the Guugu Yimithirr in Australia, don't have words for relative space, like left and right, but do have terms for north, south, east and west. Studies have shown that they tend to be unusually skilled at keeping track of where they are in unfamiliar places. There is also some evidence that the direction in which your first language is written can influence your sense of time, with speakers of Mandarin more likely to think of time running from top to bottom than English speakers. And the language you speak may affect how you perceive others (see "Does your language shape your personality?").

More generally, language helps us understand the world by allowing us to categorize things. Children are better at grouping objects if they have already learned the names of the categories they belong to. Conversely, after a stroke, people who have lost language skills can have trouble grouping objects. "It's not that language just affects some high-level reasoning part of the brain," says Gary Lupyan of the University of Wisconsin-Madison. "It's changing our basic perceptual representations."

Does Your Language Shape Your Personality?

"To have another language is to possess a second soul," Charlemagne is rumored to have said. He may have been on to something. In the 1960s, sociolinguist Susan Ervin-Tripp of the University of California at Berkeley asked English–Japanese bilinguals to describe what was going on in ambiguous pictures. One person, for example, told a different tale depending on their storytelling language. A picture of a woman leaning against a couch elicited a story in Japanese about a woman contemplating suicide after the loss of her fiancé. The same person, asked to respond at a separate session in English, said the woman was completing a sewing project for a class. "In general, there was more emotion in the Japanese stories," Ervin-Tripp wrote in a description of the experiment. "The switch in language draws with it the cultural baggage associated with that language."

Nairán Ramírez-Esparza at the University of Connecticut asked bilingual Mexicans to rate their personalities using both English and Spanish questionnaires. English responses emphasised openness and extroversion, while Spanish responses were more humble and reserved. "Language is such a powerful thing. It obviously makes you see yourself differently," Ramírez-Esparza says.

According to Shai Danziger of Ben-Gurion University in Israel and Robert Ward of Bangor University in the UK, it can also influence how you think of others. They asked Arabic-Hebrew bilinguals to match Arab and Jewish names with positive or negative trait words by pressing a key. They say participants showed more involuntary positive attitudes towards Jews when tested in Hebrew than when tested in Arabic. Paula Rubio-Fernandez of the University of Oslo, meanwhile, has found that bilingual children perform better on tests that require them to understand a situation from someone else's perspective.

Evidence is mounting that the words we speak and think shape our brains, perceptions, and personalities. Who knows what else? Perhaps our tastes, habits, or values. The door is wide open.

Will We All One Day Speak the Same Language?

With over a billion native speakers, Mandarin Chinese is the language spoken by the greatest number of people. English comes third, after Spanish. But unlike Mandarin and Spanish—both spoken in more than 30 countries—English is found in at least 100. In addition to the 335 million people for whom it is their first language, 550 million cite it as their second. It dominates international relations, business, and science.

All this suggests English is on course to be the planet's lingua franca. It just probably won't be the English that native speakers are used to.

Millions of second-language English speakers around the world have created dialects that incorporate elements of their native languages and cultures. Anna Mauranen of the University of Helsinki in Finland calls these varieties similects: Chinese-English, Brazilian-English, Nigerian-English. Taken together they—not American or British English—will chart the language's future path, she says.

"We used to think there were two possible futures," says Jennifer Jenkins at the University of Southampton, UK. "In one we'd all end up speaking American English. In the other, English would separate like Latin did, and we'd end up with [new] languages. I don't think either of those is happening."

Instead, English similects are probably here to stay. Even in a future where China, India and Nigeria are global superpowers, English is likely to be the language of choice for international discourse, simply because is already installed. Weirdly, this puts native speakers at risk. "We're getting to the stage where all the educated people of the world have English," says Jenkins. "Once it's no longer a special thing, native speakers lose their advantage."

They could even be at a disadvantage. Nonnative speakers are all tuned to each-other's linguistic quirks. "If you put a Chilean, a Japanese and a Polish person in a discussion in English, they understand each other perfectly," says Jenkins. "Put one with two native English speakers and there might be problems."

Mauranen envisions a future in which English similects begin to blend over national borders. New dialects are likely to form around trades or regions. She says these common goals will drive the evolution of the lingua franca, regardless of whether we call it English or not.

That is not to say that all other languages will vanish. German will remain the language of choice within German borders. Even Estonian, spoken by just 1 million people, is safe. "It's a fully fledged language, used for everything [in Estonia]," says Mauranen.

Likewise, the language directly descended from Shakespeare's English has staying power with Brits and Americans. But English, like football, will soon move outside their control, pulled into something new by the rest of the planet.

How Is Technology Changing Language?

"Writing used to be very formal," says Lauren Collister of the University of Pittsburgh, Pennsylvania. "It was books, love letters or newspaper articles. Grammar and spelling were expected to be precise."

That is changing. Every day, millions of us have real-time conversations in writing, online and on our mobile phones. As a result, writing is evolving. "Chat rooms, instant messaging, they all contributed to informalisation of written language," says Collister. Goodbye "To whom this may concern"; hello txtspk, and DBEYR.* This evolution is happening so quickly that we are already seeing it move offline and back into speech and formal lexicons. In 2011, "lol" was added to the Oxford English Dictionary.

The question is, what new language is coming down the internet pipeline?

Internet-speak often bypasses language barriers, so the next netspeak could have foreign roots. Japanese forums use "Orz" to signify kneeling down: the O is the head, r the arms and body, and z is the kneeling legs. Depending on context, it is used to signify failure and despair, or sarcastic admiration. Chinese netspeak has adapted Orz to Chinese script, rz, to convey a facial expression. Xiangxi Liu of the University of Massachusetts, Amherst, foresees an explosion of such online language, especially in Chinese, which can draw on thousands of characters.

Even the traditional building blocks of language—letters and words—are being upgraded. Ramesh Jain of the University of California, Irvine, thinks images will play a bigger role in future online communication, precisely because they cross language barriers. You only have to look at how Facebook, Google and chat companies like Line are continually growing their emoticon and sticker libraries to see the evidence for this.

This has created a strange new linguistic barrier: money. Line users pay for stickers. The company made $75 million from this scheme in its first year. Don't be deflated, though. If there is anything the explosion of internet memes and netspeak shows, it's how quick and crafty we are at inventing our own new words, which are adopted (or not) by the ruthless natural selection of social media.

*Don't believe everything you read.

Could We One Day Communicate Without Speaking?

Private thoughts fill your head every second of the day, safe from prying ears—for now. Lately, researchers have begun exploring ways to decipher our internal monologues from a distance. Don't jump for your tin foil hat just yet. The aim is to give a voice to people who are paralyzed and unable to communicate, but fully aware of their surroundings.

Adrian Owen at the University of Western Ontario in Canada showed in 2010 that it was possible to communicate with such "lockedin" people through questions with yes or no answers. The person would imagine walking around their home for "yes," or playing tennis for "no." A scanner picked up on the distinct brain activity patterns that each scenario produces. With a small delay, the team was able to decode yes/home and no/tennis.

But a one-sided conversation isn't much fun. Philip Kennedy of Neural Signals in Duluth, Georgia, has designed a brain implant that records activity in areas that control the movement of your mouth when you shape a word. He is investigating whether this could be used to interpret a person's intention to speak, and command a speech synthesizer to do the actual talking.

An alternative is to decode brain activity associated with concepts, rather than words. João Correia at Maastricht University in the Netherlands has done this using noninvasive EEG recordings. He reckons this could one day give people enough mental "vocabulary" to form whole sentences, or at the very least a few vital words.

Meanwhile, Brian Pasley and his colleagues at the University of California, Berkeley have found that groups of neurons in the auditory areas are tuned to certain frequencies and rhythms. The activity is the same whether you hear a word or merely think it. Pasley has built an algorithm that analyses which neurons are active when people think about talking and converts that information back into speech.

It's a little rough and ready, and electrodes have to be implanted in the brain, but the outcome is impressive. Listening to one of the recordings, I was able to recognize the word "Waldo," produced from imagined speech. It may be far-fetched, says Correia, but it's also "the closest we've come to speaking with the mind."

Critical Thinking

1. What have been the benefits of language to the human species and why?
2. How does learning a new language rewire the brain and shape the way we see the world?
3. How are changes in the world going to affect the way we communicate?

Internet References

Exploratorium Magazine: "The Evolution of Languages"
https://www.exploratorium.edu/exploring/language/

Linguistic Society of America
https://www.linguisticsociety.org/

MIT Press Journals: "Linguistic Inquiry"
http://www.mitpressjournals.org/loi/ling

Article

Prepared by: Elvio Angeloni

War of Words

Mark Pagel

Learning Outcomes

After reading this article, you will be able to:

- Discuss the origins and functions of linguistic diversity in human societies.
- Discuss the future of linguistic diversity in terms of its direction and causes.

For anyone interested in languages, the north-eastern coastal region of Papua New Guinea is like a well-stocked sweet shop. Korak speakers live right next to Brem speakers, who are just up the coast from Wanambre speakers, and so on. I once met a man from that area and asked him whether it is true that a different language is spoken every few kilometres. "Oh no," he replied, "they are far closer together than that."

Around the world today, some 7,000 distinct languages are spoken. That's 7,000 different ways of saying "good morning" or "it looks like rain"—more languages in one species of mammal than there are mammalian species. What's more, these 7,000 languages probably make up just a fraction of those ever spoken in our history. To put human linguistic diversity into perspective, you could take a gorilla or chimpanzee from its troop and plop it down anywhere these species are found, and it would know how to communicate. You could repeat this with donkeys, crickets or goldfish and get the same outcome.

This highlights an intriguing paradox at the heart of human communication. If language evolved to allow us to exchange information, how come most people cannot understand what most other people are saying? This perennial question was famously addressed in the Old Testament story of the Tower of Babel, which tells of how humans developed the conceit that they could use their shared language to cooperate in the building of a tower that would take them to heaven. God, angered at this attempt to usurp his power, destroyed the tower and to ensure it would not be rebuilt he scattered the people and confused them by giving them different languages. The myth leads to the amusing irony that our separate languages exist to prevent us from communicating. The surprise is that this might not be far from the truth.

The origins of language are difficult to pin down. Anatomical evidence from fossils suggests that the ability to speak arose in our ancestors sometime between 1.6 million and 600,000 years ago (*New Scientist,* 24 March, p. 34). However, indisputable evidence that this speech was conveying complex ideas comes only with the cultural sophistication and symbolism associated with modern humans. They emerged in Africa perhaps 200,000 to 160,000 years ago, and by 60,000 years ago had migrated out of the continent—eventually to occupy nearly every region of the world. We should expect new languages to arise as people spread out and occupy new lands because as soon as groups become isolated from one another their languages begin to drift apart and adapt to local needs (*New Scientist,* 10 December 2011, p. 34). But the real puzzle is that the greatest diversity of human societies and languages arises not where people are most spread out, but where they are most closely packed together.

Papua New Guinea is a classic case. That relatively small land mass—only slightly larger than California—is home to between 800 and 1,000 distinct languages, or around 15 per cent of all languages spoken on the planet. This linguistic diversity is not the result of migration and physical isolation of different populations. Instead, people living in close quarters seem to have chosen to separate into many distinct societies, leading lives so separate that they have become incapable of talking to one another. Why?

Thinking about this, I was struck by an uncanny parallel between linguistic and biological diversity. A well-known phenomenon in ecology called Rapoport's rule states that the greatest diversity of biological species is found near to the equator, with numbers tailing off as you approach the poles. Could this be true for languages too? To test the idea, anthropologist Ruth Mace from University College London and I looked at the distribution of around 500 Native American tribes before the arrival of Europeans and used this to plot the number of different language groups per unit area at each degree of latitude (*Nature,* vol 428, p. 275). It turned out that the distribution matched Rapoport's rule remarkably well.

The congruity of biological species and cultures with distinct languages is probably not an accident. To survive the harsh polar landscape, species must range far and wide, leaving little opportunity for new ones to arise. The same is true of human groups in the far northern regions. They too must cover wide geographical areas to find sufficient food, and this tends to blend languages and cultures. At the other end of the spectrum, just as the bountiful, sun-drenched tropics are a cradle of biological speciation, so this rich environment has allowed humans to thrive and splinter into a profusion of societies.

Of course that still leaves the question of why people would want to form into so many distinct groups. For the myriad biological species in the tropics, there are advantages to being different because it allows each to adapt to its own ecological niche. But humans all occupy the same niche, and splitting into distinct cultural and linguistic groups actually brings disadvantages, such as slowing the movement of ideas, technologies and people. It also makes societies more vulnerable to risks and plain bad luck. So why not have one large group with a shared language?

An answer to this question is emerging with the realisation that human history has been characterised by continual battles. Ever since our ancestors walked out of Africa, beginning around 60,000 years ago, people have been in conflict over territory and resources. In my book *Wired for Culture* (Norton/Penguin, 2012) I describe how, as a consequence, we have acquired a suite of traits that help our own particular group to outcompete the others. Two traits that stand out are "groupishness"—affiliating with people with whom you share a distinct identity—and xenophobia, demonising those outside your group and holding parochial views towards them. In this context, languages act as powerful social anchors of our tribal identity. How we speak is a continual auditory reminder of who we are and, equally as important, who we are not. Anyone who can speak your particular dialect is a walking, talking advertisement for the values and cultural history you share. What's more, where different groups live in close proximity, distinct languages are an effective way to prevent eavesdropping or the loss of important information to a competitor.

In support of this idea, I have found anthropological accounts of tribes deciding to change their language, with immediate effect, for no other reason than to distinguish themselves from neighbouring groups. For example, a group of Selepet speakers in Papua New Guinea changed its word for "no" from *bia* to *bune* to be distinct from other Selepet speakers in a nearby village. Another group reversed all its masculine and feminine nouns—the word for he became she, man became woman, mother became father, and so on. One can only sympathise with anyone who had been away hunting for a few days when the changes occurred.

The use of language as identity is not confined to Papua New Guinea. People everywhere use language to monitor who is a member of their "tribe." We have an acute, and sometimes obsessive, awareness of how those around us speak, and we continually adapt language to mark out our particular group from others. In a striking parallel to the Selepet examples, many of the peculiar spellings that differentiate American English from British—such as the tendency to drop the "u" in words like colour—arose almost overnight when Noah Webster produced the first American Dictionary of the English Language at the start of the 19th century. He insisted that: "As an independent nation, our honor [sic] requires us to have a system of our own, in language as well as government."

Use of language to define group identity is not a new phenomenon. To examine how languages have diversified over the course of human history, my colleagues and I drew up family trees for three large language groups—Indo-European languages, the Bantu languages of Africa, and Polynesian languages from Oceania (*Science,* vol 319, p. 588). These "phylogenies," which trace the history of each group back to a common ancestor, reveal the number of times a contemporary language has split or "divorced" from related languages. We found that some languages have a history of many divorces, others far fewer.

When languages split, they often experience short episodes during which they change rapidly. The same thing happens during biological evolution, where it is known as punctuational evolution (*Science,* vol 314, p. 119). So the more divorces a language has had, the more its vocabulary differs from its ancestral language. Our analysis does not say why one language splits into two. Migration and isolation of groups is one explanation, but it also seems clear that bursts of linguistic change have occurred at least in part to allow speakers to assert their own identities. There really has been a war of words going on.

So what of the future? The world we live in today is very different from the one our ancestors inhabited. For most of our history, people would have encountered only their own cultural group and immediate neighbours. Globalisation and electronic communication mean we have become far more connected and culturally homogenised, making the benefits of being understood more apparent. The result is a mass extinction of languages to rival the great biological extinctions in Earth's past.

Although contemporary languages continue to evolve and diverge from one another, the rate of loss of minority languages now greatly exceeds the emergence of new languages. Between 30 and 50 languages are disappearing every year as the young people of small tribal societies adopt majority languages. As a percentage of the total, this rate of loss equals or exceeds the decline in biological species diversity through loss of habitat and climate change. Already a mere 15 of the Earth's 7,000 languages account for about 40 per cent of the world's speakers, and most languages have very few speakers.

Still, this homogenisation of languages and cultures is happening at a far slower pace than it could, and that is because of the powerful psychological role language plays in marking out our cultural territories and identities. One consequence of this is that languages resist "contamination" from other languages, with speakers often treating the arrival of foreign words with a degree of suspicion—witness the British and French grumblings about so-called Americanisms. Another factor is the role played by nationalistic agendas in efforts to save dying languages, which can result in policies such as compulsory Welsh lessons for schoolchildren up to the age of 16 in Wales.

Linguistic Creativity

This resistance to change leaves plenty of time for linguistic diversity to pop up. Various street and hip-hop dialects, for example, are central to the identity of specific groups, while mass communication allows them easily to reach their natural constituencies. Another interesting example is Globish, a pared-down form of English that uses just 1,000 or so words and simplified language structures. It has spontaneously evolved among people who travel extensively, such as diplomats and international business people. Amusingly, native English speakers can be disadvantaged around Globish because they use words and grammar that others cannot understand.

In the long run, though, it seems virtually inevitable that a single language will replace all others. In evolutionary terms, when otherwise equally good solutions to a problem compete, one of them tends to win out. We see this in the near worldwide standardisation of ways of telling time, measuring weights and distance, CD and DVD formats, railway gauges, and the voltages and frequencies of electricity supplies. It may take a very long time, but languages seem destined to go the same way—all are equally good vehicles of communication, so one will eventually replace the others. Which one will it be?

Today, around 1.2 billion people—about 1 in 6 of us—speak Mandarin. Next come Spanish and English with about 400 million speakers each, and Bengali and Hindi follow close behind. On these counts Mandarin might look like the favourite in the race to be the world's language. However, vastly more people learn English as a second language than any other. Years ago, in a remote part of Tanzania, I was stopped while attempting to speak Swahili to a local person who held up his hand and said: "My English is better than your Swahili." English is already the worldwide lingua franca, so if I had to put money on one language eventually to replace all others, this would be it.

In the ongoing war of words, casualties are inevitable. As languages become extinct we are not simply losing different ways of saying "good morning," but the cultural diversity that has arisen around our thousands of distinct tribal societies. Each language plays a powerful role in establishing a cultural identity—it is the internal voice that carries the memories, thoughts, hopes and fears of a particular group of people. Lose the language and you lose that too.

Nevertheless, I suspect a monolinguistic future may not be as bad as doomsayers have suggested. There is a widely held belief that the language you speak determines the way you think, so that a loss of linguistic diversity is also a loss of unique styles of thought. I don't believe that. Our languages determine the words we use but they do not limit the concepts we can understand and perceive. Besides, we might draw another, more positive, moral from the story of Babel: With everyone speaking the same language, humanity can more easily cooperate to achieve something monumental. Indeed, in today's world it is the countries with the least linguistic diversity that have achieved the most prosperity.

Critical Thinking

1. Discuss the linguistic diversity among humans in comparison to animal communication.
2. What is the "intriguing paradox" at the heart of human communication?
3. How does the author explain the original diversity of human languages?
4. Where on earth is the greatest diversity of human languages and why?
5. How do *groupishness* and *xenophobia* both play a role in linguistic diversity? Be familiar with the evidence cited by the author in support of this idea.
6. What are the factors involved in why a language splits into two?
7. What is the future for linguistic diversity and why? Why is the pace of "homogenization" slower than it could be?
8. In what contexts does linguistic diversity continue to pop up?
9. What does the author see as the future for linguistic diversity? Why might a "monolinguistic future" not be as bad as doomsayers have suggested?

Internet References

Exploratorium Magazine: "The Evolution of Languages"
www.exploratorium.edu/exploring/language

Language and Culture
http://anthro.palomar.edu/language/default.htm

Language Extinction
www.colorado.edu/iec

Showcase Anthropology
www.anthropology.wisc.edu

Article

Prepared by: Elvio Angeloni

Armor against Prejudice

ED YONG

Learning Outcomes

After reading this article, you will be able to:

- Discuss the impact of negative stereotypes on many minorities.
- Discuss the effect of "stereotype threat" on individual performance.
- Explain the interventionist approach to stereotype threat and its possible positive outcome.

Neil deGrasse Tyson, the renowned science communicator, earned his PhD in astrophysics from Columbia University in 1991. About 4,000 astrophysicists resided in the country at the time. Tyson brought the total number of African-Americans among them to a paltry seven. In a convocation address, he spoke openly about the challenges he faced: "In the perception of society, my academic failures are expected and my academic successes are attributed to others." Tyson said. "To spend most of my life fighting these attitudes levies an emotional tax that is a form of intellectual emasculation. It is a tax that I would not wish upon my enemies."

Tyson's words speak to a broad truth: negative stereotypes impose an intellectual burden on many minorities and on others who think that the people around them perceive them as inferior in some way. In many different situations—at school, at work or in sports stadiums—these individuals worry that they will fail in a way that affirms derogatory stereotypes. Young white athletes fear that they will not perform as well as their black peers, for example, and women in advanced math classes worry that they will earn lower grades than the men. This anxiety—Tyson's "emotional tax"—is known as stereotype threat. Hundreds of studies have confirmed that stereotype threat undermines performance, producing the very failure they dread. Sometimes, people become trapped in a vicious cycle in which poor performance leads to more worry, which further impedes performance.

In recent years, psychologists have greatly improved their understanding of how stereotype threat affects individuals, why it happens and, most important, how to prevent it. Although the threat is real, some researchers question how well some of the relevant laboratory studies mirror anxiety in real-world settings; they also note that it is just one of many factors that contribute to social and academic inequality. Yet it is also one of the factors that can be easily changed. In studies conducted in actual schools, relatively simple interventions—such as self-esteem-boosting writing exercises completed in less than an hour—have produced dramatic and long-lasting effects, shrinking achievement gaps, and expelling stereotype threat from the classroom and students' minds. Some educators are working on ways to scale up these interventions to statewide education programs.

Identifying the Threat

Two psychologists, Claude Steele of Stanford University and Joshua Aronson, then also at Stanford, coined the term "stereotype threat" in 1995. Then, as now, black students across the U.S. earned worse grades on average than their peers and were more likely to drop out early at all levels of education. The various explanations for this gap included the pernicious idea that black students were innately less intelligent. Steele and Aronson were not convinced. Instead, they reasoned, the very existence of this negative stereotype might impair a student's performance.

In a now classic experiment, they presented more than 100 college students with a frustrating test. When they told the students that the exam would not measure their abilities, black and white students with comparable SAT scores did equally well. When Steele and Aronson told the students that the test would assess their intellectual ability, however, the black students' scores fell, but those of their white peers did not. Simply asking the students to record their race beforehand had the same effect.

The study was groundbreaking. Steele and Aronson showed that standardized tests are far from standardized. When presented in a way that invokes stereotype threat, even subtly, they put some students at an automatic disadvantage. "There was a lot of skepticism at first, but it's reducing with time," Aronson says. "In the beginning, even I didn't believe how strong the effects were. I thought, 'Somebody else has to replicate this.'"

Many researchers have. To date, hundreds of studies have found evidence of stereotype threat in all manner of groups. It afflicts students from poorer backgrounds in academic tests and men in tasks of social sensitivity. White students suffer from it when pitted against Asian peers in math tests or against black peers in sports. In many of these studies, the strongest students suffer the greatest setbacks. The ones who are most invested in succeeding are most likely to be bothered by a negative stereotype and most likely to underperform as a result. Stereotype threat is nothing if not painfully ironic.

Exactly how pervasive stereotype threat is in real-world settings remains somewhat unclear, however, largely because the relevant studies face the same problems that plague much of social psychology. Most were conducted with small numbers of college students—which increases the chances of statistical flukes—and not all studies found a strong effect. Some critics also note that laboratory experiments are often a poor substitute for the real world. Paul Sackett of the University of Minnesota has argued that outside the lab, stereotype threat could be less common and more easily overcome. Last year Gijsbert Stoet, then at the University of Leeds in England, and David C. Geary of the University of Missouri—Columbia examined every study that looked for stereotype threat among women taking math tests—a phenomenon that Steele and his colleagues first identified in 1999. Out of 20 that repeated the 1999 experiment, only 11 concluded that women performed worse than men. Geary is not ready to discount stereotype threat, but he thinks it may not be as strong as it is sometimes portrayed.

Ann Marie Ryan of Michigan State University has identified some plausible reasons for such inconsistent conclusions. In 2008 she and Hanna-Hanh Nguyen, then at California State University, Long Beach, compared the results of 76 different studies on stereotype threat in high schoolers and undergraduates. They found that in the lab, scientists are able to detect the threat only under certain conditions, such as when they give volunteers an especially difficult test or when they work with people who strongly identify with their social group.

In the past decade, psychologists have shifted from showing that stereotype threat exists to understanding how it works. Researchers have demonstrated that the threat operates in the same way across different groups of people. Anxiety arrives; motivation falls; expectations lower. Building on these findings, Toni Schmader of the University of British Columbia surmised that the threat preys on something fundamental. The most obvious culprit was working memory—the collection of cognitive skills that allows us to temporarily hold and manipulate information in our mind. This suite of skills is a finite resource, and stereotype threat can drain it. Individuals might psychologically exhaust themselves by worrying about other people's prejudices and thinking about how to prove them wrong. To test this idea, Schmader gave 75 volunteers a difficult working memory test, during which they had to memorize a list of words while solving mathematical equations. She told some volunteers that the test would assess their memory skills and that men and women may have inborn differences in their abilities. Sure enough, women who were told of this supposed discrepancy kept fewer words in mind, whereas their male colleagues had no such problems.

This depletion of working memory creates various stumbling blocks to success. People tend to overthink actions that would otherwise be automatic and become more sensitive to cues that might indicate discrimination. An ambiguous expression can be misread as a sneer, and even one's own anxiety can become a sign of imminent failure. Minds also wander, and self-control weakens. When Schmader stopped women in the middle of a math test and asked them what they were thinking of, those under stereotype threat were more likely to be daydreaming.

Expelling Stereotypes

Most recently, researchers have moved the study of stereotype threat out of the lab and into schools and lecture halls, where they try to dispel or prevent the threat altogether. "I see three waves of research," Schmader says. "The first was identifying the phenomenon and how far it travels. The second was looking at who experiences the effect and its mechanisms. The third wave is now to translate these results into interventions."

Geoffrey Cohen, also at Stanford, has achieved particularly impressive results. His method is disarmingly simple: he asks people to consider what is important to them, be it popularity or musical ability, and write about why it matters. The 15-minute exercise acts like a mental vaccine that boosts students' self-confidence, helping them combat any future stereotype threat.

In 2003 Cohen visited racially diverse middle schools in California and put his exercise through a randomized controlled trial—the gold-standard test in medicine that checks if an intervention works by pitting it against a placebo. Cohen administered his exercise to seventh graders: half wrote about their own values, and the rest wrote about things that were unimportant to them. The trial was double-blinded, meaning that neither Cohen nor the students knew who was in which group.

At the end of the term, black students who completed the exercise had closed a 40 percent academic gap between them and their white peers. Best of all, the students at the bottom of the class benefited most. Over the next two years, the same students took two or three booster versions of the original exercise. Only 5 percent of the poorest students who wrote about their values ended up in remedial classes or repeated a grade, compared with 18 percent of those in the control group. Ultimately, the black students' grade point averages rose by a quarter of a point and by 0.4 point among the worst performers.

A few fractions of a point here and there might not seem like a huge improvement, but even small changes in confidence—whether positive or negative—have a cumulative effect. Children who do poorly at first can quickly lose self-confidence or a teacher's attention; conversely, signs of modest progress can motivate far greater success. By intervening early on, Cohen asserts, educators can turn vicious cycles into virtuous ones.

Cohen's task is so simple that Ryan and others are not entirely convinced by his results. "It was hard for us to believe, but we've replicated it since," Cohen says. In the past five years ,he has used his exercise to swing the fortunes of black students in three different middle schools and to largely close the gender gap in a college-level physics class. Skeptics, though, still hope that independent researchers will try to replicate these studies.

Meanwhile Cohen is seeking new ways to help students. He has collaborated with Greg Walton, also at Stanford, to counter a kind of isolation that stereotype threat often induces. Many minorities worry that their academic peers will not fully accept them. Walton combated these worries with survey statistics and quotes from older students showing that such feelings are common to everyone regardless of race and that they disappear with time. "It makes them reframe their own experiences through the lens of this message, rather than of race," Walton explains.

Walton and Cohen tested their hour-long exercise with college students in their first spring term. Three years later, when the students graduated, the achievement gap between blacks and whites had been halved. The black students were also happier and healthier than their peers who did not take part in Walton's exercise. In the past three years, they had made fewer visits to the doctor. Walton acknowledges that such a simple exercise may look trivial to an outsider. But, he says, for students who are "actively worried about whether they fit in, the knowledge that those concerns are shared and temporary is actually very powerful."

Cohen and Walton are now scaling up their simple and inexpensive interventions from individual schools to entire states. The pair—as well as Carol Dweck and Dave Paunesku—both also at Stanford, created PERTS (the Project for Education Research That Scales), which allows them to rapidly administer their interventions online. They can also combine the programs or pit them against one another to see which have the greatest effects.

Even if the programs work as planned, researchers who study stereotype threat admit that undoing it is not a panacea against inequality. Cohen, for example, tested his initial writing exercise only in schools with mixed ethnicities, and he is unsure if it would work in predominantly minority schools. "There are many reasons why we have achievement gaps—inequality of resources, bad schools, less well-trained teachers," Walton adds. "There doesn't seem to be much hope of addressing these structural barriers. What's exciting about stereotype threat is that we can make headway in the face of those things."

Recent work on the phenomenon not only offers realistic hope for alleviating some truly tenacious problems—it also upends pervasive beliefs. By thwarting stereotype threat, researchers have shown that the stereotypes themselves are unfounded. Performance gaps between black and white students or between male and female scientists do not indicate differences in ability; rather they reflect prejudices that we can change. "The things we thought were so intractable 15 years ago aren't," Aronson says, "and that's a hugely positive message."

Critical Thinking

1. In what ways do negative stereotypes impose an intellectual burden on many minorities?
2. Discuss the effect of "stereotype threat" on performance and how it can be changed.
3. How did the experiment by Steele and Aronson illustrate the effects of stereotype threat?
4. Discuss the findings of the various studies on stereotype threat.
5. Why has it been difficult to assess the effects of stereotype threat outside the lab settings?
6. How does Ann Marie Ryan explain the inconsistent conclusions?
7. Discuss the ways in which stereotype threat actually works.
8. Discuss the interventionist methods of Geoffrey Cohen and Greg Walton and why they seem to reduce the effects of stereotype threat.
9. Explain why undoing stereotype threat is not a panacea and yet offers a realistic hope.

Internet References

Language and Culture
http://anthro.palomar.edu/language/default.htm

Linguistic Society of America
www.linguisticsociety.org/resource/sociolinguistics

Understanding Prejudice
http://www.understandingprejudice.org/apa/

Ed Yong is a science writer based in England. He has written for *Nature, Wired, National Geographic* and *New Scientist,* among other publications.

Article Prepared by: Elvio Angeloni

Speak Up, I Can't Hear You

Can It Really Be True That Men and Women Understand Language in Different Ways?

DEBORAH CAMERON

Learning Outcomes

After reading this article, you will be able to:

- Discuss the evidence pertaining to the question as to whether or not men and women speak different languages, as raised in John Gray's book, *Men Are from Mars, Women Are from Venus*.
- Discuss the "Mars versus Venus" issue in terms of its effect on cases of sexual assault.
- Discuss the evidence showing that both men and women use the same linguistic strategies, such as indirect communication, with respect to refusing an invitation.

John Gray's *Men Are from Mars, Women Are from Venus* contains a chapter entitled *Speaking Different* Languages. In it, Gray says that the "original" Martians and Venusians communicated without difficulty because they knew their languages were mutually incomprehensible. Modern men and women, by contrast, are under the illusion that they speak the same language. But though the words they use may be the same, their meanings for each sex are different. The result is that men and women often do not understand one another.

The idea that men and women metaphorically "speak different languages" is not, of course, new, but the myth of Mars and Venus has given it new currency and legitimacy. What was once just a metaphor has acquired the status of literal, scientific truth. Today, it is widely believed that misunderstanding between men and women is a widespread and serious problem. But is our concern about it justified by the evidence or is "male–female miscommunication" a myth?

Before the myth of Mars and Venus, the idea that women communicate less directly than men was associated with concerns about women's alleged lack of assertiveness and confidence. The importance of speaking directly was a staple topic in assertiveness training, and advice based on the same principle was common in self-help books and women's magazines, especially those addressed to professional women. For instance, a 1992 article in *Options* magazine on "10 classic career mistakes all women make" lists using "tentative language" as number nine.

"How many times have you heard someone say things like, 'I'm not really sure if I'm right, but perhaps . . . '?" the article asked. "With that kind of talk, who is going to believe we are confident in what we are saying?. . . . Too often we make statements as if they were questions, such as, 'We'll bring the deadline forward, OK?'"

Options counsels women to avoid tentative language on the grounds that it makes them sound weak and indecisive—the argument put forward by Robin Lakoff in her influential 1970s text, Language and Woman's Place. But, over time, a different argument has become more popular. The following tip comes from *Glamour* magazine: "speak directly to male subordinates. Women tend to shy away from giving a blatant order, but men find the indirect approach manipulative and confusing." Here, women are told to speak directly to men, not because indirectness undermines their authority but because men find it "manipulative and confusing." The substance of the advice has not changed, but the theory behind it has shifted from a "deficit model" of gender difference (women's ways of speaking are inferior to men's) to a "cross-cultural approach" (the two styles are equally valid, but the difference between them can lead to misunderstanding).

This raises two questions. First, if the male and female styles are equally valid, why does it always seem to be women who are told they must accommodate to men's preferences—even, apparently, when the men are their subordinates? Is avoiding male–female miscommunication an exclusively female responsibility? Second, though, why is it assumed that indirectness causes miscommunication in the first place? What is the evidence that men are confused by it?

Glamour is not the only source for this allegation. In a section of his book which explains how to ask men to do things, Gray says that women should avoid using indirect requests. For instance, they should not signal that they would like a man to bring in the shopping by saying, "The groceries are in the car": they should ask him directly, by saying, "Would you bring in the groceries?" Another mistake women make is to formulate requests using the word "could" rather than "would." "Could you empty the trash?" says Gray, "is merely a question gathering information. 'Would you empty the trash?' is a request."

Gray seems to be suggesting that men hear utterances such as "Could you empty the trash?" as purely hypothetical questions about their ability to perform the action mentioned. But that is a patently ridiculous claim. No competent user of English would take "Could you empty the trash?" as "merely a question gathering information," any more than they would take "Could you run a mile in four minutes?" as a polite request to start running. Gray is right to think that the "Could you do X?" formula has both functions but wrong to suppose that this causes confusion. Human languages are not codes in which each word or expression has a single, predetermined meaning. Rather, human communication relies on the ability of humans to put the words someone utters together with other information about the world and on that basis infer what the speaker intended to communicate to them.

Some individuals—for instance, people with autism—may indeed find indirectness confusing; they find a great deal of human communication confusing because their condition impairs their ability to make inferences about what is going on in other people's minds. But this kind of problem is exceptional: we define it as a disability precisely because the ability to infer others' intentions plays such a crucial role in communication. Does Gray think that maleness is a disability? And if he really believes men cannot process indirect requests from women, how does he explain the fact that men quite frequently make indirect requests to women?

A friend once told me a story about the family dinners of her childhood. Each night as the family sat down to eat, her father would examine the food on his plate and then say to his wife something like, "Is there any ketchup, Vera?" His wife would then get up and fetch whatever condiment he had mentioned. According to Gray's theory, he should have reacted with surprise: "oh, I didn't mean I wanted ketchup, I was just asking whether we had any." Needless to say, that was not his reaction. Both he and his wife understood "Is there any ketchup?" as an indirect request to get the ketchup, rather than "merely a question gathering information."

Yet if my friend made the same request, her mother's response was different: she treated it as an information question and said, "Yes, dear, it's in the cupboard." Presumably, that was not because she had suddenly become incapable of understanding indirectness. Rather, she pretended to hear her daughter's request as an information question because she wanted to send her a message along the lines of, "I may get ketchup for your father, but I don't feel obliged to do the same for you."

What this example illustrates is that some "misunderstandings" are tactical rather than real. Pretending not to understand what someone wants you to do is one way to avoid doing it. This may be what is really going on when a man claims not to have recognized a woman's "Could you empty the trash?" or "The groceries are in the car" as a request. The "real" conflict is not about what was meant, it is about who is entitled to expect what services from whom.

By recasting this type of domestic dispute as a problem of "male–female miscommunication," the myth of Mars and Venus just obscures the real issue. And while arguments about who empties the trash or unloads the groceries may be petty, there are other conflicts between men and women where far more is at stake.

At a Canadian university in the 1990s, two women students made complaints against the same male student after they discovered by chance that they had both, on separate occasions, gone out on a date with him and been sexually assaulted at the end of the evening. Their complaints were heard by a university tribunal whose proceedings were recorded for a linguistic research project.

Like many rape and sexual assault cases, this one turned on whether or not the defendant could reasonably have believed that the complainants consented to sex. Both incidents had begun consensually, with the women inviting the man into their room and engaging in activities such as kissing and touching, but they claimed he had gone on to force them into further sexual activity which they made clear they did not want. He maintained that they did want it—or at least, had said nothing to make him think they did not.

In this extract from the hearing, one of the complainants, MB, has just told the tribunal that the defendant persisted in touching her even after she had repeatedly communicated to him that she did not want to have sex. A tribunal member, GK, then asks her the following question: "and did it occur to you through the persistent behavior that maybe your signals were not coming across loud and clear, that 'I'm not getting through what I want and what I don't want?' . . . This is the whole thing about getting signals mixed up. We all socialize in one way or the other to read signals and to give signals. In that particular context, were you at all concerned your signals were not being read exactly and did you think, since signals were not being read correctly for you, 'Should I do something different with my signals?'"

GK evidently interprets the incident as a case of miscommunication (getting signals mixed up). She also appears to hold the complainant responsible for the breakdown in communication. She phrases her initial question using a formula ("Did it occur to you that . . . ?") which usually implies that the point should have occurred to the addressee. Her subsequent questions ("Were you at all concerned that . . . ?," "Did you think that . . . [you] should . . . ?") are phrased in a similarly loaded way. GK is not so much asking about MB's view of events as communicating her own: MB should have realized that her signals were not getting through, and she should have acted on that realization by "doing something different with [her] signals."

Susan Ehrlich, the linguist who analyzed the tribunal proceedings, notes that the defendant is never challenged in the same way about his response to the complainants' signals. At one point, he is asked why he persisted in sexual activity with MB when she was either asleep or pretending to be asleep. He replies, "She said that she was tired, you know, she never said like 'Don't', you know, 'Don't do this', uhm, 'Get out of bed.'" Nobody asks him why he did not consider the possibility that by saying she was tired and then apparently falling asleep, MB was communicating that she wanted him to stop. You don't have to be a rocket scientist to work out that someone who feigns unconsciousness while in bed with you probably doesn't want to have sex. But nobody criticizes the defendant for being so obtuse. In these proceedings, the assumption does seem to be that avoiding miscommunication is not a shared responsibility but specifically a female one.

This assumption both reflects and reinforces the traditional tendency of rape trials—especially where the parties are acquainted—to focus more on the character and behavior of the complainant than on that of the alleged perpetrator. Her clothing, her alcohol consumption, her previous sexual conduct, and reputation are all scrutinized minutely for any sign that she might have been willing all along. By suggesting that men have trouble understanding any refusal which is not maximally direct, the myth of Mars and Venus has added to the burden judicial proceedings place on women who claim to have been raped. They can now be challenged not only to prove that they did not consent to sex but also that they refused in a manner sufficiently direct to preclude misunderstanding. The women in the Canadian case were unable to satisfy the tribunal on that point. The tribunal's written judgment criticized their behavior: "there is little doubt that both complainants did not expressly object to some of the activity that took place that evening. It is also clear that their actions at times did not unequivocally indicate a lack of willing participation."

The defendant was found guilty, but the tribunal declined to impose the recommended punishment, expulsion from the university. Instead, they banned him from campus dormitory buildings. This decision reflected their view that the complainants were partly responsible for what had happened to them. Had they communicated differently, they could have prevented it.

That idea also features prominently in sex education and "rape prevention" programs, which instruct women that if they do not want to have sex they should "Just say no." It is stressed that a woman's refusal should take the form of a firm, unvarnished "No" (spoken in a tone and accompanied by body language that make clear it is a real, rather than a token, refusal), and that it is not necessary—in fact, it is counterproductive—to give reasons for refusing. Only by keeping the message short and simple can you be sure that it will not be misunderstood. This advice may be well-intentioned, but linguistic research suggests it is highly questionable.

The researchers Celia Kitzinger and Hannah Frith conducted focus-group interviews with 58 women and asked them how, in practice, they communicated to men that they did not wish to have sex. Despite being familiar with the standard rape-prevention advice, all but a tiny handful of the women said they would never "Just say no." They judged this to be an unacceptable way of doing things and likely to make matters worse by giving men an additional reason to feel aggrieved.

The strategies the women actually reported using were designed to "soften the blow," as one put it, in various ways. One popular tactic was to provide a reason for refusing which made reference to a woman's inability, as opposed to her unwillingness, to have sex. Examples included the time-honored "I've got a headache," "I'm really tired," and "I've got my period." As one woman explained, such excuses would prevent the man from "getting really upset" or "blaming you." Another softening tactic was to preface the refusal with something like "I'm incredibly flattered, but. . . ." Women also reported telling men that they were not yet ready for sex, when they knew in reality that they would never be interested.

All this might seem like depressing evidence that psychologists are right about women lacking assertiveness, confidence, or self-esteem—except for one crucial fact. All the strategies the women reported using in this situation are also used, by both sexes, in every other situation where it is necessary to verbalize a refusal. Research on conversational patterns shows that in everyday contexts, refusing is never done by "just saying no." Most refusals do not even contain the word "No." Yet, in nonsexual situations, no one seems to have trouble understanding them.

If this sounds counterintuitive, let us consider a concrete example. Suppose a colleague says to me casually as I pass her in the corridor: "a few of us are going to the pub after work, do you want to come?" This is an invitation, which calls for me to respond with either an acceptance or a refusal. If I am going to accept, I can simply say "Yes, I'd love to" or "Sure, see you there." If I am going to refuse, by contrast, I am unlikely to communicate that by just saying "No, I can't" (let alone "No, I don't want to").

Why the difference? Because refusing an invitation—even one that is much less sensitive than a sexual proposal—is a more delicate matter than accepting one. The act of inviting someone implies that you hope they will say yes: if they say no, there is a risk that you will be offended, upset, or just disappointed. To show that they are aware of this, and do not want you to feel bad, people generally design refusals to convey reluctance and regret.

Because this pattern is so consistent and because it contrasts with the pattern for the alternative response, acceptance and refusals are immediately recognizable as such. In fact, the evidence suggests that people can tell a refusal is coming as soon as they register the initial hesitation. And when I say "people," I mean people of both sexes. No one has found any difference between men's and women's use of the system I have just described.

As Kitzinger and Frith comment, this evidence undermines the claim that men do not understand any refusal less direct than a firm "No." If "ordinary," nonsexual refusals do not generally take the form of saying "No" but are performed using conventional strategies such as hesitating, hedging, and offering excuses, then sexual refusals which use exactly the same strategies should not present any special problem. "For men to claim that they do not understand such refusals to be refusals," Kitzinger and Frith say, "is to lay claim to an astounding and implausible ignorance."

Even so, you might think that if a woman is worried about being assaulted, she should err on the side of caution: forget the usual social niceties and "unequivocally indicate a lack of willing participation." The Canadian tribunal was clearly puzzled by MB's failure to do this. They pressed her about it until she finally offered an explanation. Like the women in Kitzinger and Frith's study, MB felt it was prudent to try to "soften the blow." She did not confront her assailant directly, she said, because she was afraid of him—and of what, beyond sexual assault, he might do to her if she provoked him: "you do whatever you have to to survive. [Crying] I mean, I was just thinking how to survive that second. I mean, I didn't care if that meant getting back into bed with him. If he didn't hurt me I didn't care at that second . . . I did whatever I could to get by."

This raises doubts about the wisdom of expert advice on rape prevention, which tells women to do the opposite of "softening the blow": in essence, it tells them to aggravate the offence of rejecting a man's advances by verbalizing their refusals in a highly confrontational way. This advice presupposes that men who persist in making unwanted sexual advances are genuinely confused and will be happy to have their confusion dispelled by a simple, firm "No." It does not allow for the possibility that men who behave in this way are not so much confused about women's wishes as indifferent to them. Confronting a violent and determined aggressor is not necessarily the safest option and, to a woman who is terrified, it may well seem like the most dangerous, putting her at risk of being beaten as well as raped.

Women are not wrong to fear the consequences of following advice to "just say no." But thanks to the myth of Mars and Venus, they are not only receiving bad advice on how to prevent rape, they are also being held responsible for preventing it and blamed if they do not succeed.

The 1967 prison film *Cool Hand Luke* is remembered, among other things, for a line spoken by the prison warden to Luke, an inmate who persistently rebels against authority. "What we have here," says the warden, "is failure to communicate." Both of them know that communication is not the issue. Luke understands the warden but chooses to defy him. What the warden really means is "failure to do what I want you to do."

A similar (mis)use of the word "communication" has become increasingly common in our culture. Conflicts which are really caused by people wanting different things (he wants her to have sex and she does not want to; she wants him to do his share of the housework and he wants her to stop nagging about it) are persistently described as "misunderstandings" or "communication problems." If someone does not respond in the way we want them to, it means they cannot have understood us—the problem is "failure to communicate," and the solution is better communication.

This belief, or hope, is undoubtedly one of the things that make the idea of male–female miscommunication appealing to many people. In the words of Deborah Tannen: "understanding style differences for what they are takes the sting out of them. Believing that 'You're not interested in me,' 'You don't care about me as much as I care about you,' or 'You want to take away my freedom' feels awful. Believing that 'You have a different way of showing you're listening' or 'Showing you care' allows for no-fault negotiation: you can ask for or make adjustments without casting or taking blame."

It is comforting to be told that nobody needs to "feel awful": that there are no real conflicts, only misunderstandings, and no disagreements of substance, only differences of style. Acknowledging that many problems between men and women go deeper than "failure to communicate" would make for a much bleaker and less reassuring message.

But the research evidence does not support the claims made by Tannen and others about the nature, the causes, and the prevalence of male–female miscommunication. No doubt some conflicts between individual men and women are caused by misunderstanding: the potential for communication to go awry is latent in every exchange between humans, simply because language is not telepathy. But the idea that men and women have a particular problem because they differ systematically in their ways of using language, and that this is the major source of conflict between them, does not stand up to scrutiny.

Critical Thinking

1. Do men and women really use different linguistic strategies? Explain.
2. What has been the impact of "Mars versus Venus" on women in the workplace and regarding claims of sexual assault?

Internet References

Gender and Language: Websites
http://libguides.wwu.edu/c.php?g=309073&p=2057702

WOMANSPEAK Training Blog
https://www.womenspeaktraining.com/womenspeaktrainingblogspotcom

Article

Prepared by: Elvio Angeloni

Vanishing Languages

Russ Rymer

Learning Outcomes

After reading this article, you will be able to:

- Explain the importance of the variety of human languages in today's world.
- Discuss the different ways in which languages highlight the varieties of human experience.

Tuvan

The Compassion of Khoj Özeeri

One morning in early fall Andrei Mongush and his parents began preparations for supper, selecting a black-faced, fat-tailed sheep from their flock and rolling it onto its back on a tarp outside their livestock paddock. The Mongush family's home is on the Siberian taiga, at the edge of the endless steppes, just over the horizon from Kyzyl, the capital of the Republic of Tuva, in the Russian Federation. They live near the geographic center of Asia, but linguistically and personally, the family inhabits a borderland, the frontier between progress and tradition. Tuvans are historically nomadic herders, moving their *aal*—an encampment of yurts—and their sheep and cows and reindeer from pasture to pasture as the seasons progress. The elder Mongushes, who have returned to their rural aal after working in the city, speak both Tuvan and Russian. Andrei and his wife also speak English, which they are teaching themselves with pieces of paper labeled in English pasted onto seemingly every object in their modern kitchen in Kyzyl. They work as musicians in the Tuvan National Orchestra, an ensemble that uses traditional Tuvan instruments and melodies in symphonic arrangements. Andrei is a master of the most characteristic Tuvan music form: throat singing, or *khöömei.*

When I ask university students in Kyzyl what Tuvan words are untranslatable into English or Russian, they suggest khöömei, because the singing is so connected with the Tuvan environment that only a native can understand it, and also *khoj özeeri,* the Tuvan method of killing a sheep. If slaughtering livestock can be seen as part of humans' closeness to animals, khoj özeeri represents an unusually intimate version. Reaching through an incision in the sheep's hide, the slaughterer severs a vital artery with his fingers, allowing the animal to quickly slip away without alarm, so peacefully that one must check its eyes to see if it is dead. In the language of the Tuvan people, khoj özeeri means not only slaughter but also kindness, humaneness, a ceremony by which a family can kill, skin, and butcher a sheep, salting its hide and preparing its meat and making sausage with the saved blood and cleansed entrails so neatly that the whole thing can be accomplished in two hours (as the Mongushes did this morning) in one's good clothes without spilling a drop of blood. Khoj özeeri implies a relationship to animals that is also a measure of a people's character. As one of the students explained, "If a Tuvan killed an animal the way they do in other places"—by means of a gun or knife—"they'd be arrested for brutality."

Tuvan is one of the many small languages of the world. The Earth's population of seven billion people speaks roughly 7,000 languages, a statistic that would seem to offer each living language a healthy one million speakers, if things were equitable. In language, as in life, things aren't. Seventy-eight percent of the world's population speaks the 85 largest languages, while the 3,500 smallest languages share a mere 8.25 million speakers. Thus, while English has 328 million first-language speakers, and Mandarin 845 million, Tuvan speakers in Russia number just 235,000. Within the next century, linguists think, nearly half of the world's current stock of languages may disappear. More than a thousand are listed as critically or severely endangered—teetering on the edge of oblivion.

In an increasingly globalized, connected, homogenized age, languages spoken in remote places are no longer protected by national borders or natural boundaries from the languages that dominate world communication and commerce. The reach of

Mandarin and English and Russian and Hindi and Spanish and Arabic extends seemingly to every hamlet, where they compete with Tuvan and Yanomami and Altaic in a house-to-house battle. Parents in tribal villages often encourage their children to move away from the insular language of their forebears and toward languages that will permit greater education and success.

Who can blame them? The arrival of television, with its glamorized global materialism, its luxury-consumption proselytizing, is even more irresistible. Prosperity, it seems, speaks English. One linguist, attempting to define what a language is, famously (and humorously) said that a language is a dialect with an army. He failed to note that some armies are better equipped than others. Today any language with a television station and a currency is in a position to obliterate those without, and so residents of Tuva must speak Russian and Chinese if they hope to engage with the surrounding world. The incursion of dominant Russian into Tuva is evident in the speaking competencies of the generation of Tuvans who grew up in the mid-20th century, when it was the fashion to speak, read, and write in Russian and not their native tongue.

Yet Tuvan is robust relative to its frailest counterparts, some of which are down to a thousand speakers, or a mere handful, or even one individual. Languages like Wintu, a native tongue in California, or Siletz Dee-ni, in Oregon, or Amurdak, an Aboriginal tongue in Australia's Northern Territory, retain only one or two fluent or semifluent speakers. A last speaker with no one to talk to exists in unspeakable solitude.

Increasingly, as linguists recognize the magnitude of the modern language die-off and rush to catalog and decipher the most vulnerable tongues, they are confronting underlying questions about languages' worth and utility. Does each language have boxed up within it some irreplaceable beneficial knowledge? Are there aspects of cultures that won't survive if they are translated into a dominant language? What unexpected insights are being lost to the world with the collapse of its linguistic variety?

Fortunately, Tuvan is not among the world's endangered languages, but it could have been. Since the breakup of the Soviet Union, the language has stabilized. It now has a well-equipped army—not a television station, yet, or a currency, but a newspaper and a respectable 264,000 total speakers (including some in Mongolia and China). Yet Tofa, a neighboring Siberian language, is down to some 30 speakers. Tuvan's importance to our understanding of disappearing languages lies in another question linguists are struggling to answer: What makes one language succeed while another dwindles or dies?

Aka

The Respect of Mucrow

I witnessed the heartrending cost of broken languages among the Aka people in Palizi, a tiny, rustic hamlet perched on a mountainside in Arunachal Pradesh, India's rugged northeastern most state. It is reachable by a five-hour drive through palm and hardwood jungles on single-track mountain roads. Its one main street is lined with unpainted board-faced houses set on stilts and roofed with thatch or metal. Villagers grow their own rice, yams, spinach, oranges, and ginger; slaughter their own hogs and goats; and build their own houses. The tribe's isolation has bred a radical self-sufficiency, evidenced in an apparent lack of an Aka word for job, in the sense of salaried labor.

The Aka measure personal wealth in mithan, a breed of Himalayan cattle. A respectable bride price in Palizi, for instance, is expressed as eight mithan. The most cherished Aka possession is the precious *tradzy* necklace—worth two mithan—made from yellow stones from the nearby river, which is passed down to their children. The yellow stones for the tradzy necklaces can no longer be found in the river, and so the only way to have a precious necklace is to inherit one.

Speaking Aka—or any language—means immersing oneself in its character and concepts. "I'm seeing the world through the looking glass of this language," said Father Vijay D'Souza, who was running the Jesuit school in Palizi at the time of my visit. The Society of Jesus established the school in part because it was concerned about the fragility of the Aka language and culture and wanted to support them (though classes are taught in English). D'Souza is from southern India, and his native language is Konkani. When he came to Palizi in 1999 and began speaking Aka, the language transformed him.

"It alters your thinking, your worldview," he told me one day in his headmaster's office, as children raced to classes through the corridor outside. One small example: *mucrow.* A similar word in D'Souza's native language would be an insult, meaning "old man." In Aka "mucrow" means something more. It is a term of respect, deference, endearment. The Aka might address a woman as mucrow to indicate her wisdom in civic affairs, and, says D'Souza, "an Aka wife will call her husband mucrow, even when he's young," and do so affectionately.

American linguists David Harrison and Greg Anderson have been coming to Arunachal Pradesh to study its languages since 2008. They are among the scores of linguists worldwide engaged in the study of vanishing languages. Some have academic and institutional affiliations (Harrison and Anderson are both connected with National Geographic's Enduring Voices Project), while others may work for Bible societies that translate Scripture into new tongues. The authoritative index of world languages is *Ethnologue,* maintained by SIL International, a faith-based organization. The researchers' intent may be hands-off, to record a grammar and lexicon before a language is lost or contaminated, or it may be interventionist, to develop a written accompaniment for the oral language, compile a dictionary, and teach native speakers to write.

Linguists have identified a host of language hotspots (analogous to biodiversity hotspots) that have both a high level of linguistic diversity and a high number of threatened languages. Many of these are in the world's least reachable, and often least hospitable, places—like Arunachal Pradesh. Aka and its neighboring languages have been protected because Arunachal Pradesh has long been sealed off to outsiders as a restricted border region. Even other Indians are not allowed to cross into the region without federal permission, and so its fragile microcultures have been spared the intrusion of immigrant labor, modernization—and linguists. It has been described as a black hole of linguistics because its incredible language variety remains so little explored.

Much of public life in Palizi is regulated through the repetition of mythological stories used as forceful fables to prescribe behavior. Thus a money dispute can draw a recitation about a spirit whose daughters are eaten by a crocodile, one by one, as they cross the river to bring him dinner in the field. He kills the crocodile, and a priest promises to bring the last daughter back to life but overcharges so egregiously that the spirit seeks revenge by becoming a piece of ginger that gets stuck in the greedy priest's throat.

Such stories were traditionally told by the elders in a highly formal version of Aka that the young did not yet understand and according to certain rules, among them this: Once an elder begins telling a story, he cannot stop until the story is finished. As with linguistic literacy, disruption is disaster. Yet Aka's young people no longer follow their elders in learning the formal version of the language and the stories that have governed daily life. Even in this remote region, young people are seduced away from their mother tongue by Hindi on the television and English in the schools. Today Aka's speakers number fewer than 2,000, few enough to put it on the endangered list.

One night in Palizi, Harrison, Anderson, an Indian linguist named Ganesh Murmu, and I sat cross-legged around the cooking fire at the home of Pario Nimasow, a 25-year-old teacher at the Jesuit school. A Palizi native, Nimasow loved his Aka culture even as he longed to join the outside world. In his sleeping room in an adjacent hut was a television waiting for the return of electricity, which had been out for many months thanks to a series of landslides and transformer malfunctions. After dinner Nimasow disappeared for a moment and came back with a soiled white cotton cloth, which he unfolded by the flickering light of the cooking fire. Inside was a small collection of ritual items: a tiger's jaw, a python's jaw, the sharp-toothed mandible of a river fish, a quartz crystal, and other objects of a shaman's sachet. This sachet had belonged to Nimasow's father until his death in 1991.

"My father was a priest," Nimasow said, "and his father was a priest." And now? I asked. Was he next in line? Nimasow stared at the talismans and shook his head. He had the kit, but he didn't know the chants; his father had died before passing them on. Without the words, there was no way to bring the artifacts' power to life.

Linguistics has undergone two great revolutions in the past 60 years, on seemingly opposite ends of the discipline. In the late 1950s Noam Chomsky theorized that all languages were built on an underlying universal grammar embedded in human genes. A second shift in linguistics—an explosion of interest in small and threatened languages—has focused on the variety of linguistic experience. Field linguists like David Harrison are more interested in the idiosyncrasies that make each language unique and the ways that culture can influence a language's form. As Harrison points out, some 85 percent of languages have yet to be documented. Understanding them can only enrich our comprehension of what is universal to all languages.

Different languages highlight the varieties of human experience, revealing as mutable aspects of life that we tend to think of as settled and universal, such as our experience of time, number, or color. In Tuva, for example, the past is always spoken of as ahead of one, and the future is behind one's back. "We could never say, I'm looking forward to doing something," a Tuvan told me. Indeed, he might say, "I'm looking forward to the day before yesterday." It makes total sense if you think of it in a Tuvan sort of way: If the future were ahead of you, wouldn't it be in plain view?

Smaller languages often retain remnants of number systems that may predate the adoption of the modern world's base-ten counting system. The Pirahã, an Amazonian tribe, appear to have no words for any specific numbers at all but instead get by with relative words such as "few" and "many." The Pirahã's lack of numerical terms suggests that assigning numbers may be an invention of culture rather than an innate part of human cognition. The interpretation of color is similarly varied from language to language. What we think of as the natural spectrum of the rainbow is actually divided up differently in different tongues, with many languages having more or fewer color categories than their neighbors.

Language shapes human experience—our very cognition—as it goes about classifying the world to make sense of the circumstances at hand. Those classifications may be broad—Aka divides the animal kingdom into animals that are eaten and those that are not—or exceedingly fine-tuned. The Todzhu reindeer herders of southern Siberia have an elaborate vocabulary for reindeer; an *iyi düktüg myiys,* for example, is a castrated former stud in its fourth year.

If Aka, or any language, is supplanted by a new one that's bigger and more universally useful, its death shakes the foundations of the tribe. "Aka is our identity," a villager told me one day as we walked from Palizi down the path that wound past the rice fields to the forests by the river. "Without it, we are the general public." But should the rest of the world mourn too? The question would not be an easy one to frame in Aka, which seems to lack a single term for world. Aka might suggest an answer, though, one embodied in the concept of mucrow—a regard for tradition, for long-standing knowledge, for what has come before, a conviction that the venerable and frail have something to teach the callow and the strong that they would be lost without.

Critical Thinking

1. In what respects does the Mongush family "inhabit a borderland"?
2. Why are some Tuvan words untranslatable?
3. How many languages are there in the world? Why are so many of them disappearing?
4. What are some of the underlying questions about languages' worth and utility? How is the language of Tuvan important to our understanding of disappearing languages?
5. In what ways does the Aka language reflect Aka culture?
6. What is the difference between a linguist's "hands-off" approach versus an "interventionist approach"?
7. In what respects is the Aka language located in a "language hotspot"? How have they been protected?
8. Why are Aka youth no longer learning the stories that have governed daily life?
9. How does the author illustrate the fact that different languages highlight the varieties of human experience?

Internet References

Intute: Anthropology
www.intute.ac.uk/anthropology

Russ Rymer is the author of *Genie: A Scientific Tragedy,* the story of an abused child whose case helped scientists study the acquisition of language.

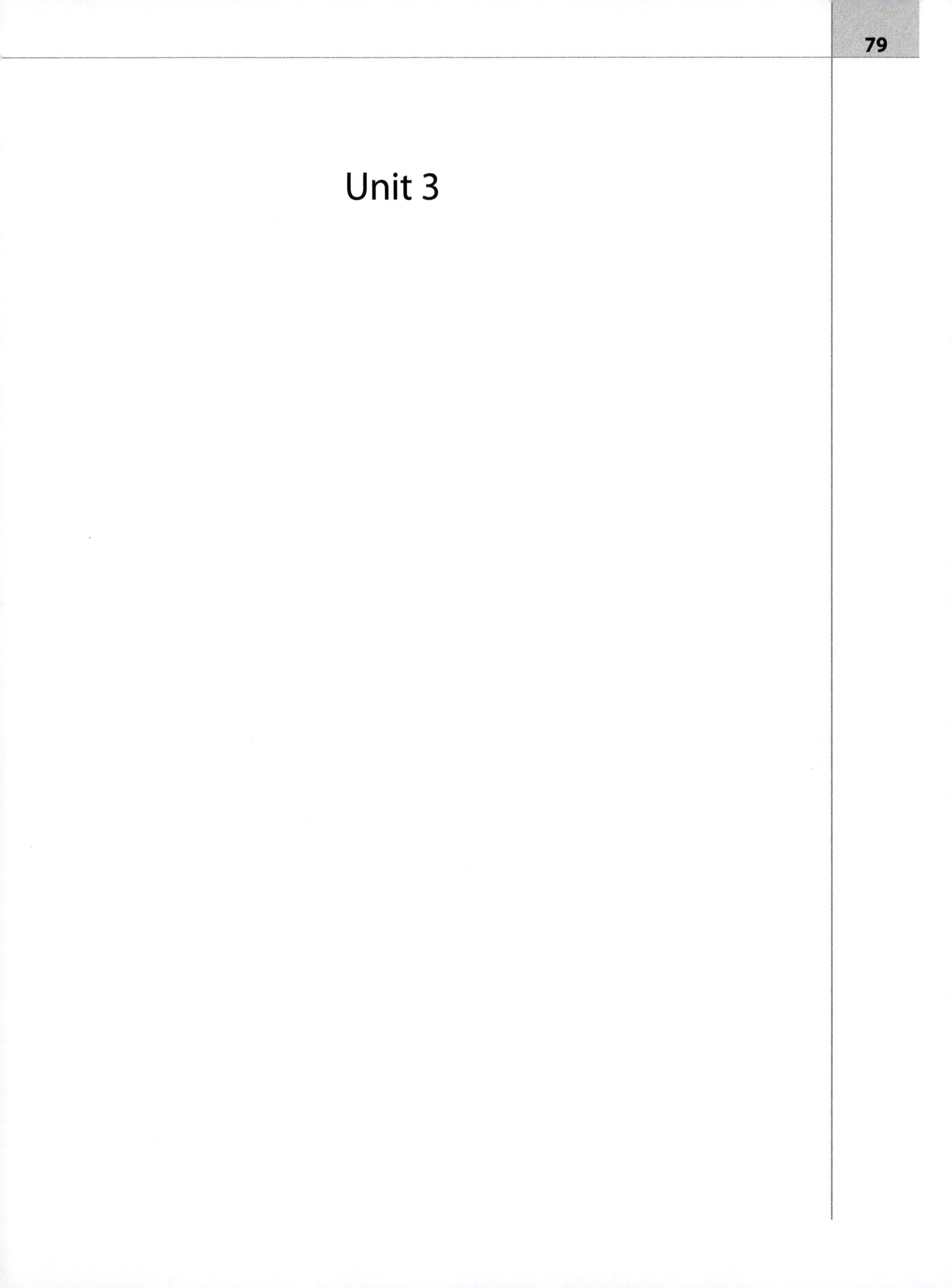

Unit 3

UNIT

Prepared by: Elvio Angeloni

The Organization of Society and Culture

Human beings do not interact with one another or think about their world in random fashion. They engage in structured and recurrent physical and mental activities. Such patterns of behavior and thought—referred to here as the organization of society and culture—may be seen in a number of different contexts, from the mating preferences of hunter-gatherer bands to whether a mother breastfeeds her child to the decisions made by neighboring tribes as to whether they shall go to war or establish peaceful relations with each other.

Of special importance are the ways in which people make a living—in other words, the production, distribution, and consumption of goods and services. It is only by knowing the basic subsistence systems that we can hope to gain insight into other levels of social and cultural phenomena, for they are all inextricably bound together. Noting the various aspects of a sociocultural system in harmonious balance, however, does not imply an anthropological seal of approval. To understand infanticide (killing of the newborn) in the manner that it is practiced among some peoples is neither to condone nor condemn it. The adaptive patterns that have been in existence for a great length of time, such as many of the patterns of hunters and gatherers, probably owe their existence to their contributions to long-term human survival.

Anthropologists, however, are not content with the data derived from their individual experiences with others. On the contrary, personal descriptions must become the basis for sound anthropological theory. Otherwise, they remain meaningless, isolated relics of culture in the manner of museum pieces. In other words, while anthropological accounts of field are to some extent descriptive, they should also serve to challenge both the academic and "commonsense" notions about why people behave and think the way they do. They remind us that assumptions are never really safe and if anthropologists are kept on their toes, it is the field as a whole that benefits.

Article

Prepared by: Elvio Angeloni

Generous by Nature

BOB HOLMES

Learning Outcomes

After reading this article, you will be able to:

- Discuss and explain the Maasai concept of "osotua" as a sometimes one-sided, need-based giving that can last for generations.
- Discuss the importance of reputation as a way of encouraging giving.
- Discuss the method suggested by research to persuade people in modern societies to give more generously to charity.

An ancient form of giving holds clues on how to promote human kindness.

Life isn't easy as a Maasai herder on the Serengeti plain in Eastern Africa. At any moment, disease could sweep through your livestock, the source of almost all your wealth. Drought could parch your pastures, or bandits could steal the herd. No matter how careful you are, or how hard you work, fate could leave you destitute. What's a herder to do?

The answer is simple: ask for help. Thanks to a Maasai tradition known as osotua—literally, umbilical cord—anyone in need can request aid from their network of friends. Anyone who's asked is obliged to help, often by giving livestock, as long as it doesn't jeopardise their own survival. No one expects a recipient to repay the gift, and no one keeps track of how often a person asks or gives.

Osotua runs counter to the way we usually view cooperation, which is all about reciprocity—you scratch my back, I'll scratch yours. Yet similar forms of generosity turn out to be common in cultures around the world. Some anthropologists think it could represent one of the earliest forms of generosity in human society.

That's not the only curiosity about generosity. In biological and evolutionary terms, it makes no sense to give and get nothing in return. Altruism is rare in other animals, yet humans can be inexplicably kind. Are we generous by nature? How did we get to be this way? What role does culture play in kindness? These are the big questions now being addressed by researchers in the Human Generosity Project, who are using fieldwork, experiments, and modelling to explore osotua and other examples of human cooperation. Their aim is to find how best to make the milk of human kindness flow.

A Friend in Need

Osotua isn't a responsibility the Maasai take lightly. "It is the connecting fibre in society," says anthropologist Dennis ole Sonkoi at Rutgers University in New Jersey, who is Maasai. Each individual maintains their own network of osotua partners. Once formed, the relationships can last for generations, with parents passing osotua partners on to their children. And it's not just the Maasai. "In every society we're studying, we have found need-based transfers," says Human Generosity Project co-director Athena Aktipis at Arizona State University in Tempe. Fijians, Tanzanian slum dwellers and American cattle ranchers all pitch in to help neighbours in need, with no expectation of being paid back. Even the Ik of Uganda, whom one anthropologist once vilified as the least generous people in the world, do it.

But the giving is often one-sided. "Since I was a kid, there were families that I knew to have a lot of cows. Those families would be the ones that are always approached," says Sonkoi. On the face of it, they seem to lose much and gain little by participating. Why do they continue to be generous, against their apparent best interests?

A clue lies in the trigger for such generosity: an unpredictable crisis. This suggests that these practices persist because they help manage risk, which pays off for everyone in the long run. Even the best-prepared family can fall prey to catastrophe, such as a sudden illness. These types of risk cannot be prevented, so need-based giving may have emerged as a proto-insurance policy. Prosperous members of many societies share so that this social insurance will be available if they need it—just as wealthy homeowners insure their belongings against fire. "You're exchanging the possibility of a catastrophic loss for the certainty of a small, controllable loss," says Lee Cronk at Rutgers University, who heads up the Human Generosity Project with Aktipis.

Thinking of osotua-style generosity as insurance could explain why participants don't keep a tally of who owes whom. "If you don't help partners they may not survive, and then they may not be around to help you," says Aktipis.

To investigate this idea, Aktipis and her colleagues made a computer simulation of a Maasai herding society. Each virtual household had a herd of cattle, which would grow through reproduction but occasionally be hit by a disaster. If numbers fell below 64 cattle—about what it takes to support a Maasai family—the household would die.

Aktipis's team ran the simulation under three scenarios: one with no giving, one in which potential donors would only give if the asker had paid back previous gifts, and one resembling osotua. Their newly published results show that households survived much longer, on average, with osotua-style giving, supporting the idea that even habitual donors benefit in the long run from keeping their neighbours going.

However, need-based giving works best when risks are "asynchronous"—when hardship is likely to strike one family and spare their neighbours. Herding tribes in northern Mongolia, for example, use such generosity to help families crippled by illness. However, the system breaks down when they face their biggest threat, a zud—a winter storm that prevents livestock from feeding. With everyone affected, helping one's neighbours isn't really an option.

This may also explain how the Ik got their reputation for selfishness, says Cronk. When anthropologist Colin Turnbull visited in the 1960s, he described them as "unfriendly, uncharitable, inhospitable and generally mean as any people can be." But they had been pushed out of their traditional territory and were struggling with famine and war. Under such circumstances, they may have had little ability to help one another.

However, the ability to help isn't enough in itself. To benefit from osotua-style generosity, you need to prevent cheating, for example asking when not truly in need. In some societies the solution is easy. "In the context of the Maasai, the things they're most concerned with are livestock," says Cronk. "It's hard to hide them, so you can't cheat." In addition, osotua requests tend to be made in public, so everyone knows who has asked and given—or refused to give—says Sonkoi.

Where wealth is easier to hide, reputation is the key. In Fiji, for example, there is an osotua-like practice called kerekere. "People can get reputations for being habitual kerekereers, implying they're lazy," says Matthew Gervais at Rutgers University. That makes them think carefully before making kerekere requests, which bring a slight taint of shame.

In fact, reputation doesn't just inhibit cheating in kerekere: it appears to be the rock upon which generosity is built. Gervais gave 51 Fijian men a sum of money roughly equal to a day's wages, and the choice of sharing their windfall with any of the other 50 men, all of whom they knew. Despite being told their decision would remain undisclosed, they proved surprisingly generous. On average, they kept just 12 per cent of the money for themselves, and 22 men kept nothing. When Gervais asked them how they chose who to share their money with, almost all said they gave to people who needed it. However, closer statistical analysis showed reputation was almost as important as need. Men with a reputation for giving tended to be the ones who received more.

Cronk believes that in day-to-day life, norms of generosity, love and respect drive decisions about sharing more than cold cost-benefit calculations do. This reinforces the idea that generosity is good. But the Human Generosity Project focuses on close-knit societies. Do humans become less generous when they live in more complex societies?

Of course, there is still need-based giving. "When natural disasters occur, people donate," says Aktipis. "And they donate because they know there is need, not because they expect they're going to get good dividends on their donation to the Red Cross." On the other hand, people in Western countries often walk past beggars on the street. But that could be because social institutions exist that they expect to step in and help. In fact, Westerners often give generously to strangers, whereas people living in smaller-scale societies tend to direct their generosity towards people they know. Fijians, for example, are very generous within their village. "But when we've had Fijians do games that involve giving to distant poor people, they seem almost baffled as to why anyone would send money to someone they don't know far away," says Joseph Henrich at Harvard University.

Nevertheless, osotua-style generosity offers some ideas about how to encourage charitable giving worldwide (see "Encouraging generosity"). And insights from the Human Generosity Project could help with some seemingly intractable problems. For example, Aktipis is working with the authorities that manage southern Arizona's scarce supply of water. The city of Phoenix has dozens of independent water providers that draw from a range of wells and other sources. These vary seasonally and with the weather, so water availability can be unpredictable, leaving individual managers unable to meet demand. Aktipis hopes that by borrowing knowledge from need-based sharing, they will learn to cooperate more effectively.

In the future, this form of generosity could have a far more widespread and important part to play. It is possible that the social upheavals that accompany climate change and sea-level rise could overwhelm conventional insurance and social-assistance programmes. If that happens, it would be comforting to know that we can count on our neighbours for help.

Encouraging Generosity

Research suggests ways to persuade people to give more generously to charity

1. Let givers build their prestige through donating. "That's what Bill Gates is trying to do when he gets billionaires to give away half their wealth," says Joseph Henrich at Harvard University. This works for ordinary people, too, says behavioural scientist David Rand at Yale University.
2. Appeal in person, preferably to acquaintances. Wesley Allen-Arave at the University of New Mexico surveyed the charitable giving of 515 New Mexican households and found that they were most likely to agree to a request from someone they knew—that criterion being more important than severity of need, says Allen-Arave.
3. Build empathy for the needy. That's why so many charitable appeals feature photos of sad-looking children. Reading fiction featuring an unfortunate protagonist could make people more empathetic, and thus more willing to help someone in need—an idea that Henrich hopes to test.

Critical Thinking

1. What is meant by the Maasai concept of "osotua" and how does it function?
2. What does research suggest that we do to encourage generosity in modern society?

Internet References

Center for African Studies
https://africanstudies.stanford.edu

Center for Human Evolutionary Studies
evolution.rutgers.edu/people/ches

Article

Prepared by: Elvio Angeloni

Breastfeeding and Culture

KATHERINE DETTWYLER

Learning Outcomes

After reading this article, you will be able to:

- Discuss the benefit of breastfeeding for child, mother, and society.
- Discuss the factors that affect the practices of breastfeeding in various cultures.

In a perfect world—one where child health and cognitive development were optimal—all children would be breastfed for as long as they wanted. As large-bodied, highly intelligent primates, that would be for a minimum of 2.5 years and as long as 6 or 7 years, or longer. In a perfect world, all mothers would know how to breastfeed and be supported in their efforts to do so by health care providers, spouses, friends, neighbors, co-workers, and the general beliefs of their culture.

Breastfeeding is, first and foremost, a way to provide protective immunities and health-promoting factors to children. Breast milk should be the primary source of nutrition for the first two years of life, complemented by appropriate solid foods around six months of age. Breast milk provides important immunities and nutrients, especially for growing brains, for as long as the child is breastfed. It is a source of physical and emotional comfort to a child, and for the mother it is the wellspring of the important mothering hormones, prolactin and oxytocin.

Ordinarily, childbirth is followed by breastfeeding, with its flood of prolactin, the "mothering hormone," and oxytocin, "the hormone of love." Both hormones elicit caretaking, affective, and protective behaviors by the mother towards her child. If the mother does not breastfeed, her body interprets this as "the baby died," and enters a state of hormonal grieving, preparing for a new attempt at reproduction. The mother, however, still has to cope with a newborn, and later a toddler, without the calming and nurturing influence of prolactin and oxytocin.

Like childbirth, however, breastfeeding is influenced by a variety of cultural beliefs, some directly related to breastfeeding itself, and others pertaining to a woman's role in society, to the proper relationship between mother and child, to the proper relationship between mother and father, and even to beliefs about breasts themselves.

One way of thinking about cultural influences on breastfeeding initiation and duration is based on the Demographic Transition, in which societies move from a pre-transition state of high birth and death rates, through a transitional stage of high birth but low death rates (resulting in rapid population growth), and eventually into a post-transition stage of low birth and death rates. Margaret Mead was the first to recognize an "Infant Feeding Transition." A culture begins in a pre-transition state of almost everyone breastfeeding for several years, then moves through a transitional stage of bottle-feeding. Three main forces conspire to move women away from breastfeeding: (1) the separation of their productive labor and their reproductive labor, as societies shift from subsistence-based economies to wage labor-based economies, and/or women are taken away from both productive and reproductive work to be their husband's social partners; (2) increasing confidence in the power of science to provide "better living through chemistry" coupled with decreasing confidence in the ability of women's bodies to function normally, and (3) the rise of commercial interests intent on making a profit by convincing women that breastfeeding is less healthy, difficult, primitive, and/or shameful. The transition is initiated by women with more education and higher incomes turning to shorter and shorter durations of breastfeeding, and eventually only wet-nursing (in previous centuries) or bottle-feeding (in the 20th and 21st centuries) from birth.

As time goes by, women with less education and lower income levels emulate their social superiors and adopt bottle-feeding as well. By the time the last of the lower classes have adopted bottle-feeding as being "modern and scientific," the well-educated upper-class women are returning to breastfeeding, first for short periods, and then for increasing durations. They have moved on to the post-transition stage. The return to breastfeeding by well-educated upper-class women is fueled by several factors, including research during the last few decades clearly documenting the superiority of breastfeeding over formula in terms of maternal and child health and child cognitive development, feminism's insistence that women's reproductive powers are of great value, and a general backlash against the infant formula companies for promoting their products in unethical ways. Primarily, in the United States it has been well-educated middle- and upper-class women who have fought for legislation to protect the rights of mothers to breastfeed in public, and for better maternity care and on-site child care facilities.

In the late 1950s, anthropologist Margaret Mead urged researchers to: "Find out how we can get from the working class mothers who breastfeed to the upper middle-class women who also breastfeed, without a generation of bottle feeders in between" (Raphael 1979). We still haven't figured out how to do this.

There are still a number of "pre-transition" cultures in the world, in which all women breastfeed each child for several years, but Western influence—particularly in the form of aggressive infant formula marketing strategies and the export of Western cultural beliefs about breasts as sex objects—is affecting even the remotest regions of the world. Korea, for example, is in the early stages of the transition from universal long-term breastfeeding to the adoption of bottles. Survey data reveal a decline in breastfeeding incidence and duration from the 1960s to the 1990s, led by upper-class, well-educated urban Korean women. China, likewise, has begun the transition to bottle-feeding, experiencing a rapid decline in the prevalence of breastfeeding in urban and periurban areas. Not surprisingly, China has been targeted by the infant formula companies as the next great market for their products.

Cuba is at the beginning of the infant feeding transition, with mothers of higher educational levels having the shortest duration of breastfeeding. Cuba seems to be well ahead of the United States in meeting established goals for maternal and child health through breastfeeding, with national strategies for supporting and promoting breastfeeding, including having all government hospitals participate in the World Health Organization's Baby-Friendly Hospital Initiative, and developing educational programs for day care centers and elementary and secondary schools to try to create a breastfeeding-friendly culture among both males and females from an early age. Cuba may be able to avoid a complete switch to bottle-feeding.

The Arabian Gulf countries (Bahrain, Kuwait, Oman, Qatar, Saudi Arabia, and the United Arab Emirates) are fully into the transitional phase, with middle- and upper-class women seldom breastfeeding, or only for a few weeks, and older women nursing longer than younger women. The influence of oil revenues on the lifestyles of these women, including the common employment of foreign housemaids and nannies, who bottle-feed the children, is fascinating and disturbing. The transition from full breastfeeding to almost full bottle-feeding has been particularly swift in this part of the world. "Westernized" hospital practices have been especially harmful, with hospital personnel and private clinics being used to promote the use of formula.

Australia, Canada, and the United States represent societies farthest along this "Infant Feeding Transition," with women of higher incomes and more education initiating breastfeeding in great numbers, and with increasing durations as well. This trend began in the 1970s, but was helped by the 1997 statement by the American Academy of Pediatrics that all children in the United States should be nursed for a minimum of one year (and thereafter as long as both mother and child wish), as well as by recent research showing that formula-fed children have lower IQs than their breastfed counterparts. In the United States, breastfeeding to the age of three years or beyond is becoming more and more common, as is breastfeeding siblings of different ages, known as "tandem nursing" (Dettwyler 2001). In the last decades, the biggest leaps in initiating breastfeeding in the United States have been among WIC clients (women, infants, and children), who tend to be poor and less well-educated, indicating a trickle-down effect of breastfeeding from the upper classes, as well as the success of WIC Peer Counselor training programs.

Exactly how a particular region responds to influence from the Western industrialized nations and from the multinational infant formula companies depends on many different social, political, and economic factors. This makes it difficult to predict how the infant feeding transition will look in a specific region, or how long the bottle-feeding stage will last.

Cultural beliefs affect breastfeeding in other ways as well. Among the Bambara of Mali, people believe that because breast milk is made from a woman's blood, the process of breastfeeding creates a special relationship between a child and the woman who breastfeeds that child, whether or not she is the child's biological mother. In addition, breastfeeding creates a bond among all of the children who nurse from the same woman, whether or not they are biological siblings.

Having milk-siblings expands one's kinship network, providing more people one can call on for help in times of need. However, these kinship ties also prohibit marriage between the related children. In order to reduce the impact on potential marriage partners, women try to breastfeed other women's children only if they would already be excluded as marriage partners. Thus, a woman might wet-nurse the children of her co-wives, the children of her husband's brothers, or her grandchildren, while avoiding breastfeeding the children of her best friend, who she hopes will grow up to marry her own children. Similar beliefs about the "milk tie" are found among people in Haiti, Papua New Guinea, the Balkans, Burma, and among the Badawin of Kuwait and Saudi Arabia. In cultures where everyone is breastfed, or where everyone is bottle-fed, one's identity does not hinge on how one was fed. But in cultures entering or leaving the transition, feeding practices can be very important to one's identity. In a culture just entering the transition, to be bottle-fed is to have high status and be wealthy and modern. In a culture entering the final stage, to be breastfed is to have high status and be wealthy and modern.

In a wide variety of cultures, males are breastfed longer than females, sometimes much longer. These practices are supported by a variety of cultural beliefs, including the ideas that earlier weaning for girls insures a much-desired earlier menopause (Taiwan), that boys must be nursed longer so they will be willing to take care of their aged parents (Ireland), and that breast milk is the conduit for machismo, something boys need, but girls do not (Ecuador). Additionally, a number of societies have noted that males are physiologically weaker than females, more prone to illness and early death, so mothers nurse their sons longer to help ensure their survival.

Cultural beliefs about birth can have a profound influence on the success or failure of breastfeeding. Breastfeeding works best when the mother and baby are un-drugged at delivery, when they are kept together after birth, when the baby is not washed, when the baby is fed at the first cue (long before crying), when breastfeeding occurs early and often, when free formula samples and other gifts are not given to the mother, and when all those who surround the mother are knowledgeable and supportive of breastfeeding. Where the culture of birthing meets most or all of these criteria, we find higher rates of breastfeeding as well as longer durations. The World Health Organization's Baby-Friendly Hospital Initiative provides both a blueprint for optimal breastfeeding conditions and references to support their recommendations.

Cultural beliefs about how often children should breastfeed can help or hinder the process. The composition of human milk, as well as studies of human populations where children are allowed to breastfeed on demand, suggests that the natural frequency of breastfeeding is several times an hour for a few minutes each time, rather than according to a schedule, with longer feedings separated by several hours. Infrequent feeding in the early days and weeks of breastfeeding can permanently affect a mother's milk supply. As control of breast milk production gradually shifts from primarily endocrine (prolactin) to primarily autocrine (based on breast fullness) during the first few months postpartum, women who have been nursing on a three- to four-hour schedule may find that they no longer have sufficient milk to meet their babies' needs. A simple strategy of unrestricted breastfeeding from birth onwards would prevent this supply problem.

Perhaps the most pernicious cultural belief affecting breastfeeding is the one found in the United States and a small number of other (mostly Western) cultures—the belief that women's breasts are naturally erotic. American culture is obsessed with the sexual nature of women's breasts and their role in attracting and keeping male attention, as well as their role in providing sexual pleasure. This is reflected by the "normal" circumstances under which breasts are exposed in the United States (*Playboy* centerfolds, low-cut evening gowns, bikinis), by the phenomenon of breast augmentation surgery, by the association of breasts with sexual pleasure, and by the reactions of some people when they see women breastfeeding (embarrassment, horror, disgust, disapproval). In fact, the cultural belief that breasts are intrinsically erotic is just that, a cultural belief of limited distribution—one that has devastating consequences for women who want to breastfeed their children.

The mammary glands play no role in sexual behavior in any species other than humans. Among humans, the cross-cultural evidence clearly shows that most cultures do not define the breasts as sex objects. Extensive cross-cultural research in the 1940s and 1950s, published by Ford and Beach, found that, of 190 cultures surveyed, only 13 viewed women's breasts as sexually attractive. Likewise, 13 cultures out of 190 involved women's breasts in sexual activity. Of these latter 13, only three are also listed among the 13 where breasts are considered sexually attractive.

In most cultures, breasts are viewed solely as functional body parts, used to feed children—similar to how the typical American male views women's elbows, as devices to bend arms. Thus, in most cultures, it doesn't matter whether they are covered or not, or how big they are; husbands do not feel jealous of their nursing children, and women are never accused of breastfeeding for their own sexual pleasure. In the United States, and increasingly where Western ideas about breasts as sex objects are taking hold, women find that they must be extremely discreet about where and how they breastfeed. They may get little support for breastfeeding, or even active resistance from jealous husbands; they may receive dirty looks or rude comments or be asked to go elsewhere (often the bathroom) to nurse. Still others are accused of sexually abusing their children for breastfeeding them longer than a year (Dettwyler 2001).

The evolution of cultural beliefs about breasts is difficult to pin down. Carolyn Latteier and Marilyn Yalom provide the most thorough research on the history of Western culture's obsession with breasts. The rise of both the infant formula industry and commercial pornography following World War II contributed to modern views of breasts as sex objects, rather than glands for producing milk for children.

Among health care providers themselves, a culture of denial about the health risks of formula contributes to the persistence of bottle-feeding. Many physicians view bottle-feeding as "almost as good" in spite of overwhelming research to the contrary. It is estimated that for every 1,000 deaths of infants in the United States, four of those deaths can be directly attributed to the use of infant formula. Additionally, children who are formula-fed have higher rates of many illnesses during childhood including diabetes, ear infections, gastrointestinal and upper respiratory infections, lymphoma, Sudden Infant Death Syndrome, and allergies. They continue to have higher rates of illnesses throughout life, including heart disease, some types of cancer, and multiple sclerosis. Children who are formula-fed likewise have lower average scores on intelligence tests and lower grades in school. Mothers who breastfeed their children, especially for longer durations, have lower rates of reproductive cancers (especially breast cancer), and lower rates of osteoporosis.

Unfortunately, obstetricians often view infant nutrition as the responsibility of the pediatrician, while the pediatrician claims that by the time the child is born, the mother has long since made up her mind about how she will feed her child. Many health care professionals say that they hesitate to discuss the dangers of formula for fear of "making women feel guilty." This is patronizing of parents and robs them of their chance to make an informed decision about this important area of child care.

In a perfect world, all cultural beliefs would support breastfeeding. The World Health Organization's Baby-Friendly Hospital Initiative and the Coalition for Improving Maternity Services' Mother-Friendly Childbirth Initiative are two attempts to clarify the best cultural practices for initiating breastfeeding. The Internet has also had a major impact on the culture of breastfeeding support. LactNet is an e-mail list for professionals who work in the lactation field. Kathleen Bruce and Kathleen Auerbach, both lactation consultants in the United States, began the list in March of 1995. It has grown to include more than 3,000 individuals from 38 countries who share ideas, beliefs, research studies, and clinical experience. Documents such as the Baby-Friendly Hospital Initiative and the Mother-Friendly Childbirth Initiative, and resources such as LactNet, are creating and sustaining a global culture of breastfeeding support.

Additional Resources

For Internet links related to this chapter, please visit our website at www.mhhe.com/dettwyler,

Ford, C. S., and F. A. Beach. *Patterns of Sexual Behavior.* New York: Harper & Row, 1951.

Giuliani, Rudolph W. (Introduction) and the editors of LIFE Magazine. *One Nation: America Remembers September 11, 2001.* New York: Little Brown & Company, 2001.

Kear, Adrian, and Deborah Lynn Steinberg, eds. *Mourning Diana: Nation, Culture and the Performance of Grief.* New York: Routledge, 1999.

Latteier, C. *Breasts: The Women's Perspective on an American Obsession.* Binghamton, NY: Haworth Press, 1998.

Podolefsky, Aaron, and Peter J. Brown, eds. *Applying Anthropology: An Introductory Reader.* 7th ed. New York: McGraw-Hill Higher Education, 2002.

Raphael, D. "Margaret Mead—A Tribute." *The Lactation Review* 4, no. 1 (1979), pp. 1–3.

Simopoulos, A. P., J. E. Dutra de Oliveira, and I. D. Desai, eds. *Behavioral and Metabolic Aspects of Breastfeeding: International Trends. World Review of Nutrition and Dietetics, Volume 78.* Basel, Switzerland: S. Karger, 1995.

Stuart-Macadam, Patricia, and Katherine A. Dettwyler, eds. *Breastfeeding: Biocultural Perspectives.* New York: Aldine de Gruyter Publishers, 1995.

Walker, M. "A Fresh Look at the Hazards of Artificial Infant Feeding, II." 1998. Available from the International Lactation Consultants Association.

Yalom, M. *A History of the Breast.* New York: Random House, Inc., 1997.

Critical Thinking

1. Discuss the importance of breastfeeding for both mother and child.
2. What kinds of cultural factors influence breastfeeding?
3. Discuss the main forces that move women away from breastfeeding.
4. What factors have fueled the return to breastfeeding?
5. How has Western influence brought about bottle-feeding in countries that are undergoing a transition? Why might Cuba be an exception in this regard?
6. Why are the Arabian Gulf countries "fully into the transitional phase"?
7. Describe the "Infant Feeding Transition" and why it is occurring.
8. How do cultural beliefs affect breastfeeding?
9. Why are males breastfed more often than females?
10. What are some of the detrimental effects of not breastfeeding?

Internet References

Journal of Human Lactation
http://jhl.sagepub.com

American Anthropological Association Children and Childhood Interest Group
http://aaacig.usu.edu

Article

Prepared by: Elvio Angeloni

Children Playing and Learning

DAVID F. LANCY

Learning Outcomes

After reading this article, you will be able to:

- Describe the laissez-faire attitude on the part of elders regarding "teaching" children in traditional cultures.
- Contrast the way children learn in traditional cultures with the way they are educated in our society.
- Discuss the importance of "gamesmanship" in terms of its importance and how it is gradually learned.

Across cultures, with very few exceptions, early childhood is a time for play. Parents may vary in how positively they view this activity, but, at a minimum, they see its value for keeping kids busy and out of the way. Toddlers are supervised during the play by explicitly delegated sib-caretakers, with adults in the vicinity alert to the sounds of trouble. However, virtually all scholars who've observed children at play in village settings cite a wealth of opportunities for learning the culture. And many would agree that play is a "form of buffered learning through which the child can make . . . step-by-step progress toward adult behavior." I argued that learning through play was more efficient than learning from instruction for several reasons, not least because instruction is often boring to the young, while play is arousing, and because instruction "requires an investment by a second party, the teacher."

From my earliest fieldwork in the Liberian hinterland bush, I was struck by this enduring phenomenon—children are active, hands-on, and engaged learners. And a great deal of their learning occurs in the context of play. Even when physically inactive, they are intently watching what the adults are up to, gathering material for later make-believe scripts. In the next essay, I describe boys watching from the periphery as a court case unfolds in the town chief's open-air courtroom. While watching, the boys discuss the case sotto voce and the chief offers up frequent homilies that lift some mundane element in the case to the level of moral imperative or customary practice. The boys absorb all these lessons, as evidenced by the reenactment of the court drama in their make-believe play later on. A key element in the watching, discussing, and reenacting is that it is entirely child-initiated. This is one "classroom, "among many in the village, where attendance is optional and there are no quizzes.

This laissez-faire attitude on the part of the elders regarding "teaching" children is consistent with four widely held beliefs about children. First, children want to learn their culture, so they strive for competence. Second, they learn best without adult direction and at their own pace. Third, they are motivated to learn useful skills in order to "fit in" and be accepted by their families. And fourth, expecting children to strive to "fit in" means that when they appear to lack this motivation, they will be called to account. In the chief's court, "fitting in" meant being quiet and not interfering. Contrast these views with our own beliefs that children learn little without teaching and need to meet certain specific age- or grade-determined milestones in their learning. Nor are they really required to "fit in" as their parents give them a free pass—to the despair of their teachers.

As the essays in this chapter illustrate, within tightly defined limits, parents may accord autonomy to children—to acquire and use a large library of interactive media or to choose from a self-constructed menu of food offerings, as examples. But unlike the villagers' anthropologists study, their lives are, otherwise, tightly managed, including their play.

Cowboys and Indians and the Origin of the Couch Potato

Many years ago, I undertook an ethnographic study of childhood in a remote West African village called Gbarngasuakwelle. Ethnography is the method used by cultural anthropologists. It involves living with the people they're trying to understand; speaking the local language; learning and respecting their customs; and, above all, observing and listening, recording faithfully what is heard and seen, and then trying to make sense of it as a nonnative. One of the prominent themes in my report (published as *Playing on the Mother-Ground*) was the importance of observation in the lives of children. As just mentioned, one venue where I hung out was the town chief's court.

With apologies to fans of Court TV, the average court case is just slightly more interesting than watching grass grow. And this was certainly true of the local court presided over by Chief Wolliekollie. Imagine a 40-minute debate about the failure to promptly return a borrowed lantern or an even longer debate over the amount of compensation appropriate in the case of an adulterous liaison (the juicy details discretely glossed over). And yet the court never failed to attract a good crowd of juvenile spectators. While the boys watching the chief's court were quiet and blended in with their surroundings, it was obvious that the chief saw them as "pupils" in an open-air classroom. His rhetorical questions and judicial "opinions" often reflected basic principles of Kpelle morality. Most societies are keenly aware of the child as voyeur and fully expect to use public events for their didactic value.

Among the Yakutat of British Columbia, "Children learned a great deal by listening to the older people talk, especially when the old men gathered in the sweathouse to bathe and chat." Among the Tale of Ghana, "children learn who their . . . ancestors were by listening at sacrifices." Anthropologists note that little is private or off-limits to children in the village, and they learn about the birds and the bees quite early. For example, Australian Arunta children play at being husbands and wives, making separate windbreaks and fires and pretending to cook food. Sometimes they also play at adultery, with a boy running away with the "wife" of another boy.

So one of the first clues an anthropologist might note as evidence of children's autonomy to learn on their own is that the culture is displayed like an open book. There is no censorship and children can browse at will. In contemporary society, we seem to embrace a philosophy of "do as I say, not as I do." Because we focus so narrowly on children learning through explicit lessons, we ignore the many lessons we teach without intending to. Sociologist Peter McClaren recorded this scene some years ago:

> Georgette and Wendy picked up some dolls at the activity center. Georgette chose G.I. Joe and Wendy picked up a Farah Fawcett doll. "Let's pretend we're married," Georgette said. "Okay," Wendy agreed. Georgette took G.I. Joe and promptly slapped the Farah doll across the face with it, shouting: "That's what you get for talkin' to me like that."

Years after recording the African scenes of children as spectators, I had an epiphany and realized that what I had witnessed in Gbarngasuakwelle was the fertile field in which couch potatoes might grow. It turns out to be a small step from watching interesting things happen in the village, to watching television. In the village, however, the court case eventually ends and the juvenile spectators disperse for new, usually more active, adventures. By contrast, in many contemporary homes, the television/video game/iPhone is never off. While village children's prolonged and intense observation and eavesdropping on adults may be vital in learning their culture, interest is bound to fall off once they've "mastered" particular aspects of the "curriculum." Older boys do not hang around the court; it is all too familiar. The boredom that comes with overfamiliarization and lack of challenge is all too common in our classrooms, in contrast to the perpetually novel and challenging interactivity found in contemporary recreational and social media. Unfortunately, attempts to hybridize academic content with video game interactivity have not been notably successful.

Boys in Gbarngasuakwelle were also enthralled by their elders' success in hunting and trapping, and spent countless hours in chasing games and "play" hunting that evolved into the real thing. In my childhood, I was a cowboy. I grew up without a village; my windows on the world were books and television. But I didn't become a couch potato either. As exciting as those Saturday morning Westerns were, I took equal or greater pleasure from replicating the heroic exploits of the Lone Ranger or Hopalong Cassidy. My parents could not afford, nor did they approve of, building a toy treasury for me. But they believed that fantasy play stimulated the imagination and contracted with Santa one year to provide me some "props" including a cowboy hat and six-shooter. We do, occasionally, see village parents supplying cast-off or scaled-down tools and weapons as toys to encourage children to use play as a learning medium. Even more important is the belief that, while playing and learning outdoors, children are distracted and don't get in adults' way.

This is a belief my mother shared. So I spent hours each day "roamin' the range." In the process, I remained lean and healthy, and hence, according to Nigel Barber (blog = The Human Beast) would have more easily evaded predators in an earlier incarnation during the Paleolithic.

In contrast, television and video games, and the comfortable environment in which they are situated, may be so compelling that the child never shifts from observation to replication. Couch potatoes not only miss out on physical exercise but may be shortchanged in their mental exercise as well. In fact, there are numerous studies showing a strong inverse correlation between time spent with video games (current average = 13 hours a week) and school grades. So parents may need to intervene (minimally) to nudge children from passive receptors to active creators and, above all, to get them off the couch and into the backyard or the neighborhood at large. Recent studies highlight how few families spend any time at all outdoors in leisure activity in the typical week. "Children not only don't wander through their neighborhood playing with peers; ¾ of them don't even play in their own backyards." Parenthetically, on the subject of toy guns and modern derivatives, many child advocates worry about the impact of violent video games on aggressive behavior. And this is one parental anxiety that is justified. A thorough survey of the huge literature on the relationship between violent video games and later aggressive behavior found that the "evidence strongly suggests that exposure to violent video games is a causal risk factor for increased aggressive behavior, aggressive cognition, and aggressive affect and for decreased empathy and prosocial behavior." At least some of these negative effects may be due to diminished face-to-face (see the "Gamesmanship" essay below) social interaction that is associated with children who are absorbed in media for hours on end. That said, if children use guns to harm or kill themselves or others, the culprit is far more likely to be the careless gun owner who often justifies ready access to a lethal weapon by the need to "protect" themselves and their family. Virtually any day of the week in the United States one can find a minor news item of the "Boy, 4, shot by sibling while waiting in car" variety.

What can we take away from all this? Children are endowed with several predilections that facilitate their learning culture with little or no direct instruction. Those predilections can still be useful today in helping a child learn to construct narratives (stories) and to learn many aspects of the culture. However, in the village, there is no lens through which the culture is distorted on its way to the child's brain, except for their own naivety. But if electronic media represent the window our children have on society and history, it is "through a glass darkly." Product advertising dominates the cultural "lessons" conveyed. Other "lessons" seem almost anticultural, gaining their audience through the egregious violation of cultural standards and mores—think The Simpsons. In the village, common "child-produced" content emerges in make-believe play in which children take pride in replicating the skills and pursuits of those older. In contemporary society, child-constructed narratives may be telegraphic, barely literate prose, sexting, and cyberbullying.

Toys or Tools?

Archaeologist Bob Dawe was intrigued by a puzzle. His field is the prehistory of the Plains Indians, which he reconstructs from studying early sites that were utilized by these people. Many of the sites contain the remains of large mammals that were hunted as a staple of the diet. These "kill" sites include buffalo jumps, where large numbers of animals were killed and butchered. Among the bones are the tools used by hunters, including stone arrow points. The puzzling thing is that these often include large numbers of small, poorly knapped arrowheads that would have made no more impression on a bison than a mosquito bite. Dawe's hypothesis is that the points were quickly and crudely made to give to children who would use them in "toy" arrows. He buttresses his argument with material from ethnographic studies and travelers' recollections. Many observers of the Plains Indians (including John James Audubon) took note of adults giving children scaled-down tools—especially for hunting—which they were expected to use to gradually perfect their skill. Dawe writes, "Toys should not be considered nonfunctional. Rather they are small-scale tools which functioned and suffered the same tool use-life as their adult-sized counterparts."

> While not universal, in many societies, tools are made for children to play with, they are given cast-off tools to convert into toys, and/or the raw materials to make their own. Franz Boas—one of anthropology's founding fathers (and mentor of founding mother Margaret Mead)—described how Inuit (Eskimo) boys played a game that simulated the hunting of ringed seals through the ice. The materials used in the game, such as pieces of sealskin and miniature harpoons, were often supplied by parents to encourage this kind of learning through play. Similarly, Inuit "girls make dolls out of scraps of skin and clothe them like real men and women." Their mothers encourage them, for it is in this way that they learn to sew and cutout patterns. "Girls from the Conambo tribe in Ecuador will, as their mothers before them, become potters. While quite young, they can be found playing with balls of clay donated by their mothers. They turn the clay into snakes, miniature animals, and hollow vessels, all baby steps on the way to learning to produce useable ceramics. In a Chiga farming village, a small child is given a gourd to play with, to balance on his orher head and, trailing after older siblings, takes it "to the watering-place . . . brings it back with a little water in it."

Even more common, I've found many cases where children are free to handle and play with adult-sized tools. Most striking are children literally "playing with knives," a few examples of which follow (all referenced in D. F. Lancy, "Playing with knives: The socialization of self-initiated learners," Child Development, 87, 2016):

- "[An Amazonian Pirahã child] was playing with a sharp kitchen knife about nine inches in length. He was swinging the knife blade around him, often coming close to his eyes, his chest, his arm, and other body parts, when he dropped the knife, his mother—talking to someone else—reached backward nonchalantly without interrupting her conversation, picked up the knife and handed it back to the toddler."

- "[A Tanzanian Hadza] infant may grab a sharp knife, put it in its mouth, and suck on it without adults showing the least bit of concern until they need the knife again."
- "I don't like it when our children play with machetes, but if the baby decides to play, I leave it. And if the baby cuts themself and if they see the blood, they themselves will decide not to play with the machete."(Aka [Central Africa] mother)

Appearances to the contrary, I do not think this nonchalant attitude reflects indifference or callousness toward the fate of one's children. Rather, this extreme laissez-faire attitude reflects a bedrock belief in the power of children to learn autonomously. More than this, parents often express the view that parental intervention of any sort, including teaching, is a waste of time (children will learn without it) and may even be harmful if children become reluctant to explore and learn on their own. This "folk" wisdom was recently confirmed in a series of experiments, undertaken by psychologists in the United States, using a multiaction toy. Four- and five-year-old subjects "who were taught a function of the toy performed fewer kinds of actions on the toy and discovered fewer of its other functions" than children who were not taught anything about the toy.

Village children not given toys made by adults, or not finding any full-scale tool available, make their own. These constructions often display enormous ingenuity, persistence, and skill. An unusual case is found in Kutch, where Rabari boys start their education in animal husbandry by creating a "flock" out of dried camel and sheep droppings and then moving the flock, corralling it, taking it to water, and so on. I have observed dozens of toys that were created from recycled materials, many quite elaborate, such as wire cars or trucks made throughout Africa. Even when toys have no obvious connection to useful skills or knowledge, children may learn a great deal through the process of invention and construction. I was enthralled by a youngster during a trip to Yemen. He had scavenged a cast-off plastic jerry can, modified it to use as a sled, and proceeded to launch himself, repeatedly, down a stone parapet.

Figure 4.1 shows a pair of boys from the Bara tribal area of south central Madagascar playing with clay figurines they've made themselves. The author of the photo, Gabriel Scheidecker, writes:

> The boys are playing with vehicles made from clay. The toys are modeled after sarety (borrowing from French charrette, ox cart) and mainly used for transporting the harvest (rice and manioc). The toy versions are called kisarety. The prefix ki- signifies small, not serious, and is used for all children's games and toys that reflect adult activities/things. The boys have "loaded" one cart with "rice" (sand) pulled by a Zebu (note the hump) ox. Humans are depicted with their arms bent in a way that suggests they may be engaged in an "ox fight."

In 2010, I visited a Vezo fishing village in southwest Madagascar. The community depends, for its livelihood, almost entirely on collecting marine resources. From adolescence, villagers will venture out into the Zanzibar channel in colorful outrigger canoes to fish and hunt turtles. The wide expanse of beach fronting on the sea—from which these expeditions are launched—serves as a kind of mixed-age, teacherless classroom. Babies are placed in tide pools to splash around and grow accustomed to saltwater; three boys around age five clamber over a beached canoe, learning an agile dance from thwart to gunwale; six-year-olds convert discarded planks or logs into "canoes" they ride on and paddle. The first lesson in sail-handling probably occurs as the boy maneuvers a miniature sailboat he has made himself. In short, a significant part of the "canoe curriculum: can be acquired through play with "toys."

Am I suggesting that our children be given free rein in the garage, workshop, barn, kitchen? Hardly, but most parents and teachers could widen the safety zone for them and provide many more opportunities to explore and learn independently. My own childhood was greatly enriched by having many opportunities to "build" things with cast-off construction materials, using my father's tools—unobserved by an adult. Ultimately, I'm not sure which practice is more harmful for children—playing with knives or the opposite. A Korean American journalist remarked, "I was surprised in the United States when a nine-year-old asked me to butter his bread because he wasn't 'allowed to use a knife,' even a butter knife."

What lessons do *our* children learn from toys? It could very well be that they are primarily learning to be avid consumers. In my view, "Black Friday" is aptly named. It is a black day on the nation's calendar. A few years ago, while watching the nightly news, I was treated to a horrific scene of a crowd bursting through the doors of Toys "R" Us. I watched as a cute blond cherub got knocked down in the crush and, for all I know, trampled. The announcer's commentary—completely upbeat—extolled the social and economic benefits of this phenomenon, ignoring the anarchic behavior on the screen. One study relevant to my question looked at "Dear Santa" letters in the United Kingdom versus Sweden. The latter bans television advertising aimed at children, the former offers no such prohibition. The results, unsurprisingly, showed that British kids had longer wish lists and requested primarily "branded" toys. Another study in Britain reported, anecdotally, about 11-year-old Philip who was particularly pleased on his birthday because his auntie had followed his directions and made the right choice. He proudly declared, "I wanted a Huffy [scooter] because they're the best at the moment and so I gave her the product code number and price and everything in case she got it wrong." Eric Clark has reviewed these studies and notes, sardonically:

> Kids get bored with their toys before they break them, sometimes even before they have played with them. In fact, many toys are no longer created for play. They are designed to be purchased, to be possessed, to be a badge of status. The more toys, the happier the child. A survey in 2005 showed that 80 percent of children under 12 were given more than 10 toys a year, but 60 percent of those toys were soon thrown out even though there was nothing wrong with them. . . . For most toy companies, the role of children is clear: they are cash cows to be milked.

It turns out that childhood observers saw this coming from a long way off. In a history of American childhood, published in 1917, the author laments, "two days playing with [contemporary toys] exhausts the pleasure. They are too complete—the fun of making them has been taken away from the child."

Whatever lessons are being learned, they are different lessons. Historian Gary Cross charts the steady decline in popularity of construction sets and other toys that can serve as tools. As he says, "Toys that prepare children for adult life seem harder to find." Five years ago, Stinky the Garbage Truck was hot. I noted three salient attributes of this toy. First, it was expensive (70 dollars) but available at a discount. Second, and lamentably, it promised to fill the void for a friend- or siblingless child. "Who could believe a trash-gobbling garbage truck could be SO loveable? There's a ton of fun surprises in store with your new pal: chats, joke telling, exercise partner, and sing-along silliness, too. Friendship with Stinky never smelled sweeter!" But Stinky's central lesson seems to be that toys are trash: "he can 'eat' garbage. [And the] garbage your child feeds him can consist of anything from other toy cars to several tiny toys your child is sure to have lying around his or her room." By 2015, it was passé and no longer in production.

Unfortunately, manufacturers of traditional, sturdy, creative, and constructive toys have not fared well. My favorite company, now deceased, was Back to Basics Toys. Instead, children and their parents seem to prefer toys that come with a narrative already provided (via television, video games, or commercials). But I'm being overly pessimistic. Fine construction toys are still made (although I'd buy the more generic Lego block set over the single-purpose "movie-themed" sets). Lincoln Logs is celebrating their 100th anniversary. Venerable board games like monopoly still have valid lessons to teach, including the meaning of "friendly competition." Most of the tools of the domestic kitchen are harmless and should be accessible to children, especially when they want to "help" make dinner. The same is true for garden tools. Parents and prospective parents may need to reexamine their leisure time—first by increasing it! Can one's hobbies be selected with eager-to-learn children in mind? Cooking? Gardening? Sewing? Volunteering at the humane society? Taking up a musical instrument? Learning a foreign language? How about the "urban farming" movement? Williams Sonoma has lovely chicken coops ranging from $300–1,500.

Gamesmanship

In his study of "moral" development, the great Swiss psychologist Jean Piaget observed children of different ages playing marbles and used the game to illustrate the child's passing through numerous stages before arriving at a mature (fully moral) understanding of social conventions.

In watching players, we first see the refinement of manual dexterity. Humans are tool users, and young humans, as a consequence, are object manipulators. In its most refined form, using perfectly polished and round orbs, playing marbles calls forth tremendous small motor skill and digital finesse. Then we see "gamesmanship," where children manipulate the rules and each other to enhance the quality of play as well as their own success. Lastly, we see the development of social understanding of an appreciation of rules qua rules.

By at least the Roman era, and probably earlier, children used knucklebones as projectiles to try and dislodge each other's stationery targets. In other words, the basic pattern of marbles—whereby a player shoots a hard object at one or more similar objects to drive it, or them, out of a demarcated area—is probably quite old. Marbles, as we know the game, is clearly shown in Breughel's 1560 painting Children's Games. In Adriaen van Ostade's Children and Dog from 1673, boys are playing marbles outside a tavern. More recently, I have found marbles (and its kin) being played all over the world.

Renowned British folklorists Iona and Peter Opie document three basic versions of the game, but the variation in rules of play is staggering. What was critical, from Piaget's perspective, was that the game could be played at various levels so that very young children might play, even without understanding most of the rules. He wrote, "Children's games constitute the most admirable social institutions. The game of marbles, for instance . . . contains an extremely complex system of rules, that is to say, a code of laws, a jurisprudence of its own." After documenting the primary dimensions of the game, Piaget begins to probe the players' cognitive representation of the rules.

> You begin by asking the child if he could invent a new rule. . . . Once the new rule has been formulated, you ask the child whether it could give rise to a new game. . . . The child either agrees to the suggestion or disputes it. If he agrees, you immediately ask him whether the new rule is a "fair" rule, a "real" rule, one "like the others,"

and try to get at the various motives that enter into the answers.

Piaget teases out distinct age-dependent styles in children's approach to marbles. Initially, the child plays with the marbles as interesting objects, but there's no game per se. By about age four, the child can play the game, knows how to make the right moves physically, and understands the necessity for turn-taking. "The child's chief interest is no longer psychomotor; it is social." He is able to imitate the model provided by a more mature player, but he really has no sense of strategy or of what to do to increase the likelihood of winning. Then, around age seven, players focus on winning, even though their grasp of the rules—as revealed through questioning—is still vague. By age 11, the child is an expert on marbles and can explain every rule and exception. Nevertheless, the child still hasn't grasped rules qua rules. He still sees them as immutable. But, by 13, boys understand that the rules are arbitrary and conventional.

There are hundreds of illustrations of children's games from history and anthropology. Unfortunately, relatively few describe children actually in the process of playing, as opposed to a dry catalog of the rules and mechanics. But we can make a number of generalizations from the descriptions that are available. First, because toddlers are usually under the care and supervision of their older siblings, games are flexible enough to permit their participation. Older, more expert players will handicap themselves, for example, to ensure that learners can enjoy some success.

Complexities in the rules are introduced gradually. Games are played in a neighborhood playgroup of mixed age and gender. "Winning" is far less important than maintaining amicable relations. Players, in their roles as child caretakers, do not want the cries of an unhappy charge to attract the scrutiny of an angry adult.

The playgroup is hardly awash in a constant flow of good feelings, however. We have vivid accounts of protracted arguments about rules and their application. Particularly in the groups of older children—which tend to be homogeneous with respect to age and gender—games are not so much about learning and adhering to rules as about a running exercise in negotiation. As the Opies document for marbles, and Candy Goodwin for hopscotch and jump rope, there is a constant alteration between individual attempts to gain an advantage, cries of "foul" by opponents, and negotiated agreements that permit the game to proceed. Collectively, I've referred to these diplomatic skills as "gamesmanship."

In many cases, games support particular cultural ends. Aymara boys in the Andes play marbles—girls play jacks—while herding their flocks far from the village. Ben Smith's careful description of these games complements his in-depth analyses of speech and social-interaction patterns during play. Smith discusses the importance of qhincha (bad luck) in marbles. By confronting and enduring qhincha in the game, boys successfully fend off accusations of being feminine or homosexual. By implication, a boy who keeps control of himself when something goes wrong (a pebble in the path deflects his shot, say, or a toddler tramps through the ring of marbles) demonstrates the "chacha-ness" or "toughness" that reflects masculinity.

> The very ethos of the culture may dictate the nature of play. In the emerging Israeli state, the kibbutz was created as a utopian alternative to the competition and status differentials inherent in Western society. Not surprisingly, a study of children's games revealed a bias toward egalitarian outcomes—no winners, no losers. In Oceania, one finds examples of societies that are so egalitarian that, in children's play, "competitiveness is almost never in evidence." Among the Tangu of Papua New Guinea, children in teams play a game called taketak, which is designed—in keeping with local values—to end in a tie.

In small-scale, band societies, the playgroup, necessarily of mixed ages, must allow all players, no matter how inept, to participate; the playing field is always level, so to speak, and supports the prevailing egalitarian ethos. !Kung children throw a weighted feather in the air, and, as it floats down, they strike it with a stick or flick it back up into the air. The "game," called zeni, is played solo, and children make no attempt to compare skill or success. Aka foragers are highly egalitarian, and Boyette notes the absence of rough-and-tumble play and competitive games. Ndanga is a popular game in which "there is no winner in the game and there is no score kept."

In contemporary, middle-class, Western society, marbles and similar amusements are rapidly becoming extinct. The Opies blame this decline on the rise of adult-managed games and sports, but we might also cite video games as a major factor. Should we be at all concerned about this? Is a fondness for old-fashioned games purely sentimental? I don't think so. As opportunities for children to "negotiate" through rule-governed play dwindle, scholars are increasingly excited by the possibilities of Machiavellian intelligence (MI). There is a revolution under way in our thinking about the sapiens part of *Homo sapiens*. One useful starting point is Richard Byrne's The Thinking Ape. He writes:

> the essence of the Machiavellian intelligence hypothesis is that intelligence evolved in social circumstances. Individuals would be favored who were able to use and exploit others in their social group, without causing the disruption and potential group fission liable to result from naked aggression. Their manipulations might as easily involve cooperation as conflict, sharing as hoarding.

The theory has garnered a steady stream of empirical support. Extrapolating from it, I would argue that, if children have Machiavellian brains and, further, that brains need to be exercised to fully develop, marbles and the like are the perfect mental gym. The key elements here are rule-governed play, flexibility in applying the rules, and an absence of adult umpires. That is, children must be free to construct successful gaming sessions without adult guidance or interference. That's the essence of gamesmanship.

Unfortunately, current child-rearing practices have largely expropriated the opportunities for children to exercise gamesmanship and MI through unsupervised play. Adults now thoroughly manage and script most children's activities. Gary Fine's ethnography of Little League has become the definitive study of adult-managed play. He notes that the official *Little League* rule book ran to 62 pages in 1984 (and to 100 pages as of 2009) and that, in dramatic contrast to games organized by children, in "Little League, negotiation by players is unthinkable." Indeed, when players attempt to protest an umpire's call, for example, coaches and others call them "unsportsmanlike."

In addition to adult management of what were once child-initiated games and pickup sports, growing evidence indicates that parents—at least those among the contemporary intelligentsia—are taking control of make-believe play as well. This recent change in the way parents behave arises from their attempt to fill in for the siblings and peers their increasingly isolated children do not have, especially in urban settings. Parents also seem to feel that a child's unguided play will not yield the kind of academic payoff that parent-directed play yields. And, importantly, parents fear their offspring may suffer physical or psychological harm if they play with "neighborhood" kids. Parents may view marbles as dangerous because a child might swallow and choke on one. Despite such worries and good intentions, curtailing play initiated by children seems likely to attenuate—if not destroy altogether—opportunities to develop the skills associated with gamesmanship. One unintended consequence, for example, may be the rise in bullying as children lose opportunities to nurture and develop the ability to bargain and argue their way through disagreements.

But we can fight back. For starters, we can weigh in on the debate regarding the overly academic atmosphere in many preschools and the shift toward a more play-based curriculum. We should get behind the drive to restore recess to the elementary-school program. Some school districts and municipalities hire playground or recess coaches "who hope to show children that there is good old-fashioned fun to be had without iPods and video games and [who'll help] students learn to settle petty disputes, like who had the ball first or who pushed whom, not with fists but with the tried and true 'rock-paper-scissors.'"

Social critics warn parents to allow children greater freedom, particularly in play. As evidence that further decline is not inevitable, consider that March was declared Marbles Month at the Horsham Primary School in western Victoria, Australia. The game, school officials promised, would be vigorously promoted.

Critical Thinking

1. How is it that children become active, hands-on, engaged learners in traditional cultures?
2. What is "gamesmanship," how is it learned, and why is it important for social maturity?

Internet References

American Academy of Pediatrics
https://www.aap.org/en-us/Pages/Default.aspx

Attachment Parenting
http://www.attachmentparenting.org/

Fatherhood Institute
http://www.fatherhoodinstitute.org/

Family Lives
https://www.familylives.org.uk/advice/toddler-preschool/learning-play/how-children-learn-through-play/

Society for the Anthropology of Religion
Sar.americananthro.org/

The Ounce
https://www.theounce.org/

Article

Prepared by: Elvio Angeloni

The Inuit Paradox

How can people who gorge on fat and rarely see a vegetable be healthier than we are?

Patricia Gadsby

Learning Outcomes

After reading this article, you will be able to:

- Identify the traditional Inuit (Eskimo) practices that are important for their survival in the circumstances they live in and contrast them with the values professed by the society you live in.
- Discuss what contemporary hunter-collector societies teach us about the quality of life in the prehistoric past.
- Define the "Inuit paradox" and explain what we can learn from it with regard to modern-day eating practices.

Patricia Cochran, an Inupiat from Northwestern Alaska, is talking about the native foods of her childhood: "We pretty much had a subsistence way of life. Our food supply was right outside our front door. We did our hunting and foraging on the Seward Peninsula and along the Bering Sea."

"Our meat was seal and walrus, marine mammals that live in cold water and have lots of fat. We used seal oil for our cooking and as a dipping sauce for food. We had moose, caribou, and reindeer. We hunted ducks, geese, and little land birds like quail, called ptarmigan. We caught crab and lots of fish—salmon, whitefish, tomcod, pike, and char. Our fish were cooked, dried, smoked, or frozen. We ate frozen raw whitefish, sliced thin. The elders liked stinkfish, fish buried in seal bags or cans in the tundra and left to ferment. And fermented seal flipper, they liked that too."

Cochran's family also received shipments of whale meat from kin living farther north, near Barrow. Beluga was one she liked; raw muktuk, which is whale skin with its underlying blubber, she definitely did not. "To me it has a chew-on-a-tire consistency," she says, "but to many people it's a mainstay." In the short subarctic summers, the family searched for roots and greens and, best of all from a child's point of view, wild blueberries, crowberries, or salmonberries, which her aunts would mix with whipped fat to make a special treat called *akutuq*—in colloquial English, Eskimo ice cream.

Now Cochran directs the Alaska Native Science Commission, which promotes research on native cultures and the health and environmental issues that affect them. She sits at her keyboard in Anchorage, a bustling city offering fare from Taco Bell to French cuisine. But at home Cochran keeps a freezer filled with fish, seal, walrus, reindeer, and whale meat, sent by her family up north, and she and her husband fish and go berry picking—"sometimes a challenge in Anchorage," she adds, laughing. "I eat fifty-fifty," she explains, half traditional, half regular American.

No one, not even residents of the northernmost villages on Earth, eats an entirely traditional northern diet anymore. Even the groups we came to know as Eskimo—which include the Inupiat and the Yupiks of Alaska, the Canadian Inuit and Inuvialuit, Inuit Greenlanders, and the Siberian Yupiks—have probably seen more changes in their diet in a lifetime than their ancestors did over thousands of years. The closer people live to towns and the more access they have to stores and cash-paying jobs, the more likely they are to have westernized their eating. And with westernization, at least on the North American continent, comes processed foods and cheap carbohydrates—Crisco, Tang, soda, cookies, chips, pizza, fries. "The young and urbanized," says Harriet Kuhnlein, director of the Centre for Indigenous Peoples' Nutrition and Environment at McGill University in Montreal, "are increasingly into fast food." So much so that type 2 diabetes, obesity, and other diseases of Western civilization are becoming causes for concern there too.

Today, when diet books top the best-seller list and nobody seems sure of what to eat to stay healthy, it's surprising to learn how well the Eskimo did on a high-protein, high-fat diet. Shaped by glacial temperatures, stark landscapes, and protracted winters, the traditional Eskimo diet had little in the way of plant food, no agricultural or dairy products, and was unusually low in carbohydrates. Mostly people subsisted on what they hunted and fished. Inland dwellers took advantage of caribou feeding on tundra mosses, lichens, and plants too tough for humans to stomach (though predigested vegetation in the animals' paunches became dinner as well). Coastal people exploited the sea. The main nutritional challenge was avoiding starvation in late winter if primary meat sources became too scarce or lean.

These foods hardly make up the "balanced" diet most of us grew up with, and they look nothing like the mix of grains, fruits, vegetables, meat, eggs, and dairy we're accustomed to seeing in conventional food pyramid diagrams. How could such a diet possibly be adequate? How did people get along on little else but fat and animal protein?

The diet of the Far North shows that there are no essential foods—only essential nutrients.

What the diet of the Far North illustrates, says Harold Draper, a biochemist and expert in Eskimo nutrition, is that there are no essential foods—only essential nutrients. And humans can get those nutrients from diverse and eye-opening sources.

One might, for instance, imagine gross vitamin deficiencies arising from a diet with scarcely any fruits and vegetables. What furnishes vitamin A, vital for eyes and bones? We derive much of ours from colorful plant foods, constructing it from pigmented plant precursors called carotenoids (as in carrots). But vitamin A, which is oil soluble, is also plentiful in the oils of cold-water fishes and sea mammals, as well as in the animals' livers, where fat is processed. These dietary staples also provide vitamin D, another oil-soluble vitamin needed for bones. Those of us living in temperate and tropical climates, on the other hand, usually make vitamin D indirectly by exposing skin to strong sun—hardly an option in the Arctic winter—and by consuming fortified cow's milk, to which the indigenous northern groups had little access until recent decades and often don't tolerate all that well.

As for vitamin C, the source in the Eskimo diet was long a mystery. Most animals can synthesize their own vitamin C, or ascorbic acid, in their livers, but humans are among the exceptions, along with other primates and oddballs like guinea pigs and bats. If we don't ingest enough of it, we fall apart from scurvy, a gruesome connective-tissue disease. In the United States today we can get ample supplies from orange juice, citrus fruits, and fresh vegetables. But vitamin C oxidizes with time; getting enough from a ship's provisions was tricky for early 18th- and 19th-century voyagers to the polar regions. Scurvy—joint pain, rotting gums, leaky blood vessels, physical and mental degeneration—plagued European and U.S. expeditions even in the 20th century. However, Arctic peoples living on fresh fish and meat were free of the disease.

Impressed, the explorer Vilhjalmur Stefansson adopted an Eskimo-style diet for five years during the two Arctic expeditions he led between 1908 and 1918. "The thing to do is to find your antiscorbutics where you are," he wrote. "Pick them up as you go." In 1928, to convince skeptics, he and a young colleague spent a year on an Americanized version of the diet under medical supervision at Bellevue Hospital in New York City. The pair ate steaks, chops, organ meats like brain and liver, poultry, fish, and fat with gusto. "If you have some fresh meat in your diet every day and don't overcook it," Stefansson declared triumphantly, "there will be enough C from that source alone to prevent scurvy."

In fact, all it takes to ward off scurvy is a daily dose of 10 milligrams, says Karen Fediuk, a consulting dietitian and former graduate student of Harriet Kuhnlein's who did her master's thesis on vitamin C. (That's far less than the U.S. recommended daily allowance of 75 to 90 milligrams—75 for women, 90 for men.) Native foods easily supply those 10 milligrams of scurvy prevention, especially when organ meats—preferably raw—are on the menu. For a study published with Kuhnlein in 2002, Fediuk compared the vitamin C content of 100-gram (3.55-ounce) samples of foods eaten by Inuit women living in the Canadian Arctic: Raw caribou liver supplied almost 24 milligrams, seal brain close to 15 milligrams, and raw kelp more than 28 milligrams. Still higher levels were found in whale skin and muktuk.

As you might guess from its antiscorbutic role, vitamin C is crucial for the synthesis of connective tissue, including the matrix of skin. "Wherever collagen's made, you can expect vitamin C," says Kuhnlein. Thick skinned, chewy, and collagen rich, raw muktuk can serve up an impressive 36 milligrams in a 100-gram piece, according to Fediuk's analyses. "Weight for weight, it's as good as orange juice," she says. Traditional Inuit practices like freezing meat and fish and frequently eating them raw, she notes, conserve vitamin C, which is easily cooked off and lost in food processing.

Hunter-gatherer diets like those eaten by these northern groups and other traditional diets based on nomadic herding or subsistence farming are among the older approaches to human eating. Some of these eating plans might seem strange to us—diets centered around milk, meat, and blood among the East African pastoralists, enthusiastic tuber eating by the Quechua living in the High Andes, the staple use of the mongongo nut in the southern African !Kung—but all proved resourceful adaptations to particular eco-niches. No people, though, may have been forced to push the nutritional envelope further than those living at Earth's frozen extremes. The unusual makeup of the far-northern diet led Loren Cordain, a professor of evolutionary nutrition at Colorado State University at Fort Collins, to make an intriguing observation.

Four years ago, Cordain reviewed the macronutrient content (protein, carbohydrates, fat) in the diets of 229 hunter-gatherer groups listed in a series of journal articles collectively known as the Ethnographic Atlas. These are some of the oldest surviving human diets. In general, hunter-gatherers tend to eat more animal protein than we do in our standard Western diet, with its reliance on agriculture and carbohydrates derived from grains and starchy plants. Lowest of all in carbohydrate, and highest in combined fat and protein, are the diets of peoples living in the Far North, where they make up for fewer plant foods with extra fish. What's equally striking, though, says Cordain, is that these meat-and-fish diets also exhibit a natural "protein ceiling." Protein accounts for no more than 35 to 40 percent of their total calories, which suggests to him that's all the protein humans can comfortably handle.

Wild-animal fats are different from other fats. Farm animals typically have lots of highly saturated fat.

This ceiling, Cordain thinks, could be imposed by the way we process protein for energy. The simplest, fastest way to make energy is to convert carbohydrates into glucose, our body's primary fuel. But if the body is out of carbs, it can burn fat, or if necessary, break down protein. The name given to the convoluted business of making glucose from protein is gluconeogenesis. It takes place in the liver, uses a dizzying slew of enzymes, and creates nitrogen waste that has to be converted into urea and disposed of through the kidneys. On a truly traditional diet, says Draper, recalling his studies in the 1970s, Arctic people had plenty of protein but little carbohydrate, so they often relied on gluconeogenesis. Not only did they have bigger livers to handle the additional work but their urine volumes were also typically larger to get rid of the extra urea. Nonetheless, there appears to be a limit on how much protein the human liver can safely cope with: Too much overwhelms the liver's waste-disposal system, leading to protein poisoning—nausea, diarrhea, wasting, and death.

Whatever the metabolic reason for this syndrome, says John Speth, an archaeologist at the University of Michigan's Museum of Anthropology, plenty of evidence shows that hunters through the ages avoided protein excesses, discarding fat-depleted animals even when food was scarce. Early pioneers and trappers in North America encountered what looks like a similar affliction, sometimes referred to as rabbit starvation because rabbit meat is notoriously lean. Forced to subsist on fat-deficient meat, the men would gorge themselves, yet wither away. Protein can't be the sole source of energy for humans, concludes Cordain. Anyone eating a meaty diet that is low in carbohydrates must have fat as well.

Stefansson had arrived at this conclusion, too, while living among the Copper Eskimo. He recalled how he and his Eskimo companions had become quite ill after weeks of eating "caribou so skinny that there was no appreciable fat behind the eyes or in the marrow." Later he agreed to repeat the miserable experience at Bellevue Hospital, for science's sake, and for a while ate nothing but defatted meat. "The symptoms brought on at Bellevue by an incomplete meat diet [lean without fat] were exactly the same as in the Arctic . . . diarrhea and a feeling of general baffling discomfort," he wrote. He was restored with a fat fix but "had lost considerable weight." For the remainder of his year on meat, Stefansson tucked into his rations of chops and steaks with fat intact. "A normal meat diet is not a high-protein diet," he pronounced. "We were really getting three-quarters of our calories from fat." (Fat is more than twice as calorie dense as protein or carbohydrate, but even so, that's a lot of lard. A typical U.S diet provides about 35 percent of its calories from fat.)

Stefansson dropped 10 pounds on his meat-and-fat regimen and remarked on its "slenderizing" aspect, so perhaps it's no surprise he's been co-opted as a posthumous poster boy for Atkins-type diets. No discussion about diet these days can avoid Atkins. Even some researchers interviewed for this article couldn't resist referring to the Inuit way of eating as the "original Atkins." "Superficially, at a macronutrient level, the two diets certainly look similar," allows Samuel Klein, a nutrition researcher at Washington University in St. Louis, who's attempting to study how Atkins stacks up against conventional weight-loss diets. Like the Inuit diet, Atkins is low in carbohydrates and very high in fat. But numerous researchers, including Klein, point out that there are profound differences between the two diets, beginning with the type of meat and fat eaten.

Fats have been demonized in the United States, says Eric Dewailly, a professor of preventive medicine at Laval University in Quebec. But all fats are not created equal. This lies at the heart of a paradox—the Inuit paradox, if you will. In the Nunavik villages in northern Quebec, adults over 40 get almost half their calories from native foods, says Dewailly, and they don't die of heart attacks at nearly the same rates as other Canadians or Americans. Their cardiac death rate is about half of ours, he says. As someone who looks for links between diet and cardiovascular health, he's intrigued by that reduced risk. Because the traditional Inuit diet is "so restricted," he says, it's easier to study than the famously heart-healthy Mediterranean diet, with its cornucopia of vegetables, fruits, grains, herbs, spices, olive oil, and red wine.

A key difference in the typical Nunavik Inuit's diet is that more than 50 percent of the calories in Inuit native foods come from fats. Much more important, the fats come from wild animals.

Wild-animal fats are different from both farm-animal fats and processed fats, says Dewailly. Farm animals, cooped up and stuffed with agricultural grains (carbohydrates) typically have lots of solid, highly saturated fat. Much of our processed food is also riddled with solid fats, or so-called trans fats, such as the reengineered vegetable oils and shortenings cached in baked goods and snacks. "A lot of the packaged food on supermarket shelves contains them. So do commercial french fries," Dewailly adds.

Trans fats are polyunsaturated vegetable oils tricked up to make them more solid at room temperature. Manufacturers do this by hydrogenating the oils—adding extra hydrogen atoms to their molecular structures—which "twists" their shapes. Dewailly makes twisting sound less like a chemical transformation than a perversion, an act of public-health sabotage: "These man-made fats are dangerous, even worse for the heart than saturated fats." They not only lower high-density lipoprotein cholesterol (HDL, the "good" cholesterol) but they also raise low-density lipoprotein cholesterol (LDL, the "bad" cholesterol) and triglycerides, he says. In the process, trans fats set the stage for heart attacks because they lead to the increase of fatty buildup in artery walls.

Wild animals that range freely and eat what nature intended, says Dewailly, have fat that is far more healthful. Less of their fat is saturated, and more of it is in the monounsaturated form (like olive oil). What's more, cold-water fishes and sea mammals are particularly rich in polyunsaturated fats called n-3 fatty acids or omega-3 fatty acids. These fats appear to benefit the heart and vascular system. But the polyunsaturated fats in most Americans' diets are the omega-6 fatty acids supplied by vegetable oils. By contrast, whale blubber consists of 70 percent monounsaturated fat and close to 30 percent omega-3s, says Dewailly.

Dieting is the price we pay for too little exercise and too much mass-produced food.

Omega-3s evidently help raise HDL cholesterol, lower triglycerides, and are known for anticlotting effects. (Ethnographers have remarked on an Eskimo propensity for nosebleeds.) These fatty acids are believed to protect the heart from life-threatening arrhythmias that can lead to sudden cardiac death. And like a "natural aspirin," adds Dewailly, omega-3 polyunsaturated fats help put a damper on runaway inflammatory processes, which play a part in atherosclerosis, arthritis, diabetes, and other so-called diseases of civilization.

You can be sure, however, that Atkins devotees aren't routinely eating seal and whale blubber. Besides the acquired taste problem, their commerce is extremely restricted in the United States by the Marine Mammal Protection Act, says Bruce Holub, a nutritional biochemist in the department of human biology and nutritional sciences at the University of Guelph in Ontario.

"In heartland America it's probable they're not eating in an Eskimo-like way," says Gary Foster, clinical director of the Weight and Eating Disorders Program at the Pennsylvania School of Medicine. Foster, who describes himself as open-minded about Atkins, says he'd nonetheless worry if people saw the diet as a green light to eat all the butter and bacon—saturated fats—they want. Just before rumors surfaced that Robert Atkins had heart and weight problems when he died, Atkins officials themselves were stressing saturated fat should account for no more than 20 percent of dieters' calories. This seems to be a clear retreat from the diet's original don't-count-the-calories approach to bacon and butter and its happy exhortations to "plow into those prime ribs." Furthermore, 20 percent of calories from saturated fats is *double* what most nutritionists advise. Before plowing into those prime ribs, readers of a recent edition of the *Dr. Atkins' New Diet Revolution* are urged to take omega-3 pills to help protect their hearts. "If you watch carefully," says Holub wryly, "you'll see many popular U.S. diets have quietly added omega-3 pills, in the form of fish oil or flaxseed capsules, as supplements."

Needless to say, the subsistence diets of the Far North are not "dieting." Dieting is the price we pay for too little exercise and too much mass-produced food. Northern diets were a way of life in places too cold for agriculture, where food, whether hunted, fished, or foraged, could not be taken for granted. They were about keeping weight on.

This is not to say that people in the Far North were fat: Subsistence living requires exercise—hard physical work. Indeed, among the good reasons for native people to maintain their old way of eating, as far as it's possible today, is that it provides a hedge against obesity, type 2 diabetes, and heart disease. Unfortunately, no place on Earth is immune to the spreading taint of growth and development. The very well-being of the northern food chain is coming under threat from global warming, land development, and industrial pollutants in the marine environment. "I'm a pragmatist," says Cochran, whose organization is involved in pollution monitoring and disseminating food-safety information to native villages. "Global warming we don't have control over. But we can, for example, do cleanups of military sites in Alaska or of communication cables leaching lead into fish-spawning areas. We can help communities make informed food choices. A young woman of childbearing age may choose not to eat certain organ meats that concentrate contaminants. As individuals, we do have options. And eating our salmon and our seal is still a heck of a better option than pulling something processed that's full of additives off a store shelf."

Not often in our industrial society do we hear someone speak so familiarly about "our" food animals. We don't talk of "our pig" and "our beef." We've lost that creature feeling, that sense of kinship with food sources. "You're taught to think in boxes," says Cochran. "In our culture the connectivity between humans, animals, plants, the land they live on, and the air they share is ingrained in us from birth.

"You truthfully can't separate the way we get our food from the way we live," she says. "How we get our food is intrinsic to our culture. It's how we pass on our values and knowledge to the young. When you go out with your aunts and uncles to hunt or to gather, you learn to smell the air, watch the wind, understand the way the ice moves, know the land. You get to know where to pick which plant and what animal to take."

"It's part, too, of your development as a person. You share food with your community. You show respect to your elders by offering them the first catch. You give thanks to the animal that gave up its life for your sustenance. So you get all the physical activity of harvesting your own food, all the social activity of sharing and preparing it, and all the spiritual aspects as well," says Cochran. "You certainly don't get all that, do you, when you buy prepackaged food from a store."

"That's why some of us here in Anchorage are working to protect what's ours, so that others can continue to live back home in the villages," she adds. "Because if we don't take care of our food, it won't be there for us in the future. And if we lose our foods, we lose who we are." The word Inupiat means "the real people." "That's who we are," says Cochran.

Critical Thinking

1. What kinds of diseases are on the increase among the Inuit and why?
2. How does their traditional high-protein, high-fat diet compare with the "balanced diet" most of us grew up with? What does this mean, according to Harold Draper?
3. What are the contrasting sources of vitamins A, D, and C between our diet and the diet of the Inuit? What is the advantage of eating meat and fish raw?
4. What is a "protein ceiling"? How did hunter-gatherers cope with this problem?
5. Where do the more healthful fats (monounsaturated and omega-3 fatty acids) come from? What are their benefits?
6. Why is it that Atkins-dieters are not really eating in an "Eskimo-like way"?
7. What are the differences between the subsistence diets of the Far North and "dieting"?
8. Were people of the Far North fat? Why not? In what ways did the old way of eating protect them?
9. How is the northern food chain threatened?
10. In what sense is there a kinship with food sources in the Far North that our industrial societies do not have? Why is it also a part of one's development as a person?

Internet References

The Paleolithic Diet Page
www.paleodiet.com

The Institute for Intercultural Studies
www.interculturalstudies.org/main.html

Sociology Guy's Anthropology Links
www.trinity.edu/~mkearl/anthro.html

Article

Prepared by: Elvio Angeloni

Cell Phones, Sharing, and Social Status in an African Society

DANIEL JORDAN SMITH

Learning Outcomes

After reading this article, you will be able to:

- Discuss the economics, the politics, and the sociality of cell phone use in Nigeria.
- Discuss the ways in which cell phones are perceived as status symbols in Nigeria.

Contemporary processes of globalization have stimulated many anthropologists to begin asking new research questions. One important area of innovative research pertains to the global spread of technology and its influence on local people, practices, values, and behaviors. Globalization involves the worldwide transfer of technology, capital, industry, people, and cultural ideas. It has made the world a smaller place, but it has also increased social inequalities across the "digital divide."

In the twentieth century, radio and television played powerful roles in creating linkages between previously disconnected areas of the world. Without a doubt, new mass media brought the signs, symbols, images, and cultural values of the industrialized "First World" to people and communities in poorer "Third World" regions. The globalization of technology is not a top-down, unidirectional process. New technologies create new ways in which small groups of people can shape the ideas, values, political opinions, and even the actions of large groups of people within a particular town, district, country, or world region.

Recent technological developments are influencing people and communities in new ways, raising new research questions for anthropologists. One such development is the Internet, although on a global scale fewer people have access to that technology than the topic of this selection: cell phones. Like radio and television before them, cell phones create new and unprecedented opportunities for communication across distances. As this selection vividly demonstrates, the ways in which people use cell phones are powerfully influenced by local ideas, values, customs, and practices. In other words, global processes always take place within local contexts. Both the symbolic meaning and the social rules for using cell phones change in different cultural contexts.

Introduction

On July 19, 2004, the popular BBC Africa Service morning news program, *Network Africa,* carried a curious story from its Nigeria correspondent. He described a recent epidemic of rumors circulating in the country, purporting that anyone who answered calls on their cellular telephones originating from several specific numbers risked madness, and even death. I had heard a similar story in the previous few days from dozens of friends and acquaintances in and around the towns of Owerri and Umuahia in southeastern Nigeria, where I was conducting research. Ironically, cell phone usage around the country surged in the wake of the rumors, as people phoned and sent text messages to friends and relatives, warning them of the "killer numbers."

Once the popular rumors circulated widely, Nigerian newspapers carried stories printing some of the suspected numbers and incorporating quotations from citizens who allegedly witnessed the effects of these sinister calls (Akinsuyi 2004). But the newspapers also published statements from spokespersons for the country's major mobile telephone service providers, denying that such killer numbers existed (Ikhemuemhe 2004). Further, they published interviews with government authorities and university scientists disputing the technological feasibility of transmitting witchcraft through cell phones. Radio call-in programs and television talk shows buzzed with debate about the story, mesmerizing the nation for the better part of two weeks. Eventually, popular attention faded, as it had with regard to a previous rumor suggesting that men who carried cell phones in their pockets or strapped them to their belts risked becoming infertile.

The rumors that mobile phones might be implicated in infertility, madness, and murder are a testament to how dramatically this new technology has affected Nigeria. A few elite Nigerians had access to older cellular telephone technologies beginning in the 1990s, but the number of such phones was minuscule. The introduction of the Global System for Mobile Communications (GSM) technology to Nigeria in 2001 and the liberalization of Nigeria's previously government-controlled telecommunications industry transformed cell phones from an extreme rarity into an everyday technology to which literally millions of ordinary citizens have access. When GSM technology was first introduced in Nigeria, the country had only approximately 500,000 landlines for over 100 million people (Obadare 2004), a number which had not increased significantly in many years. By the end of 2004, less than four years after the first GSM cellular phones and services went on sale to the Nigerian public, the country had over 7 million subscribers (Mobile Africa 2005), with some recent estimates putting the number of mobile phones users in Nigeria at over 11 million (PANA 2005).

In addition, millions more people without their own phones were provided easy access to cell phone service, as individual cell phone owners became small-scale entrepreneurs, converting their personal phones into informal businesses. By the time the BBC story was broadcast, thousands of call centers, most with just one or two phones and a single attendant, dotted Nigeria's landscape. Every major city and many small towns are now connected, and countless rural and urban communities that have no running water and little or no electricity service are integrated into the country's vast and expanding mobile telephone network.

Cell phones have produced dramatic changes in communication in Nigeria, with many positive effects. Mobile phones have been integrated into long-standing patterns of social relationship, enabling Nigerians separated by great distances to continue to interact based on expectations of sharing and reciprocity. But just as important, they have become symbols of social status. Nigerians assert and express modern identities by purchasing, using, and publicly displaying the latest consumer commodities. Mastery of the new phone technology is a marker of being middle class, educated, and urban. Yet the reality is that cell phones represent a level of economic achievement that is out of reach to most Nigerians. The majority of new cell phone consumers experience the costs of usage as exorbitant, reinforcing the sense that middle-class status remains elusive. Thus, while the burgeoning popularity of cell phones in Nigeria, and throughout sub-Saharan Africa, represents the aspirations of ordinary people for better lives, this new technology exposes the pronounced and enduring nature of social inequality.

Cell Phone Economics

Owning and using a cell phone in Nigeria requires three primary investments: (1) buying a phone; (2) accessing service from one of the country's four major providers through the purchase of a SIM (Subscriber Identity Module) card that is installed in the back of the phone to connect it to the service network; and (3) procuring "recharge cards," through which call time is paid for by loading a unique pin number each time one wants to add credit to an individual account. While the phone and the SIM card are one-time acquisitions, access to service depends on the regular purchase of the recharge cards to load call time as previously purchased amounts are exhausted.

In 2005, new phones are available in Nigeria for as little as 6,000 naira (approximately 45 U.S. dollars), and as much as 60,000 naira (over U.S. $450), depending on the brand, the model, and the complexity of features offered on the phone. The price of SIM cards declined dramatically in the past several years, to about five to ten dollars, with companies sometimes offering free SIM cards as part of periodic marketing campaigns. The vast majority of customers use the "pay as you go" recharge card system.

Most crucial from the perspective of ordinary Nigerians is the cost of calls themselves. As with every other feature of cell phone service, the cost of calls has declined significantly over the four years since GSM service was introduced. But the price of calls per minute and per second (a choice between these rates is now available to most consumers) is still expensive, relative to both Nigerians' purchasing power and the cost of cell phone service in other countries (Obadare 2004). Importantly, although incoming calls are free, every outgoing call is charged—there are no free minutes per month or at night and on weekends, though lower rates apply in off-peak hours. Further, recharge cards expire. Credit not utilized within a specified period of time is forever lost. For example, ten dollars of credit would typically need to be used within about two weeks.

Initially, when GSM cell phone service was first introduced, domestic calls cost approximately 50 naira (37 U.S. cents) per minute. Recently, the cost has declined to about 25 naira (19 cents) per minute, with the precise amount depending upon the volume of calls per month, whether the call is in or out of network, the time of day, and so on. Each of the country's four main service providers (Glomobile, Mtel, MTN, and Vmobile) offers a diverse range of service packages and special deals, but most consumers cannot afford to make enough calls to qualify for the plans that offer the cheapest calling rates. Indeed, an entire discourse of complaint about the high cost of cell phone calls has emerged in Nigeria (Obadare 2004). Popular reaction to the economics of personal cell phone use has generated a new lexicon and a growing repertoire of behaviors designed to mitigate the financial burdens of cell phone ownership.

"The Fire That Consumes Money"

In southeastern Nigeria, where I work, and where the predominant language is Igbo, the vernacular name for a cell phone is *oku na iri ego,* which translates literally as "the fire that consumes money." This popular local name reflects ordinary citizens' frustrations with the perceived exorbitant costs of cell phone calls. New linguistic turns of phrase and innovative social practices that have evolved with the proliferation of cell phone technology build on people's aggravation over the strain of cell phone ownership, but they also indicate the degree to which cell phone culture has taken root in everyday life.

Nigerians have adapted their cell phone usage to suit their economic circumstances, and some aspects of the service plans offered by the country's main providers are clearly designed to attract and keep customers who cannot afford to make a high volume of phone calls. For example, the Short Messaging Systems (SMS), through which customers can send "text messages," is extremely popular in Nigeria and typically costs only 15 naira (about 10 U.S. cents) per message. Text messages must be limited in size, usually no more than 160 characters. Text messaging is particularly popular with younger customers and it has generated its own lexicon of abbreviations, an economy of language that has also become part of Nigeria's youth culture, as it has in other settings (for literature on text messaging generally see Fox 2001; Dooring 2002; and Sylvia and Hady 2004).

Text messaging has become a common way for Nigerians who cannot afford regular phone calls to communicate using the new technology. But for older people, and even among young folks, using text messages too frequently without also calling can be interpreted as sign of unwillingness to spend money on a particular relationship—reflecting either stinginess or a lack of deep concern about the relationship or both. As a consequence, although text messaging is extremely popular, people are careful not to rely on it too exclusively, lest they become objects of criticism. In times of economic hardship, the willingness to spend money on a phone call is evidence of interest or commitment to a relationship, whether it is a friendship, a family tie, a business partnership, or a romance. The consequences of the microeconomics of cell phone use reflect the importance and the complexity of how issues of wealth, inequality, and status are negotiated in human relationships.

"Flash Me, I Flash You"

Other common practices besides text messaging illustrate the economics and micropolitics of cell phone behavior, and the importance of these behaviors in navigating issues of inequality in social relationships. For example, a major consequence of the fact that many cell phone owners cannot afford to maintain credit on a regular basis is the innovation of what Nigerians call "flashing." To "flash" someone means to call the recipient's line and allow the phone to ring just once, so that the incoming number is displayed to the recipient, but the caller hangs up before the recipient answers. This way, the recipient knows the number of the person trying to reach him or her, and hopefully has enough credit to call back. Flashing is possible because one can make a call without paying for it as long as no one picks up. Under the prevailing plans in Nigeria, it is possible to receive incoming calls even when one does not have any credit.

From my experience observing scores of friends and acquaintances receiving flashes, whether or not the recipient of the flash could identify the caller from the incoming number was not necessarily a good predictor of a callback. Sometimes knowledge of the identity of the incoming caller created the incentive to call back immediately, perhaps out of obligation, affection, or some prior awareness about the reason for the call. Conversely, on other occasions, knowledge of the identity of the caller had the opposite effect, the attitude being that anyone who had something important to communicate would find a way to pay for a call, even if only for a minute or two. People often refused to call back after a flash out of suspicion that the caller wanted the recipient to bear the cost of the conversation. Nevertheless, unidentified flashes often sparked curiosity, and people frequently responded to them.

Given that countless Nigerians who own cell phones are often in a position where credit is exhausted or very low, and therefore very precious, flashing can sometimes become a comical exchange in which no one wants to bear the costs of a call. In the Pidgin English that is often the lingua franca in Nigeria, people expressed the phenomenon of reciprocal flashing, in which no one was willing to pay for a call, with the phrase "flash me, I flash you." Mostly in good humor, friends frequently suspected each other of trying to transfer and defray the costs of communication through flashing. As a consequence, people sometimes tried to answer their phones before the end of the first ring, engaging the call before the flasher could hang up. This practice was particularly common when someone flashed more than once, giving the recipient time to prepare for a quick answer. Over the past couple of years I witnessed numerous comic scenes where people plotted to "catch" flashers before they could hang up, making them pay for the connection.

Sharing Credit: Inequality and Sociality

Of course most people who communicate by telephone eventually see each other in person, and past episodes of flashing are often topics of discussion. A typical face-to-face conversation about flashing might include a query by the flasher as to why the recipient did not call back, followed by an admission (or assertion) by the recipient that he or she did not have any credit. The recipient, in turn, may accuse the flasher of having credit and being unwilling to use it. These mostly good-natured conversations reproduce some of the complexity of how people in Nigeria navigate the social representation of wealth more generally. On the one hand, using and sharing one's cell phone liberally are clear signals of wealth, and, like many kinds of conspicuous consumption in Nigeria, seemingly carefree cell phone usage can be rewarded with recognition and prestige. On the other hand, in Nigeria's current economic climate, in which most people are struggling to make ends meet, a strong ethos prevails in which even the relatively affluent portray themselves as just getting by, particularly among people who are otherwise their peers.

These contradictory dimensions of people's public representations of wealth play out constantly in the arena of cell phone socioeconomics. For those who really are struggling, claiming one has no credit can be a strategy for protecting a precious and dwindling resource. Conversely, using one's cell phone generously even when one cannot actually afford it can be a way of portraying or maintaining social status that is threatened by economic hardship. For those who are better off, claiming not to have credit can be a form of humility, representing oneself as just as much of a victim of Nigeria's unjust political economy as one's peers. But the balance can be precarious. Humility can easily be interpreted as stinginess if a wealthy person persists too long in feigning hardship. However, acting too carefree can be seen as ostentatious or arrogant. Ultimately, affluent people are meant to demonstrate and share their prosperity, but in ways that do not humiliate their peers. The proliferation of cell phones has created a very prominent sphere in which the micropolitics of social inequality in Nigeria are enacted (for other examples see Barber 1995; Cornwall 2002; and Smith 2004).

Although Nigerians' cell phone-related social behaviors illustrate the importance of economics in how people manage their phone usage, including strategizing about the social representation of one's wealth, it would be a mistake to emphasize only the economic dimensions of Nigeria's emerging cell phone culture and its associated behavior. A good deal of cell phone-related behavior requires a social rather than an economic interpretation.

Perhaps the most striking example is the way that Nigerians conceptualize cell phone credit. Clearly, everyone who uses cell phones knows how much phone calls cost, and people are aware of the exact amounts in which recharge cards are sold. Further, as the discussion above regarding the phenomenon of flashing suggests, there is a considerable degree of conscious jockeying with regard to sharing and spending one's credit. However, to a remarkable extent, Nigerians seem to think of cell phone credit in much different terms than they think of money. Once money is transformed into cell phone credit through the purchase and loading of recharge cards, cell phone credit becomes much more like food or drink than money, in the sense that people feel more entitled to share in it without the strict incursion of a debt that would be the case if one asked to borrow money. As with food or drink, there is a strong social expectation that cell phone credit should be shared if one has it.

My awareness of the difference between Nigerian and Western (or at least American) sensibilities in this matter was driven home to me by the experience of an American student who worked as my summer research assistant. She lived with a Nigerian family and found them amazingly hospitable and generous, to the point where they refused to allow her to pay rent or contribute to the household budget for food. She felt guilty about this, knowing the family's limited means, and we devised ways that she could contribute without offending her hosts. But when it came to the student's cell phone, the situation was quite the opposite. She had acquired a cell phone mainly so that her parents could call her at any time from the United States. Over the course of the summer, she found that people in the household had no compunctions about asking if she had credit, and, if she did, they had no hesitation in asking to use her phone to make calls. One young woman in the household asked to use her phone so often that the student finally became exasperated and reported it to me. She could not understand how the same family that was so generous and so unwilling to accept her money could expect to use her cell phone in ways that, from her perspective, seemed so insensitive.

Conceived of as a consumable commodity, cell phone credit was easily incorporated into long-standing traditions of sharing, gift giving, and reciprocity, in which people are expected and often genuinely desire to share without incurring the equivalent of a monetary debt. Of course money too is highly implicated in social relationships, and it can be gifted and shared as well as borrowed, lent, or spent, but it was clear from my student's experience, and from numerous similar interactions that I have since participated in and observed, that cell phone credit is transformed into a medium of social exchange that is much different from money once it is loaded into a phone. Nigerians routinely ask their friends and family, and even acquaintances of less intimacy, whether or not they have credit, in ways they would rarely, if ever, ask so openly about money.

The politics of sharing cell phone credit is nonetheless complicated, both because forms of nonmonetary sharing and reciprocity have their own moral economy, with numerous unspoken rules and expectations, and because cell phone credit is, in fact, in some ways more like money than are consumable commodities like food or drink. Even in the sharing of food and drink, in which Nigerians, like people in many societies, are extremely generous and social, there are expectations of generalized reciprocity (Bearman 1997). Although one does not incur a quantifiable debt by sharing someone's food, if, over time, one only takes and never gives, this will be recognized and admonished in some way. Similarly, with the sharing of cell phone credit, someone asking to make calls on another's phone cannot expect indefinite cooperation if favors are not eventually reciprocated.

However, cell phone credit is still more like money than is a beer or a plate of cooked meat. Although ordinary Nigerians have obviously participated in the conversion of cell phone credit from money into a commodity that carries a more social definition, this transformation is not complete. People routinely lied to their friends about their credit, and I observed countless instances in which people were "caught" misrepresenting their credit. At a club in Nigeria where I play tennis, men would commonly pick up a person's phone while he was on the court to check how much credit was available. Someone caught underreporting his credit would almost certainly have to relent and share his phone. Through such actions people contribute to the demonetization of cell phone credit. But this demonetization did not occur without ambivalence. Indeed, the social expectation that one must share phone credit contributed further to the notion that cell phones are a "fire that consumes money."

As these anecdotes suggest, sociality is at least as important a dynamic in Nigerian social life as inequality, and not just in terms of sharing, but also with regard to the importance of regularly greeting and communicating with people in one's social network. The preeminent value of sociality has greatly influenced cell phone usage, in ways that have significant economic implications, even if economic calculations are not always foremost in the minds of cell phone users. Although much of what I have described above demonstrates that Nigerians are highly conscious of the economics of cell phone use and deeply aware of the social implications of cell phone behavior, it is also true that people's penchant for regular communication for purely social purposes means that people make many calls just to say hello and to be in touch. To have a phone and not use it to reach out to family and friends is similar to the idea of living alone or preferring solitude and privacy to social interaction. For most Nigerians it is not only unconscionable, it is unthinkable (Uchendu 1965). As a consequence, although many Nigerians rightly extol the virtues of the country's new cell phone services for promoting business and facilitating a more effective and productive commercial sector, my observations suggest that the vast majority of ordinary customers use a good deal of their credit making calls that are the cellular telephone version of a friendly visit. All this suggests that while cell phone technology has sparked some changes in social life, in many ways the new technology has also adapted to and been incorporated into longer-standing behavioral customs.

"Glo with Pride:" Cell Phones as Status Symbols

As I sat down in the parlor of my friend's house in the southeastern town of Owerri, her twenty-three-year-old son, Uzoma, inquired whether I owned a cell phone. I said I did, and he asked to see it. After a quick inspection of my very simple and obviously low-end Motorola phone, Uzoma declared dismissively: "This phone doesn't fit you." He meant that a person of my status should have a fancier and more expensive phone, preferably the type currently most popular in Nigeria, where the face flips open, the phone has numerous elaborate technical features, and the screen looks like a computer LCD. I defended my simple phone, but I was not surprised at Uzoma's evaluation. I had encountered this reaction to my phone many times before in a society where cell phones have become important markers of social status.[1]

The relatively educated, mostly urban, and at least marginally economically successful Nigerians who own the majority of the country's more than ten million cell phones are acutely aware of the status distinctions conferred by different models. People are constantly noting the quality of their peers' phones, openly conveying approval or disapproval in ways that consciously connect cell phones to social status. Even where people cannot afford to upgrade their phones, the quality of one's cell phone cover and the type and number of accessories owned can be the subject of more fine-grained attempts to assert both status and fashion. Indeed, as status symbols, the cell phones operate at the cusp between economics and fashion, marking both financial position and sense of style. Uzoma assumed I could afford a more expensive phone, so he concluded that I was either too cheap to own a phone fit for a man of my means or too fashion-challenged to know that my phone was a disgrace.

In a huge country like Nigeria, where many people migrate from their villages of origin to cities and towns in search of education, employment, and economic advancement (Geschiere and Gugler 1998; Gugler 2002), the advent of cell phones in a context where landlines served less than 1 percent of the population has revolutionized communication between family and friends separated by long distances. It is little wonder that so many people want cell phones, or that people who can barely afford some of the basic necessities of everyday life make extraordinary efforts to acquire one. But aside from the practical advantages of cell phone ownership, there is no doubt that cell phones have become an important form of symbolic capital, and that the social status conferred by owning a cell phone is a major motivation for many people (Bourdieu 1984). The cell phone companies cultivate and exploit the symbolic dimensions of cell phone ownership in their advertising, and the pressure of seeing peers enjoy the benefits and social recognition of cell phone ownership induces ever larger numbers of consumers to take the leap.

Whereas just ten years ago, before the advent of GSM technology in Nigeria, cell phones were the exclusive province of the superelite, by 2004 many Nigerians who were not wealthy enough to own their own houses and could not afford to buy a used car were able to acquire the latest marker of modernity. The transition from an elite exoticism to an almost essential accessory for an aspiring middle class happened remarkably fast. Just two years ago, Umuahia, a small city of less than 200,000 that is the capital of Abia State, had not yet been linked to the network of any of the four main service providers. However, for those who really wanted cell phone service, a regional company called Baudex provided a mostly effective but very expensive service.

At the social club where I frequently played tennis, a playground for the town's elite, approximately fifteen to twenty men owned these Baudex phones in the summer of 2003. To call further attention to the status they displayed by owning and sporting these expensive phones, the owners formed a club within the club. They called themselves "*Ofo* United." "*Ofo*" refers to a mystical staff that is the emblem of traditional authority in Igbo society, a symbol that implies supernatural backing. "United" presumably refers to the name of famous football teams, most notably the world-famous Manchester United, but also to teams in Nigeria that use "United" in their names. The members of *Ofo* United sometimes further separated themselves from other members of the larger club, sharing a roasted goat and several cartons of beer, greeting each other saying "*Ofo* United," and brandishing their phones like some sort of secret society symbol. Just a year later, all this changed dramatically, as both MTN and Glomobile had established full service in Umuahia. By the time I left Nigeria in December of 2004, literally every member of the tennis club had a phone, as did the club's receptionists, one of the bar girls, and some of the kitchen staff. *Ofo* United was no more.

As cell phones have come within the reach of more ordinary citizens, their availability has only intensified the status competition associated with the new technology. Just as the poorest Nigerians have for many years worn watches that do not keep time in order to appear better off than they are, one now sees many young people carrying cell phones that are just shells—though being exposed in such a deception is worse than having no phone at all. Because so many people can aspire to having a cell phone, the distinctions noticed with regard to brands, models, and accessories have become even more fine-grained. Many wealthier people now own multiple phones, with one line for each provider, and they carry them wherever they go. Having a cell phone is no longer so distinctive, but having two or three is still notable. Similarly, making calls to friends or relatives in London or New York, seemingly without a care about the higher cost, can still impress one's peers. In late 2004, camera phones were just hitting the Nigerian market, and I have no doubt they will be all the rage in a very short time.

Conclusion

Although it is impossible to pinpoint the origin of the "killer numbers" rumors described at the start of this article, I suggest that their currency and appeal were related to popular discontents about the role of cell phones in highlighting and sometimes aggravating social inequality. Some speculated that the rumors were the work of one provider trying to undermine the business of another (the killer numbers were first associated with the phone numbers of one company, though, in time, it spread to them all). Others argued that the rumors were a form of consumer revenge, with the allegations meant to damage the reputation and profits of companies toward which customers felt increasing anger. Still others suggested that the rumors were started by some among the vast majority of Nigerians who still cannot afford to own cell phones, in order to strike fear into those who were intimidating their economic inferiors with their ostentatious use of this flashy new technology. More important than these theories about origin is the speed with which the rumors spread and the extent to which they captured popular imagination. The fascination they generated reflects the fact that, as happy as most Nigerians are for their newfound access to a modern communications technology, ordinary citizens remain extremely discontented over the extent of inequality in their society. The new technology is being interpreted, to a large extent, in relation to these discontents.

Note

1. In 2000, *The New York Times* published an article suggesting the importance of cell phones not only for displaying social status generally, but for the attraction of mates. The newspaper account drew on an article in the journal *Human Nature,* entitled "Mobile Phones as Lekking Devices among Human

Males" (Lycett and Dunbar 2000). Regardless of whether one finds a sociobiological argument convincing, the association of cell phones with social status seems to strike a chord across many societies.

References

Akinsuyi, Yemi. 2004. Anxiety Over 'Satanic' GSM Phone Numbers. *This Day* (Nigeria), July 23.

Barber, Karin. 1995. Money, Self-Realization, and the Person Yoruba Texts. In *Money Matters: Instability, Values and Social Payments in the Modern History of West African Communities,* ed. J. Guyer, 205–224. Portsmouth, NH: Heinemann.

Bearman, Peter. 1997. Generalized Exchange. *American Journal of Sociology* 102(5): 1383–1415.

Bourdieu, Pierre. 1984. *Distinction: A Social Critique of the Judgement of Taste.* Translated by Richard Nice. Cambridge: Harvard University Press.

Cornwall, Andrea. 2002. Spending Power: Love, Money, and the Reconfiguration of Gender Relations in Ado-Odo, Southwestern Nigeria. *American Ethnologist* 29(4): 963–980.

Dooring, Nicolas. 2002. 'Kurzm-wird-gesendet'—Abbreviations and Acronyms in SMS Communication (Short-Message-Service). *Muttersparche.*

Fox, Barry. 2001. No 2MORO for Text Messaging Lingo. *New Scientist* 171(2298): 24.

Geschiere, Peter, and Josef Gugler. 1998. The Urban-Rural Connection: Changing Issues of Belonging and Identification. *Africa* 68(3): 309–319.

Gugler, Josef. 2002. The Son of a Hawk Does Not Remain Abroad: The Urban-Rural Connection in Africa. *African Studies Review* 45(1): 21–41.

Ikhemuemhe, Godfrey. 2004. The Killer Phone Rumour—Operators Cry Foul. *Vanguard* (Nigeria), July 26, 2004.

Lycett, John, and Robin Dunbar. 2000. Mobile Phones as Lekking Devices among Human Males. *Human Nature* 11(1): 93–104.

Mobile Africa. 2005. Cellular/Mobile Phone Networks in Africa, www.mobileafrica.net/mobile-phone-networks-in-africa.php. (Accessed June 7, 2005).

Obadare, Ebenezer. 2004. "The Great GSM (cell phone) Boycott: Civil Society, Big Business and the State in Nigeria." Dark Roast Occasional Paper Series, No. 18. Cape Town: South Africa: Isandla Institute.

PANA (Pan African News Agency). 2005. Nigeria's Phone Subscriber Base Hits 12 Million. *PanAfrican News Agency Daily Newswire,* May 4.

Smith, Daniel Jordan. 2004. Burials and Belonging in Nigeria: Rural-Urban Relations and Social Inequality in a Contemporary African Ritual. *American Anthropologist* 106(3): 569–579.

Sylvia, K. N., and S. W. Hady. 2004. Communication Pattern with SMS: Short Message Service and MMS: Multimedia Message Service as a Trend of Conduct of Modern Teenagers. *International Journal of Psychology* 39(5–6): 289.

Uchendu, Victor. 1965. *The Igbo of Southeast Nigeria.* Fort Worth, TX: Holt, Reinhart, Winston.

Critical Thinking

1. How and why does cell phone use touch upon wealth, inequality, and status in Nigeria? How are these issues reflected in the vernacular name, "the fire that eats money" and in the use of text messaging? In "flashing"?
2. Describe the economic dimensions of cell phone use and sharing.
3. How do Nigerians think about cell phone credit in different terms than they think of money?
4. In what sense is cell phone use a reflection of sociality?
5. In what respects can cell phones be seen as status symbols in Nigeria?

Internet References

Smithsonian Institution

www.si.edu

The Royal Anthropological Institute of Great Britain and Ireland (RAI)

www.therai.org.uk

Daniel Jordan Smith, "Cell Phones, Sharing, and Social Status in African Society." Reprinted with permission of the author.

Article

Prepared by: Elvio Angeloni

Wanted: Compassion

When empathy wanes, the best response might be to strengthen compassion.

BRYAN GOODWIN

Learning Outcomes

After reading this article, you will be able to:

- Discuss the evidence that we Americans have lost our collective sense of empathy. Describe and explain the anti-intellectualism that is rampant today in America.
- Discuss the importance of compassion and how it can be promoted among young people. The polarization implicit in today's "tribalism" and the author's suggestion as to how scientists should deal with it.

Incivility in America has risen to the level of a national crisis, according to a survey of U.S. adults by the public relations firm Weber Shandwick (2017). Respondents said they see rudeness at every turn—not just the stuff spewing from TV news, politicians, and social media, but even while driving, shopping, and working. Many perceive that at the heart of this, lack of civility is unwillingness to understand or show concern for others' feelings—basically, a troubling loss of *empathy*.

Have we Americans lost our collective sense of *empathy*?

Caring Less about Caring

One answer to that question might be found in a series of studies conducted over the past few decades designed to measure college students' empathic concern and perspective taking. The studies asked students to respond to statements like "I often have tender, concerned feelings for people less fortunate than me" and "I try to look at everybody's side of a disagreement before I make a decision." Affirmative responses predict more prosocial behaviors, like volunteering and donating money, and fewer antisocial behaviors, like verbal aggression. Thus, we might find it alarming that these studies find that between 1979 and 2009, levels of empathic concern and perspective taking dropped by 48 percent and 34 percent, respectively (Konrath, O'Brien, & Hsing, 2011).

More recently, a team of Harvard researchers reported that when they asked 10,000 middle and high school students whether achievement, happiness, or caring for others was most important, 80 percent chose achievement or happiness over benevolence. As one student put it, "If you're not happy, life is nothing. After that, you want to do well. And after that, expend any excess energy on others" (Weissbourd & Jones, 2014, p. 1).

Where, we might wonder, are kids getting such antisocial messages? Movies? Video games? Well, no—it's from us. In the Harvard study, 80 percent of students said their parents were more concerned about their achievement than about them caring for others. Students were three times more likely to agree than disagree with the statement, "My parents are prouder if I get good grades in my classes than if I'm a caring community member in class and school" (Weissbourd & Jones, 2014, p. 1). The same went for students' perceptions of what teachers value.

So, if we've somehow rewired kids' brains to feel less empathy, what we can do to bring it back?

Feeling Your Pain

Let's first examine what happens in our brains when we experience empathy—that is, feel with others. We humans have an amazing capacity to experience others' emotions. Brain research shows that we fire almost identical neural networks when we see others in pain as when we experience pain ourselves (Singer & Klimecki, 2014). In other words, we actually feel other people's pain—which can prompt us to rush to their aid.

Yet this can also create *empathic distress* or *burnout* when we feel others' pain too intensely or for too long. For example, the longer students stay in medical school, the less empathy they feel (Neumann et al., 2011). Studies also reveal that we mute our empathic responses when we view those in pain as members of a different group (such as players on a different team) or as deserving of their pain (for instance, if we saw them playing unfairly; Singer & Klimecki, 2014).

So, in a world of 24-hour access to other people's suffering on television and computer screens, we might be forgiven for experiencing some empathic burnout. One response to such distress might be to insulate ourselves from those feelings by casting others as members of an out-group or chalking up their misfortunes to their own misdeeds.

Compassion: Mightier than Empathy?

A better response, however, would be to recognize that what's often more important than empathy is a different emotion, one that fires entirely different neural networks in our brains and causes us to feel *for* other people—becoming concerned for their well-being and wanting to help them, yet not necessarily mirroring their emotions. This emotion is compassion. As it turns out, we're more likely to help others when we feel compassion versus empathy (Batson, 2009). Moreover, it's possible to cultivate compassion. "Loving kindness training" is a type of meditative exercise during which people generate feelings of kindness toward those close to them and then apply those feelings toward strangers and those with whom they disagree. After such training, people are not only more likely to engage in altruistic acts, they also feel happier (Frederickson et al., 2008).

So perhaps instead of encouraging kids to feel empathy, we should help them develop compassion for others by, for instance:

- *Strengthening perspective taking*. Educators can help students consider what other people are thinking, feeling, and motivated by as we discuss literature, history, and science—or listen to different approaches to solving math problems.
- *Helping kids practice caring*. As with anything, compassion takes daily practice—which we can provide students through well-chosen classroom jobs or community service.
- *Measuring and valuing compassion*. What we measure is what we get. Schools might include measures of compassion in climate surveys, tally total hours of community service, and celebrate students who engage in "random acts of kindness."

As the Harvard team noted in its report, the sad irony of parents' overemphasis on kids' personal achievement and happiness is that it produces neither; if anything, such emphasis creates stressed-out kids who lack the coping skills to bounce back from disappointment. Meanwhile, numerous studies have shown that when we help others, we increase our own sense of well-being (Weissbourd & Jones, 2014). Therein lies, perhaps, the key lesson to offer students: that the most important achievements and the greatest happiness are to be found in helping others.

References

Batson, C. D. (2009). These things called empathy: Eight related but distinct phenomena. In J. Decety & W. Ickes (Eds.), *The social neuroscience of empathy* (pp. 3–15). Cambridge, MA: MIT Press.

Frederickson, B. L., Cohn, M. A., Coffey, K. A., Pek, J., & Finkel, S. M. (2008). Open hearts build lives: Positive emotions, induced through loving-kindness meditation, build consequential resources. *Journal of Personal Social Psychology*, 95(5), 1045–1062.

Konrath, S. H., O'Brien, E. H., & Hsing, C. (2011). Changes in dispositional empathy in American college students over time: A meta-analysis. *Personality and Social Psychology Review*, 15(2), 180–198.

Neumann, M., Edelhäuser, F., Tauschel, D., Fischer, M. R., Wirtz, M., et al. (2011). Empathy decline and its reasons: A systematic review of studies with medical students and residents. *Academic Medicine*, 86(8), 996–1009.

Singer, T., & Klimecki, O. M. (2014). Empathy and compassion. *Current Biology*, 24(18), R875–R878.

Weber Shandwick. (2017). *Civility in America VII: The state of civility*. New York: Author.

Weissbourd, R., & Jones, S. M., with Anderson, T. R., Kahn, J., & Russell, M. (2014). *The children we mean to raise: The real messages adults are sending about values*. Cambridge, MA: Making Caring Common Project, Harvard Graduate School of Education.

Critical Thinking

1. Why has there been a loss of empathy in America?
2. How can we best promote kindness and happiness in America?

Internet References

How to Teach Civility During Divisive Times

https://www.parentmap.com/article/teaching-children-empathy-civility-politics

Parents Value Grades Over Kindness, Kids Say In New Study

https://www.today.com/parents/parents-value-grades-over-kindness-kids-say-new-study-1D79845326

Positive Psychology Promotes Civility

https://www.psychologytoday.com/us/blog/positive-psychology-in-the-classroom/201302/positive-psychology-promotes-civility

Promoting Civility and Tolerance in Our Schools and Communities

http://ipsinstitute.org/wp-content/uploads/2017/12/Promoting-Civility-and-Tolerance-Report.pdf

Bryan Goodwin (bgoodwin@mcrel.org) is president and CEO of McREL International, Denver, CO. He is the lead author of *Balanced Leadership for Powerful Learning* (ASCD, 2015).

Unit 4

UNIT

Prepared by: Elvio Angeloni

Other Families, Other Ways

Because most people in small-scale societies of the past spent their whole lives within a local area, it is understandable that their primary interactions—economic, religious, and otherwise—were with their relatives. It also makes sense that, through marriage customs, they strengthened those kinship relationships that clearly defined their mutual rights and obligations. More recently, the family structure has had to be surprisingly flexible and adaptive.

For these reasons, anthropologists have looked upon family and kinship as the key mechanisms for transmitting culture from one generation to the next. Social changes may have been slow to take place throughout the world, but as social horizons have widened, family relationships and community alliances are increasingly based upon new principles. Even when birth rates have increased, kinship networks have diminished in size and strength. As people have increasingly become involved with others as coworkers in a market economy, our associations depend more and more upon factors such as personal aptitudes, educational backgrounds, and job opportunities. Yet the family still exists. Except for some rather unusual exceptions, the family is small, but still functions in its age-old nurturing and protective role, even under conditions where there is little affection or under conditions of extreme poverty and a high infant mortality rate. Beyond the immediate family, the situation is in a state of flux. Certain ethnic groups, especially those in poverty, still have a need for the broader network and in some ways seem to be reformulating those ties.

We do not know where these changes will lead us and which ones will ultimately prevail. One thing is certain: Anthropologists will be there to document the trends, because the discipline of anthropology has had to change as well. Indeed, anthropologists exhibit a growing interest in the study of complex societies where old theoretical perspectives are inadequate. The current trends, however, do not necessarily depict the decline of the kinship unit. The large family network is still the best guarantee of individual survival and well-being in an urban setting.

Article

Prepared by: Elvio Angeloni

When Brothers Share a Wife

Among Tibetans, the Good Life Relegates Many Women to Spinsterhood

MELVYN C. GOLDSTEIN

Learning Outcomes

After reading this article, you will be able to:

- Discuss why "fraternal polyandry" is socially acceptable in Tibet but not in our society.
- Explain the disappearance and subsequent revival of fraternal polyandry in Tibet.

Eager to reach home, Dorje drives his yaks hard over the 17,000-foot mountain pass, stopping only once to rest. He and his two older brothers, Pema and Sonam, are jointly marrying a woman from the next village in a few weeks, and he has to help with the preparations.

Dorje, Pema, and Sonam are Tibetans living in Limi, a 200-square-mile area in the northwest corner of Nepal, across the border from Tibet. The form of marriage they are about to enter—fraternal polyandry in anthropological parlance—is one of the world's rarest forms of marriage but is not uncommon in Tibetan society, where it has been practiced from time immemorial. For many Tibetan social strata, it traditionally represented the ideal form of marriage and family.

The mechanics of fraternal polyandry are simple. Two, three, four, or more brothers jointly take a wife, who leaves her home to come and live with them. Traditionally, marriage was arranged by parents, with children, particularly females, having little or no say. This is changing somewhat nowadays, but it is still unusual for children to marry without their parents' consent. Marriage ceremonies vary by income and region and range from all the brothers sitting together as grooms to only the eldest one formally doing so. The age of the brothers plays an important role in determining this: very young brothers almost never participate in actual marriage ceremonies, although they typically join the marriage when they reach their mid-teens.

The eldest brother is normally dominant in terms of authority, that is, in managing the household, but all the brothers share the work and participate as sexual partners. Tibetan males and females do not find the sexual aspect of sharing a spouse the least bit unusual, repulsive, or scandalous, and the norm is for the wife to treat all the brothers the same.

Offspring are treated similarly. There is no attempt to link children biologically to particular brothers, and a brother shows no favoritism toward his child even if he knows he is the real father because, for example, his other brothers were away at the time the wife became pregnant. The children, in turn, consider all of the brothers as their fathers and treat them equally, even if they also know who is their real father. In some regions children use the term "father" for the eldest brother and "father's brother" for the others, while in other areas they call all the brothers by one term, modifying this by the use of "elder" and "younger."

Unlike our own society, where monogamy is the only form of marriage permitted, Tibetan society allows a variety of marriage types, including monogamy, fraternal polyandry, and polygyny. Fraternal polyandry and monogamy are the most common forms of marriage, while polygyny typically occurs in cases where the first wife is barren. The widespread practice of fraternal polyandry, therefore, is not the outcome of a law requiring brothers to marry jointly. There is choice, and in fact, divorce traditionally was relatively simple in Tibetan society. If a brother in a polyandrous marriage became dissatisfied and wanted to separate, he simply left the main house and set up his own household. In such cases, all the children stayed in the main household with the remaining brother(s), even if the departing brother was known to be the real father of one or more of the children.

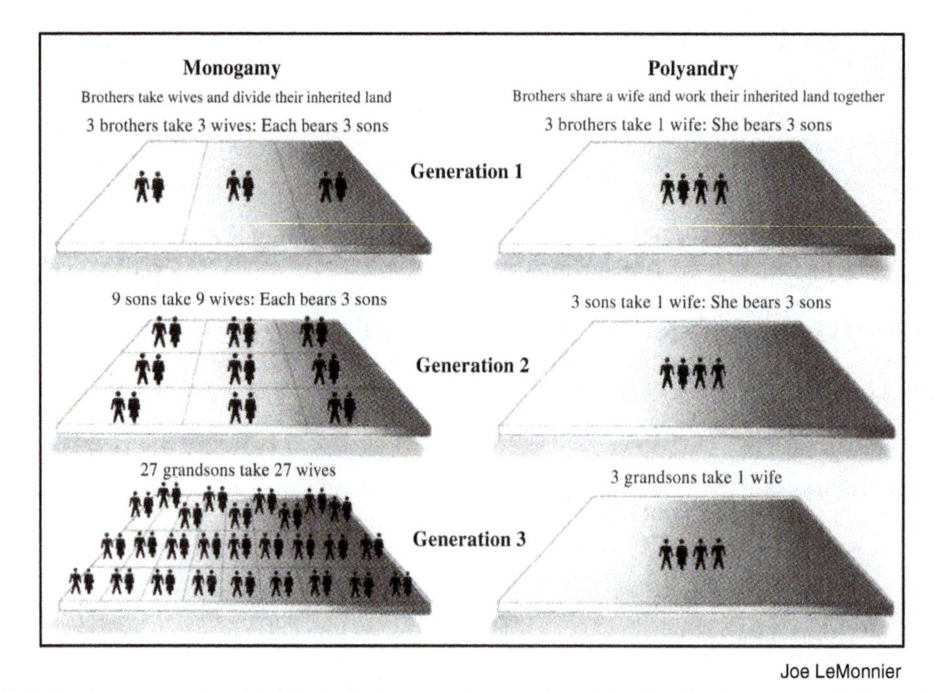

Joe LeMonnier

Family Planning in Tibet An economic rationale for fraternal polyandry is outlined in the diagram, which emphasizes only the male offspring in each generation. If every wife is assumed to bear three sons, a family splitting up into monogamous households would rapidly multiply and fragment the family land. In this case, a rule of inheritance, such as primogeniture, could retain the family land intact, but only at the cost of creating many landless male offspring. In contrast, the family practicing fraternal polyandry maintains a steady ratio of persons to land.

The Tibetans' own explanation for choosing fraternal polyandry is materialistic. For example, when I asked Dorje why he decided to marry with his two brothers rather than take his own wife, he thought for a moment, then said it prevented the division of his family's farm (and animals) and thus facilitated all of them achieving a higher standard of living. And when I later asked Dorje's bride whether it wasn't difficult for her to cope with three brothers as husbands, she laughed and echoed the rationale of avoiding fragmentation of the family and land, adding that she expected to be better off economically, since she would have three husbands working for her and her children.

Exotic as it may seem to Westerners, Tibetan fraternal polyandry is thus in many ways analogous to the way primogeniture functioned in nineteenth-century England. Primogeniture dictated that the eldest son inherited the family estate, while younger sons had to leave home and seek their own employment—for example, in the military or the clergy. Primogeniture maintained family estates intact over generations by permitting only one heir per generation. Fraternal polyandry also accomplishes this but does so by keeping all the brothers together with just one wife so that there is only one *set* of heirs per generation.

While Tibetans believe that in this way fraternal polyandry reduces the risk of family fission, monogamous marriages among brothers need not necessarily precipitate the division of the family estate: brothers could continue to live together, and the family land could continue to be worked jointly. When I asked Tibetans about this, however, they invariably responded that such joint families are unstable because each wife is primarily oriented to her own children and interested in their success and well-being over that of the children of the other wives. For example, if the youngest brother's wife had three sons while the eldest brother's wife had only one daughter, the wife of the youngest brother might begin to demand more resources for her children since, as males, they represent the future of the family. Thus, the children from different wives in the same generation are competing sets of heirs, and this makes such families inherently unstable. Tibetans perceive that conflict will spread from the wives to their husbands and consider this likely to cause family fission. Consequently, it is almost never done.

Although Tibetans see an economic advantage to fraternal polyandry, they do not value the sharing of a wife as an end in itself. On the contrary, they articulate a number of problems inherent in the practice. For example, because authority is customarily exercised by the eldest brother, his younger male siblings have to subordinate themselves with little hope of changing their status within the family. When these younger brothers are aggressive and individualistic, tensions and difficulties often occur despite there being only one set of heirs.

In addition, tension and conflict may arise in polyandrous families because of sexual favoritism. The bride normally sleeps with the eldest brother, and the two have the responsibility to see to it that the other males have opportunities for sexual access. Since the Tibetan subsistence economy requires males to travel a lot, the temporary absence of one or more brothers facilitates this, but there are also other rotation practices. The cultural ideal unambiguously calls for the wife to show equal affection and sexuality to each of the brothers (and vice versa), but deviations from this ideal occur, especially when there is a sizable difference in age between the partners in the marriage.

Dorje's family represents just such a potential situation. He is fifteen years old and his two older brothers are twenty-five and twenty-two years old. The new bride is twenty-three years old, eight years Dorje's senior. Sometimes such a bride finds the youngest husband immature and adolescent and does not treat him with equal affection; alternatively, she may find his youth attractive and lavish special attention on him. Apart from that consideration, when a younger male like Dorje grows up, he may consider his wife "ancient" and prefer the company of a woman his own age or younger. Consequently, although men and women do not find the idea of sharing a bride or bridegroom repulsive, individual likes and dislikes can cause familial discord.

Two reasons have commonly been offered for the perpetuation of fraternal polyandry in Tibet: that Tibetans practice female infanticide and therefore have to marry polyandrously, owing to a shortage of females; and that Tibet, lying at extremely high altitudes, is so barren and bleak that Tibetans would starve without resort to this mechanism. A Jesuit who lived in Tibet during the eighteenth century articulated this second view: "One reason for this most odious custom is the sterility of the soil, and the small amount of land that can be cultivated owing to the lack of water. The crops may suffice if the brothers all live together, but if they form separate families they would be reduced to beggary."

Both explanations are wrong, however. Not only has there never been institutionalized female infanticide in Tibet, but Tibetan society gives females considerable rights, including inheriting the family estate in the absence of brothers. In such cases, the woman takes a bridegroom who comes to live in her family and adopts her family's name and identity. Moreover, there is no demographic evidence of a shortage of females. In Limi, for example, there were (in 1974) sixty females and fifty-three males in the fifteen- to thirty-five-year age category, and many adult females were unmarried.

The second reason is also incorrect. The climate in Tibet is extremely harsh, and ecological factors do play a major role perpetuating polyandry, but polyandry is not a means of preventing starvation. It is characteristic, not of the poorest segments of the society, but rather of the peasant landowning families.

In the old society, the landless poor could not realistically aspire to prosperity, but they did not fear starvation. There was a persistent labor shortage throughout Tibet, and very poor families with little or no land and few animals could subsist through agricultural labor, tenant farming, craft occupations such as carpentry, or by working as servants. Although the per person family income could increase somewhat if brothers married polyandrously and pooled their wages, in the absence of inheritable land, the advantage of fraternal polyandry was not generally sufficient to prevent them from setting up their own households. A more skilled or energetic younger brother could do as well or better alone, since he would completely control his income and would not have to share it with his siblings. Consequently, while there was and is some polyandry among the poor, it is much less frequent and more prone to result in divorce and family fission.

An alternative reason for the persistence of fraternal polyandry is that it reduces population growth (and thereby reduces the pressure on resources) by relegating some females to lifetime spinsterhood. Fraternal polyandrous marriages in Limi (in 1974) averaged 2.35 men per woman, and not surprisingly, 31 percent of the females of child-bearing age (twenty to forty-nine) were unmarried. These spinsters either continued to live at home, set up their own households, or worked as servants for other families. They could also become Buddhist nuns. Being unmarried is not synonymous with exclusion from the reproductive pool. Discreet extramarital relationships are tolerated, and actually half of the adult unmarried women in Limi had one or more children. They raised these children as single mothers, working for wages or weaving cloth and blankets for sale. As a group, however, the unmarried woman had far fewer offspring than the married women, averaging only 0.7 children per woman, compared with 3.3 for married women, whether polyandrous, monogamous, or polygynous. While polyandry helps regulate population, this function of polyandry is not consciously perceived by Tibetans and is not the reason they consistently choose it.

If neither a shortage of females nor the fear of starvation perpetuates fraternal polyandry, what motivates brothers, particularly younger brothers, to opt for this system of marriage? From the perspective of the younger brother in a land-holding family, the main incentive is the attainment or maintenance of the good life. With polyandry, he can expect a more secure and higher standard of living, with access not only to this family's land and animals but also to its inherited collection of clothes, jewelry, rugs, saddles, and horses. In addition, he will experience less work pressure and much greater security because all responsibility does not fall on one "father." For Tibetan brothers, the question is whether to trade off the greater personal freedom inherent in monogamy for the real or potential economic security, affluence, and social prestige associated with life in a larger, labor-rich polyandrous family.

A brother thinking of separating from his polyandrous marriage and taking his own wife would face various disadvantages. Although in the majority of Tibetan regions all brothers theoretically have rights to their family's estate, in reality Tibetans are reluctant to divide their land into small fragments. Generally, a younger brother who insists on leaving the family will receive only a small plot of land, if that. Because of its power and wealth, the rest of the family usually can block any attempt of the younger brother to increase his share of land through litigation. Moreover, a younger brother may not even get a house and cannot expect to receive much above the minimum in terms of movable possessions, such as furniture, pots, and pans. Thus, a brother contemplating going it on his own must plan on achieving economic security and the good life not through inheritance but through his own work.

The obvious solution for younger brothers—creating new fields from virgin land—is generally not a feasible option. Most Tibetan populations live at high altitudes (above 12,000 feet), where arable land is extremely scarce. For example, in Dorje's village, agriculture ranges only from about 12,900 feet, the lowest point in the area, to 13,300 feet. Above that altitude, early frost and snow destroy the staple barley crop. Furthermore, because of the low rainfall caused by the Himalayan rain shadow, many areas in Tibet and northern Nepal that are within the appropriate altitude range for agriculture have no reliable sources of irrigation. In the end, although there is plenty of unused land in such areas, most of it is either too high or too arid.

Even where unused land capable of being farmed exists, clearing the land and building the substantial terraces necessary for irrigation constitute a great undertaking. Each plot has to be completely dug out to a depth of two to two and half feet so that the large rocks and boulders can be removed. At best, a man might be able to bring a few new fields under cultivation in the first years after separating from his brothers, but he could not expect to acquire substantial amounts of arable land this way.

In addition, because of the limited farmland, the Tibetan subsistence economy characteristically includes a strong emphasis on animal husbandry. Tibetan farmers regularly maintain cattle, yaks, goats, and sheep, grazing them in the areas too high for agriculture. These herds produce wool, milk, cheese, butter, meat, and skins. To obtain these resources, however, shepherds must accompany the animals on a daily basis. When first setting up a monogamous household, a younger brother like Dorje would find it difficult to both farm and manage animals.

In traditional Tibetan society, there was an even more critical factor that operated to perpetuate fraternal polyandry—a form of hereditary servitude somewhat analogous to serfdom in Europe. Peasants were tied to large estates held by aristocrats, monasteries, and the Lhasa government. They were allowed the use of some farmland to produce their own subsistence but were required to provide taxes in kind and corvée (free labor) to their lords. The corvée was a substantial hardship, since a peasant household was in many cases required to furnish the lord with one laborer daily for most of the year and more on specific occasions such as the harvest. This enforced labor, along with the lack of new land and ecological pressure to pursue both agriculture and animal husbandry, made polyandrous families particularly beneficial. The polyandrous family allowed an internal division of adult labor, maximizing economic advantage. For example, while the wife worked the family fields, one brother could perform the lord's corvée, another could look after the animals, and a third could engage in trade.

Although social scientists often discount other people's explanations of why they do things, in the case of Tibetan fraternal polyandry, such explanations are very close to the truth. The custom, however, is very sensitive to changes in its political and economic milieu and, not surprisingly, is in decline in most Tibetan areas. Made less important by the elimination of the traditional serf-based economy, it is disparaged by the dominant non-Tibetan leaders of India, China, and Nepal. New opportunities for economic and social mobility in these countries, such as the tourist trade and government employment, are also eroding the rationale for polyandry, and so it may vanish within the next generation.

Author's Note

The Revival of Fraternal Polyandry in Tibet: Old Solutions for New Problems

In spite of my observation at the end of this article—that political and economic changes were eroding the rationality for fraternal polyandry—there has been a remarkable revival of polyandry in the Tibet Autonomous Region.

After the failed Tibetan Uprising in 1959, the Chinese government acted to end the traditional land-holding system and replace it with communes in which individual commune members worked under a set of managers. Fraternal polyandry ended, as families had no land to conserve and farm.

The rise to power of Deng Xiaoping in 1978 changed China radically. China now opened its doors to the West and adopted Western-style market economics complete with the reintroduction of the profit motive and individual wealth seeking.

In rural Tibet, this resulted in communes closing in 1980–81, with each commune member receiving an equal share of the commune's land regardless of age or sex. Thus, if each person received 1 acre, a family of 6 received 6 acres, on which it now managed to maximize production and income. However, families actually held this land as a long-term lease from the government so land could not be bought or sold. Consequently, as children were born and the size of families grew, land per capita began to decrease. At the same time, as sons reached the age of marriage, it was obvious that if families with several sons allowed each to marry and set up nuclear families, the land the family received from the commune would decline dramatically, and with no way to buy more land, each of the family units would have difficulty growing enough grain for subsistence. Families, therefore, as in the old society, began to utilize traditional fraternal polyandry to keep their sons together at marriage to conserve the family's land intact across generations.

A second factor underlying the widespread revival of fraternal polyandry concerned its concentration of male labor in the family. However, in the new socioeconomic environment, this has not been used to fulfill corvée labor obligations to one's lord (as mentioned in the article), but rather to increase family income by sending surplus labor (one or more of the set of siblings) to "go for income," i.e., to go outside the village as migrant laborers to earn cash income working for part of the year in cities or on rural construction projects. By the time of my last stint of fieldwork in rural Tibet in 2009, this had become the largest source of rural family income.

Fraternal polyandry has therefore undergone an unexpected revival in Tibet because its traditional functions of conserving land intact across generations and concentrating male labor in the family has offered families in the new economic system old solutions to new problems. Rapidly changing socioeconomic conditions, therefore, do not necessarily erode traditional cultural practices. They can, as in this case, revive and sustain them as well.

Critical Thinking

1. What is "fraternal polyandry"? How is it arranged?
2. How do marriage ceremonies vary? When do younger brothers typically join the marriage?
3. How are authority, work, and sex dealt with?
4. Describe the relationship between fathers and children. How is family structure reflected in kinship terminology?
5. What types of marriage are allowed in Tibetan society? Which are the most common? When does polygyny typically occur? Is fraternal polyandry a matter of law or choice? What happens if a brother is dissatisfied? What about his children?
6. How do the Tibetans explain fraternal polyandry? How is this analogous to primogeniture in 19th-century England?
7. Why does it seem that monogamous marriages among brothers in the same household would not work?
8. What kinds of problems occur with fraternal polyandry that make it less than ideal?
9. What two reasons have been commonly offered for the perpetuation of fraternal polyandry in Tibet and how does the author refute these?
10. What percentage of women remain unmarried in Tibetan society? What happens to them? To what extent does polyandry thereby limit population growth? Are the Tibetans aware of this effect?
11. Why would a younger brother accept such a marriage form?
12. How is the polyandrous family more adaptive to the system of hereditary servitude in traditional Tibet?
13. Why is the custom of fraternal polyandry in decline?
14. Explain the disappearence and subsequent revival of fraternal polyandry in Tibet.

Internet References

Sex and Marriage
http://anthro.palomar.edu/marriage/default.htm

Wedding Traditions and Customs
http://worldweddingtraditions.com

Melvyn C. Goldstein, now a professor of anthropology at Case Western Reserve University in Cleveland, has been interested in the Tibetan practice of fraternal polyandry (several brothers marrying one wife) since he was a graduate student in the 1960s.

Article

Prepared by: Elvio Angeloni

No More Angel Babies on the Alto do Cruzeiro

A dispatch from brazil's revolution in child survival.

NANCY SCHEPER-HUGHES

Learning Outcomes

After reading this article, you will be able to:

- Describe and explain the "normalization" of infant death as it once occurred on the Alto do Cruzeiro in Brazil.
- Discuss the economic and political changes in Brazil that led to the decline in "angel babies."

It was almost 50 years ago that I first walked to the top of the Alto do Cruzeiro (the Hill of the Crucifix) in Timbaúba, a sugar-belt town in the state of Pernambuco, in Northeast Brazil. I was looking for the small mud hut, nestled in a cliff, where I was to live. It was December 1964, nine months after the coup that toppled the left-leaning president, João Goulart. Church bells were ringing, and I asked the woman who was to host me as a Peace Corps volunteer why they seemed to ring at all hours of the day. "Oh, it's nothing," she told me. "Just another little angel gone to heaven."

That day marked the beginning of my life's work. Since then, I've experienced something between an obsession, a trauma, and a romance with the shantytown. Residents of the newly occupied hillside were refugees from the military junta's violent attacks on the peasant league movement that had tried to enforce existing laws protecting the local sugarcane cutters. The settlers had thrown together huts made of straw, mud, and sticks or, lacking that, lean-tos made of tin, cardboard, and scrap materials. They had thrown together families in the same makeshift fashion, taking whatever was at hand and making do. In the absence of husbands, weekend play fathers did nicely as long as they brought home the current baby's powdered milk, if not the bacon. Households were temporary; in such poverty women were the only stable force, and babies and fathers were circulated among them. A man who could not provide support would be banished to take up residence with another, even more desperate woman; excess infants and babies were often rescued by older women, who took them in as informal foster children.

Premature death was an everyday occurrence in a shantytown lacking water, electricity, and sanitation and beset with food scarcity, epidemics, and police violence. My assignment was to immunize children, educate midwives, attend births, treat infections, bind up festering wounds, and visit mothers and newborns at home to monitor their health and refer them as needed to the district health post or to the emergency room of the private hospital—owned by the mayor's brother—where charity cases were sometimes attended, depending on the state of local patron-client relations.

I spent several months making the rounds between the miserable huts on the Alto with a public-health medical kit strapped on my shoulder. Its contents were pathetic: a bar of soap, scissors, antiseptics, aspirin, bandages, a glass syringe, some ampules of vaccine, several needles, and a pumice stone to sharpen the needles, which were used over and over again for immunizations. Children ran away when they saw me coming, and well they might have.

But what haunted me then, in addition to my own incompetence, was something I did not have the skill or maturity to understand: Why didn't the women of the Alto grieve over the deaths of their babies? I tucked that question away. But as Winnicott, the British child psychoanalyst, liked to say, "Nothing is ever forgotten."

Sixteen years elapsed before I was able to return to the Alto do Cruzeiro, this time as a medical anthropologist. It was in 1982—during the period known as the abertura, or opening, the beginning of the end of the military dictatorship—that I made the first of the four trips that formed the basis for my 1992 book, *Death Without Weeping: The Violence of Everyday Life in Brazil.* My goal was to study women's lives, specifically mother love and child death under conditions so dire that the Uruguayan writer Eduardo Galeano once described the region as a concentration camp for 30 million people. It was not a gross exaggeration. Decades of nutritional studies of sugarcane cutters and their families in Pernambuco showed hard evidence of slow starvation and stunting. These nutritional dwarfs were surviving on a daily caloric intake similar to that of the inmates of the Buchenwald concentration camp. Life on the Alto resembled prison-camp culture, with a moral ethic based on triage and survival.

If mother love is the cultural expression of what many attachment theorists believe to be a bioevolutionary script, what could this script mean to women living in these conditions? In my sample of three generations of mothers in the sugar plantation zone of Pernambuco, the average woman had 9.5 pregnancies, 8 live births, and 3.5 infant deaths. Such high rates of births and deaths are typical of societies that have not undergone what population experts call the demographic transition, associated with economic development, in which first death rates and, later, birth rates drop as parents begin to trust that more of their infants will survive. On the contrary, the high expectation of loss and the normalization of infant death was a powerful conditioner of the degree of maternal attachments. Mothers and infants could also be rivals for scarce resources. Alto mothers renounced breastfeeding as impossible, as sapping far too much strength from their own "wrecked" bodies.

Scarcity made mother love a fragile emotion, postponed until the newborn displayed a will to live—a taste (gusto) and a knack (jeito) for life. A high expectancy of death prepared mothers to "let go" of and to hasten the death of babies that were failing to thrive, by reducing the already insufficient food, water, and care. The "angel babies" of the Alto were neither of this Earth nor yet fully spirits. In appearance they were ghostlike: pale and wispy-haired; their arms and legs stripped of flesh; their bellies grossly distended; their eyes blank and staring; and their faces wizened, a cross between startled primate and wise old sorcerer.

The experience of too much loss, too much death, led to a kind of patient resignation that some clinical psychologists might label "emotional numbing" or the symptoms of a "masked depression." But the mothers' resignation was neither pathological nor abnormal. Moreover, it was a moral code. Not only had a continual exposure to trauma obliterated rage and protest, it also minimized attachment so as to diminish sorrow.

Infant death was so commonplace that I recall a birthday party for a four-year-old in which the birthday cake, decorated with candles, was placed on the kitchen table next to the tiny blue cardboard coffin of the child's nine-month-old sibling, who had died during the night. Next to the coffin a single vigil candle was lit. Despite the tragedy, the child's mother wanted to go ahead with the party. "Parabens para pace," we sang, clapping our hands. "Congratulations to you!" the Brazilian birthday song goes. And on the Alto it had special resonance: "Congratulations, you survivor you—you lived to see another year!"

When Alto mothers cried, they cried for themselves, for those left behind to continue the struggle. But they cried the hardest for their children who had almost died, but who surprised everyone by surviving against the odds. Wiping a stray tear from her eye, an Alto mother would speak with deep emotion of the child who, given up for dead, suddenly beat death back, displaying a fierce desire for life. These tough and stubborn children were loved above all others.

Staying alive in the shantytown demanded a kind of egoism that often pits individuals against each other and rewards those who take advantage of those weaker than themselves. People admired toughness and strength; they took pride in babies or adults who were cunning and foxy. The toddler that was wild and fierce was preferred to the quiet and obedient child. Men and women with seductive charm, who could manipulate those around them, were better off than those who were kind. Poverty doesn't ennoble people, and I came to appreciate what it took to stay alive.

Theirs were moral choices that no person should be forced to make. But the result was that infants were viewed as limitless. There was a kind of magical replaceability about them, similar to what one might find on a battlefield. As one soldier falls, another takes his place. This kind of detached maternal thinking allowed the die-offs of shantytown babies—in some years, as many as 40 percent of all the infants born on the Alto died—to pass without shock or profound grief. A woman who had lost half her babies told me, "Who could bear it, Nanci, if we are mistaken in believing that God takes our infants to save us from pain? If that is not true, then God is a cannibal. And if our little angels are not in heaven flying around the throne of Our Lady, then where are they, and who is to blame for their deaths?"

If mothers allowed themselves to be attached to each newborn, how could they ever live through their babies' short lives and deaths and still have the stamina to get pregnant and give birth again and again? It wasn't that Alto mothers did not experience mother love at all. They did, and with great intensity. But mother love emerged as their children developed strength and vitality. The apex of mother love was not the image of Mary and her infant son, but a mature Mary, grieving the death of her young adult son. The Pieta, not the young mother at the crèche, was the symbol of motherhood and mother love on the Alto.

In *Death Without Weeping*, I first told of a clandestine extermination group that had begun to operate in Timbaúba in the 1980s. The rise of these vigilantes seemed paradoxical, insofar as it coincided with the end of the 20-year military dictatorship. What was the relationship between democracy and death squads? No one knew who was behind the extrajudicial limpeza ("street cleaning," as their supporters called it) that was targeting "dirty" street children and poor young Black men from the shantytowns. But by 2000 the public was well aware of the group and the identity of its leader, Abdoral Gonçalves Queiroz. Known as the "Guardian Angels," they were responsible for killing more than 100 victims. In 2001 I was invited, along with my husband, to return to Timbaúba to help a newly appointed and tough-minded judge and state prosecutor to identify those victims whose relatives had not come forward. In the interim, the death squad group had infiltrated the town council, the mayor's office, and the justice system. But 11 of them, including their semiliterate gangster-boss, Queiroz, had been arrested and were going on trial.

The death squad was a residue of the old military regime. For 20 years, the military police had kept the social classes segregated, with "dangerous" street youths and unemployed rural men confined to the hillside slums or in detention. When the old policing structures loosened following the democratic transition, the shantytowns ruptured and poor people, especially unemployed young men and street children, flooded downtown streets and public squares, once the preserve of gente fina (the cultivated people). Their new visibility betrayed the illusion of Brazilian modernity and evoked contradictory emotions of fear, aversion, pity, and anger.

Excluded and reviled, unemployed Black youths and loose street kids of Timbaúba were prime targets of Queiroz and his gang. Depending on one's social class and politics, the band could be seen as hired serial killers or as justiceiros (outlaw heroes) who were protecting the community. Prominent figures—well-known businessmen and local politicians—applauded the work of the death squad, whom they also called "Police 2," and some of these leading citizens were active in the extrajudicial "courts" that were deciding who in Timbaúba should be the next to die.

During the 2001 death-squad field research expedition, I played cat-and-mouse with Dona Amantina, the dour manager of the cartorio civil, the official registry office. I was trying to assemble a body count of suspicious homicides that could possibly be linked to the death squad, focusing on the violent deaths of street kids and young Black men. Since members of the death squad were still at large, I did not want to make public what I was doing. At first, I implied that I was back to count infant and child deaths, as I had so many years before. Finally, I admitted that I was looking into youth homicides. The manager nodded her head. "Yes, it's sad. But," she asked with a shy smile, "haven't you noticed the changes in infant and child deaths?" Once I began to scan the record books, I was wearing a smile, too.

Brazil's national central statistics bureau, the Instituto Brasileiro de Geografia e Estatística (IBGE), began reporting data for the municipality of Timbaúba in the late 1970s. In 1977, for example, IBGE reported 761 live births in the municipality and 311 deaths of infants (up to one year of age) for that same year, yielding an infant mortality rate of 409 per 1,000. A year later, the IBGE data recorded 896 live births and 320 infant deaths, an infant mortality rate of 357 per 1,000. If reliable, those official data indicated that between 36 and 41 percent of all infants in Timbaúba died in the first 12 months of life.

During the 1980s, when I was doing the research for *Death Without Weeping,* the then mayor of Timbaúba, the late Jacques Ferreira Lima, disputed those figures. "Impossible!" he fumed "This municipio is growing, not declining." He sent me to the local private hospital built by, and named for, his father, Joío Ferreira Lima, to compare the IBGE statistics with the hospital's records on births and deaths. There, the head nurse gave me access to her records, but the official death certificates only concerned stillbirths and perinatal deaths. In the end, I found that the best source of data was the ledger books of the cartorio civil, where births and infant and child deaths were recorded by hand. Many births were not recorded until after a child had died, in order to register a death and receive a free coffin from the mayor's office. The statistics were as grim as those of the IBGE.

In 2001, a single afternoon going over infant and toddler death certificates in the same office was enough to document that something radical had since taken place—a revolution in child survival that had begun in the 1990s. The records now showed a completed birth rate of 3.2 children per woman and a mortality rate of 35 per 1,000 births. Subsequent field trips in 2006 and 2007 showed even further reductions. The 2009 data from the IBGE recorded a rate of 25.2 child deaths per 1,000 births for Timbaúba.

Though working on other topics in my Brazilian field trips in 2001, 2006, and 2007, I took the time to interview several young women attending a pregnancy class at a newly constructed, government-run clinic. The women I spoke with—some first-time mothers, others expecting a second or third child—were confident in their ability to give birth to a healthy baby. No one I spoke to expected to have, except by accident, more than two children. A pair—that was the goal. Today, young women of the Alto can expect to give birth to three or fewer infants and to see all of them live at least into adolescence. The old stance of maternal watchful waiting accompanied by deselection of infants viewed as having no "talent" for life had been replaced by a maternal ethos of "holding on" to every infant, each seen as likely to survive. As I had noted in the past as well, there was a preference for girl babies. Boys, women feared, could disappoint their mothers—they could kill or be killed as adolescents and young men. The Alto was still a dangerous place, and gangs, drug dealers, and the death squads were still in operation. But women in the state-run clinic spoke of having control over their reproductive lives in ways that I could not have imagined.

By 2001 Timbaúba had experienced the demographic transition. Both infant deaths and births had declined so precipitously that it looked like a reproductive workers' strike. The numbers—though incomplete—were startling. Rather than the more than 200 annual infant and child mortalities of the early 1980s, by the late 1990s there were fewer than 50 childhood deaths recorded per year. And the causes of death were specific. In the past, the causes had been stated in vague terms: "undetermined," "heart stopped, respiration stopped," "malnutrition," or the mythopoetic diagnosis of "acute infantile suffering."

On my latest return, just this June, the reproductive revolution was complete. The little two-room huts jumbled together on the back roads of the Alto were still poor, but as I visited the homes of dozens of Alto residents, sometimes accompanied by a local community health agent, sometimes dropping in for a chat unannounced, or summoned by the adult child of a former key informant of mine, I saw infants and toddlers who were plump and jolly, and mothers who were relaxed and breastfeeding toddlers as old as three years. Their babies assumed a high status in the family hierarchy, as precious little beings whose beauty and health brought honor and substance—as well as subsistence—to the household.

Manufactured cribs with pristine sheets and fluffy blankets, disposal diapers, and plastic rattles were much in evidence. Powdered milk, the number one baby killer in the past, was almost a banned substance. In contrast, no one, literally, breastfed during my early years of research on the Alto. It was breast milk that was banned, banned by the owners of the sugar plantations and by the bourgeois patrons (mistresses of the house) for whom the women of the Alto washed clothes and cleaned and cooked and served meals. Today, those jobs no longer exist. The sugar mills and sugar estates have closed down, and the landowning class has long since moved, leaving behind a population of working-class poor, a thin middle class (with washing machines rather than maids), and a displaced rural labor force that is largely sustained by the largesse of New Deal–style federal assistance.

Direct cash transfers are made to poor and unemployed families, and grants (bolsas, or "purses") are given to women, mothers, babies, schoolchildren, and youth. The grants come with conditions. The balsa familiar (family grant), a small cash payment to each mother and up to five of her young children, requires the mother to immunize her babies, attend to their medical needs, follow medical directions, keep the children in school, monitor their homework, help them prepare for exams, and purchase school books, pens and pencils, and school clothes. Of the 30 Alto women between the ages of 17 and 40 my research associate, Jennifer S. Hughes, and I interviewed in June, the women averaged 3.3 pregnancies—higher than the national average, but the real comparison here is with their own mothers, who (based on the 13 of the 30 who could describe their mothers' reproductive histories) averaged 13.6 pregnancies and among them counted 61 infant deaths. Jennifer is my daughter and a professor of colonial and postcolonial Latin American history at the University of California, Riverside. I like to think that her awesome archival skills were honed more than 20 years ago when I enlisted her, then a teenager, to help me count the deaths of Alto babies in the civil registry office. She agreed to help me on this most recent field trip, and it was our first professional collaboration.

Jennifer, for example, looked up Luciene, the first-born daughter of Antonieta, one of my earliest key informants and my neighbor when I lived on the Alto do Cruzeiro. Now in her 40s, Luciene had only one pregnancy and one living child. Her mother had given birth to 15 babies, 10 of whom survived. Daughter and mother now live next door to each other, and they spoke openly and emotionally about the "old days," "the hungry times," "the violent years," in comparison to the present. "Today we are rich," Antonieta declared, "really rich," by which she meant her modernized home on the Alto Terezinha, their new color television set, washing machine, and all the food and delicacies they could want.

Four of the 30 women we interviewed had lost an infant, and one had lost a two year old who drowned playing with a large basin of water. Those deaths were seen as tragic and painful memories. The mothers did not describe the deaths in a monotone or dismiss them as inevitable or an act of mercy that relieved their suffering. Rather, they recalled with deep sadness the date, the time, and the cause of their babies' deaths, and remembered them by name, saying that Gloria would be 10 today or that Marcos would be eight years old today, had she or he lived.

What has happened in Timbaúba over the past decades is part of a national trend in Brazil. Over the past decade alone, Brazil's fertility rate has decreased from 2.36 to 1.9 children per family—a number that is below the replacement rate and lower than that of the United States. Unlike in China or India, this reproductive revolution occurred without state coercion. It was a voluntary transition and a rapid one.

A footnote in *Death Without Weeping* records the most common requests that people made of me in the 1960s and again in the 1980s: Could I possibly help them obtain false teeth?

[A] pair of eyeglasses? [A] better antibiotic for a sick older child? But most often I was asked—begged—by women to arrange a clandestine sterilization. In Northeast Brazil, sterilization was always preferable to oral contraceptives, IUDs, and condoms. Reproductive freedom meant having the children you wanted and then "closing down the factory." "A fábrica é fechada!" a woman would boastfully explain, patting her abdomen. Until recently, this was the privilege of the upper middle classes and the wealthy. Today, tubal ligations are openly discussed and arranged. One woman I interviewed, a devout Catholic, gushed that God was good, so good that he had given her a third son, her treasure trove, and at the same time had allowed her the liberty and freedom of a tubal ligation. "Praise to God!" she said. "Amen," I said.

In Brazil, the reproductive revolution is linked to democracy and the coming into political power of President Fernando Henrique Cardoso (1995–2002), aided by his formidable wife, the anthropologist and women's advocate Ruth Cardoso. It was continued by Luiz Inacio Lula da Silva, universally called "Lula," and, since 2011, by his successor, Dilma Rousseff. President Lula's Zero Hunger campaign, though much criticized in the popular media as a kind of political publicity stunt, in fact has supplied basic foodstuffs to the most vulnerable households.

Today food is abundant on the Alto. Schoolchildren are fed nutritious lunches, fortified with a protein mixture that is prepared as tasty milk shakes. There are food pantries and state and municipal milk distribution programs that are run by women with an extra room in their home. The monthly stipends to poor and single mothers to reward them for keeping their children in school has turned elementary school pupils into valuable household "workers," and literacy has increased for both the children and their mothers, who study at home alongside their children.

When I first went to the Alto in 1964 as a Peace Corps volunteer, it was in the role of a visitadora, a public-health community worker. The military dictatorship was suspicious of the program, which mixed health education and immunizations with advocating for water, street lights, and pit latrines as universal entitlements—owed even to those who had "occupied public land" (like the people of the Alto, who had been dispossessed by modernizing sugar plantations and mills). The visitadora program, Brazil's version of Chinese "barefoot doctors," was targeted by the military government as subversive, and the program ended by 1966 in Pernambuco. Many years later President Cardoso fortified the national health care system with a similar program of local "community health agents," who live and work in their micro-communities, visiting at-risk households, identifying crises, diagnosing common symptoms, and intervening to rescue vulnerable infants and toddlers from premature death. In Timbaúba, there are some 120 community health agents, male and female, working in poor micro-communities throughout the municipality, including dispersed rural communities. On the Alto do Cruzeiro 12 health agents each live and work in a defined area, each responsible for the health and well-being of some 150 families comprising 500 to 600 individuals. The basic requirement for a health worker is to have completed ensino fundamental, the equivalent of primary and middle school. Then, he or she must prepare for a public concurso, a competition based on a rigorous exam.

The community health agent's wage is small, a little more than the Brazilian minimum wage, but still less than US $700 a month for a 40-hour work week, most of it on foot up and down the hillside "slum" responding to a plethora of medical needs, from diaper rash to an emergency home birth. The agent records all births, deaths, illnesses, and other health problems in the micro-community; refers the sick to health posts, emergency rooms, and hospitals; monitors pregnancies and the health of newborns, the disabled, and the elderly. He or she identifies and reports communicable diseases and acts as a public-health and environmental educator. The agent participates in public meetings to shape health policies. Above all, the community health agent is the primary intermediary between poor people and the national health care system.

I am convinced that the incredible decline in premature deaths and useless suffering that I witnessed on the Alto is primarily the result of these largely unheralded medical heroes, who rescue mothers and their children in a large town with few doctors and no resident surgeons, pediatricians, and worst of all, obstetricians. A pregnant woman of the Alto suffers today from one of the worst dilemmas and anxieties a person in her condition can face: no certain location to give birth. The only solution at present is to refer women in labor to distant obstetric and maternity wards in public hospitals in Recife, the state capital, a 67-mile drive away. The result can be fatal: at least one woman in the past year was prevented (by holding her legs together) from delivering her baby in an ambulance, and both mother and child died following their arrival at the designated hospital in Recife. For this reason, Alto women and their health agents often choose prearranged cesarian sections well in advance of due dates, even though they know that C-sections are generally not in the best interest of mothers or infants.

Then, beyond the human factor, environmental factors figure in the decline in infant mortality in the shantytowns of Timbaúba and other municipalities in Northeast Brazil. The most significant of these is the result of a simple, basic municipal public-health program: the installation of water pipes that today reach nearly all homes with sufficient clean water. It is amazing to observe the transformative potential of material conditions: water = life!

Finally, what about the role of the Catholic Church? The anomaly is that, in a nation where the Catholic Church predominates in the public sphere and abortion is still illegal except in the case of rape or to save a mother's life, family size has dropped so sharply over the last two decades. What is going on? For one thing, Brazilian Catholics are independent, much like Catholics in the United States, going their own way when it comes to women's health and reproductive culture. Others have simply left Catholicism and joined evangelical churches, some of which proclaim their openness to the reproductive rights of women and men. Today only 60 percent of Brazilians identify as Roman Catholic. In our small sample of 30 women of the Alto, religion—whether Catholic, Protestant, Spiritist, or Afro-Brazilian—did not figure large in their reproductive lives.

The Brazilian Catholic Church is deeply divided. In 2009, the Archbishop of Recife announced the Vatican's excommunication of the doctors and family of a nine-year-old girl who had an abortion. She had been raped by her stepfather (thus the abortion was legal), and she was carrying twins—her tiny stature and narrow hips putting her life in jeopardy. After comparing abortion to the Holocaust, Archbishop José Cardoso Sobrinho told the media that the Vatican rejects believers who pick and choose their moral issues. The result was an immediate decline in church attendance throughout the diocese.

While the Brazilian Catholic hierarchy is decidedly conservative, the rural populace, their local clerics, and liberation theologians such as the activist ex-priest Leonardo Boff are open in their interpretations of Catholic spirituality and corporeality. The Jesus that my Catholic friends on the Alto embrace is a sensitive and sentient Son of God, a man of sorrows, to be sure, and also a man of compassion, keenly attuned to simple human needs. The teachings of liberation theology, while condemned by Pope John Paul II, helped to dislodge a baroque folk Catholicism in rural Northeast Brazil that envisioned God and the saints as authorizing and blessing the deaths of angel babies.

Padre Orlando, a young priest when I first met him in 1987, distanced himself from the quaint custom of blessing the bodies of dead infants as they were carried to the municipal graveyard in processions led by children. He also invited me and my Brazilian research assistant to give an orientation on family planning to poor Catholic women in the parish hall. When I asked what form of contraception I could teach, he replied, "I'm a celibate priest, how should I know? Teach it all, everything you know." When I reminded him that only the very unpredictable rhythm method was approved by the Vatican, he replied, "Just teach it all, everything you know, and then say, but the Pope only approves the not-so-safe rhythm method."

The people of the Alto do Cruzeiro still face many problems. Drugs, gangs, and death squads have left their ugly mark. Homicides have returned with a vengeance, but they are diffuse and chaotic, the impulsive murders one comes to expect among poor young men—the unemployed, petty thieves, and small-time drug dealers—and between rival gangs. One sees adolescents and young men of the shantytowns, who survived that dangerous first year of life, cut down by bullets and knives at the age of 15 or 17 by local gangs, strongmen, bandidos, and local police in almost equal measure. The old diseases also raise their heads from time to time: schistosomiasis, Chagas disease, tuberculosis, and even cholera.

But the bottom line is that women on the Alto today do not lose their infants. Children go to school rather than to the cane fields, and social cooperatives have taken the place of shadow economies. When mothers are sick or pregnant or a child is ill, they can go to the well-appointed health clinic supported by both state and national funds. There is a safety net, and it is wide, deep, and strong.

Just as we were leaving in mid-June, angry, insurgent crowds were forming in Recife, fed up with political corruption, cronyism, and the extravagant public expenditures in preparation for the 2014 World Cup in Brazil—when the need was for public housing and hospitals. Those taking to the streets were mostly young, urban, working-class, and new middle-class Brazilians. The rural poor were generally not among them. The people of the Alto do Cruzeiro (and I imagine in many other communities like it) are strong supporters of the government led by the PT (Partido dos Trabalhadores, or Workers' Party). Under the PT, the government has ended hunger in Pernambuco and has opened family clinics and municipal schools that treat them and their children with respect for the first time in their lives.

The protesters in the streets are among the 40 million Brazilians who were added to the middle class between 2004 and 2010, under the government of President Lula, and whose rising expectations are combustible. When the healthy, literate children of the Alto do Cruzeiro grow up, they may yet join future protests demanding more accountability from their elected officials.

Critical Thinking

1. Discuss the conditions on the Alto do Cruzeiro that help to explain the "normalization" of infant death.
2. Describe the demographic transition and the effect it has on a mother's trust that her infant will survive.
3. When and why do Alto mothers cry?
4. Describe and explain the egoism that is admired and demanded in the shantytown.
5. Explain "magical replaceability" regarding children.

6. Discuss the "detached maternal thinking" and the emergence of mother love in the context of religious beliefs.
7. Explain the appearance of the death squads.
8. Describe the demographic transition in terms of what has brought it about and the resulting attitudes toward having children.
9. Describe the deep divisions within the Brazilian Catholic Church with respect to family planning.

Internet References

American Anthropological Association Children and Childhood Interest Group
http://aaacig.usu.edu/

Journal of Medical Ethics
http://jme.bmj.com/

Latin American Studies
www.library.arizona.edu/search/subjects

Nancy Scheper-Hughes is Chancellor Professor (Emerita) at UC Berkeley. A central theme unifying her research and writing is how violence comes to mark the bodies and psyches of the vulnerable, poor, and the dispossessed. Her multiple award winning book, *Death without Weeping: The Violence of Everyday life in Brazil* (1993), is a life's work as she constantly returns to the community of Alto do Cruzeiro to Northeast Brazil to write about the changing context of mother love and child death. She is writing a sequel, Longing for Brazil: Radical Hope During Difficult Times, to be published by University of California Press.

Article

Prepared by: Elvio Angeloni

Arranging a Marriage in India

SERENA NANDA

Learning Outcomes

After reading this article, you will be able to:

- List the pros and cons of arranged marriages versus love marriages.
- Discuss the factors that must be taken into account in arranging a marriage in India.

> Sister and doctor brother-in-law invite correspondence from North Indian professionals only, for a beautiful, talented, sophisticated, intelligent sister, 5'3", slim, M.A. in textile design, father a senior civil officer. Would prefer immigrant doctors, between 26–29 years. Reply with full details and returnable photo.
>
> A well-settled uncle invites matrimonial correspondence from slim, fair, educated South Indian girl, for his nephew, 25 years, smart, M.B.A., green card holder, 5'6". Full particulars with returnable photo appreciated.
>
> —*Matrimonial Advertisements,* India Abroad

In India, almost all marriages are arranged. Even among the educated middle classes in modern, urban India, marriage is as much a concern of the families as it is of the individuals. So customary is the practice of arranged marriage that there is a special name for a marriage which is not arranged: It is called a "love match."

On my first field trip to India, I met many young men and women whose parents were in the process of "getting them married." In many cases, the bride and groom would not meet each other before the marriage. At most they might meet for a brief conversation, and this meeting would take place only after their parents had decided that the match was suitable. Parents do not compel their children to marry a person who either marriage partner finds objectionable. But only after one match is refused will another be sought.

As a young American woman in India for the first time, I found this custom of arranged marriage oppressive. How could any intelligent young person agree to such a marriage without great reluctance? It was contrary to everything I believed about the importance of romantic love as the only basis of a happy marriage. It also clashed with my strongly held notions that the choice of such an intimate and permanent relationship could be made only by the individuals involved. Had anyone tried to arrange my marriage, I would have been defiant and rebellious!

At the first opportunity, I began, with more curiosity than tact, to question the young people I met on how they felt about this practice. Sita, one of my young informants, was a college graduate with a degree in political science. She had been waiting for over a year while her parents were arranging a match for her. I found it difficult to accept the docile manner in which this well-educated young woman awaited the outcome of a process that would result in her spending the rest of her life with a man she hardly knew, a virtual stranger, picked out by her parents.

"How can you go along with this?" I asked her, in frustration and distress. "Don't you care who you marry?"

"Of course I care," she answered. "This is why I must let my parents choose a boy for me. My marriage is too important to be arranged by such an inexperienced person as myself. In such matters, it is better to have my parents' guidance."

I had learned that young men and women in India do not date and have very little social life involving members of the opposite sex. Although I could not disagree with Sita's reasoning, I continued to pursue the subject.

Young men and women do not date and have very little social life involving members of the opposite sex.

"But how can you marry the first man you have ever met? Not only have you missed the fun of meeting a lot of different people, but you have not given yourself the chance to know who is the right man for you."

"Meeting with a lot of different people doesn't sound like any fun at all," Sita answered. "One hears that in America the girls are spending all their time worrying about whether they will meet a man and get married. Here we have the chance to enjoy our life and let our parents do this work and worrying for us."

She had me there. The high anxiety of the competition to "be popular" with the opposite sex certainly was the most prominent feature of life as an American teenager in the late fifties. The endless worrying about the rules that governed our behavior and about our popularity ratings sapped both our self-esteem and our enjoyment of adolescence. I reflected that absence of this competition in India most certainly may have contributed to the self-confidence and natural charm of so many of the young women I met.

And yet, the idea of marrying a perfect stranger, whom one did not know and did not "love," so offended my American ideas of individualism and romanticism, that I persisted with my objections.

"I still can't imagine it," I said. "How can you agree to marry a man you hardly know?"

"But of course he will be known. My parents would never arrange a marriage for me without knowing all about the boy's family background. Naturally we will not rely only on what the family tells us. We will check the particulars out ourselves. No one will want their daughter to marry into a family that is not good. All these things we will know beforehand."

Impatiently, I responded, "Sita, I don't mean know the family, I mean, know the man. How can you marry someone you don't know personally and don't love? How can you think of spending your life with someone you may not even like?"

"If he is a good man, why should I not like him?" she said. "With you people, you know the boy so well before you marry, where will be the fun to get married? There will be no mystery and no romance. Here we have the whole of our married life to get to know and love our husband. This way is better, is it not?"

Her response made further sense, and I began to have second thoughts on the matter. Indeed, during months of meeting many intelligent young Indian people, both male and female, who had the same ideas as Sita, I saw arranged marriages in a different light. I also saw the importance of the family in Indian life and realized that a couple who took their marriage into their own hands was taking a big risk, particularly if their families were irreconcilably opposed to the match. In a country where every important resource in life—a job, a house, a social circle—is gained through family connections, it seemed foolhardy to cut oneself off from a supportive social network and depend solely on one person for happiness and success.

Six years later I returned to India to again do fieldwork, this time among the middle class in Bombay, a modern, sophisticated city. From the experience of my earlier visit, I decided to include a study of arranged marriages in my project. By this time I had met many Indian couples whose marriages had been arranged and who seemed very happy. Particularly in contrast to the fate of many of my married friends in the United States who were already in the process of divorce, the positive aspects of arranged marriages appeared to me to outweigh the negatives. In fact, I thought I might even participate in arranging a marriage myself. I had been fairly successful in the United States in "fixing up" many of my friends, and I was confident that my matchmaking skills could be easily applied to this new situation, once I learned the basic rules. "After all," I thought, "how complicated can it be? People want pretty much the same things in a marriage whether it is in India or America."

An opportunity presented itself almost immediately. A friend from my previous Indian trip was in the process of arranging for the marriage of her eldest son. In India there is a perceived shortage of "good boys," and since my friend's family was eminently respectable and the boy himself personable, well educated, and nice looking, I was sure that by the end of my year's fieldwork, we would have found a match.

The basic rule seems to be that a family's reputation is most important. It is understood that matches would be arranged only within the same caste and general social class, although some crossing of subcastes is permissible if the class positions of the bride's and groom's families are similar. Although dowry is now prohibited by law in India, extensive gift exchanges took place with every marriage. Even when the boy's family do not "make demands," every girl's family nevertheless feels the obligation to give the traditional gifts, to the girl, to the boy, and to the boy's family. Particularly when the couple would be living in the joint family—that is, with the boy's parents and his married brothers and their families, as well as with unmarried siblings—which is still very common even among the urban, upper-middle class in India, the girls' parents are anxious to establish smooth relations between their family and that of the boy. Offering the proper gifts, even when not called "dowry," is often an important factor in influencing the relationship between the bride's and groom's families and perhaps, also, the treatment of the bride in her new home.

Even today, almost all marriages in India are arranged. It is believed that parents are much more effective at deciding whom their daughters should marry.

In a society where divorce is still a scandal and where, in fact, the divorce rate is exceedingly low, an arranged marriage is the beginning of a lifetime relationship not just between the bride and groom but between their families as well.

In a society where divorce is still a scandal and where, in fact, the divorce rate is exceedingly low, an arranged marriage is the beginning of a lifetime relationship not just between the bride and groom but between their families as well. Thus, while a girl's looks are important, her character is even more so, for she is being judged as a prospective daughter-in-law as much as a prospective bride. Where she would be living in a joint family, as was the case with my friend, the girls's ability to get along harmoniously in a family is perhaps the single most important quality in assessing her suitability.

My friend is a highly esteemed wife, mother, and daughter-in-law. She is religious, soft-spoken, modest, and deferential. She rarely gossips and never quarrels, two qualities highly desirable in a woman. A family that has the reputation for gossip and conflict among its womenfolk will not find it easy to get good wives for their sons. Parents will not want to send their daughter to a house in which there is conflict.

My friend's family were originally from North India. They had lived in Bombay, where her husband owned a business, for forty years. The family had delayed in seeking a match for their eldest son because he had been an Air Force pilot for several years, stationed in such remote places that it had seemed fruitless to try to find a girl who would be willing to accompany him. In their social class, a military career, despite its economic security, has little prestige and is considered a drawback in finding a suitable bride. Many families would not allow their daughters to marry a man in an occupation so potentially dangerous and which requires so much moving around.

The son had recently left the military and joined his father's business. Since he was a college graduate, modern, and well traveled, from such a good family, and, I thought, quite handsome, it seemed to me that he, or rather his family, was in a position to pick and choose. I said as much to my friend.

While she agreed that there were many advantages on their side, she also said, "We must keep in mind that my son is both short and dark; these are drawbacks in finding the right match." While the boy's height had not escaped my notice, "dark" seemed to me inaccurate; I would have called him "wheat" colored perhaps, and in any case, I did not realize that color would be a consideration. I discovered, however, that while a boy's skin color is a less important consideration than a girl's, it is still a factor.

An important source of contacts in trying to arrange her son's marriage was my friend's social club in Bombay. Many of the women had daughters of the right age, and some had already expressed an interest in my friend's son. I was most enthusiastic about the possibilities of one particular family who had five daughters, all of whom were pretty, demure, and well educated. Their mother had told my friend, "You can have your pick for your son, whichever one of my daughters appeals to you most."

I saw a match in sight. "Surely," I said to my friend, "we will find one there. Let's go visit and make our choice." But my friend held back; she did not seem to share my enthusiasm, for reasons I could not then fathom.

When I kept pressing for an explanation of her reluctance, she admitted, "See, Serena, here is the problem. The family has so many daughters, how will they be able to provide nicely for any of them? We are not making any demands, but still, with so many daughters to marry off, one wonders whether she will even be able to make a proper wedding. Since this is our eldest son, it's best if we marry him to a girl who is the only daughter, then the wedding will truly be a gala affair." I argued that surely the quality of the girls themselves made up for any deficiency in the elaborateness of the wedding. My friend admitted this point but still seemed reluctant to proceed.

"Is there something else," I asked her, "some factor I have missed?" "Well," she finally said, "there is one other thing. They have one daughter already married and living in Bombay. The mother is always complaining to me that the girl's in-laws don't let her visit her own family often enough. So it makes me wonder, will she be that kind of mother who always wants her daughter at her own home? This will prevent the girl from adjusting to our house. It is not a good thing." And so, this family of five daughters was dropped as a possibility.

Somewhat disappointed, I nevertheless respected my friend's reasoning and geared up for the next prospect. This was also the daughter of a woman in my friend's social club. There was clear interest in this family and I could see why. The family's reputation was excellent; in fact, they came from a subcaste slightly higher than my friend's own. The girl, who was an only daughter, was pretty and well educated and had a brother studying in the United States. Yet, after expressing an interest to me in this family, all talk of them suddenly died down and the search began elsewhere.

"What happened to that girl as a prospect?" I asked one day. "You never mention her any more. She is so pretty and so educated, what did you find wrong?"

"She is too educated. We've decided against it. My husband's father saw the girl on the bus the other day and thought her forward. A girl who 'roams about' the city by herself is not the girl for our family." My disappointment this time was even greater, as I thought the son would have liked the girl very much. But then I thought, my friend is right, a girl who is going to live in a joint family cannot be too independent or she will make life miserable for everyone. I also learned that if the family of the girl has even a slightly higher social status than the family of the boy, the bride may think herself too good for them, and this too will cause problems. Later my friend admitted to me that this had been an important factor in her decision not to pursue the match.

The next candidate was the daughter of a client of my friend's husband. When the client learned that the family was looking for a match for their son, he said, "Look no further, we have a daughter." This man then invited my friends to dinner to see the girl. He had already seen their son at the office and decided that "he liked the boy." We all went together for tea, rather than dinner—it was less of a commitment—and while we were there, the girl's mother showed us around the house. The girl was studying for her exams and was briefly introduced to us.

After we left, I was anxious to hear my friend's opinion. While her husband liked the family very much and was impressed with his client's business accomplishments and reputation, the wife didn't like the girl's looks. "She is short, no doubt, which is an important plus point, but she is also fat and wears glasses." My friend obviously thought she could do better for her son and asked her husband to make his excuses to his client by saying that they had decided to postpone the boy's marriage indefinitely.

By this time almost six months had passed and I was becoming impatient. What I had thought would be an easy matter to arrange was turning out to be quite complicated. I began to believe that between my friend's desire for a girl who was modest enough to fit into her joint family, yet attractive and educated enough to be an acceptable partner for her son, she would not find anyone suitable. My friend laughed at my impatience:

Appendix
Further Reflections on Arranged Marriage . . .

This essay was written from the point of view of a family seeking a daughter-in-law. Arranged marriage looks somewhat different from the point of view of the bride and her family. Arranged marriage continues to be preferred, even among the more educated, Westernized sections of the Indian population. Many young women from these families still go along, more or less willingly, with the practice, and also with the specific choices of their families. Young women do get excited about the prospects of their marriage, but there is also ambivalence and increasing uncertainty, as the bride contemplates leaving the comfort and familiarity of her own home, where as a "temporary guest" she had often been indulged, to live among strangers. Even in the best situation she will now come under the close scrutiny of her husband's family. How she dresses, how she behaves, how she gets along with others, where she goes, how she spends her time, her domestic abilities—all of this and much more—will be observed and commented on by a whole new set of relations. Her interaction with her family of birth will be monitored and curtailed considerably. Not only will she leave their home, but with increasing geographic mobility, she may also live very far from them, perhaps even on another continent. Too much expression of her fondness for her own family, or her desire to visit them, may be interpreted as an inability to adjust to her new family, and may become a source of conflict. In an arranged marriage the burden of adjustment is clearly heavier for a woman than for a man. And that is in the best of situations.

In less happy circumstances, the bride may be a target of resentment and hostility from her husband's family, particularly her mother-in-law or her husband's unmarried sisters, for whom she is now a source of competition for the affection, loyalty, and economic resources of their son or brother. If she is psychologically, or even physically abused, her options are limited, as returning to her parents' home, or divorce, are still very stigmatized. For most Indians, marriage and motherhood are still considered the only suitable roles for a woman, even for those who have careers, and few women can comfortably contemplate remaining unmarried. Most families still consider "marrying off" their daughters as a compelling religious duty and social necessity. This increases a bride's sense of obligation to make the marriage a success, at whatever cost to her own personal happiness.

The vulnerability of a new bride may also be intensified by the issue of dowry, which although illegal, has become a more pressing issue in the consumer conscious society of contemporary urban India. In many cases, where a groom's family is not satisfied with the amount of dowry a bride brings to her marriage, the young bride will be constantly harassed to get her parents to give more. In extreme cases, the bride may even be murdered, and the murder disguised as an accident or suicide. This also offers the husband's family an opportunity to arrange another match for him, thus bringing in another dowry. This phenomena, called dowry death, calls attention not just to the "evils of dowry" but also to larger issues of the powerlessness of women as well.

Serena Nanda
March 1998

"Don't be so much in a hurry," she said. "You Americans want everything done so quickly. You get married quickly and then just as quickly get divorced. Here we take marriage more seriously. We must take all the factors into account. It is not enough for us to learn by our mistakes. This is too serious a business. If a mistake is made we have not only ruined the life of our son or daughter, but we have spoiled the reputation of our family as well. And that will make it much harder for their brothers and sisters to get married. So we must be very careful."

If a mistake is made we have not only ruined the life of our son or daughter, but we have spoiled the reputation of our family as well.

What she said was true and I promised myself to be more patient, though it was not easy. I had really hoped and expected that the match would be made before my year in India was up. But it was not to be. When I left India my friend seemed no further along in finding a suitable match for her son than when I had arrived.

Two years later, I returned to India and still my friend had not found a girl for her son. By this time, he was close to thirty, and I think she was a little worried. Since she knew I had friends all over India, and I was going to be there for a year, she asked me to "help her in this work" and keep an eye out for someone suitable. I was flattered that my judgment was respected, but knowing now how complicated the process was, I had lost my earlier confidence as a matchmaker. Nevertheless, I promised that I would try.

It was almost at the end of my year's stay in India that I met a family with a marriageable daughter whom I felt might be a good possibility for my friend's son. The girl's father was related to a good friend of mine and by coincidence came from the same village as my friend's husband. This new family had a successful business in a medium-sized city in central India and were from the same subcaste as my friend. The daughter was pretty and chic; in fact, she had studied fashion design in college. Her parents would not allow her to go off by herself to any of the major cities in India where she could make a career, but they had compromised with her wish to work by allowing her to run a small dress-making boutique from their home. In spite of her desire to have a career, the daughter was both modest and home-loving and had had a traditional, sheltered upbringing. She had only one other sister, already married, and a brother who was in his father's business.

I mentioned the possibility of a match with my friend's son. The girl's parents were most interested. Although their daughter was not eager to marry just yet, the idea of living in Bombay—a sophisticated, extremely fashion-conscious city where she could continue her education in clothing design—was a great inducement. I gave the girl's father my friend's address and suggested that when they went to Bombay on some business or whatever, they look up the boy's family.

Returning to Bombay on my way to New York, I told my friend of this newly discovered possibility. She seemed to feel there was potential but, in spite of my urging, would not make any moves herself. She rather preferred to wait for the girl's family to call upon them. I hoped something would come of this introduction, though by now I had learned to rein in my optimism.

A year later I received a letter from my friend. The family had indeed come to visit Bombay, and their daughter and my friend's daughter, who were near in age, had become very good friends. During that year, the two girls had frequently visited each other. I thought things looked promising.

Last week I received an invitation to a wedding: My friend's son and the girl were getting married. Since I had found the match, my presence was particularly requested at the wedding. I was thrilled. Success at last! As I prepared to leave for India, I began thinking, "Now, my friend's younger son, who do I know who has a nice girl for him . . . ?"

Critical Thinking

1. To what extent are marriages arranged in India? How do middle class families in modern urban India feel about marriage? What is a "love match"?
2. How does the author describe the process of the parents' "getting them married" (with regard to young men and women)? Why did the author find this "oppressive"?
3. Describe the arguments and counter-arguments regarding arranged marriages as revealed in the verbal exchanges between the author and Sita.
4. In what sense did the author see arranged marriage as successful in contrast to marriage in the United States?
5. Why was the author so sure that a match could be made quickly for her friend's son?
6. What factors must be taken into account in arranging a marriage?
7. Why was the friend's son originally not considered a good match? What happened that would change his prospects? What drawbacks remained?
8. Describe the "problems" that arose with regard to the various "prospects" as well as the positive factors involved in the final match.

Internet References

Kinship and Social Organization
www.umanitoba.ca/anthropology

Sex and Marriage
http://anthro.palomar.edu/marriage/default.htm

Wedding Traditions and Customs
http://worldweddingtraditions.com

Edited by Philip R. DeVita.

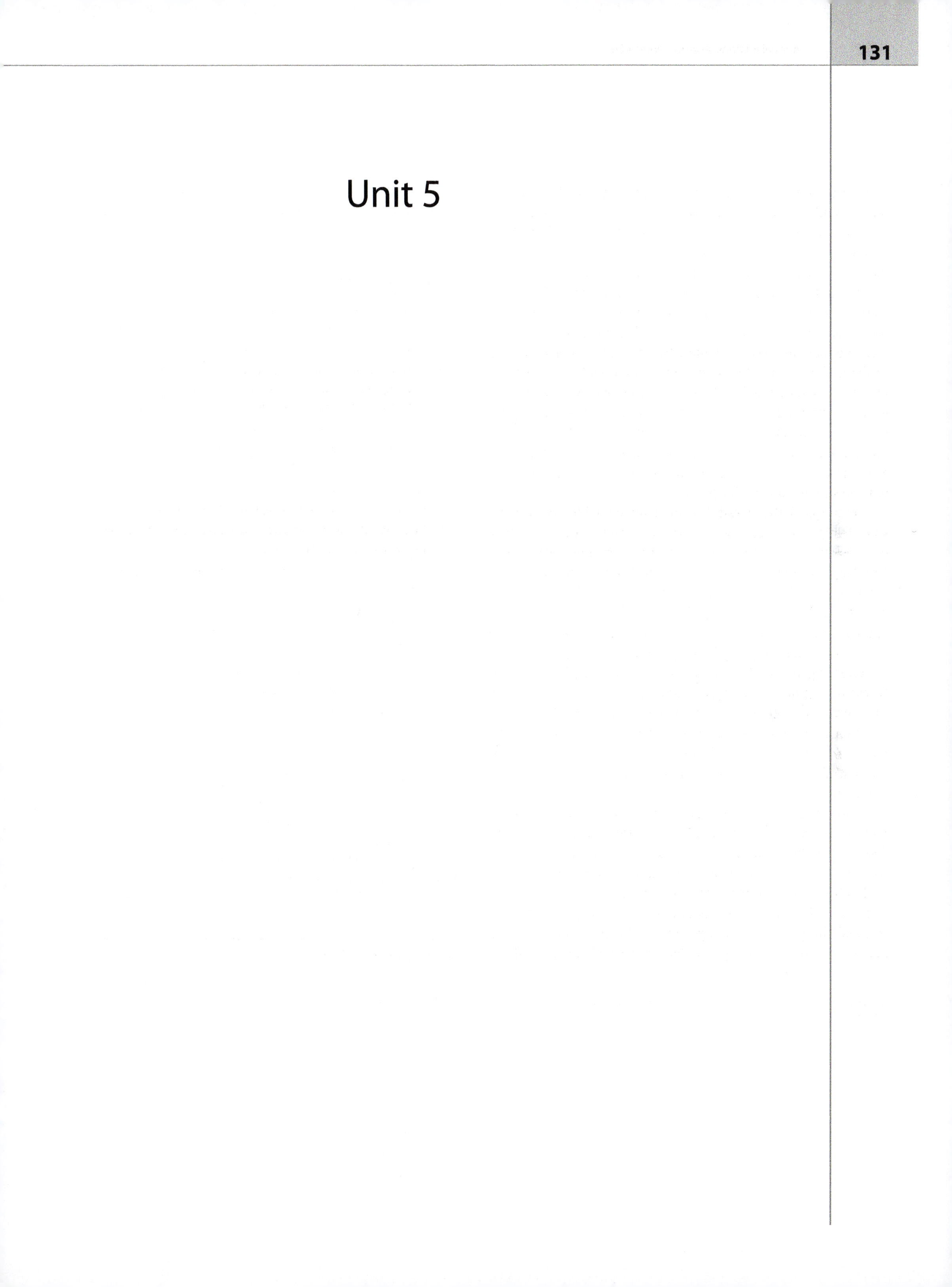

Unit 5

UNIT

Prepared by: Elvio Angeloni

Gender and Status

The feminist movement in the United States has had a significant impact upon the development of anthropology. Feminists have rightly charged that anthropologists have tended to gloss over the lives of women in studies of society and culture. In part this is because, until recent times, most anthropologists have been men. The result has been an undue emphasis on male activities as well as male perspectives in descriptions of particular societies.

These charges, however, have proven to be a firm corrective. In the last few decades, anthropologists have studied women and, more particularly, the division of labor based on gender and its relation to biology, as well as to social and political status. In addition, these changes in emphasis have been accompanied by an increase in the number of women in the field.

Feminist anthropologists have critically attacked many of the established anthropological beliefs. They have shown, for example, that field studies of nonhuman primates, which were often used to demonstrate the evolutionary basis of male dominance, distorted the actual evolutionary record by focusing primarily on baboons. While male baboons, for instance, have been shown to be especially dominant and aggressive, other, less-quoted primate studies show how dominance and aggression are highly situational phenomena, sensitive to ecological variation. Feminist anthropologists have also shown that the subsistence contribution of women was likewise ignored by anthropologists. A classic case is that of the !Kung, a hunting and gathering group in southern Africa, where women provide the bulk of the foodstuffs, including most of the available protein, and who, not coincidentally, enjoy a more egalitarian relationship than usual with men. Thus, since political control is a matter of cultural variation, male authority is not biologically predetermined. In fact, there are many cultures in which some men may play a more feminine or, at least, asexual role, showing that gender relationships are deeply embedded in social experience and that the gender categories employed in any given culture may be inadequate to the task of doing justice to the actual diversity that exists.

Lest we think that gender issues are primarily academic, we should keep in mind that gender equality in this world is still a distant dream.

Article

Prepared by: Elvio Angeloni

Return of the Missing Daughters

MONICA DAS GUPTA

Learning Outcomes

After reading this article, you will be able to:

- Explain why sons have been traditionally more valued than daughters in Asia.
- Discuss recent demographic changes in Asia with respect to gender in terms of its causes and its consequences for gender equality and family life in general.

Traditions That Favor Sons in Asia—Resulting in Millions of Dead or Neglected Girls—Have Started to Change

DAUGHTERS ARE USELESS AND UNWORTHY!" shouted an elderly woman in a village near Busan in South Korea in 1996. Other old women sitting with her, as we talked about families, nodded their agreement. Why, I asked? It was not because daughters were lazy, she said. "No, women did a lot of hard labor in the fields, and their marriage costs virtually nothing. People don't want daughters because they are not helpful to the family—they leave the family when they marry. It is sons who stay home, inherit assets, and keep the rituals of ancestor worship."

In China, I heard similar stories. A man said that when his daughter was born, "my wife was so upset that she did not want to care for the child, and I had to persuade her to nurse it."

These attitudes have had life-and-death effects. The natural human male–female birth ratio is only about 5–6 percent more boys than girls. But in China in 2000, there were 20 percent more boys born. This kind of skewed sex ratio has been found across much of East Asia, South Asia, the southern Caucasus, and parts of the Balkans. Female babies are aborted in these areas, killed at birth, or die through neglect. Why? As the woman from Busan said, it is brutal economics. These cultures have historically excluded adult daughters from helping in their parents' households or inheriting property, which diminishes their value to their birth family.

But recently, the demographic bias against females has begun to shift. South Korea has shown a rebalancing of child sex ratios since the mid-1990s, with proportions of boys to girls dropping from high levels to biologically normal ones. There is even a shift toward a preference for daughters in South Korea today. In India, the 2011 census shows a sharp drop in sex ratios in children in the northwestern part of the country, where they had been very high. In China, the climb in such sex ratios has leveled off.

These shifts coincide with rapid urbanization and social changes that have helped make daughters more valuable to their parents. Daughters no longer vanish from their birth families, and in some cases, they bring in additional men from outside. Twenty years after my original fieldwork in Busan, one woman in South Korea told me, "My mother suffered a lot of abuse when she was young because she had three daughters and no sons. Now that we are grown, she is very happy because we all remain close to her. She says that her sons-in-law treat her better than sons."

Shoving Women Out

FOR CENTURIES, the social organization of rural society in China, South Korea, and northwestern India pushed daughters away from their parents' households. When women married, they were absorbed into their husband's family. New labor in their birth family was provided by daughters-in-law marrying in, further emphasizing the value of sons. A similar social structure appears in other regions with strong son preference, including northern Vietnam and the southern Caucasus countries.

To cement this daughter transfer, when a woman joins her husband's family, her "slot" in her birth family is eliminated. A new slot is created for incoming brides. If women do return—a rare occurrence—they and their parents have to struggle hard to make the unusual situation work. Other members of the family and the village resist because of the potential reduction of their property rights. Once a woman from rural China has been married and her land entitlement reallocated among village residents, for example, her return can be met with a fair amount of antagonism.

The impact of these cultural norms can be seen in the contrast between elder living arrangements in countries such as Taiwan and South Korea and those in countries such as the Philippines. The first two have rigidly patrilineal (male-oriented) kinship systems, whereas the third has a system of kinship that does not favor children of any one gender. In Taiwan and South Korea, a substantial proportion of parents live with married sons, but almost none live with married daughters, according to a forthcoming study I conducted with Doo-Sub Kim of Hanyang University in Seoul. In the Philippines, parents are equally likely to live with married children of either gender. It is not surprising that child sex ratios are normal in the Philippines but have been lopsided in Taiwan and South Korea.

The results of devaluation of females are not surprising, either. Unwanted girls have been removed through infanticide and neglect, producing male-skewed child sex ratios. Beginning in the 1980s, sonograms and other technologies for prenatal sex detection made it possible to act on sex bias even before birth. The new methods made it easier for parents to avoid having unwanted daughters—through abortion—and sex ratios at birth showed more imbalance.

Major disruptions such as famine and war heighten the pressure on parents to get rid of children they perceive to be superfluous. Beginning in 1937, Japanese troops swept through eastern China, and girls went "missing:" 17 percent more girls died than one would expect from typical mortality rates in this situation. Parents in war-torn regions felt that they had to make some harsh choices. A woman in the province of Zhejiang told me of her own experience in the 1930s: "when I was six years old, my mother said that I should be sold. I begged my father not to do this, that I would eat very little if only they would let me stay at home." The collapse of governmental institutions can have similar effects. In the southern Caucasus countries, for instance, birth ratios favoring boys shot up when the USSR was dissolved.

A shift from large to small family size also increases the pressure on parents to select for sons. In large-family, high-fertility settings, parents can afford to have several daughters and still go on to have one or two sons. In small families with fewer births, there are only limited chances to have sons. The second girl born into such families in son-favoring cultures has a much higher chance of dying before birth or during early childhood.

When Brides Are in Short Supply

THE DEATHS of these female babies are a shocking result of gender inequality. The damaging effects ripple through society. Eventually they translate into a shortage of adult women. And after heightened periods of sex selection in earlier decades, a "marriage squeeze" now grips China, South Korea, and northwestern India. China presents the starkest scenario. In 2010, the Chinese Academy of Social Sciences estimated that by 2020, one in five men in China will be unable to find a wife.

The bride shortage affects poorer men most severely. In China, Shang-Jin Wei of Columbia University and his colleague report that poorer parents in areas with imbalanced sex ratios struggle to improve their sons' chances in the marriage market. The parents resort to desperate measures such as taking on dangerous work to earn more and build a nicer house, one who can attract this newly scarce and valuable commodity: a bride to marry into the family.

At the same time, the marriage squeeze can benefit women. In areas of China with fewer potential brides, a study by Maria Porter of Michigan State University found that women have greater bargaining power within their marriage, enabling them to provide greater support for their parents than before. Women from poor areas can marry men who offer higher living standards, either locally or by migrating to other parts of their country. Some migrate to other countries to marry better-off men. In China, South Korea, and India, several studies show these long-distance suitors are typically socioeconomically disadvantaged compared with other men in their own locale. They are unable to attract a local wife but still can offer an improved standard of living to women from impoverished regions.

These migration marriages do come with risks for women, however. Some research suggests that women who come from different ethnic or linguistic groups face problems in assimilation, are viewed as outsiders, do not know the local language and customs, and have limited social networks in their new setting. Many such marriages are to men who live in rural areas, and rural life further isolates the brides.

Difficulties can go beyond social isolation and cultural misunderstandings. In a 2010 study of Vietnamese brides in Taiwan, done by researchers at Viet Nam National University, Ho Chi Minh City, most women said that they were happy because they were able to help their birth families financially. But some mentioned problems, such as being humiliated by their husband and in-laws for their poverty, suffering domestic violence, or being made to work like a slave. In Taiwan, in fact, a 2006 study found that marriage migration was a risk factor in domestic violence. And in South Korea, Hanyang's Kim found a greater likelihood of divorce among such marriages.

Some researchers and policy makers have also suggested that the creation of a generation of enforced bachelors may raise levels of crime and violence, including violence against women. Crime levels climbed in areas with higher male-to-female ratios, according to a study in India led by Jean Drèze of the Delhi School of Economics, as well as another study, which was conducted in China by Lena Edlund of Columbia and her colleagues.

The Value of Women

OVER THE PAST TWO DECADES, the bias against girls has begun to diminish. My colleague Woojin Chung and I documented this phenomenon in a study of South Korean women's changing attitudes toward children's gender. When interviewed in 1991, 35 percent of women born between 1955 and 1964 said that they "must have a son." But by 2003, only 19 percent of women born in that same period held this view. Changes in attitude have swept across society. Even after accounting for differences in education levels and urban versus rural residence, the odds of women aged 15–49 stating they "must have a son" in 2003 were roughly ⅓ of the 1991 level. Changes in social norms account for as much as 73 percent of this decline. Only 27 percent of the drop is caused solely by increases in individual levels of education and urbanization. When attitudes changed, child sex ratios followed, as shown in the box on the opposite page.

What turned the corner, enhancing girls' value? It is a hard answer to tease out, but the increasing urbanization and education of parents play a major role. South Korea, for example, has urbanized at blistering speed, with the percentage of people living in and around cities doubling between 1966 and 1986, from 33 to 67 percent. By 1991, 75 percent of the population lived in urban areas. The effects of urban life on son preference are both social and economic. Living in a city reduces the centrality of sons' roles in their parents' lives. While villagers spend their days surrounded by clan members, urban residents live and work in the more impersonal settings of apartment blocks and office complexes. This shift relieves pressure to conform to traditional expectations of filial duty and to have sons to continue the lineage.

In urban areas, children who support their parents tend to do so less because of formal rules and more because they happen to live in the same city and have strong relationships with their parents. In this way, urbanization helps to bridge the gap between the value placed on daughters and sons. Female education and employment also enhance the potential support they can offer. And with growing access to pensions and social protection systems, people become less dependent on their children for financial support.

Government policies have also nudged male preference into decline by encouraging mainstream equality for women. India has used affirmative action to increase women's political participation, putting a female quota in place for candidates for local government positions. Social scientists have found that after the policy was created, gender stereotypes weakened in the population as a whole, and girls' aspirations for themselves rose.

Extensive media outreach has also been a staple feature of family-planning programs in India, China, and South Korea. Posters and commercials encourage parents to have small families even if they do not include sons. These efforts promote the view that daughters are just as good as sons for family happiness.

Female characters in popular Indian television soap operas now work outside the home and are active in public life. The values and roles illustrated in these programs challenge traditional views of a woman's place in society. Studies show that exposure to these messages is associated with reduced son preference.

There have also been direct attempts to change sex ratios by banning the use of technology for prenatal sex detection and selection. These bans have been put into place in several countries, but there has been little rigorous evaluation of the impact of these measures because of a lack of data. India's ban on sex selection appears to have had at most a modest effect. A vigorous effort in China to ban birth selection has shown little effect on the national sex ratio of babies.

Countries in Asia are still urbanizing rapidly, so I believe the preference for sons will continue to decline. Policy makers can accelerate this process through legal and other measures enhancing gender equity. They can also expand media advocacy and portray women helping their own aging parents (not just their in-laws). Such steps help to change gender stereotypes and overcome parents' preference for sons. For women—and for society in general—such approaches may have better outcomes than outright attempts to ban the selection of sex at birth.

...

Critical Thinking

1. Why were sons favored over daughters in traditional Asia? What were the consequences of this attitude with respect to gender inequality?

2. Why has there been a "marriage squeeze" in Asia in recent times?
3. Why has gender inequality been diminishing in Asia lately?

Internet References

Asian Journal of Women's Studies
https://www.tandfonline.com/toc/rajw20/current

East Asia Forum
www.eastasiaforum.org/2016/06/20/gender-and-sexuality-in-asia-today/

International Journal of Gender & Women's
ijgws.com/

Monica Das Gupta is a research professor at the University of Maryland's sociology department and is a former senior demographer for the World Bank.

Das Gupta, Monica. "Return of the Missing Daughters," *Scientific American*, vol. 317, no. 3, September 2017.

Article

Prepared by: Elvio Angeloni

The Berdache Tradition

WALTER L. WILLIAMS

Learning Outcomes

After reading this article, you will be able to:

- Define berdache and explain how it highlights the ways in which different societies accommodate atypical individuals.
- Discuss Native American beliefs regarding the berdache.

Because it is such a powerful force in the world today, the Western Judeo-Christian tradition is often accepted as the arbiter of "natural" behavior of humans. If Europeans and their descendant nations of North America accept something as normal, then anything different is seen as abnormal. Such a view ignores the great diversity of human existence.

This is the case of the study of gender. How many genders are there? To a modern Anglo-American, nothing might seem more definite than the answer that there are two: men and women. But not all societies around the world agree with Western culture's view that all humans are either women or men. The commonly accepted notion of "the opposite sex," based on anatomy, is itself an artifact of our society's rigid sex roles.

Among many cultures, there have existed different alternatives to "man" or "woman." An alternative role in many American Indian societies is referred to by anthropologists as *berdache*. . . . The role varied from one Native American culture to another, which is a reflection of the vast diversity of aboriginal New World societies. Small bands of hunter-gatherers existed in some areas, with advanced civilizations of farming peoples in other areas. With hundreds of different languages, economies, religions, and social patterns existing in North America alone, every generalization about a cultural tradition must acknowledge many exceptions.

This diversity is true for the berdache tradition as well, and must be kept in mind. My statements should be read as being specific to a particular culture, with generalizations being treated as loose patterns that might not apply to peoples even in nearby areas.

Briefly, a berdache can be defined as a morphological male who does not fill a society's standard man's role, who has a non-masculine character. This type of person is often stereotyped as effeminate, but a more accurate characterization is androgyny. Such a person has a clearly recognized and accepted social status, often based on a secure place in the tribal mythology. Berdaches have special ceremonial roles in many Native American religions, and important economic roles in their families. They will do at least some women's work, and mix together much of the behavior, dress, and social roles of women and men. Berdaches gain social prestige by their spiritual, intellectual, or craftwork/artistic contributions, and by their reputation for hard work and generosity. They serve a mediating function between women and men, precisely because their character is seen as distinct from either sex. They are not seen as men, yet they are not seen as women either. They occupy an alternative gender role that is a mixture of diverse elements.

In their erotic behavior berdaches also generally (but not always) take a nonmasculine role, either being asexual or becoming the passive partner in sex with men. In some cultures the berdache might become a wife to a man. This male-male sexual behavior became the focus of an attack on berdaches as "sodomites" by the Europeans who, early on, came into contact with them. From the first Spanish conquistadors to the Western frontiersmen and the Christian missionaries and government officials, Western culture has had a considerable impact on the berdache tradition. In the last two decades, the most recent impact on the tradition is the adaptation of a modern Western gay identity.

To Western eyes berdachism is a complex and puzzling phenomenon, mixing and redefining the very concepts of what is considered male and female. In a culture with only two recognized genders, such individuals are gender nonconformist, abnormal, deviant. But to American Indians, the institution of another gender role means that berdaches are not deviant—indeed, they do conform to the requirements of a custom in which their culture tells them they fit. Berdachism is a way for society to recognize and assimilate some atypical individuals without imposing a change on them or stigmatizing them as deviant. This cultural institution confirms their legitimacy for what they are.

Societies often bestow power upon that which does not neatly fit into the usual. Since no cultural system can explain everything, a common way that many cultures deal with these inconsistencies is to imbue them with negative power, as taboo, pollution, witchcraft, or sin. That which is not understood is seen as a threat. But an alternative method of dealing with such things, or people, is to take them out of the realm of threat and to sanctify them.[1] The berdaches' role as mediator is thus not just between women and men, but also between the physical and the spiritual. American Indian cultures have taken what Western culture calls negative, and made it a positive; they have successfully utilized the different skills and insights of a class of people that Western culture has stigmatized and whose spiritual powers have been wasted.

Many Native Americans also understood that gender roles have to do with more than just biological sex. The standard Western view that one's sex is always a certainty, and that one's gender identity and sex role always conform to one's morphological sex is a view that dies hard. Western thought is typified by such dichotomies of groups perceived to be mutually exclusive: male and female, black and white, right and wrong, good and evil. Clearly, the world is not so simple; such clear divisions are not always realistic. Most American Indian worldviews generally are much more accepting of the ambiguities of life. Acceptance of gender variation in the berdache tradition is typical of many native cultures' approach to life in general.

Overall, these are generalizations based on those Native American societies that had an accepted role for berdaches. Not all cultures recognized such a respected status. Berdachism in aboriginal North America was most established among tribes in four areas: first, the Prairie and western Great Lakes, the northern and central Great Plains, and the lower Mississippi Valley; second, Florida and the Caribbean; third, the Southwest, the Great Basin, and California; and fourth, scattered areas of the Northwest, western Canada, and Alaska. For some reason it is not noticeable in eastern North America, with the exception of its southern rim. . . .

American Indian Religions

Native American religions offered an explanation for human diversity by their creation stories. In some tribal religions, the Great Spiritual Being is conceived as neither male nor female but as a combination of both. Among the Kamia of the Southwest, for example, the bearer of plant seeds and the introducer of Kamia culture was a man-woman spirit named Warharmi.[2] A key episode of the Zuni creation story involves a battle between the kachina spirits of the agricultural Zunis and the enemy hunter spirits. Every four years an elaborate ceremony commemorates this myth. In the story a kachina spirit called *ko'lhamana* was captured by the enemy spirits and transformed in the process. This transformed spirit became a mediator between the two sides, using his peacemaking skills to merge the differing lifestyles of hunters and farmers. In the ceremony, a dramatic reenactment of the myth, the part of the transformed *ko'lhamana* spirit, is performed by a berdache.[3] The Zuni word for berdache is *lhamana,* denoting its closeness to the spiritual mediator who brought hunting and farming together.[4] The moral of this story is that the berdache was created by the deities for a special purpose, and that this creation led to the improvement of society. The continual reenactment of this story provides a justification for the Zuni berdache in each generation.

In contrast to this, the lack of spiritual justification in a creation myth could denote a lack of tolerance for gender variation. The Pimas, unlike most of their Southwestern neighbors, did not respect a berdache status. *Wi-kovat,* their derogatory word, means "like a girl," but it does not signify a recognized social role. Pima mythology reflects this lack of acceptance in a folk tale that explains male androgyny as due to Papago witchcraft. Knowing that the Papagos respected berdaches, the Pimas blamed such an occurrence on an alien influence.[5] While the Pimas' condemnatory attitude is unusual, it does point out the importance of spiritual explanations for the acceptance of gender variance in a culture.

Other Native American creation stories stand in sharp contrast to the Pima explanation. A good example is the account of the Navajos, which presents women and men as equals. The Navajo origin tale is told as a story of five worlds. The first people were First Man and First Woman, who were created equally and at the same time. The first two worlds that they lived in were bleak and unhappy, so they escaped to the third world. In the third world lived two twins, Turquoise Boy and White Shell Girl, who were the first berdaches. In the Navajo language the world for berdache is *nadle,* which means "changing one" or "one who is transformed." It is applied to hermaphrodites—those who are born with the genitals of both male and female—and also to "those who pretend to be *nadle,*" who take on a social role that is distinct from either men or women.[6]

In the third world, First Man and First Woman began farming, with the help of the changing twins. One of the twins noticed some clay and, holding it in the palm of his/her hand, shaped it into the first pottery bowl. Then he/she formed a plate, a water dipper, and a pipe. The second twin observed some reeds and began to weave them, making the first basket. Together they shaped axes and grinding stones from rocks, and hoes from bone. All these new inventions made the people very happy.[7]

The message of this story is that humans are dependent for many good things on the inventiveness of *nadle.* Such individuals were present from the earliest eras of human existence, and their presence was never questioned. They were part of the natural order of the universe, with a special contribution to make.

Later on in the Navajo creation story, White Shell Girl entered the moon and became the Moon Bearer. Turquoise Boy, however, remained with the people. When First Man realized that Turquoise Boy could do all manner of women's work as well as women, all the men left the women and crossed a big river. The men hunted and planted crops. Turquoise Boy ground the corn, cooked the food, and weaved cloth for the men. Four years passed with the women and men separated, and the men were happy with the *nadle.* Later, however the women wanted to learn how to grind corn from the *nadle,* and both the men and women had decided that it was not good to continue living separately. So the women crossed the river and the people were reunited.[8]

They continued living happily in the third world, until one day a great flood began. The people ran to the highest mountaintop, but the water kept rising and they all feared they would be drowned. But just in time, the ever-inventive Turquoise Boy found a large reed. They climbed upward inside the tall hollow reed, and came out at the top into the fourth world. From there, White Shell Girl brought another reed, and they climbed again to the fifth world, which is the present world of the Navajos.[9]

These stories suggest that the very survival of humanity is dependent on the inventiveness of berdaches. With such a mythological belief system, it is no wonder that the Navajos held *nadle* in high regard. The concept of the *nadle* is well formulated in the creation story. As children were educated by these stories, and all Navajos believed in them, the high status accorded to gender variation was passed down from generation to generation. Such stories also provided instruction for *nadle* themselves to live by. A spiritual explanation guaranteed a special place for a person who was considered different but not deviant.

For American Indians, the important explanations of the world are spiritual ones. In their view, there is a deeper reality than the here-and-now. The real essence or wisdom occurs when one finally gives up trying to explain events in terms of "logic" and "reality." Many confusing aspects of existence can better be explained by actions of a multiplicity of spirits. Instead of a concept of a single god, there is an awareness of "that which we do not understand." In Lakota religion, for example, the term *Wakan Tanka* is often translated as "god." But a more proper translation, according to the medicine people who taught me, is "The Great Mystery."[10]

While rationality can explain much, there are limits to human capabilities of understanding. The English language is structured to account for cause and effect. For example, English speakers say, "It is raining," with the implication that there is a cause "it" that leads to rain. Many Indian languages, on the other hand, merely note what is most accurately translated as "raining" as an observable fact. Such an approach brings a freedom to stop worrying about causes of things, and merely to relax and accept that our human insights can go only so far. By not taking ourselves too seriously, or overinflating human importance, we can get beyond the logical world.

The emphasis of American Indian religions, then, is on the spiritual nature of all things. To understand the physical world, one must appreciate the underlying spiritual essence. Then one can begin to see that the physical is only a faint shadow, a partial reflection, of a supernatural and extrarational world. By the Indian view, everything that exists is spiritual. Every object—plants, rocks, water, air, the moon, animals, humans, the earth itself—has a spirit. The spirit of one thing (including a human) is not superior to the spirit of any other. Such a view promotes a sophisticated ecological awareness of the place that humans have in the larger environment. The function of religion is not to try to condemn or to change what exists, but to accept the realities of the world and to appreciate their contributions to life. Everything that exists has a purpose.[11]

One of the basic tenets of American Indian religion is the notion that everything in the universe is related. Nevertheless, things that exist are often seen as having a counterpart: sky and earth, plant and animal, water and fire. In all of these polarities, there exist mediators. The role of the mediator is to hold the polarities together, to keep the world from disintegrating. Polarities exist within human society also. The most important category within Indian society is gender. The notions of Woman and Man underlie much of social interaction and are comparable to the other major polarities. Women, with their nurtural qualities, are associated with the earth, while men are associated with the sky. Women gatherers and farmers deal with plants (of the earth), while men hunters deal with animals.

The mediator between the polarities of woman and man, in the American Indian religious explanation, is a being that combines the elements of both genders. This might be a combination in a physical sense, as in the case of hermaphrodites. Many Native American religions accept this phenomenon in the same way that they accept other variations from the norm. But more important is their acceptance of the idea that gender can be combined in ways other than physical hermaphroditism. The physical aspects of a thing or a person, after all, are not nearly as important as its spirit. American Indians use the concept of a person's *spirit* in the way that other Americans use the concept of a person's *character*. Consequently, physical hermaphroditism is not necessary for the idea of gender mixing. A person's character, their spiritual essence, is the crucial thing.

The Berdache's Spirit

Individuals who are physically normal might have the spirit of the other sex, might range somewhere between the two sexes, or might have a spirit that is distinct from either women or men. Whatever category they fall into, they are seen as being different from men. They are accepted spiritually as "Not Man." Whichever option is chosen, Indian religions offer spiritual explanations. Among the Arapahos of the Plains, berdaches are called *haxu'xan* and are seen to be that way as a result of a supernatural gift from birds or animals. Arapaho mythology recounts the story of Nih'a'ca, the first *haxu'xan.* He pretended to be a woman and married the mountain lion, a symbol for masculinity. The myth, as recorded by ethnographer Alfred Kroeber about 1900, recounted that "These people had the natural desire to become women, and as they grew up gradually became women. They gave up the desires of men. They were married to men. They had miraculous power and could do supernatural things. For instance, it was one of them that first made an intoxicant from rainwater."[12] Besides the theme of inventiveness, similar to the Navajo creation story, the berdache role is seen as a product of a "natural desire." Berdaches "gradually became women," which underscores the notion of woman as a social category rather than as a fixed biological entity. Physical biological sex is less important in gender classification than a person's desire—one's spirit.

They myths contain no prescriptions for trying to change berdaches who are acting out their desires of the heart. Like many other cultures' myths, the Zuni origin myths simply sanction the idea that gender can be transformed independently of biological sex.[13] Indeed, myths warn of dire consequences when interference with such a transformation is attempted. Prince Alexander Maximilian of the German state of Wied, traveling in the northern Plains in the 1830s, heard a myth about a warrior who once tried to force a berdache to avoid women's clothing. The berdache resisted, and the warrior shot him with an arrow. Immediately the berdache disappeared, and the warrior saw only a pile of stones with his arrow in them. Since then, the story concluded, no intelligent person would try to coerce a berdache.[14] Making the point even more directly, a Mandan myth told of an Indian who tried to force *mihdake* (berdaches) to give up their distinctive dress and status, which led the spirits to punish many people with death. After that, no Mandans interfered with berdaches.[15]

With this kind of attitude, reinforced by myth and history, the aboriginal view accepts human diversity. The creation story of the Mohave of the Colorado River Valley speaks of a time when people were not sexually differentiated. From this perspective, it is easy to accept that certain individuals might combine elements of masculinity and femininity.[16] A respected Mohave elder, speaking in the 1930s, stated this viewpoint simply: "From the very beginning of the world it was meant that there should be [berdaches], just as it was instituted that there should be shamans. They were intended for that purpose."[17]

This elder also explained that a child's tendencies to become a berdache are apparent early, by about age nine to twelve, before the child reaches puberty: "That is the time when young persons become initiated into the functions of their sex. . . . None but young people will become berdaches as a rule."[18] Many tribes have a public ceremony that acknowledges the acceptance of berdache status. A Mohave shaman related the ceremony for his tribe: "When the child was about ten years old his relatives would begin discussing his strange ways. Some of them disliked it, but the more intelligent began envisaging an initiation ceremony." The relatives prepare for the ceremony without letting the boy know of it. It is meant to take him by surprise, to be both an initiation and a test of his true inclinations. People from various settlements are invited to attend. The family wants the community to see it and become accustomed to accepting the boy as an *alyha.*

On the day of the ceremony, the shaman explained, the boy is led into a circle: "If the boy showed a willingness to remain standing in the circle, exposed to the public eye, it was almost certain that he would go through with the ceremony. The singer, hidden behind the crowd, began singing the songs. As soon as the sound reached the boy he began to dance as women do." If the boy is unwilling to assume *alyha* status, he would refuse to dance. But if his character—his spirit—is *alyha,* "the song goes right to his heart and he will dance with much intensity. He cannot help it. After the fourth song he is proclaimed." After the ceremony, the boy is carefully bathed and receives a woman's skirt. He is then led back to the dance ground, dressed as an *alyha,* and announces his new feminine name to the crowd. After that he would resent being called by his old male name.[19]

Among the Yuman tribes of the Southwest, the transformation is marked by a social gathering, in which the berdache prepares a meal for the friends of the family.[20] Ethnographer Ruth Underhill, doing fieldwork among the Papago Indians in the early 1930s, wrote that berdaches were common among the Papago Indians, and were usually publicly acknowledged in childhood. She recounted that a boy's parents would test him if they noticed that he preferred female pursuits. The regular pattern, mentioned by many of Underhill's Papago informants, was to build a small brush enclosure. Inside the enclosure they placed a man's bow and arrows, and also a woman's basket. At the appointed time the boy was brought to the enclosure as the adults watched from outside. The boy was told to go inside the circle of brush. Once he was inside, the adults "set fire to the enclosure. They watched what he took with him as he ran out and if it was the basketry materials, they reconciled themselves to his being a berdache."[21]

What is important to recognize in all of these practices is that the assumption of a berdache role was not forced on the boy by others. While adults might have their suspicions, it was only when the child made the proper move that he was considered a berdache. By doing woman's dancing, preparing a meal, or taking the woman's basket he was making an important symbolic gesture. Indian children were not stupid, and they knew the implications of these ceremonies beforehand. A boy in the enclosure could have left without taking anything, or could have taken both the man's and the woman's tools. With the community standing by watching, he was well aware that his choice would mark his assumption of berdache status. Rather than being seen as an involuntary test of his reflexes, this ceremony may be interpreted as a definite statement by the child to take on the berdache role.

Indians do not see the assumption of berdache status, however, as a free will choice on the part of the boy. People felt that the boy was acting out his basic character. The Lakota shaman Lame Deer explained:

> They were not like other men, but the Great Spirit made them *winktes* and we accepted them as such. . . . We think that if a woman has two little ones growing inside her, if she is going to have twins, sometimes instead of giving birth to two babies they have formed up in her womb into just one, into a half-man/half-woman kind of being. . . . To us a man is what nature, or his dreams, make him. We accept him for what he wants to be. That's up to him.[22]

While most of the sources indicate that once a person becomes a berdache it is a lifelong status, directions from the spirits determine everything. In at least one documented case, concerning a nineteenth-century Klamath berdache named Lele'ks, he later had a supernatural experience that led him to leave the berdache role. At that time Lele'ks began dressing and acting like a man, then married women, and eventually became one of the most famous Klamath chiefs.[23] What is important is that both in assuming berdache status and in leaving it, supernatural dictate is the determining factor.

Dreams and Visions

Many tribes see the berdache role as signifying an individual's proclivities as a dreamer and a visionary. . . .

Among the northern Plains and related Great Lakes tribes, the idea of supernatural dictate through dreaming—the vision quest—had its highest development. The goal of the vision quest is to try to get beyond the rational world by sensory deprivation and fasting. By depriving one's body of nourishment, the brain could escape from logical thought and connect with the higher reality of the supernatural. The person doing the quest simply sits and waits for a vision. But a vision might not come easily; the person might have to wait for days.

The best way that I can describe the process is to refer to my own vision quest, which I experienced when I was living on a Lakota reservation in 1982. After a long series of prayers and blessings, the shaman who had prepared me for the ceremony took me out to an isolated area where a sweat lodge had been set up for my quest. As I walked to the spot, I worried that I might not be able to stand it. Would I be overcome by hunger? Could I tolerate the thirst? What would I do if I had to go to the toilet? The shaman told me not to worry, that a whole group of holy people would be praying and singing for me while I was on my quest.

He had me remove my clothes, symbolizing my disconnection from the material would, and crawl into the sweat lodge. Before he left me I asked him, "What do I think about?" He said, "Do not think. Just pray for spiritual guidance." After a prayer he closed the flap tightly and I was left in total darkness. I still do not understand what happened to me during my vision quest, but during the day and a half that I was out there, I never once felt hungry or thirsty or the need to go to the toilet. What happened was an intensely personal experience that I cannot and do not wish to explain, a process of being that cannot be described in rational terms.

When the shaman came to get me at the end of my time, I actually resented having to end it. He did not need to ask if my vision quest was successful. He knew that it was even before seeing me, he explained, because he saw an eagle circling over me while I underwent the quest. He helped interpret the signs I had seen, then after more prayers and singing he led me back to the others. I felt relieved, cleansed, joyful, and serene. I had been through an experience that will be a part of my memories always.

If a vision quest could have such an effect on a person not even raised in Indian society, imagine its impact on a boy who from his earliest years had been waiting for the day when he could seek his vision. Gaining his spiritual power from his first vision, it would tell him what role to take in adult life. The vision might instruct him that he is going to be a great hunter, a craftsman, a warrior, or a shaman. Or it might tell him that he will be a berdache. Among the Lakotas, or Sioux, there are several symbols for various types of visions. A person becomes *wakan* (a sacred person) if she or he dreams of a bear, a wolf, thunder, a buffalo, a white buffalo calf, or Double Woman. Each dream results in a different gift, whether it is the power to cure illness or wounds, a promise of good hunting, or the exalted role of a *heyoka* (doing things backward).

A white buffalo calf is believed to be a berdache. If a person has a dream of the sacred Double Woman, this means that she or he will have the power to seduce men. Males who have a vision of Double Woman are presented with female tools. Taking such tools means that the male will become a berdache. The Lakota word *winkte* is composed of *win,* "woman," and *kte,* "would become."[24] A contemporary Lakota berdache explains, "To become a *winkte,* you have a medicine man put you up on the hill, to search for your vision. "You can become a *winkte* if you truly are by nature. You see a vision of the White Buffalo Calf Pipe. Sometimes it varies. A vision is like a scene in a movie."[25] Another way to become a *winkte* is to have a vision given by a *winkte* from the past.[26]. . .

By interpreting the result of the vision as being the work of a spirit, the vision quest frees the person from feeling responsible for his transformation. The person might even claim that the change was done against his will and without his control. Such a claim does not suggest a negative attitude about berdache status, because it is common for people to claim reluctance to fulfill their spiritual duty no matter what vision appears to them. Becoming any kind of sacred person involves taking on various social responsibilities and burdens.[27]. . .

A story was told among the Lakotas in the 1880s of a boy who tried to resist following his vision from Double Woman. But according to Lakota informants "few men succeed in this effort after having taken the strap in the dream." Having rebelled against the instructions given him by the Moon Being, he committed suicide.[28] The moral of that story is that one should not resist spiritual guidance, because it will lead only to grief. In another case, an Omaha young man told of being addressed by a spirit as "daughter," whereupon he discovered that he was unconsciously using feminine styles of speech. He tried to use male speech patterns, but could not. As a result of this vision, when he returned to his people he resolved himself to dress as a woman.[29] Such stories function to justify personal peculiarities as due to a fate over which the individual has no control.

Despite the usual pattern in Indian societies of using ridicule to enforce conformity, receiving instructions from a vision inhibits others from trying to change the berdache. Ritual explanation provides a way out. It also excuses the community from worrying about the cause of that person's difference, or the feeling that it is society's duty to try to change him.[30] Native American religions, above all else, encourage a basic respect for nature. If nature makes a person different, many Indians conclude, a mere human should not undertake to counter this spiritual dictate. Someone who is "unusual" can be accommodated without being stigmatized as "abnormal." Berdachism is thus not alien or threatening; it is a reflection of spirituality.

Notes

1. Mary Douglas, *Purity and Danger* (Baltimore: Penguin, 1966), p. 52. I am grateful to Theda Perdue for convincing me that Douglas's ideas apply to berdachism. For an application of Douglas's thesis to berdaches, see James Thayer, "The Berdache of the Northern Plains: A Socioreligious Perspective," *Journal of Anthropological Research 36* (1980): 292–93.
2. E. W. Gifford, "The Kamia of Imperial Valley," *Bureau of American Ethnology Bulletin 97* (1931): 12.
3. By using present tense verbs in this text, I am not implying that such activities are necessarily continuing today. I sometimes use the present tense in the "ethnographic present," unless I use the past tense when I am referring to something that has not continued. Past tense implies that all such practices have disappeared. In the absence of fieldwork to prove such disappearance, I am not prepared to make that assumption, on the historic changes in the berdache tradition.
4. Elsie Clews Parsons, "The Zuni La' Mana," *American Anthropologist 18* (1916): 521; Matilda Coxe Stevenson, "Zuni Indians," *Bureau of American Ethnology Annual Report 23* (1903): 37; Franklin Cushing, "Zuni Creation Myths," *Bureau of American Ethnology Annual Report 13* (1894): 401–3. Will Roscoe clarified this origin story for me.
5. W. W. Hill, "Note on the Pima Berdache," *American Anthropologist 40* (1938): 339.
6. Aileen O'Bryan, "The Dine': Origin Myths of the Navaho Indians," *Bureau of American Ethnology Bulletin 163* (1956): 5; W. W. Hill, "The Status of the Hermaphrodite and Transvestite in Navaho Culture," *American Anthropologist 37* (1935): 273.
7. Martha S. Link, *The Pollen Path: A Collection of Navajo Myths* (Stanford: Stanford University Press, 1956).
8. O'Bryan, "Dine'," pp. 5, 7, 9–10.
9. Ibid.
10. Lakota informants, July 1982. See also William Powers, *Oglala Religion* (Lincoln: University of Nebraska Press, 1977).
11. For this admittedly generalized overview of American Indian religious values, I am indebted to traditionalist informants of many tribes, but especially those of the Lakotas. For a discussion of native religions see Dennis Tedlock, *Finding the Center* (New York: Dial Press, 1972); Ruth Underhill, *Red Man's Religion* (Chicago: University of Chicago Press, 1965); and Elsi Clews Parsons, *Pueblo Indian Religion* (Chicago: University of Chicago Press, 1939).
12. Alfred Kroeber, "The Arapaho," *Bulletin of the American Museum of Natural History 18* (1902–7): 19.
13. Parsons, "Zuni La' Mana," p. 525.
14. Alexander Maximilian, *Travels in the interior of North America, 1832–1834,* vol. 22 of *Early Western Travels,* ed. Reuben Gold Thwaites, 32 vols. (Cleveland: A. H. Clark, 1906), pp. 283–84, 354. Maximilian was quoted in German in the early homosexual rights book by Ferdinand Karsch-Haack, *Das Gleichgeschlechtliche Leben der Naturvölker* (The same-sex life of nature peoples) (Munich: Verlag von Ernst Reinhardt,

1911; reprinted New York: Arno Press, 1975), pp. 314, 564.

15. Oscar Koch, *Der Indianishe Eros* (Berlin: Verlag Continent, 1925), p. 61.
16. George Devereux, "Institutionalized Homosexuality of the Mohave Indians," *Human Biology 9* (1937): 509.
17. Ibid., p. 501
18. Ibid.
19. Ibid., pp. 508–9.
20. C. Daryll Forde, "Ethnography of the Yuma Indians," *University of California Publications in American Archaeology and Ethnology 28* (1931): 157.
21. Ruth Underhill, *Social Organization of the Papago Indians* (New York: Columbia University Press, 1938), p. 186. This story is also mentioned in Ruth Underhill, ed., *The Autobiography of a Papago Woman* (Menasha, Wisc.: American Anthropological Association, 1936), p. 39.
22. John Fire and Richard Erdoes, *Lame Deer, Seeker of Visions* (New York: Simon and Schuster, 1972), pp. 117, 149.
23. Theodore Stern, *The Klamath Tribe: A People and Their Reservation* (Seattle: University of Washington Press, 1965), pp. 20, 24; Theodore Stern, "Some Sources of Variability in Klamath Mythology," *Journal of American Folklore 69* (1956): 242ff; Leshe Spier, *Klamath Ethnography* (Berkeley: University of California Press, 1930), p. 52.
24. Clark Wissler, "Societies and Ceremonial Associations in the Oglala Division of the Teton Dakota," *Anthropological Papers of the American Museum of Natural History 11*, pt. 1 (1916): 92; Powers, *Oglala Religion*, pp. 57–59.
25. Ronnie Loud Hawk, Lakota informant 4, July 1982.
26. Terry Calling Eagle, Lakota informant 5, July 1982.
27. James S. Thayer, "The Berdache of the Northern Plains: A Socioreligious Perspective," *Journal of Anthropological Research 36* (1980): 289.
28. Fletcher, "Elk Mystery," p. 281.
29. Alice Fletcher and Francis La Flesche, "The Omaha Tribe," *Bureau of American Ethnology Annual Report 27* (1905–6): 132.
30. Harriet Whitehead offers a valuable discussion of this element of the vision quest in "The Bow and the Burden Strap: A New Look at Institutionalized Homosexuality in Native North America," in *Sexual Meanings*, ed. Sherry Ortner and Harriet Whitehead (Cambridge: Cambridge University Press, 1981), pp. 99–102. See also Erikson, "Childhood," p. 329.

Critical Thinking

1. What is a berdache? What special roles have berdaches played in Native American societies?
2. What kinds of erotic behavior have they exhibited?
3. How have Europeans and American Indians differed in their treatment of the berdaches? How does the author explain these two different approaches?
4. How does the author contrast Western thought with Native American views regarding gender?
5. Why do Native Americans explain things in spiritual terms rather than "logic" and "reality"?
6. What is the emphasis of American Indian religions? What is the function of such religion?
7. What is one of the most basic tenets of American Indian religion? What kinds of polarities exist? Why are mediators necessary?
8. What is the most important category within Indian society? How do men and women differ?
9. Describe some of the Native American beliefs regarding the berdache.

Internet References

Sexualities
http://sexualities.sagepub.com

Sexuality Studies
https://sxs.sfsu.edu

Sexuality Studies.net
http://sexualitystudies.net/programs

The Kinsey Institute
www.kinseyinstitute.org/about

Gender & History
www.blackwellpublishing.com/journal.asp?ref=0953-5233&site=1

Article

Prepared by: Elvio Angeloni

The Hijras: An Alternative Gender in India

SERENA NANDA

Learning Outcomes

After reading this article, you will be able to:

- Describe the transgender hijra of India in terms of their traditional social and religious roles.
- Discuss the ways in which the hijra of India challenge the binary sex/gender notions of the West.

My first encounter with the hijras was in 1971. While walking on Churchgate in Bombay with an Indian friend one day, we were confronted by two persons in female clothing, who stood before us, blocking our passage. They clapped their hands in a peculiar manner and then put out their upturned palms in the traditional Indian gesture of a request for alms. My friend hurriedly dropped a few rupees into the outstretched palms in front of us, and pulled me along at a quick pace, almost shoving me in front of her. Startled at her abrupt reaction, I took another look at the two people who had intercepted us. It was only then that I realized that they were not females at all, but men, dressed in women's clothing. Now curious, I asked my friend who these people were and why she had reacted so strongly to their presence, but she just shook her head and would not answer me. Sensing her discomfort, I let the subject drop but raised it with other friends at a later time. In this way I found out a little about the hijras, and became determined to learn more.

For the next 10 years my professional interests as an anthropologist centered on culture and gender roles. As part of my interest in sexual variation I read what little I could find on the hijras, asking my Indian friends and relatives about them, and extending this interest through several field trips over the next twenty years. I learned that the hijras, described as neither men nor women, performed on auspicious occasions such as births and marriages, where they are believed to have the power to confer blessings of fertility; from some male acquaintances I discovered that hijras may also be prostitutes. Hijras were called eunuchs, but also said to be born intersexed, a contradiction I could not untangle. I realized that without talking with hijras themselves, I could not distinguish fact from fiction, myth from reality.

In 1981 I lived in India for a year with my family and decided to learn more about the hijras. During this time I met and interviewed many hijras in several of the major cities in North and South India. I spent days with them in their homes, attended their performances, met their husbands and customers, and also members of their families, and formed some good friendships among them. As a result of one of these friendships, I was made a ritual younger sister to a hijra guru. I also visited the temple of Bahuchara Mataji, the special deity of the hijras, located close to Ahmadabad. In addition, I spoke at length with doctors and social scientists in India who had personal knowledge of individual hijras or had written about them. All of these investigators were males, however, and I think being a woman gave me a great advantage in getting to know individual hijras in a more personal, and therefore, deeper way.

While hijras are regarded as deviant, and even bizarre, perhaps, in Indian society, in my hundreds of conversations with them, I was most forcibly struck by them as individuals who share in our common humanity. Like human beings everywhere, hijras are both shaped by their culture and the role they play in society, but are also individuals who vary in their emotions, behavior, and outlook on life. Some hijras were outgoing, flirtatious, and jolly, and loved to dress up, perform, and have their photos taken. They met the difficulties of their lives with a good sense of humor, which they often turned on themselves. Kamladevi was one of these: she was a favorite friend of mine because she was so amusing and she spoke fluent English, having graduated from a convent high school. She was a great gossip and imitated her hijra friends and elders in funny and very insightful ways. In telling a story of how she and several other hijra prostitutes were picked up by the police one evening, she captured to perfection the intimidating attitude of the police, the arrogance of the magistrate, and the combination of innocence and boldness she had used in telling them off. Like many hijra prostitutes, Kamladevi worked very hard under the watchful and demanding eye of the hijra "madam" who swallowed most of her earnings. Although she made a fair living as a prostitute, Kamladevi always spent more than she had as she could not resist buying saris and jewelry. But in spite of her poverty, and ill health as well, she always had an eye for the humorous side of things.

Other hijras I knew were very serious and even shy. They saw their life as a fate "written on their forehead," and accepted with resignation whatever insults or abuses were meted out to them. They worked all day, every day, at whatever they did to earn a living, whether begging alms from shops, or serving in bathhouses, or at various domestic chores within their households, which included cooking, cleaning, or small tasks such as grinding spices, which they did for outsiders to earn a few extra rupees. These hijras had few interests or social contacts, some even relatively isolated within the hijra community itself. Hijras who earned a living performing at marriages and childbirths were the elite of their community. Although they also worked very hard, they were better rewarded financially and gained status within the hijra community for earning a living in this traditional manner, rather than practicing prostitution or eking out a living begging for alms. Kavita, for example, one of the hijra performers I knew well, was determined to sing and dance whenever she got the opportunity. She not only performed at marriages and childbirths, but also in more contemporary settings, such as "stag parties" and college functions. Her energy in dancing for hours at a time, as well as her ability to "keep her cool" in the face of the teasing and rowdiness of large crowds of men was a well deserved source of pride to her.

While younger hijras are often playful and sometimes even outrageously bold in public, hijra elders, or gurus, as they are called, most often maintain a great degree of dignity. They, like other middle aged and elderly Indian women, tend to wear simple clothing and little jewelry, though what they wear is often real gold. They are modest in their manner, and also, like many middle class housewives, do not "roam about" but stay close to home, supervising the households of which they are in charge. Hijra gurus are also the ones who are most familiar with their place in India, which is rooted both in Hindu mythology, which incorporates many transgender figures, and in Islam, with its tradition of eunuchs who served at the courts of kings (Nanda 1999). Most gurus I met were happy to share this information with me, as it is the basis of their power and respect in Indian society.

But whatever their personality, their age, or social status within the hijra community, I almost always found a very courteous, and even hospitable reception among the hijras I visited. Occasionally hijras in the largest cities were hostile or even aggressive, an attitude undoubtedly fostered by the abuse or prurient curiosity they sometimes receive from the larger society, including foreigners. Given the many reasons hijras have to resent outsiders, I was overcome by the welcome I received, and the several close relationships that I formed. But even when courteous and hospitable, not all the hijras I met were interested in being interviewed. Some hijras would reveal nothing about their lives before they joined the community, while others were more forthcoming.

My interviews convince me, however, that the common belief in India that all hijras are born intersexed (hermaphrodites) and are taken away from their parents and brought into the hijra community as infants, is not correct. Most hijras are physically normal men, whose effeminacy, sometimes accompanied by an interest in homosexual activity, led them to seek out the hijra community in their late childhood or adolescence. Their childhood effeminacy, expressed in a wish to wear girl's clothing and imitate girl's behavior was the source of ridicule or abuse by their peers and family and the only solution appeared to be that of leaving their families and joining up with the hijras. While many hijras subsequently lose all contact with their families, others maintain a connection; they may occasionally visit their parents or siblings or these family members may visit them.

Rukhmini was a hijra whose break with her family was permanent and complete. She came from a middle class family and her father was a high ranking police officer. In spite of the many attempts of her father and brothers to prevent her, she persisted in acting and dressing as a girl. When it became known to her father that Rukhmini had had sexual relations with the gardener's son, he almost killed her by holding her head down in a barrel of water and beating her with his cross belt. "My mother cried tears of blood," she said. After this incident, Rukhmini ran away from her home and never returned.

In Sushila's case, she lived at home until her late teens, in relative peace with her family, until one night an elder brother falsely accused her of stealing some money from him. In his anger he told her to "use your own money that you get from selling your anus." She was more outraged at the false accusation of theft than the insult about her homosexuality and then and there left her home to join a hijra commune in a nearby city. Sushila keeps in touch with her family, and sends them gifts on the occasion of her brothers' and sisters' marriage. Meera, a hijra guru, joined the hijra community from a different and less typical route. She had grown up with the desires to be like a female, but followed the conventions of society by having her family arrange her marriage. She was married for over twenty years, and the father of several children, before she "upped one day and joined the hijras." She, too, keeps track of her family and occasionally sends them money when they need it.

As physically normal men, Kavita, Kamladevi, Rukhmini, Sushila, Rekha, and Meera were required to undergo an "operation" which removed their male genitals and transformed them into hijras. This operation, called "nirvana" or rebirth, is a religious ritual for hijras which positions them as ascetics, whose creative powers derive from their rejecting and thus transcending normal sexuality. This role connects them to Shiva, the great Hindu deity, who through his asceticism was given powers to create by Lord Brahma. The operation also identifies hijras with their special goddess and gives them the power to confer blessings of fertility, and equally, curse those who resist their demand for alms. For the small percentage of hijras who are born intersexed, no such operation is necessary. Salima, for example, a hijra from Bombay, told me that from a very early age she had "an organ that was very small." Her mother thought it would grow as she grew older, but when this did not happen her mother took her to many doctors, all to no avail. When Salima was about ten years old, a doctor told her mother, "nothing can be done, your child is neither a man nor a woman," and so Salima's mother gave her to a household of hijras who lived nearby. Salima lived with this group very happily and reported that they treated her with great kindness when she was a child.

But whatever their former lives had been, whether they had joined the hijras voluntarily, or been given to the community in despair by their parents, once an individual joins the community, they become subject to its rules and must adapt to its restrictions. This is not easy. In return for the emotional and economic security provided by the hijra community, an individual must give up some freedom, although probably not more than a young woman gives up when she becomes a bride living in a joint family. Unlike similar persons in the United States, who primarily live and work on their own, the hijras, shaped as they are by Indian culture in spite of their deviance, seem to prefer, like most Indians, to live in groups.

The Hijra Community

The hijra community in India has the qualities of both a religious cult and a caste and takes its customs, social organization and history from both Hinduism and Islam (Nanda 1999; Reddy 2005). Hijras find great pride in citing their identification with many of the great male figures of Hindu mythology who take on female forms in various situations. Familiar to all Hindus is Arjun's disguise as a eunuch in the Mahabharata and Shiva's form as Ardhanarisvara, half man/half woman, just two examples of powerful males in Hindu culture who act or dress as women or who partake of feminine qualities.

Many Hindu festivals include male transgenderism, like the one in south India that attracts thousands of hijras from all over India. This festival is based on a story of a king, who, in order to avert defeat in a war, promised to sacrifice his eldest son to the Gods, asking only that he first be allowed to arrange his son's marriage. Because no woman could be found who would marry a man about to be sacrificed, Lord Krishna came to earth as a woman to marry the King's son and the king won the battle, as the gods had promised. For the festival, men dress as women and go through a marriage ceremony with the deity. The priest performs the marriage, tying on the traditional wedding necklace. The next day the deity is carried to a burial ground and all of those who have "married" him remove their wedding necklaces, cry and beat their breasts, break their bangles, and remove the flowers from their hair, as a widow does in mourning. Hijra participation in this ritual affirms their identification with Krishna, one of the most important Indian deities.

The identification of males with female deities, expressed by the hijras through their cross dressing and emasculation, is a traditional part of Hinduism. This identification reinforces the legitimacy of the hijras as devotees of the Mother Goddess and vehicles of her power, which they use to confer blessings of fertility and prosperity at the births and weddings where they perform. The importance of the mother goddess in India is thus critical to understanding the role of the hijras. Hijra devotion to the goddess, Bahucharaji, a version of the Mother Goddess, closely identified with Durga, is central to their community. Bahucharaji's temple, near Ahmedabad, always has several hijra attendants present who bless visitors and tell them the stories of the powers of the goddess, which has specific references to transgenderism. It is in the name of the goddess that the hijras undergo their emasculation operation, which to them is a ritual of rebirth, transforming them from men to hijras.

Hindu, Muslim, and even Christian hijras revere the goddess, while at the same time embracing elements of Islamic culture. The Indian tradition among both Hindus and Muslims of seeking blessings from saint-like figures whose personal power and charisma supersedes their ascribed religion permits the hijras to find some respect in both these religious communities. In pre-independence India, for example, Muslim rulers gave land grants and special rights to hijras in their kingdoms. And while the hijra role is definitely rooted in early Hinduism, the use of eunuchs in the Mughal courts also strengthened its emergence as a distinct sub-culture. The incorporation of both Hinduism and Islam in the hijras' identity and community is characteristic of the power of Indian culture to incorporate seeming contradictions and paradoxes, into itself, including gender ambiguity, variation, and contradictions (O'Flaherty 1980).

As a caste (jati), or community (quam), hijras have a highly structured social organization whose dominant feature is a hierarchical relationship between the elders, or gurus, and the juniors, or chelas (the guru/chela relationship models itself on the teacher/disciple relationships which are an important feature of Hinduism). Each hijra joins the community under the sponsorship of a guru, and the guru/chela relationship ideally lasts a lifetime. Chelas of the same guru consider themselves "sisters" and adopt fictive kinship relations, such as "aunty" and "grandmother" with hijra elders. As chelas get older, they may become gurus by recruiting chelas for themselves. This process both offers scope for social mobility within the hijra community and also helps maintain the community over time. Hijra social organization, particularly in the guru/chela relationship, thus attempts to substitute for the family life which hijras have abandoned: the guru offers protection, care, and security to the chela and receives in return obedience, loyalty, and a portion of their earnings. Another important advantage of belonging to the hijra community is that it provides a haven when a hijra becomes aged or ill, and can no longer work. A hijra guru with many chelas will be well taken care of, but even a hijra with no chelas will be taken care of by the members of her community.

The typical effective working group of hijras is a communal household, consisting of 5–15 people, headed by a guru. The household members contribute part or all of their earnings to the household and share household chores. In return they get a roof over their heads, food, protection from the police for those who engage in prostitution, and a place from which to carry on their business. Most importantly, as all of the work hijras do, whether begging, entertaining, or prostitution, is strictly divided up among all the hijra households in a city, joining a hijra commune is practically the only way a hijra can get work. The hijra household is thus both an economic and a residential unit, as well as a family-like group which provides emotional satisfaction and a network of social relationships.

Living in a hijra household puts many restrictions on behavior. Just as an Indian bride must make adjustments to her inlaws when she moves into a joint family, so a new hijra must make many accommodations to her new "family" in a hijra commune. Kumari, an independent sort of person, who, with her guru's permission, eventually moved out to her own place, told me that "living with the hijras was very difficult. There were so many jobs to do . . . like cooking and housework. After coming home from a whole day of dancing, I then had to cook and do other chores. If I did the household chores during the day, I wouldn't have time to go out and the whole day would be lost. Gurus are very strict. If you don't keep your hair covered with your sari, if you don't cook properly, if the house is not spotlessly clean, for all these things they give you trouble. You can't just throw your dirty clothes down anywhere, you have to hang them up. If you don't serve food on the proper dishes, they will shout, 'What, are you a man that you cannot do these things properly!' I got tired of all that and so asked my guru permission to live on my own."

But even for hijras like Kumari, who prefer to live on their own, the idea of living as a hijra without the support of a guru is unthinkable. "You can never be without a guru," says Kumari, "anymore than you people (non-hijras) can be without a mother. Just as a daughter is known by her mother, so we are known by our guru. To belong to the hijra community, to live in a sari like this, you must have a guru; otherwise you will have no respect in society."

An individual can only join the hijra community under the sponsorship of a guru, and as a member of her guru's "house" (gharana). The "houses" into which the hijra community is divided are similar to symbolic descent groups, like clans or lineages. Although there are few meaningful distinctions between these "houses," each has its own founder and history. Hijras say the "houses" are like several brothers from the same mother, or two countries, like England and America, which have a common origin. A hijra remains in the "house" of her guru even if she moves her residence to some other household or even some other city. When a hijra dies, it is the elders of her "house," rather than her household, who arrange for her funeral; and a guru will pass her property to chelas belonging to her "house" when she dies.

Each "house" has a naik, or chief and it is the naiks who get together locally, and also nationally, to decide on major policy issues for the hijra community, or to celebrate some event within the community, such as the death anniversary of a famous guru. At the local level, it is the naiks who get together in a jamaat (meeting of the elders) to resolve conflict among hijra individuals or households within a city or region.

One of the most important tasks of the jamaat is to make sure that hijras do not violate the rules of their community. Honesty is one of the unshakable hijra norms. Hijras frequently change their residence, both within and between cities, and a hijra who has been found guilty of stealing someone's property will not be accepted in any hijra household. Without a household, a hijra will find herself without friends, and more important, without access to work. In respectable hijra households, individuals are expected to behave with some propriety, and hijras who drink heavily, or who are quarrelsome, or cannot control their aggression, will find themselves out on the street. The punishment for misbehavior varies with the crime: in some cases fines are levied; in more serious cases a hijra's hair will be cut as a way of stigmatizing her within the community, as hijras are obliged to wear their hair long, like women. For the most serious offenses, such as abusing or assaulting one's guru, a hijra may be cast out of the community altogether and have to pay a very heavy fine to re-enter.

This had happened to Rehka. Rehka had been in the hijra community for the last 15 years, earning her keep by playing the dholak (drum) which always accompanies hijra performances. Several years ago, provoked in an argument over men and money, Rehka insulted her guru and struck her. A meeting of the naiks determined that she should be cast out of the hijra community. From living very comfortably and with her future secure, Rehka now found herself, literally, on the street. Her sister chelas would no longer talk to her, not even, she said, "give me a drink of water." There was no place within walking distance she could work that was not already part of another hijra group's territory. If she tried to perform or even beg, she would be chased away by other hijras. With no money, and no work, Rehka took up residence on the street, earning a few rupees caring for some neighbor's children, or sometimes walking miles to a suburb to beg for alms. When it rained she slept under a bus. Living in the open, her clothes became tattered, her appearance and her health deteriorated and she was constantly insulted by neighborhood rowdies. It was a vicious cycle: Rekha was cast out of the community until she could raise the substantial fine of over 1,000 rupees that the naiks determined as the price of her re-entry into the community and apart from the community it was hopeless to even think of earning that sum, never mind saving it. Rehka's transformation was not lost on the hijras in her city. For all who knew her, it acted as a powerful incentive to maintain their own obedience and loyalty to their gurus.

The most important conflicts that naiks resolve are those that occur when the rigid territorial allotment of work within a city is violated. Naiks reach agreement about which hijra groups may work—whether begging alms from shop owners or in traditional performances—in particular areas of a city. When a hijra group finds others encroaching on their assigned territory, there may be arguments or even fist fights, and the naiks must negotiate new allotments of territory or maintain traditional boundaries. Because hijras can hardly go to the police or courts to settle their disputes—nor would they wish to give up such power to outsiders—disputes are settled within the community.

The hijras today are an example of a highly successful cultural adaptation. Their structured social organization, which imitates both a family and a caste, the use of the guru/chela relationship as a recruitment strategy, their willingness to move into new economic niches, and the effective control over economic rights exercised within the community, provide hijras with both the flexibility and control needed to succeed in today's complex and highly competitive society. In the face of dwindling opportunities for their traditional performances, prostitution, always a lucrative profession, has expanded. Hijras now bless girl infants as well as boys; they have become tax collectors, and have successfully run for political office. In politics, hijras have largely succeeded by emphasizing that their ascetic role as neither man nor woman, with no families to support, which they contrast to the widespread nepotism and corruption engaged in by so many Indian politicians (Reddy 2003).

Hijras have also successfully weathered the attempts of the Indian government to outlaw their emasculation operation, which serves as the definitive symbol of their identity. Indeed, they have become politically organized and have petitioned various state governments to grant them, as members of the "sexually marginalized," rights to jobs, marriage, legal recognition as a third gender and to consider sending a hijra into space as part of India's space program (Reddy 2010:140).

Gender Variation in Other Cultures

The assumption by a man of a woman's character, sex/gender role and identity in a spiritual or religious context, and even as a means of salvation, which has long been part of the Hindu tradition, is found in many other cultural traditions as well (Herdt 1996), particularly in Southeast Asia (Peletz 2009). In many great agricultural civilizations of the ancient world, arising around 10,000 years ago, Mother Goddess cults were prominent. Some of these goddesses were attended by a priesthood that included men who acted and dressed as women, either specifically during religious rituals, or permanently, while other cults involved male priests who castrated themselves while in ecstasy, in a gesture of renunciation and identification with her, very similar to the hijra nirvana ritual. The numerous images of Hermaphroditus (from which the English term hermaphrodite derives) found in Greek mythology and statuary, make it clear that androgyny and sex-change also had special meaning for the ancient Greeks.

By the end of the 4th century, B.C.E., however, cultural diffusion, through the spread of Christianity and later, in the 8th century C.E. through the spread of Islam, led to the dominance of male deities. By the 8th century C.E., mother goddess worship had virtually disappeared (India is one of the few places where it remained culturally central), and with it, of course, the sexually ambiguous priesthoods. Still later, European colonialism began to have its effect in repressing sexual and gender diversity in the New World as well as the old. The British, for example, outlawed the land grants to hijras in India, which had been awarded in various princely states, and repressed the many transgender roles in Southeast Asia (Peletz 2009), while the 19th century American occupation of Hawai'i, led to the decline of the indigenous role of the mahu (Matzner 2001).

In the mid-20th century, the European medical model, which pathologized gender diversity and homosexuality, spread throughout Asia, and had a particularly negative impact in

Thailand. The kathoey, a third gender, mentioned in ancient Buddhist scriptures and tolerated by society, as well as homosexuality, came to be viewed as "social problems," and were subject to both attempted "treatment" and repression (Jackson 1999; Costa and Matzner 2007). The contemporary global spread of fundamental Islam has also affected Islamic states such as Malaysia and Indonesia, whose previous casual toleration of indigenous transgender roles and male same-sex relationships, is now replaced by increasing public surveillance; in Indonesia a ban on the transsexual operation is being proposed.

At the same time, in recent decades, there has been a countercurrent to the decline of gender diversity, as the effects of ethnography, international human rights, the internet, and global media have sent information and images all over the world. Transgender beauty contests, long practiced in the Philippines—and based on American images of beauty rooted in the American occupation of the turn of the 20th century—have proliferated throughout Asia and the Pacific (Johnson 1997; Besnier 2011). In Indonesia, the waria, an indigenous transgender role, has become a symbol of nationalism and warias dominate beauty salons which prepare brides for traditional Indonesian weddings (Boellstorff 2005). The diffusion of a global gay identity, which is now associated with many different transgender roles throughout Asia, is spread by the media and by internet-based solidarity, even as it is transformed in local cultures in a variety of ways. Similarly, many international NGOs have set up HIV/AIDS clinics throughout Asia and Africa, which form a nexus of homosexual and transgender relationships, although in fact, AIDS in Asia and Africa is spread more by heterosexual than by same-sex relationships. Global migration, too, has been an important source of cultural diffusion, bringing for example, large numbers of transgendered Filipinos to Israel, where they dominate in the care of the aged (Heymann 2006). These globalizing dimensions of sex/gender diversity, have also affected the United States.

Sex/Gender Diversity and Change in the United States

One of the most important roles of anthropology is to increase our awareness of our own culture by reflecting on the cultures of others; as the famous anthropologist, Claude Levi-Strauss said, ethnography makes an important contribution to an ongoing critique of Western culture. The descriptions of sex/gender diversity in other cultures provokes us to re-examine the nature and assumptions of our own sex/gender system; the cultural basis of its categories; the relations between sex, sexuality, gender, and other aspects of culture; and the ways in which this impacts on individuals with alternative sex/gender identities who engage in diverse sexual practices (Nanda 2000).

Until the late 20th century, the binary Western concept of sex and gender—male and female—as well as condemnation of homosexuality, described in the book of Genesis, left no room for alternative sex/gender identities or varied sexual practices. The emergence of medical technology which enabled sex reassignment surgery both reflected and intensified this dichotomy. For an individual whose gender identity or sexual relationships were in conflict with his or her biological sex, the sex change operation provided one way out of the dilemma. Transsexuals in American culture were defined as "biologically normal persons of one sex convinced that they were members of the *opposite* sex" (Stoller, cited in Kessler and McKenna, 1978:115). The aim of sex reassignment surgery and the psychological and medical treatments (such as hormone therapy) that were required to accompany it, was the transformation of an individual from their natal sex into the sex with which they identified. An important aspect of the treatment required the individual to demonstrate to psychological and medical professionals that the individual was committed to, and was able to, make this transition.

This construction of the transsexual was consistent with the binary American sex/gender system and was supported in the larger culture by permitting various legal changes as part of a revised life story (Bolin 1988). Unlike alternative sex/gender figures in other cultures, however, transsexuals were viewed as a source of cultural anxiety, pathology, and a social problem; at best, as figures of scorn or pity. While the gay liberation movement in the United States helped our society become more humane and egalitarian in its response to sex and gender variations, our culture has not yet been able to incorporate the wide tolerance or spiritual roles for gender difference and ambiguity that traditionally existed in India and in other societies.

Even with emerging cultural and indeed legal supports of the construct of the transsexual as someone who crosses over completely to the "opposite" sex, this concept was not—and is not today—wholly accepted in our society. In a 2002 legal case in which a transsexual claimed the estate of her deceased spouse, the Kansas Supreme Court stated that both science and the courts are divided on whether transsexuals are more appropriately defined in terms of their birth sex status or their post-operative sex/gender status [*In re Marshall G. Gardiner, deceased.* (2002), in Norgren and Nanda 2006]. The Court held that, while "through surgery and hormones, a transsexual can be made to look like a woman . . . the sex assignment surgery does not create the sexual organs of a woman." The Court further held that while the plaintiff (a male to female transsexual) "wants and believes herself to be a woman [and] . . . has made every conceivable effort to make herself a female . . . her female anatomy, however, is still all man-made. The body [the plaintiff] inhabits is a male body in all aspects other than what the physicians have supplied . . . From that the Court has to conclude, that . . . as a matter of law [the plaintiff] is a male."

In spite of American resistance to changing concepts of sex and gender, illustrated by the legal decision cited above, the increasing awareness of the sex/gender systems of other cultures has led to a change in our own society. Within the last three decades America's rigid binary cultural boundaries—nature/culture, male/female, homosexual/heterosexual—have become blurred. Transgenderism is now a recognized cultural category, one that transcends the historical American "incorrigible proposition" that tells us that sex and gender are ascribed and permanent.

Transgenderism today incorporates a variety of subjective experiences, identities, and sexual practices that range widely over a sex/gender continuum, from androgynous to transsexual (Valentine 2007). Increasingly, persons defining themselves as transpeople see transgenderism as a way "out of the constraints imposed by a dichotomous sex/gender system [with the aim] . . . not to mandate anything, but to . . . be able to play with the categories, . . . to challenge the reductionism and essentialism that has accompanied these [binary] categories for so many millennia" (Ducat 2006: 48). In spite of the many differences among individuals experiencing transgender identities, one repeated theme of the transgender movement is that gender and sex categories are improperly imposed by society and its "sexual identity gatekeepers," referring here to the gender identity professionals who accepted and furthered the binary system of American sex/gender roles (Bolin 1996: 447). The transgendered are challenging and stretching the boundaries of the American system of sex/gender binary oppositions, and renouncing the American definition of gender as dependent on a consistency of genitals, body type, identity, role behaviors, sexual orientation, and sexual practice. Contemporary transgender communities include a continuum of people, from those who wish to undergo sex reassignment surgery, to those who wish to live their lives androgynously (Winter 2006). The previous split between transsexuals who viewed surgery as the only authentic expression of a feminine nature, as opposed to "part time" gender crossers who did not wish to have sex reassignment surgery, has to some extent been reconciled by the emergence of a transgender community which attempts to validate a whole range of gender roles and identities. As one transperson expressed it, " . . . you no longer have to fit into a box . . . it is okay to be transgendered. You can now lay anywhere on the spectrum from non-gendered to full transsexual" (Bolin 1996: 475). Transpeople are trying not so much to do away with maleness and femaleness as to de-naturalize them, that is, take away their privileged status in relation to all other possible combinations of behaviors, roles, and identities. The point for some transpeople is that gender categories should be something that individuals can construct for themselves, through self-reflection and observation (Cromwell 1997).

The dynamism of the contemporary transgender movement, which includes both transgender activists and mental health professionals, was recently acknowledged in a proposal by the New York City Board of Health to allow people to alter the sex on their birth certificate even if they have not had sex-change surgery (Cave 2006: A1). While this proposal, which emphasized the importance of separating anatomy from gender identity, ultimately failed, New York City has adopted other measures aimed at blurring the lines of gender identification. It has, for example, allowed beds in homeless shelters to be distributed according to appearance, applying equally to post-operative transsexuals, cross-dressers, and persons perceived to be androgynous. A Metropolitan Transit Authority policy also allows people to define their own gender when deciding whether to use men's or women's bathrooms. These new, even radical, policies are just one of the many aspects of the current transgender movement. Other aims of this movement are the redefining of gender diversity as a naturally occurring phenomenon rather than a psychological disorder; dismantling gender stereotypes, and reducing harassment and discrimination against those who do not wish to conform to current sex/gender norms (Brown 2006: A1). As Sam Winter, director of the Transgender Asia website suggests, although treating gender disorders as a mental illness, as in the United States, is useful for Western transsexuals in obtaining medical services, it extracts too high a price in substantially contributing to transphobia. For contemporary transpeople he says, "transgender is one aspect of human diversity. . . . It is a difference, not a disorder. . . . If we can speak to any gender identity disorder at all, it is in the inability of many societies to accept the particular gender identity difference we call transgender" (Winter, accessed 2006).

A core American cultural pattern which places a high value on the "authentic self"—on integrating the inner person with external actions—is central to the current transgender movement, as well as to contemporary gay activism. This core American cultural value is not universal, which makes it easier for sex/gender diversity to exist in other societies. In Thailand, for example, little value is attached to acknowledging or displaying one's private sexual orientation in public. In Thailand, how one acts is more important than how one feels. Leading a "double life" is a generally accepted feature of Thai culture, not necessarily equated with duplicity or deception as in the United States. Thus, "coming out" as a homosexual in Thailand brings shame or "loss of face" both to the individual and to the family without the compensation of expressing one's "true self" so valued in the United States. Similar values also hold in Indonesia (Wieringa 2008). In Malaysia, too, the Islamic emphasis on marriage and family takes precedence over asserting one's individuality and agency, as required in the process of "coming out" (Peletz 2009). Martin Manalansan, in his ethnography of transgendered Philippine migrants in New York, makes a similar point, quoting a "bakla" informant: "The Americans are different, darling. Coming out is their drama. When I studied at [a New England college] the queens had nothing better to talk about than coming out . . . the whites, my God, shedding tears, leaving the families. The stories are always so sad" (2003).

This contrast between cultural values, as they affect homosexuals and transgender people in Thailand, Malaysia and the Philippines, and those in the United States, casts a revealing perspective on the demand for repeal of "Don't Ask, Don't Tell," the shortsighted, politically motivated policy that banned openly gay men and women from the American military. That policy, which burdened the individual with the necessity of hiding his or her "true self" is quite simply incompatible with American culture and is now in the process of being repealed.

Unlike transsexualism, which reinforces the binary American sex/gender system, transgenderism is culturally subversive: it calls into question the rightness of binary sex/gender categories. It also provides a wider range of individual possibilities for those who experience distress by trying to conform to exclusively binary sex/gender categories, including sexual practices. The American transgender movement has been empowered by knowledge about alternative sex/gender systems throughout the world. Some of these sex/gender systems have offered American transpeople a source of meaning, and especially spiritual meaning, that they do not find in the binary, transphobic culture that is still dominant within the United States. As the West becomes more aware of alternatives and variations in gender roles in other cultures, both past and present, it can also perhaps become more accommodating of those individuals who do not fit into their traditionally prescribed—and limited—sex/gender categories.

References

Besnier, N. 2011. *On the edge of the global: Modern anxieties in a Pacific Island nation.* Stanford, CA: Stanford University Press.

Boelstorff, T. 2005. *The gay archipelago: Sexuality and nation in Indonesia.* Princeton, NJ: Princeton University Press.

Bolin, A. 1988. *In search of Eve: Transsexual rites of passage.* South Hadley, MA: Bergin and Garvey.

Bolin A. 1996. "Transcending and transgendering: Male-to-female transsexuals, dichotomy and diversity." In G. Herdt (Ed.), *Third sex third gender: Beyond sexual dimorphism in culture and history* (pp. 447–485). New York: Zone Books.

Brown, P.L. 2006. "Supporting boys or girls when the line isn't clear." *The New York Times,* December 2, p. A1.

Cave, D. 2006. "New York plans to make gender personal choice." *The New York Times,* November 7, p. A1.

Costa, L. and Andrew Matzner, A. 2007. *Male bodies, women's souls: Personal narratives of Thailand's transgendered youth.* Binghamton, NY: Haworth Press.

Cromwell, J. 1977. "Traditions of gender diversity and sexualities: A female-to-male transgendered perspective." In S. Jacobs, W. Thomas, and S. Lang (Eds.). *Two spirit people: Native American gender identity, sexuality, and spirituality.* Urbana, IL: University of Illinois Press.

Ducat, S. 2006. "Slipping into something more comfortable: Towards a liberated continuum of gender." *LiP,* Summer, pp. 46–61.

Herdt, G. 1996. *Third sex third gender: Beyond sexual dimorphism in culture and history.* New York: Zone Books.

Heymann, T. 2006. *Paper Dolls.* (film). Strand Releasing.

Jackson, P. 1999. *Lady boys, tom boys, rentboys: Male and female homosexualities in contemporary Thailand.* Binghamton, NY: Haworth Press.

Johnson, M. 1997. *Beauty and power: Transgendering and cultural transformation in the Southern Philippines.* New York: Berg.

Kessler, S.J., and W. McKenna. 1978. *Gender: An ethnomethodological approach.* New York: Wiley.

Manalansan, M. 2003. *Global divas: Filipino gay men in the diaspora.* Durham, NC: Duke University Press.

Matzner, A. 2001. *'O au no keia: Voices from Hawai'i's Mahu and transgender community.'* Philadelphia: XLibris.

Nanda, S. 1999. *Neither man nor woman: the hijras of India.* 2nd Ed. Belmont, CA: Wadsworth.

Nanda, S. 2000. *Gender diversity: crosscultural variations.* Prospect Heights, IL: Waveland.

Norgren, J. and S. Nanda. 2006. *American cultural pluralism and law.* Westport, CN: Praeger.

O'Flaherty, W.D. 1980. *Women, androgynies, and other mythical beasts.* Chicago: University of Chicago Press.

Peletz, M. 2009. *Gender pluralism: southeast asia since early modern times.* NY: Routledge.

Reddy, G. 2003. "Men" who would be kings: celibacy, emasculation and reproduction of hijras in contemporary Indian politics. *Social Research,* 70, no. 1:163–198.

Reddy, G. 2005. *With respect to sex: negotiating hijra identity in South India.* Chicago: University of Chicago Press.

Reddy, G. 2010. "Crossing 'Lines' of difference: Transnational Movements and Sexual Subjectivities In Hyderabad, India." In Diane P. Mines and Sarah Lamb (Eds.), *Everyday life in south Asia,* 2nd Ed. Bloomington, IN: University of Indiana Press.

Valentine, D. 2007. *Imagining transgender: An ethnography of a category.* Durham, NC: Duke University Press.

Wieringa, S. 2008. "If there is no feeling . . . The Dilemma between Silence and Coming Out in a Working Class Butch/Femme Community in Jakarta." In Mark B. Padilla, Jennifer S. Hirsch, Miguel Munoz-Laboy, Robert E. Sember, and Richard G. Parker (Eds.), *Love and globalization: Transformations of intimacy in the contemporary world.* Nashville, TN: University of Vanderbilt Press, pp. 70–90.

Winter, S. 2006. "Transphobia: A price worth paying for gender identity disorder? Retrieved from http://web.hku.hk/~sjwinter/TransgenderASIA/index.htm.

Critical Thinking

1. Be aware of the various social roles played by the hijra and how individuals become part of a hijra community.
2. What is the significance of the operation known as "nirvana"?
3. Be familiar with the hijra community in terms of its religious and caste qualities.
4. Be familiar with the hijra household in terms of its structure and rules.
5. What kinds of tasks are carried out by the "naiks" and the "jamaat"?
6. In what respects are the hijras an example of a highly successful cultural adaptation?
7. What evidence is there of gender variation throughout history? How did cultural diffusion and colonialism suppress it? How and why have there been countercurrents to such suppression?
8. What is meant by the American notion of a "binary sex and gender"? How has this been reinforced by medical technology?
9. What kinds of changes did the "transgender movement" bring about?
10. How and why is "coming out" treated differently in the United States and Thailand?
11. Why is "transgenderism" more subversive than "transsexualism"?

Internet References

Indian Journal of Gender Studies
http://ijg.sagepub.com

Intersections: Gender, History and Culture in the Asian Context
http://intersections.anu.edu.au

Gay, Lesbian, Bisexual, Transgender and Queer Studies, Canadian Online Journal for Queer Studies in Education
http://jqstudies.library.utoronto.ca/index.php/jqstudies

International Journal of Transgenderism
www.haworthpress.com/store/product.asp?sid=PX1MHCJ72GN18MGKKNXMG90SQVEV15K4&sku=J485&AuthType=4

SERENA NANDA is Professor Emeritus, Anthropology, at John Jay College, City University of New York. Many thanks to Joan Gregg, Mary Winslow, Cory Harris, and Barry Kass for their encouragement and suggestions.

Article

Prepared by: Elvio Angeloni

Afghan Boys Are Prized, So Girls Live the Part

JENNY NORDBERT

Learning Outcomes

After reading this article, you will be able to:

- Discuss the Afghan motivations for dressing some girls up as boys before puberty sets in.
- Explain why some Afghan girls find dressing as a boy can be both disorienting and liberating.

Six-year-old Mehran Rafaat is like many girls her age. She likes to be the center of attention. She is often frustrated when things do not go her way. Like her three older sisters, she is eager to discover the world outside the family's apartment in their middle-class neighborhood of Kabul.

But when their mother, Azita Rafaat, a member of Parliament, dresses the children for school in the morning, there is one important difference. Mehran's sisters put on black dresses and head scarves, tied tightly over their ponytails. For Mehran, it's green pants, a white shirt and a necktie, then a pat from her mother over her spiky, short black hair. After that, her daughter is out the door—as an Afghan boy.

There are no statistics about how many Afghan girls masquerade as boys. But when asked, Afghans of several generations can often tell a story of a female relative, friend, neighbor or co-worker who grew up disguised as a boy. To those who know, these children are often referred to as neither "daughter" nor "son" in conversation, but as "bacha posh," which literally means "dressed up as a boy" in Dari.

Through dozens of interviews conducted over several months, where many people wanted to remain anonymous or to use only first names for fear of exposing their families, it was possible to trace a practice that has remained mostly obscured to outsiders. Yet it cuts across class, education, ethnicity and geography, and has endured even through Afghanistan's many wars and governments.

Afghan families have many reasons for pretending their girls are boys, including economic need, social pressure to have sons, and in some cases, a superstition that doing so can lead to the birth of a real boy. Lacking a son, the parents decide to make one up, usually by cutting the hair of a daughter and dressing her in typical Afghan men's clothing. There are no specific legal or religious proscriptions against the practice. In most cases, a return to womanhood takes place when the child enters puberty. The parents almost always make that decision.

In a land where sons are more highly valued, since in the tribal culture usually only they can inherit the father's wealth and pass down a name, families without boys are the objects of pity and contempt. Even a made-up son increases the family's standing, at least for a few years. A bacha posh can also more easily receive an education, work outside the home, even escort her sisters in public, allowing freedoms that are unheard of for girls in a society that strictly segregates men and women.

But for some, the change can be disorienting as well as liberating, stranding the women in a limbo between the sexes. Shukria Siddiqui, raised as a boy but then abruptly plunged into an arranged marriage, struggled to adapt, tripping over the confining burqa and straining to talk to other women.

The practice may stretch back centuries. Nancy Dupree, an 83-year-old American who has spent most of her life as a historian working in Afghanistan, said she had not heard of the phenomenon, but recalled a photograph from the early 1900s belonging to the private collection of a member of the Afghan royal family.

It featured women dressed in men's clothing standing guard at King Habibullah's harem. The reason: the harem's women could not be protected by men, who might pose a threat to the women, but they could not be watched over by women either.

"Segregation calls for creativity," Mrs. Dupree said. "These people have the most amazing coping ability."

It is a commonly held belief among less educated Afghans that the mother can determine the sex of her unborn child, so she is blamed if she gives birth to a daughter. Several Afghan doctors and health care workers from around the country said that they had witnessed the despair of women when they gave birth to daughters, and that the pressure to produce a son fueled the practice.

"Yes, this is not normal for you," Mrs. Rafaat said in sometimes imperfect English, during one of many interviews over several weeks. "And I know it's very hard for you to believe why one mother is doing these things to their youngest daughter. But I want to say for you, that some things are happening in Afghanistan that are really not imaginable for you as a Western people."

Pressure to Have a Boy

From that fateful day she first became a mother—Feb. 7, 1999—Mrs. Rafaat knew she had failed, she said, but she was too exhausted to speak, shivering on the cold floor of the family's small house in Badghis Province.

She had just given birth—twice—to Mehran's older sisters, Benafsha and Beheshta. The first twin had been born after almost 72 hours of labor, one month prematurely. The girl weighed only 2.6 pounds and was not breathing at first. Her sister arrived 10 minutes later. She, too, was unconscious.

When her mother-in-law began to cry, Mrs. Rafaat knew it was not from fear whether her infant granddaughters would survive. The old woman was disappointed. "Why," she cried, according to Mrs. Rafaat, "are we getting more girls in the family?"

Mrs. Rafaat had grown up in Kabul, where she was a top student, speaking six languages and nurturing high-flying dreams of becoming a doctor. But once her father forced her to become the second wife of her first cousin, she had to submit to being an illiterate farmer's wife, in a rural house without running water and electricity, where the widowed mother-in-law ruled, and where she was expected to help care for the cows, sheep and chickens. She did not do well.

Conflicts with her mother-in-law began immediately, as the new Mrs. Rafaat insisted on better hygiene and more contact with the men in the house. She also asked her mother-in-law to stop beating her husband's first wife with her walking stick. When Mrs. Rafaat finally snapped the stick in protest, the older woman demanded that her son, Ezatullah, control his new wife.

He did so with a wooden stick or a metal wire. "On the body, on the face," she recalled. "I tried to stop him. I asked him to stop. Sometimes I didn't."

Soon, she was pregnant. The family treated her slightly better as she grew bigger. "They were hoping for a son this time," she explained. Ezatullah Rafaat's first wife had given birth to two daughters, one of whom had died as an infant, and she could no longer conceive. Azita Rafaat delivered two daughters, double the disappointment.

Mrs. Rafaat faced constant pressure to try again, and she did, through two more pregnancies, when she had two more daughters—Mehrangis, now 9, and finally Mehran, the 6-year-old.

Asked if she ever considered leaving her husband, she reacted with complete surprise.

"I thought of dying," she said. "But I never thought of divorce. If I had separated from my husband, I would have lost my children, and they would have had no rights. I am not one to quit."

Today, she is in a position of power, at least on paper. She is one of 68 women in Afghanistan's 249-member Parliament, representing Badghis Province. Her husband is unemployed and spends most of his time at home. "He is my house husband," she joked.

By persuading him to move away from her mother-in-law and by offering to contribute to the family income, she laid the groundwork for her political life. Three years into their marriage, after the fall of the Taliban in 2002, she began volunteering as a health worker for various nongovernmental organizations. Today she makes $2,000 a month as a member of Parliament.

As a politician, she works to improve women's rights and the rule of law. She ran for re-election on Sept. 18, and, based on a preliminary vote count, is optimistic about securing another term. But she could run only with her husband's explicit permission, and the second time around, he was not easily persuaded.

He wanted to try again for a son. It would be difficult to combine pregnancy and another child with her work, she said—and she knew she might have another girl in any case.

But the pressure to have a son extended beyond her husband. It was the only subject her constituents could talk about when they came to the house, she said.

"When you don't have a son in Afghanistan," she explained, "it's like a big missing in your life. Like you lost the most important point of your life. Everybody feels sad for you."

As a politician, she was also expected to be a good wife and a mother; instead she looked like a failed woman to her constituents. The gossip spread back to her province, and her husband was also questioned and embarrassed, she said.

In an effort to preserve her job and placate her husband, as well as fending off the threat of his getting a third wife, she proposed to her husband that they make their youngest daughter look like a son.

"People came into our home feeling pity for us that we don't have a son," she recalled reasoning. "And the girls—we can't send them outside. And if we changed Mehran to a boy we would get more space and freedom in society for her. And we can send her outside for shopping and to help the father."

No Hesitation

Together, they spoke to their youngest daughter, she said. They made it an alluring proposition: "Do you want to look like a boy and dress like a boy, and do more fun things like boys do, like bicycling, soccer and cricket? And would you like to be like your father?" Mehran did not hesitate to say yes.

That afternoon, her father took her to the barbershop, where her hair was cut short. They continued to the bazaar, where she got new clothing. Her first outfit was "something like a cowboy dress," Mrs. Rafaat said, meaning a pair of blue jeans and a red denim shirt with "superstar" printed on the back.

She even got a new name—originally called Manoush, her name was tweaked to the more boyish-sounding Mehran.

Mehran's return to school—in a pair of pants and without her pigtails—went by without much reaction by her fellow students. She still napped in the afternoons with the girls, and changed into her sleepwear in a separate room from the boys. Some of her classmates still called her Manoush, while others called her Mehran. But she would always introduce herself as a boy to newcomers.

Khatera Momand, the headmistress, with less than a year in her job, said she had always presumed Mehran was a boy, until she helped change her into sleeping clothes one afternoon. "It was quite a surprise for me," she said.

But once Mrs. Rafaat called the school and explained that the family had only daughters, Miss Momand understood perfectly. She used to have a girlfriend at the teacher's academy who dressed as a boy.

Today, the family's relatives and colleagues all know Mehran's real gender, but the appearance of a son before guests and acquaintances is just enough to keep the family functioning, Mrs. Rafaat said. At least for now.

Mr. Rafaat said he felt closer to Mehran than to his other children, and thought of her as a son. "I am very happy," he said. "When people now ask me, I say yes and they see that I have a son. So people are quiet, and I am quiet."

Economic Necessity

Mehran's case is not altogether rare.

Ten-year old Miina goes to school for two hours each morning, in a dress and a head scarf, but returns about 9 A.M. to her home in one of Kabul's poorest neighborhoods to change into boys' clothing. She then goes to work as Abdul Mateen, a shop assistant in a small grocery store nearby.

Every day, she brings home the equivalent of about $1.30 to help support her Pashtun family of eight sisters, as well as their 40-year-old mother, Nasima.

Miina's father, an unemployed mason, is often away. When he does get temporary work, Nasima said, he spends most of his pay on drugs.

Miina's change is a practical necessity, her mother said, a way for the entire family to survive. The idea came from the shopkeeper, a friend of the family, Nasima said: "He advised us to do it, and said she can bring bread for your home."

She could never work in the store as a girl, just as her mother could not. Neither her husband nor the neighbors would look kindly on it. "It would be impossible," Nasima said. "It's our tradition that girls don't work like this."

Miina is very shy, but she admitted to a yearning to look like a girl. She still likes to borrow her sister's clothing when she is home. She is also nervous that she will be found out if one of her classmates recognizes her at the store. "Every day she complains," said her mother. " 'I'm not comfortable around the boys in the store,' she says. 'I am a girl.' "

Her mother has tried to comfort her by explaining that it will be only for a few years. After all, there are others to take her place. "After Miina gets too old, the second younger sister will be a boy," her mother said, "and then the third."

Refusing to Go Back

For most such girls, boyhood has an inevitable end. After being raised as a boy, with whatever privileges or burdens it may entail, they switch back once they become teenagers. When their bodies begin to change and they approach marrying age, parents consider it too risky for them to be around boys anymore.

When Zahra, 15, opens the door to the family's second-floor apartment in an upscale neighborhood of Kabul, she is dressed in a black suit with boxy shoulders and wide-legged pants. Her face has soft features, but she does not smile, or look down, as most Afghan girls do.

She said she had been dressing and acting like a boy for as long as she could remember. If it were up to her, she would never go back. "Nothing in me feels like a girl," she said with a shrug.

Her mother, Laila, said she had tried to suggest a change toward a more feminine look several times, but Zahra has refused. "For always, I want to be a boy and a boy and a boy," she said with emphasis.

Zahra attends a girls' school in the mornings, wearing her suit and a head scarf. As soon as she is out on the steps after class, she tucks her scarf into her backpack, and continues her day as a young man. She plays football and cricket, and rides a bike. She used to practice tae kwon do, in a group of boys where only the teacher knew she was not one of them.

Most of the neighbors know of her change, but otherwise, she is taken for a young man wherever she goes, her mother said. Her father, a pilot in the Afghan military, was supportive. "It's a privilege for me, that she is in boys' clothing," he said. "It's a help for me, with the shopping. And she can go in and out of the house without a problem."

Both parents insisted it was Zahra's own choice to look like a boy. "I liked it, since we didn't have a boy," her mother said, but added, "Now, we don't really know."

Zahra, who plans on becoming a journalist, and possibly a politician after that, offered her own reasons for not wanting to be an Afghan woman. They are looked down upon and harassed, she said.

"People use bad words for girls," she said. "They scream at them on the streets. When I see that, I don't want to be a girl. When I am a boy, they don't speak to me like that."

Zahra said she had never run into any trouble when posing as a young man, although she was occasionally challenged about her gender. "I've been in fights with boys," she said. "If they tell me two bad words, I will tell them three. If they slap me once, I will slap them twice."

Time to "Change Back"

For Shukria Siddiqui, the masquerade went too far, for too long.

Today, she is 36, a married mother of three, and works as an anesthesiology nurse at a Kabul hospital. Short and heavily built, wearing medical scrubs, she took a break from attending to a patient who had just had surgery on a broken leg.

She remembered the day her aunt brought her a floor-length skirt and told her the time had come to "change back." The reason soon became clear: she was getting married. Her parents had picked out a husband whom she had never met.

At that time, Shukur, as she called herself, was a 20-year old man, to herself and most people around her. She walked around with a knife in her back pocket. She wore jeans and a leather jacket.

She was speechless—she had never thought of getting married.

Mrs. Siddiqui had grown up as a boy companion to her older brother, in a family of seven girls and one boy. "I wanted to be like him and to be his friend," she said. "I wanted to look like him. We slept in the same bed. We prayed together. We had the same habits."

Her parents did not object, since their other children were girls, and it seemed like a good idea for the oldest son to have a brother. But Mrs. Siddiqui remained in her male disguise well beyond puberty, which came late.

She said she was already 16 when her body began to change. "But I really had nothing then either," she said, with a gesture toward her flat chest.

Like many other Afghan girls, she was surprised the first time she menstruated, and worried she might be ill. Her mother offered no explanation, since such topics were deemed inappropriate to discuss. Mrs. Siddiqui said she never had romantic fantasies about boys—or of girls, either.

Her appearance as a man approaching adulthood was not questioned, she said. But it frequently got others into trouble, like the time she escorted a girlfriend home who had fallen ill. Later, she learned that the friend had been beaten by her parents after word spread through the neighborhood that their daughter was seen holding hands with a boy.

"My Best Time"

Having grown up in Kabul in a middle-class family, her parents allowed her to be educated through college, where she attended nursing school. She took on her future and professional life with certainty and confidence, presuming she would never be constricted by any of the rules that applied to women in Afghanistan.

Her family, however, had made their decision: she was to marry the owner of a small construction company. She never considered going against them, or running away. "It was my family's desire, and we obey our families," she said. "It's our culture."

A forced marriage is difficult for anyone, but Mrs. Siddiqui was particularly ill equipped. She had never cooked a meal in her life, and she kept tripping over the burqa she was soon required to wear.

She had no idea how to act in the world of women. "I had to learn how to sit with women, how to talk, how to behave," she said. For years, she was unable to socialize with other women and uncomfortable even greeting them.

"When you change back, it's like you are born again, and you have to learn everything from the beginning," she explained. "You get a whole new life. Again."

Mrs. Siddiqui said she was lucky her husband turned out to be a good one. She had asked his permission to be interviewed and he agreed. He was understanding of her past, she said. He tolerated her cooking. Sometimes, he even encouraged her to wear trousers at home, she said. He knows it cheers her up.

In a brief period of marital trouble, he once attempted to beat her, but after she hit him back, it never happened again. She wants to look like a woman now, she said, and for her children to have a mother.

Still, not a day goes by when she does not think back to "my best time," as she called it. Asked if she wished she had been born a man, she silently nods.

But she also wishes her upbringing had been different. "For me, it would have been better to grow up as a girl," she said, "since I had to become a woman in the end."

Like Mother, Like a Son

It is a typically busy day in the Rafaat household. Azita Rafaat is in the bathroom, struggling to put her head scarf in place, preparing for a photographer who has arrived at the house to take her new campaign photos.

The children move restlessly between Tom and Jerry cartoons on the television and a computer game on their mother's laptop. Benafsha, 11, and Mehrangis, 9, wear identical pink tights and a ruffled skirt. They go first on the computer. Mehran, the 6-year-old, waits her turn, pointing and shooting a toy gun at each of the guests.

She wears a bandage over her right earlobe, where she tried to pierce herself with one of her mother's earrings a day earlier, wanting to look like her favorite Bollywood action hero: Salman Khan, a man who wears one gold earring.

Then Mehran decided she had waited long enough to play on the computer, stomping her feet and waving her arms, and finally slapping Benafsha in the face.

"He is very naughty," Mrs. Rafaat said in English with a sigh, of Mehran, mixing up the gender-specific pronoun, which does not exist in Dari. "My daughter adopted all the boys' traits very soon. You've seen her—the attitude, the talking—she has nothing of a girl in her."

The Rafaats have not yet made a decision when Mehran will be switched back to a girl, but Mrs. Rafaat said she hoped it need not happen for another five or six years.

"I will need to slowly, slowly start to tell her about what she is and that she needs to be careful as she grows up," she said. "I think about this every day—what's happening to Mehran."

Challenged about how it might affect her daughter, she abruptly revealed something from her own past: "Should I share something for you, honestly? For some years I also been a boy."

As the first child of her family, Mrs. Rafaat assisted her father in his small food shop, beginning when she was 10, for four years. She was tall and athletic and saw only potential when her parents presented the idea—she would be able to move around more freely.

She went to a girls' school in the mornings, but worked at the store on afternoons and evenings, running errands in pants and a baseball hat, she said.

Returning to wearing dresses and being confined was not so much difficult as irritating, and a little disappointing, she said. But over all, she is certain that the experience contributed to the resolve that brought her to Parliament.

"I think it made me more energetic," she said. "It made me more strong." She also believed her time as a boy made it easier for her to relate to and communicate with men.

Mrs. Rafaat said she hoped the effects on Mehran's psyche and personality would be an advantage, rather than a limitation.

She noted that speaking out may draw criticism from others, but argued that it was important to reveal a practice most women in her country wished did not have to exist. "This is the reality of Afghanistan," she said.

As a woman and as a politician, she said it worried her that despite great efforts and investments from the outside world to help Afghan women, she has seen very little change, and an unwillingness to focus on what matters.

"They think it's all about the burqa," she said. "I'm ready to wear two burqas if my government can provide security and a rule of law. That's O.K. with me. If that's the only freedom I have to give up, I'm ready."

Critical Thinking

1. Why do some Afghan parents decide to raise their girls as boys?
2. What are some of the social pressures in Afghanistan to have sons rather than daughters?
3. What kind of internal conflicts do Afghan girls raised as boys experience when they reach puberty?

Internet References

Gender and Society
http://gas.sagepub.com/

International Journal of Gender & Women's Studies
http://ijgws.com/

Journal of Gender Studies
http://www.psypress.com/journals/details/0958-9236/

Article

Prepared by: Elvio Angeloni

Dethroning Miss America

The star-spangled pageant became a surprise battleground in the fight for women's rights and racial equality.

ROXANE GAY

Learning Outcomes

After reading this article, you will be able to:

- Discuss the commercial, sexist, and racial implications of the Miss American pageant as it was originally conceived.
- Discuss the backlash of some feminists to the 1968 protests as "anti-womanism."
- Describe the cyclical nature of the feminist movement.

The Miss America pageant has never been a progressive event, but in 1968, it sparked a feminist revolution. As women organized the first protest against Miss America, they were responding not only to the pageant and its antiquated, misogynistic attitudes toward women and beauty but also to how the United States, as a whole, treated women.

The 1968 uprising was conceived by a radical feminist named Carol Hanisch who popularized the phrase, "The personal is political." Disrupting the beauty contest, she thought, in the summer of that year, "just might be the way to bring the fledgling Women's Liberation Movement into the public arena."

Like so many things, the Miss America pageant began as a marketing scheme. Held in Atlantic City just after Labor Day, it started in 1921 as a way for newspapers to increase their circulation and for the resort's businesses to extend their profitable summer season. Newspapers across the country held contests judging photographs of young women, and the winners came to Atlantic City for a competition where they were evaluated on "personality and social graces." There was no equivocating. Women's beauty—white women's beauty—was a tool.

Since its inception, the pageant has evolved in some ways and not so much in others. The talent competition was introduced in 1938, so that perhaps the young women could be judged on more than just their appearance, but with that small bit of progress came regression. That same year, the pageant chose to limit the eligibility to single, never-married women between the ages of 18–28. The kind of beauty the pageant wanted to reward was very specific and very narrow—that of the demure, slender-but-not-too-thin woman, the girl next door with a bright white smile, a flirtatious but not overly coquettish manner, smart but not too smart, certainly heterosexual. There was even a "Rule 7," abandoned in 1940, that stated that Miss America contestants had to be "of good health and of the white race." The winner spent the year doing community service but also peddling sponsors' products and, later, entertaining U.S. troops.

To Hanisch and the other protest organizers, the pageant was an obvious target. On August 22, the New York Radical Women issued a press release inviting "women of every political persuasion" to the Atlantic City boardwalk on September 7, the day of the contest. They would "protest the image of Miss America, an image that oppresses women in every area in which it purports to represent us." The protest would feature a "freedom trash can" into which women could throw away all the physical manifestations of women's oppression, such as "bras, girdles, curlers, false eyelashes, wigs, and representative issues of *Cosmopolitan*, *Ladies' Home Journal*, *Family Circle*, etc."

The organizers also proposed a concurrent boycott of companies whose products were used in or sponsored the pageant. Male reporters would not be allowed to interview protesters, which remains one of the loveliest details of the protest. The organizers also issued a document offering 10 reasons why they were protesting, with detailed explanations—a womanifesto, if you will. One contention was "the degrading Mindless-Boob-Girlie Symbol." Another was racism, since a woman of color had never won—and there had never been a black contestant. "Nor has there ever been a true Miss America—an American Indian," they wrote. They also protested the military–industrial complex and the role of Miss America as a "death mascot" in entertaining the troops. They pointed to the consumeristic nature of corporate sponsorship of the pageant and the valuing of beauty as a measure of a woman's worth. They lamented that with the crowning of every new Miss America, the previous winner was forced into pop culture obsolescence. They rejected the double standard that contestants were forced to be "both sexy and wholesome, delicate but able to cope, demure yet titillatingly bitchy." The pageant represented the elevation of mediocrity—American women were encouraged to be "unoffensive, bland, apolitical"—and instilled this impoverished ambition in young girls. "NO MORE MISS AMERICA," the womanifesto proclaimed.

The organizers obtained a permit, detailing their plans for the protest, including barring men from participating, and on the afternoon of September 7, a few hundred women marched on the Atlantic City boardwalk, just outside the convention center where the pageant took place. Protesters held signs with such statements as "All Women Are Beautiful," "Cattle parades are demeaning to human beings," "Don't be a play boy accessory," and "Can make-up hide the wounds of our oppression?"

The protesters adopted guerrilla theater tactics, too. One woman performed a skit, holding her child and pots and pans, mopping the boardwalk to exemplify how a woman's work is never done. A prominent black feminist activist and lawyer, Florynce Kennedy, who went by Flo, chained herself to a puppet of Miss America "to highlight the ways women were enslaved by beauty standards." Robin Morgan, also a protest organizer, later quoted Kennedy as comparing that summer's violent protests at the Democratic National Convention to throwing a brick through a window. "The Atlantic City action," Kennedy continued, "is comparable to peeing on an expensive rug at a polite cocktail party. The man never expects the second kind of protest and very often that's the one that really gets him uptight."

The freedom trash can was a prominent feature, and the commentary about its role in the protest gave rise to one of the great misrepresentations of women's liberation—the myth of ceremonial bra-burning. It was a compelling image: angry, unshaven feminists, their breasts free from constraint, setting fire to their bras as they dared to demand their own liberation.

But it never actually happened. In fact, officials asked the women not to set the can on fire because the wooden boardwalk was quite flammable. The myth can be traced back to the *New York Post* reporter Lindsy Van Gelder who, in a piece before the protest, suggested protesters would burn bras, a nod to the burning of draft cards. After other *Post* writers reported the idea as fact, syndicated humor columnist Art Buchwald spread the myth nationwide. "The final and most tragic part of the protest," he wrote, "took place when several of the women publicly burned their brassieres." He continued to revel in his misogyny, writing, "If the average American female gave up all her beauty products she would look like Tiny Tim, and there would be no reason for the American male to have anything to do with her at all." In a handful of sentences, Buchwald neatly illustrated the urgent need for the protest.

During the actual pageant that evening, some of the protesters, including Carol Hanisch, sneaked into Boardwalk Hall and unfurled a banner reading, "Women's Liberation," while shouting, "Women's Liberation!" and "No More Miss America!" Their action gave the burgeoning movement an invaluable amount of exposure during the live broadcast.

At midnight on September 8, a few blocks away at the Atlantic City Ritz-Carlton, the inaugural Miss Black America competition was held. If the Miss America pageant wouldn't accommodate black women and black beauty, black folk decided they would create their own pageant. After his daughters expressed their desire to become Miss America, the Philadelphia entrepreneur J. Morris Anderson created Miss Black America, so his children's ambitions would not be thwarted by American racism. The 1968 winner, Saundra Williams, reveled in her win. "Miss America does not represent us because there has never been a black girl in the pageant," she said afterward. "With my title, I can show black women that they too are beautiful." In 1971, Oprah Winfrey participated in Miss Black America as Miss Tennessee. The pageant, which continues today, is the oldest pageant in the country for women of color.

While the 1968 protests may not have done much to change the nature of the Miss America pageant, they did introduce feminism into the mainstream consciousness and expand the national conversation about the rights and liberation of women. The first wave of feminism, which focused on suffrage, began in the late 19th century. Many historians now credit the '68 protest as the beginning of feminism's broader second wave.

As feminists are wont to do, the organizers were later relentless in critiquing their own efforts. In November 1968, Carol Hanisch wrote that "one of the biggest mistakes of the whole pageant was our anti-womanism . . . Miss America and all beautiful women came off as our enemy instead of our sisters who suffer with us."

History is cyclical. Women are still held to restrictive beauty standards. Certainly, the cultural definition of beauty has expanded over the years, but it has not been blown wide open. White women are still upheld as an ideal of beauty. In the

Miss America competition, women are still forced to parade around in swimsuits and high heels. "The swimsuit competition is probably the most honest part of the competition because it really is about bodies; it is about looking at women as objects," Gloria Steinem said in the 2002 film *Miss America*.

History is cyclical. As we look back on these 1968 protests, we are in the midst of another significant cultural moment led by women. After the election and inauguration of President Trump, millions of women and their allies marched in the nation's capital and in cities around the world to reaffirm women's rights, and the rights of all marginalized people, as human rights. They marched for many of the same rights the 1968 protesters were seeking. A year later, we are in the midst of a further reckoning, as women come forward to share their stories of workplace sexual harassment and sexual violence. And, for the first time, men are facing real consequences for their predation. The connective tissue between 1968 and now is stronger than ever, vibrantly alive.

Critical Thinking

1. What were the commercial, sexist, and racist aspects of the Miss America pageant?
2. In what respects has the Miss America pageant evolved in response to the feminist movement and in what respects has it retained some of its anti-feminist aspects?
3. Considering today's protests, what aspects of the women's protests are cyclical and what is new?

Internet References

The Beauty Myth
https://en.wikipedia.org/wiki/The_Beauty_Myth

Feminism in India
https://feminisminindia.com/2017/05/10/beauty-standards-ugliest-trick/

The Feminist eZine
http://www.feministezine.com/feminist/fashion/Beauty-Fashion-Vs-Feminism.html

Article

Prepared by: Elvio Angeloni

Me Too Anthropology

ELIZABETH BECKMANN

Learning Outcomes

After reading this article, you will be able to:

- Discuss the ways in which the victimization of women has been normalized in our culture and how, conversely, the #MeToo campaign has become a powerful tool for social change.
- Explain how it is that the author, as an anthropologist, is able to encourage her informants to share traumatic personal experiences while remaining reticent to speak of her own.
- Explain how anthropology can give voice to both of those who are willing to share their traumatizing stories publicly as well as those who "need a screen through which to whisper their histories."

Just over a week ago, the #MeToo campaign, originally pioneered by black activist Tarana Burke over 10 years ago, hit social media in the wake of news stories of Harvey Weinstein and the women he raped and sexually abused over the course of his career in Hollywood. Until now, the majority of the women he victimized had remained silent, pressured by the industry in which they work, confined by powerful ideologies that preach the superiority of men, the prominence of their reputations, and subsequently the validation of their actions—as heinous as they may be. This culture has endorsed the continuous violation of women's bodies and rights to the point of normalization. This is evident through the actions of a collective Hollywood cast, whose silence on the issue has put them in the role of supporting actor to Weinstein: a man whose misogynistic behaviors and attitudes are comparable to those of *President Trump*, one of the most powerful men in the world.

The ideologies that keep women from opening up about their experiences with rape and sexual abuse are not located simply in Hollywood of course but are part of a wider systemic problem the world over. Furthermore, when women *do* open up, they are immediately shut down and silenced—sending a clear message to others that they do not have power and that their experiences are negligible, unwanted reminders of the abuse committed by men against women in a society that *still* heralds men as superior. The experiences of women become labeled as insignificant. The #MeToo campaign, however, resists these normative concepts, and though this is not its first outing, this reincarnation has allowed women and girls a platform through which to share and express themselves as a group rather than simply as individuals—a powerful tool for social change.

As I sat at home that Friday morning letting my morning tea go cold scanning through my social media feeds, I looked over hundreds of stories from friends and followers, overwhelmed, shocked yet unsurprised by the multitude of women in my network who had gone through similar experiences. Some of my male friends got involved; however, many of them shared statuses expressing their appreciation that violence by men against women and femmes is a larger issue which deserves its own airtime—a sentiment I have to say I agree with vehemently. Others got involved with a simple "#MeToo," whilst some shared more extensive and painful-to-read accounts of rape, sexual, and sexist abuse. Looking at my inbox to check unopened messages, I found friends and acquaintances asking if I was going to partake in this campaign. As someone with a sizable social media following largely based on my relentless sharing of feminist articles, videos, and memes, I realized I was expected to chime in on this incredibly important movement. However, I found myself unable to craft my own #MeToo status despite having plenty of experiences and material with which to work. So what was my problem?

Although my writing career is in its infancy, I often put together papers which deal with difficult and potentially traumatizing content for academic purposes. Researching topics such as fertility, masculinity, and identity in the UK lead to the disclosure by many of my informants of varying kinds of trauma including death, physical and emotional abuse, rape, breakdowns, sexism, and drug abuse to name a few. A handful of these relayed personal struggles with sexual and emotional abuse by partners, ex-partners, colleagues, strangers, family, and acquaintances during their lives; experiences most commonly buried with years of practice and which wait quietly for a moment at which to surface. During fieldwork dealing with such topics, I make sure to express my gratitude to my informants for sharing these difficult memories and ensure to my best ability that they feel not only supported but *important*: they must be told what bravery it takes to divulge these often buried personal histories which have the potential to retraumatize them. "I've never told anyone this before" was something I heard many times last year during fieldwork. I preach to my friends, family, and informants the understated value in sharing these experiences: how will anyone know what people go through if we don't share? "Thank you for this opportunity to tell my story" one informant told me after a lengthy and emotional interview about the difficulties of wanting children with her sexually abusive ex-partner. "Now I've told you, I can think about telling my friends and family."

With this in mind, I sat considering why it was so difficult for *me* to share my own experiences when I myself have encouraged informants to do so, stressing the value in such a contribution to academic and public discourse. And I knew that there would be thousands of women, including strangers, friends, and family, sat at their computer or with phone in hand unable to pen a status that included #MeToo. Why? Shame. Guilt. The struggle to be able to use words like "rape" and "sexual abuse" in relation to the self. Shame in admitting that this had happened after believing for years that it was our fault. Guilt in believing that perhaps that person didn't intend to hurt us and that we ought to have given them the benefit of the doubt. The shame that so many women unwillingly go through during their lifetimes after experiencing rape and sexual abuse including catcalling in the street, overt sexist comments at work, a partner's disregard for your consent during acts of sex, and so on.

On my journey into campus that morning, it dawned on me that perhaps *I* needed an anthropologist through which to tell *my* stories, to locate my own trauma within a larger context, and to allow someone else to frame my words *anonymously* and with validity. I sat there as both anthropologist and informant, conversing with myself about the theoretical framings of my lived experiences. This got me thinking about the power structures in place that feed into discourses of victim as guilty are arguably fragile and in a constant state of potential demise. The #MeToo campaign has certainly caused a storm, but will this storm pass and its population revert to the way it was before, and what can modern anthropology do to ensure that it doesn't?

My discomfort in publicly sharing is certainly a problem. Though keeping traumatic events to oneself is an absolutely valid coping mechanism, the insecurity, guilt, and shame I associate with sharing is not conducive to social transformation. As a self-identifying feminist who considers herself to be a strong, independent, switched-on person, experiencing difficulty in opening up about my experiences with rape and sexual abuse is problematic. The reason for admitting this is to contribute to the emerging discourses in which women feel able to express their need to stay silent for the time being. Though the #MeToo campaign has given voice to many who were previously unable to express themselves, it has also (either intentionally or unintentionally) sought to unwilling force women into the limelight.

Although I have argued that sharing is invaluable, I would also reassure those of us who feel unable to do so just yet. Perhaps you and I feel unable to share at *this* moment due to the shame and guilt associated with victim-blaming, the retraumatizing nature of public contribution, or simply a refusal to take responsibility for educating others on what should be an obvious issue. However, this does not mean we are not part of social change. Admitting that we have a problem in sharing our experiences is part of that change. Change comes slowly, and I believe that academia as well as public platforms have a great role to play in that process, representing both those who are ready to share publically and those who need a screen through which to whisper their histories steadily. What anthropology and anthropologists can do then is to share the weight of such a burden with women in both categories but particularly the latter. Rather than leaving it to those affected by rape and sexual abuse to share and educate others on the realities of life as a woman, anthropology can give voice to those who feel unable to do this themselves—at least for the moment.

Critical Thinking

1. How has the "collective Hollywood cast" shown by example how the victimization of women can be normalized?
2. How has the #MeToo movement been able to resist the normative concepts associated with the victimization of women in our culture?
3. How is it that the field of anthropology can give voice to those women who "need a screen through which to whisper their traumatizing histories"?

Internet References

Time's Up

https://www.timesupnow.com/

The SHRMBog

https://blog.shrm.org/blog/metoo

ZOE LAWTON

https://www.zoelawton.com/metoo-blog.html

Elizabeth Beckmann is a student on the MA in the Anthropology of Development and Social Transformation at the University of Sussex.

Article

Prepared by: Elvio Angeloni

What About *The Breakfast Club*?

Revisiting the movies of my youth in the age of #MeToo.

MOLLY RINGWALD

Learning Outcomes

After reading this article, you will be able to:

- Discuss the ways in which John Hughes' films were racist, misogynistic, and homophobic.
- Discuss those aspects of John Hughes' films spoke to the needs of teenagers of the time.

Earlier this year, the Criterion Collection, which is "dedicated to gathering the greatest films from around the world," released a restored version of "*The Breakfast Club*," a film written and directed by John Hughes that I acted in, more than three decades ago. For this edition, I participated in an interview about the movie, as did other people close to the production. I don't make a habit of revisiting films I've made, but this was not the first time I'd returned to this one: a few years back, I watched it with my daughter who was 10 at the time. We recorded a conversation about it for the radio show "This American Life." I'll be the first to admit that 10 is far too young for a viewing of *The Breakfast Club*, a movie about five high-school students who befriend one other during a Saturday detention session, with plenty of cursing, sex talk, and a now-famous scene of the students' smoking pot. But my daughter insisted that her friends had already seen it, and she said she didn't want to watch it for the first time in front of other people. A writer–director friend assured me that kids tend to filter out what they don't understand, and I figured that it would be better if I were there to answer the uncomfortable questions. So I relented, thinking perhaps that it would make for a sweet if unconventional mother–daughter bonding moment.

It's a strange experience, watching a younger, more innocent version of yourself onscreen. It's stranger still—surreal, even—watching it with your child when she is much closer in age to that version of yourself than you are. My friend was right: my daughter didn't really seem to register most of the sex stuff, though she did audibly gasp when she thought I had showed my underwear. At one point in the film, the bad-boy character, John Bender, ducks under the table where my character, Claire, is sitting, to hide from a teacher. While there, he takes the opportunity to peek under Claire's skirt and, though the audience doesn't see, it is implied that he touches her inappropriately. I was quick to point out to my daughter that the person in the underwear wasn't *really* me, though that clarification seemed inconsequential. We kept watching, and despite my best intentions to give context to the uncomfortable bits, I didn't elaborate on what might have gone on under the table. She expressed no curiosity in anything sexual, so I decided to follow her lead and discuss what seemed to resonate with her more. Maybe I just chickened out.

But I kept thinking about that scene. I thought about it again this past fall, after a number of women came forward with sexual-assault accusations against the producer Harvey Weinstein, and the #MeToo movement gathered steam. If attitudes toward female subjugation are systemic, and I believe that they are, it stands to reason that the art we consume and sanction plays some part in reinforcing those same attitudes. I made three movies with John Hughes; when they were released, they made enough of a cultural impact to land me on the cover of *Time* magazine and to get Hughes hailed as a genius. His critical reputation has only grown since he died, in 2009, at the age of 59. Hughes's films play constantly on television and are even taught in schools. There is still so much that I love in them, but lately I have felt the need to examine the role that these movies have played in our cultural life: where they came from, and what they might mean now. When my daughter proposed watching *The Breakfast Club* together, I had hesitated, not knowing how she would react: if she would understand the film or if she would even like it. I worried that she would find aspects of it troubling, but I hadn't anticipated that it would ultimately be most troubling to me.

It can be hard to remember how scarce art for and about teenagers was before John Hughes arrived. Young-adult novels had not yet exploded as a genre. Onscreen, the big issues that affected teens seemed to belong largely to the world of ABC afterschool specials, which premiered in 1972 and were still around as I came of age, in the 80s. All the teens I knew would rather have died than watch one. The films had the whiff of sanctimony, the dialogue was obviously written by adults, the music was corny.

Portrayals of teenagers in movies were even worse. The actors cast in teen roles tended to be much older than their characters—they had to be, since the films were so frequently exploitative. The teen horror flicks that flourished in the 70s and 80s had them getting murdered: if you were young, attractive, and sexually active, your chances of making it to the end were basically nil (a trope spoofed, years later, by the "Scream" franchise). The successful teen comedies of the period, such as "Animal House" and "Porky's," were written by men for boys; the few women in them were either nymphomaniacs or battleaxes. (The stout female coach in "Porky's" is named Balbricker.) The boys are perverts, as one-dimensional as their female counterparts but with more screen time. In 1982, *Fast Times at Ridgemont High*, which had the rare distinction of being directed by a woman, Amy Heckerling, got closer to an authentic depiction of adolescence. But it still made room for a young male's fantasy of the actress Phoebe Cates striding topless in a soft-porny sprinkler mist.

And then Hughes came along. Hughes, who grew up in Michigan and Illinois, got work, after dropping out of college, writing ad copy in Chicago. The job brought him frequently to New York, where he started hanging around the offices of the humor magazine *National Lampoon*. He wrote a story called "Vacation '58"—inspired by his own family trips—which secured him a job at the magazine and became the basis for the movie *National Lampoon's Vacation*. Another story caught the eye of the producer Lauren Shuler Donner who encouraged him to write what became *Mr. Mom*. Those movies helped him get a deal with Universal Studios. *The Breakfast Club* was to be his directorial debut; he planned to shoot it in Chicago with local actors. He told me later that, over a July 4th weekend, while looking at headshots of actors to consider for the movie, he found me, and decided to write another movie around the character he imagined that girl to be. That script became *Sixteen Candles*, a story about a girl whose family forgets her 16th birthday. The studio loved the script, perhaps because, in form at least, it had more in common with proven successes—'Porky's" et al.—than it did with *The Breakfast Club*, which basically read like a play.

A meeting was arranged, we hit it off, and I filmed *Sixteen Candles* in the suburbs of Chicago the summer after I completed the ninth grade. Once we were done shooting and before we began filming *The Breakfast Club*, John wrote another movie specifically for me, *Pretty in Pink*, about a working-class girl navigating the social prejudices of her affluent high school. The film's dramatic arc involves getting invited and then uninvited to the prom. In synopsis, the movies can seem flimsy—a girl loses her date to a dance, a family forgets a girl's birthday—but that's part of what made them unique. No one in Hollywood was writing about the minutiae of high school and certainly not from a female point of view. According to one study, since the late 1940s, in the top-grossing family movies, girl characters have been outnumbered by boys three to one—and that ratio has not improved. That two of Hughes's films had female protagonists in the lead roles and examined these young women's feelings about the fairly ordinary things that were happening to them, while also managing to have instant cred that translated into success at the box office was an anomaly that has never really been replicated. (The few blockbuster films starring young women in recent years have mostly been set in dystopian futures or have featured vampires and were wolves.)

I had what could be called a symbiotic relationship with John during the first two of those films. I've been called his muse, which I believe I was, for a little while. But, more than that, I felt that he listened to me—though certainly not all the time. Coming out of the *National Lampoon* school of comedy, there was still a residue of crassness that clung, no matter how much I protested. In the shooting script of *The Breakfast Club*, there was a scene in which an attractive female gym teacher swam naked in the school's swimming pool as Mr. Vernon, the teacher who is in charge of the students' detention, spied on her. The scene wasn't in the first draft I read, and I lobbied John to cut it. He did, and although I'm sure the actress who had been cast in the part still blames me for foiling her break, I think the film is better for it. In *Sixteen Candles*, a character alternately called the Geek and Farmer Ted makes a bet with friends that he can score with my character, Samantha; by way of proof, he says, he will secure her underwear. Later in the film, after Samantha agrees to help the Geek by loaning her underwear to him, she has a heartwarming scene with her father. It originally ended with the father asking, "Sam, what the hell happened to your underpants?" My mom objected. "Why would a father know what happened to his daughter's underwear?" she asked. John squirmed uncomfortably. He didn't mean it that way, he said—it was just a joke, a punch line. "But it's not funny," my mother said. "It's creepy." The line was changed to "Just remember, Sam, you wear the pants in the family."

My mom also spoke up during the filming of that scene in *The Breakfast Club*, when they hired an adult woman for the shot of Claire's underwear. They couldn't even ask me to do it—I don't think it was permitted by law to ask a minor—but even having another person pretend to be me was embarrassing to me and upsetting to my mother, and she said so. That scene stayed, though. What's more, as I can see now, Bender sexually harasses Claire throughout the film. When he's not sexualizing her, he takes out his rage on her with vicious contempt, calling her "pathetic," mocking her as "Queenie." It's rejection that inspires his vitriol. Claire acts dismissively toward him, and in a pivotal scene near the end, she predicts that at school on Monday morning, even though the group has bonded, things will return, socially, to the status quo. "Just bury your head in the sand and wait for your fuckin' prom!" Bender yells. He never apologizes for any of it, but, nevertheless, he gets the girl in the end.

If I sound overly critical, it's only with hindsight. Back then, I was only vaguely aware of how inappropriate much of John's writing was, given my limited experience and what was considered normal at the time. I was well into my 30s before I stopped considering verbally abusive men more interesting than the nice ones. I'm a little embarrassed to say that it took even longer for me to fully comprehend the scene late in *Sixteen Candles*, when the dreamboat, Jake, essentially trades his drunk girlfriend, Caroline, to the Geek, to satisfy the latter's sexual urges, in return for Samantha's underwear. The Geek takes Polaroids with Caroline to have proof of his conquest; when she wakes up in the morning with someone she doesn't know, he asks her if she "enjoyed it." (Neither of them seems to remember much.) Caroline shakes her head in wonderment and says, "You know, I have this weird feeling I did." She had to have a feeling about it, rather than a thought, because thoughts are things we have when we are conscious, and she wasn't.

Thinking about that scene, I became curious how the actress who played Caroline, Haviland Morris, felt about the character she portrayed. So I sent her an e-mail. We hadn't seen or spoken to each other since she was 23 and I was 15. We met for coffee, and after we had filled each other in on all the intervening years, I asked her about it. Haviland, I was surprised to learn, does not have the same issues with the scene as I do. In her mind, Caroline bears some responsibility for what happens because of how drunk she gets at the party. "I'm not saying that its O.K. to then be raped or to have nonconsensual sex," Haviland clarified. "But . . . that's not a one-way street. Here's a girl who gets herself so bombed that she doesn't even know what's going on."

There was a time in my early 20s when I had too much to drink at a party and ended up in a bedroom sitting on the edge of a bed with a producer I didn't know, lightheaded and woozy. A good friend, who had followed me, popped her head in the door a couple of minutes later and announced, "Time to go now, Molly!" I followed her out, trying not to stumble, and spent the rest of the night violently ill and embarrassed—and the rest of my life grateful that she had been there, watching out for me, when I was temporarily incapable of watching out for myself. I shared the story with Haviland, and she listened politely, nodding.

Haviland, like me, has children, and so I decided to frame the question hypothetically, mother to mother, to see if it changed her point of view. If one of our kids had too much to drink, and something like that happened to one of them, would she say, "It's on you, because you drank too much"? She shook her head: "no. Absolutely, positively, it stays in your pants until invited by someone who is willing and consensually able to invite you to remove it." Still, she added, "I'm not going to black-and-white it. It isn't a one-way street."

After our coffee, I responded to an e-mail from Haviland to thank her for agreeing to talk to me. Later that night, I received another note. "You know," she wrote, "the more I think of it this evening, oddly, the LESS uncomfortable I am with Caroline. Jake was disgusted with her and said he could violate her 17 ways if he wanted to because she was so trashed, but he didn't. And then, Ted was the one who had to ask if they had had sex, which certainly doesn't demonstrate responsible behavior from either party but also doesn't really spell date rape. On the other hand, she was basically traded for a pair of underwear . . . Ah, John Hughes."

It's hard for me to understand how John was able to write with so much sensitivity and also have such a glaring blind spot. Looking for insight into that darkness, I decided to read some of his early writing for *National Lampoon*. I bought an old issue of the magazine on eBay and found the other stories, all from the late 70s and early 80s, online. They contain many of the same themes he explored in his films but with none of the humanity. Yes, it was a different time, as people say. Still, I was taken aback by the scope of the ugliness.

A Dog's Tale has a boy watching his mother turn into a dog. *Against His Will* features an "ugly fat" woman who tries to rape a man at gunpoint in front of the man's wife and parents because she can't have sex any other way. *My Penis* and *My Vagina* are quasi-magical-realist stories written from the points of view of teenagers who wake up in the morning with different genitalia than they were assigned at birth; the protagonist of *My Penis* literally forces her boyfriend's mouth open to penetrate him, and the male in *My Vagina* is gang-raped by his friends once they discover he has one. (The latter story ends with him having to use the money he saved for new skis on getting an abortion.) The "Hughes Engagement Guide" is an illustrated manual on how to protect yourself against women. It gives examples of women "bullshitting to not put out" and teaches readers how to do a "quickie pelvic exam," how to detect "signs of future fat," and how to determine if a woman has any ancestors of different races based on what her relatives look like—there is an accompanying drawing of an Asian person and an African American—and on and on.

The October, 1980, issue included a piece, coauthored by Ted Mann, titled "Sexual Harassment and How to Do It!" The guide explains, "If you hire a woman from another field or with a background that is not suited to the duties she is to assume, you've got the glans in the crevice, or, if you prefer, the foot in the door." It continues, "Not only will her humility prepare her for your sexual advances, it will also help steel her for her inevitable dismissal." There are sections describing different kinds of secretaries based on their ages, and how best to reward and punish them. (The older ones are "easier," the younger ones "preferable.") There's even a section on arrest: "sometimes even guys with cool sideburns and a smooth line of patter get arrested for sexual harassment and are issued summonses." It goes on to suggest different methods for cozying up to the police officer.

It's all satire, of course, but it's pretty clear that it's not the chauvinists who are being lampooned but the "women's liberation movement." Women had begun to speak out, in the mid-70s, against harassment in the workplace. (The beloved movie *9 to 5*, in which three women get revenge on a sexist boss, was released in December 1980, two months after the Hughes-Mann piece ran.) Mann is now a writer and producer who has been nominated for seven Emmys, most recently for his work on the Showtime series "Homeland." I sent him an e-mail asking what he now thought of the piece he wrote with Hughes. He replied that he didn't remember ever having written it. "It looks like one of our art director Peter's desperate page fillers," he explained, referring to Peter Kleinman. "It wouldn't fly today and it never should have flown then," he went on, adding, "These were degenerate cocaine days."

I can't vouch, personally, for any cocaine days that John may or may not have had. When I knew him, he never expressed an interest in doing drugs of any kind, including alcohol—with the exception of cigarettes, which he smoked constantly.

John believed in me, and in my gifts as an actress, more than anyone else I've known, and he was the first person to tell me that I had to write and direct one day. He was also a phenomenal grudge-keeper, and he could respond to perceived rejection in much the same way the character of Bender did in *The Breakfast Club*. But I'm not thinking about the man right now but of the films that he left behind. Films that I am proud of in so many ways. Films that, like his earlier writing, though to a much lesser extent, could also be considered racist, misogynistic, and, at times, homophobic. The words "fag" and "faggot" are tossed around with abandon; the character of Long Duk Dong, in *Sixteen Candles*, is a grotesque stereotype, as other writers have detailed far more eloquently than I could.

And yet I have been told more times than I could count, by both friends and strangers, including people in the LGBT community, that the films "saved" them. Leaving a party not long ago, I was stopped by Emil Wilbekin, a gay, African American friend of a friend, who wanted to tell me just that. I smiled and thanked him, but what I wanted to say was "Why?" There is barely a person of color to be found in the films, and no characters are openly gay. A week or so after the party, I asked my friend to put me in touch with him. In an e-mail, Wilbekin, a journalist who created an organization called Native Son, devoted to empowering gay black men, expanded upon what he had said to me as I had left the party. *The Breakfast Club*, he explained, saved his life by showing him, a kid growing up in Cincinnati in the 80s, "that there were other people like me who were struggling with their identities, feeling out of place in the social constructs of high school, and dealing with the challenges of family ideals and pressures." These kids were also "finding themselves and being 'other' in a very traditional, white, heteronormative environment." The lack of diversity didn't bother him, he added, "because the characters and story lines were so beautifully human, perfectly imperfect and flawed." He watched the films in high school, and while he was not yet out, he had a pretty good idea that he was gay.

Pretty in Pink features a character, Duckie, who was loosely based on my best friend of 40 years, Matthew Freeman. We've been friends since I was 10, and he worked as a production assistant on the film. Like Emil, he's out now but wasn't then. (It's one of the reasons I've often posited to the consternation of some fans and the delight of others, that Duckie is gay, though there's nothing to indicate that in the script.) "The characters John created spoke to feeling invisible and an outsider," Matt told me recently. They got at "how we felt as closeted gay kids who could only live vicariously through others' sexual awakenings, lest we get found out with the very real threat of being ostracized or pummelled."

John's movies convey the anger and fear of isolation that adolescents feel, and seeing that others might feel the same way is a balm for the trauma that teenagers experience. Whether that's enough to make up for the impropriety of the films is hard to say—even criticizing them makes me feel like I'm divesting a generation of some of its fondest memories or being ungrateful since they helped to establish my career. And yet embracing them entirely feels hypocritical. And yet, and yet. . . .

How are we meant to feel about art that we both love and oppose? What if we are in the unusual position of having helped create it? Erasing history is a dangerous road when it comes to art—change is essential, but so, too, is remembering the past, in all of its transgression and barbarism, so that we may properly gauge how far we have come and also how far we still need to go.

While researching this piece, I came across an article that was published in *Seventeen* magazine, in 1986, for which I interviewed John. (It was the only time I did so.) He talked about the artists who inspired him when he was younger—Bob Dylan, John Lennon—and how, as soon as they "got comfortable" in their art, they moved on. I pointed out that he had already done a lot of movies about suburbia and asked him whether he felt that he should move on as his idols had. "I think it's wise for people to concern themselves with the things they know about," he said. He added, "I'd feel extremely self-conscious writing about something I don't know."

I'm not sure that John was ever really comfortable or satisfied. He often told me that he didn't think he was a good enough writer for prose, and although he loved to write, he notoriously hated to revise. I was set to make one more Hughes film, when I was 20 but felt that it needed rewriting. Hughes refused, and the film was never made, though there could have been other circumstances I was not aware of.

In the interview, I asked him if he thought teenagers were looked at differently than when he was that age. "Definitely," he said. "My generation had to be taken seriously because we were stopping things and burning things. We were able to initiate change because we had such vast numbers. We were part of the Baby Boom, and when we moved, everything moved with us. But now, there are fewer teens, and they aren't taken as seriously as we were. You make a teenage movie, and critics say, 'How dare you?' There's just a general lack of respect for young people now."

John wanted people to take teens seriously, and people did. The films are still taught in schools because good teachers want their students to know that what they feel and say is important; that if they talk, adults and peers will listen. I think that it's ultimately the greatest value of the films, and why I hope they will endure. The conversations about them will change, and they should. It's up to the following generations to figure out how to continue those conversations and make them their own—to keep talking, in schools, in activism and art—and trust that we care.

Critical Thinking

1. In what ways were John Hughes' film characters and storylines both imperfect and flawed but also "perfectly imperfect and human"?
2. How should we treat our history with all of its flaws? Should we erase it or remember it? Explain.

Internet References

Hartford Institute for Religion Research
Hirr.hartsem.edu/ency/Anthropology.htm

Harvard Department of Anthropology
https://anthropology.fas.harvard.edu/research/religion

Sexism, Patriarchy in the Film Industry
https://www.firstpost.com/entertainment/sexism-patriarchy-in-the-film-industry-make-womens-collectives-the-need-of-the-hour-across-film-industries-3791505.html

Society for the Anthropology of Religion
Sar.americananthro.org/

10 Surprisingly Sexist Movies That You Still Love To Watch
https://www.bustle.com/articles/131195-10-surprisingly-sexist-movies-that-you-still-love-to-watch

---

Molly Ringwald is an actress, author, and singer. She lives with her family in New York.

Unit 6

UNIT

Prepared by: Elvio Angeloni

Religion, Belief, and Ritual

The anthropological interest in religion, belief, and ritual is not concerned with the scientific validity of such phenomena but rather with the way in which people relate various concepts of the supernatural to their everyday lives. From this practical perspective, some anthropologists have found that some traditional spiritual healing is just as helpful in the treatment of illness as is modern medicine; that religious beliefs and practices may be a form of social control; and that mystical beliefs and rituals are not absent from the modern world. In other words, this unit shows religion, belief, and ritual in relationship to practical human affairs. The placing of belief systems in social context thus helps to not only counter popular stereotypes, but also serves to promote a greater understanding of and appreciation for other viewpoints.

Every society is composed of feeling, thinking, and acting human beings who, at one time or another, are either conforming to or altering the social order into which they were born. Religion is an ideological framework that gives special legitimacy and validity to human experience within any given sociocultural system. In this way, monogamy as a marriage form, or monarchy as a political form, ceases to be simply one of many alternative ways in which a society can be organized, but becomes, for the believer, the only legitimate way. Religion considers certain human values and activities as sacred and inviolable. It is this mythic function that helps explain the strong ideological attachments that some people have, regardless of the scientific merits of their points of view.

While, under some conditions, religion may in fact be "the opiate of the masses," under other conditions such a belief system may be a rallying point for social and economic protest. A contemporary example of the former might be the "Moonies" (members of the Unification Church founded by Sun Myung Moon), while a good example of the latter is the role of the Black Church in the American Civil Rights movement, along with the prominence of religious figures such as Martin Luther King Jr. and Jesse Jackson. A word of caution must be set forth concerning attempts to understand belief systems of other cultures. At times, the prevailing attitude seems to be, "What I believe in is religion, and what you believe in is superstition." While anthropologists generally do not subscribe to this view, some tend to explain such behavior as incomprehensible and impractical without considering its full meaning and function within its cultural context. The articles in this unit should serve as a strong warning concerning the pitfalls of that approach.

Article

Prepared by: Elvio Angeloni

Thoughtlessly Thoughtless

Why are the ideas that come most effortlessly to us often misguided, asks Graham Lawton

GRAHAM LAWTON

Learning Outcomes

After reading this article, you will be able to:

- Explain the origins of the "zero-sum bias" and why it does function well in the modern world.
- Discuss the job of education and the difficulty in unlearning "folk theories."
- Explain why evolution favored sycophants.
- Discuss the three core components of conservative ideology in contrast to what it takes to be a liberal.
- Describe tribalism and explain why it was selected for by evolution.
- Explain the author's position that our brains are almost perfectly designed to believe in a god.
- Explain revenge as a universal human trait.

"We all have a tendency to think that the world must conform to our prejudices. The opposite view involves some effort of thought, and most people would die sooner than think—in fact they do so."

THESE words are still as true today as when Bertrand Russell wrote them in 1925. You might even argue that our predilection for fake news, conspiracy theories, and common sense politics suggests we are less inclined to think than ever. Our mental lassitude is particularly shocking given that we pride ourselves on being *Homo sapiens*, the thinking ape. How did it come to this?

The truth is, we are simply doing what people have always done. The human brain has been honed by millions of years of evolution—and it is extraordinary. However, thinking is costly in terms of time and energy, so our ancestors evolved a whole range of cognitive shortcuts. These helped them survive and thrive in a hazardous world. The problem is that the modern milieu is very different. As a result, the ideas and ways of thinking that come to us most effortlessly can get us into a lot of trouble. The first step to avoiding these pitfalls is to identify them. To that end, we bring you the *New Scientist* guide to sloppy thinking . . .

Zero Sum

We See Life as a Win–Lose Game

Children often bicker over who got the most cake or pop. But even as adults, we are acutely sensitive to the fair allocation of resources. Say there are 500 places at a local school, dished out according to who lives closest. Just before term starts, a large immigrant family is moved into a council house near the school and takes five of the places. No matter how liberal you are, it is hard not to think "Not fair!" Plenty of evidence suggests that immigrants contribute more to an economy than they take out. Yet the intuitive belief that they are extracting an unfair share of resources is hard to shake. Blame it on our zero-sum bias.

In a classic zero-sum situation, resources are finite, and your loss is my gain. Many situations in life follow this pattern—but not all. Unfortunately, this subtlety tends to pass us by. At best, seeing competition where none exists can blind us to opportunity. At worst, it has very unpleasant consequences.

Zero-sum thinking was an evolutionary adaptation to a time when we lived in small bands of hunter-gatherers, says neuroscientist Dan Meegan at the University of Guelph in Canada. Under those circumstances, resources such as food and mates were finite and often scarce, so more for one person meant less for another. Today, however, things are different.

A good example is international trade. Treaties between nations are usually designed to be win–win: the more trade that happens, the more resources there are for everybody. The basis of this is "comparative advantage," whereby trade benefits even less productive countries provided they concentrate their efforts on the goods they are most efficient at producing (see "Win-win," p. 30). Yet the bias persists. People find it hard to believe that a trading "win" for a foreign partner doesn't lead to a loss for them. This, says Meegan, is one reason why free trade is politically unpopular among people it would benefit.

Of course, sometimes our instincts are right. "For some people, free trade really is a zero-sum game," says Meegan. "Even if the nation benefits—GDP is bigger—individual people may not. They had a great job, now a Mexican has their great job." The same can happen with immigration: if school places, doctors' appointments, and decent social housing are already in short supply, then an influx of outsiders wanting all of these things will squeeze supply even further.

The trouble is, distinguishing between zero-sum and non-zero-sum situations is difficult. And even when the sum is non-zero, persuading people so is hard. "It is often easier to quantify what you're contributing than what you're getting back," says Meegan. "So it's really easy to get people upset about something when you say, 'Look at all we're putting in, but what exactly are we gaining?'"

Brexit campaigners exploited this with the notorious £350 million a week, the UK would save by leaving the European Union. In the United States, President Trump capitalizes on our zero-sum bias too, through constant carping about "bad" trade deals. It has also been blamed for the resurgence of white supremacy there. As early as 2011, during President Obama's first term, there were signs that many white Americans perceived growing "anti-white prejudice" despite overwhelming evidence that they still enjoyed privileged access to jobs, education, and justice. Research indicated that this was at least partly based on the misperception that discrimination is a zero-sum game—that less of it against minorities necessarily means more against white people.

With so much riding on it, just being aware of zero-sum thinking could go a long way to improving social relations.

Folk Knowledge
Our Childish Intuitions Haunt Us

Children, it is often said, are like little scientists. What looks like play is actually experimentation. They formulate hypotheses, test them, analyze the results, and revise their world view accordingly.

That may be true, but if kids are like scientists, they are rubbish ones. By the time they enter school, they have filled their heads with utter nonsense about how the world works. The job of education—especially science education—is to unlearn these "folk theories" and replace them with evidence-based ones. For most people, it doesn't work, and even for those who go on to become scientists, it is only partially successful. No wonder the world is so full of nonsense.

Folk theories—also known as naive theories—have been documented across all domains of science. In biology, for example, young children often conflate life with movement, seeing the sun and wind as alive, but trees and mushrooms as not. They also see purpose everywhere: birds are "for" flying, rocks are for animals to scratch themselves on, and rain falls so flowers can drink. In physics, children conclude that heat is a substance that flows from one place to another, that the sun moves across the sky, and so on. For most everyday purposes, these ideas are serviceable. Nevertheless, they aren't true.

Children cling to their folk theories, and when they encounter difficult concepts, they cling even harder. For example, many intuitively see evolution as a purposeful force that strives to endow animals and plants with the traits they need to survive. Folk theories do get knocked back as we move through education, but they never go away. "They can be suppressed by a more scientific world view but cannot be eradicated altogether," says Andrew Shtulman, a psychologist at Occidental College in Los Angeles. "Intuition can be overridden but not overwritten."

Shtulman's group has revealed this resilience by presenting people with a variety of statements about the natural world and asking them to say which were true and which false. Some were designed to be intuitively true but scientifically false, such as "fire is composed of matter"; others were intuitively false but scientifically true, such as "air is composed of matter." People who got the right answer still took significantly longer to process an intuitively false but scientifically true statement. This was even the case for those who had been scientists for decades.

Similar results come from brain scans. When people watch videos that are consistent with the laws of physics but intuitively wrong—such as light and heavy objects falling at the same rate—the error-detecting parts of their brains light up, suggesting that they are struggling to reconcile two competing beliefs. The persistence of folk theory is revealed in people with Alzheimer's disease too. Tests of their science knowledge show that they often revert to folk theories as their higher executive functions decline.

The upshot is that scientific thinking is hard-won and easily lost and that persuading most people of the validity of things like evolution, climate change, and vaccination will always be an uphill struggle.

Stereotyping
We Can't Help Pigeonholing People

We are born to judge others by how they look: our brains come hardwired with a specific face-processing area, and even shortly after birth, babies would rather look at a human face than anything else. Within their first year, they become more discerning and are more likely to crawl toward friendly looking faces than those who look a bit shifty. By the time we reach adulthood, we are snap-judgment specialists, jumping to conclusions about a person's character and status after seeing their face for just a tenth of a second. And we shun considered assessments of others in favor of simple shortcuts—for example, we judge a baby-faced individual as more trustworthy and associate a chiseled jaw with dominance.

Unfair, it may be, but it makes good evolutionary sense. Ours is an ultrasocial species, so being able to quickly assess whether someone is friend or foe and whether they have the power to help or hurt us is important survival information. But there is a problem. As psychologist Alexander Todorov of Princeton University points out, more often than not, our first impressions are wrong. It's not clear why, but he suggests that poor feedback and the fact that we meet many more strangers than our prehistoric ancestors would have both play a part.

Another problem is that we don't stick to stereotyping faces one at a time. We are just as quick to categorize groups of people—and then discriminate against them as a result. Research by Susan Fiske, also of Princeton, and her colleagues has shown that group stereotypes, too, are based on levels of trustworthiness and status—or "warmth" and "competence" as they label them. The researchers have plotted these categories on a two-by-two grid (see "Four kinds of people," below), each quarter of which is associated with a particular emotion: pity, disgust, pride, or envy. This, they have found, informs our behavior toward people in the group.

Their findings don't paint us in a great light. We tend to dehumanize groups we judge to be lacking in warmth and react violently to those with high status. "Historically, many genocides have been directed toward groups that fall into the envy quadrant," says Fiske. Even our relatively positive reactions have downsides: we may pity those of low status but react by patronizing them, and the pride we feel toward our own group can spill over into nepotism.

If you think you are above this kind of thing, think again. Even if you consciously reject stereotypes, the culture you live in does not, and experiments suggest that you are likely to share its biases. One study, for example, found that white Americans who showed no sign of racism on a standard test subconsciously dehumanize black people.

The best way to escape this evolutionary trap is to really get to know people from outside your echo chamber. Working together on a joint project is ideal because relying on someone forces you to look beyond simplistic first impressions. And don't trust social stereotypes—even your own national stereotype. The evidence suggests that we are not even accurate when it comes to judging ourselves.

Sycophancy
We're Suckers for a Celebrity

If you ever meet the queen of England, there are certain rules you are advised to follow. Do not speak until spoken to. Bow your head or curtsey. Address her first as "your majesty," then "ma'am," but "your majesty" again upon leaving. Don't make the mistake of calling her "your royal highness"—that is for other members of the royal family, pleb! And don't expect her to thank you for the £40 million plus she gets every year from the public purse or for paying to have her house done up.

Apply some rational thought and this is all very puzzling. What has the queen done to deserve such treatment? What makes her "majestic"? Why is her family "higher" than yours? If humans were a wild species of primate, you would conclude that the queen must be the dominant female. But dominance has to be earned and kept, often by physical aggression and threats, and is always up for negotiation. Nobody defers to the queen out of fear that she will beat them up if they don't, and nobody is secretly plotting a leadership challenge. Human societies do have dominant individuals, but what the queen possesses is something quite different: prestige. And we are suckers for it.

"Whatever people's political views when sober, alcohol shifts them to the right."

According to biologists, this prestige bias is an evolved feature of human cognition that goes back to the time when our ancestors were nomads living in small bands. Humans are social learners, which means we copy the behavior of other people rather than figuring everything out from scratch. People who copy successful individuals can acquire useful, survival-enhancing skills—how to hunt, for example. But to do so requires sustained and close contact with the skilled without getting on their nerves. The best way to do this is to "kiss up," as psychologist Francisco Gil-White at the University of Pennsylvania puts it. Pay them compliments, do them favors, sing their virtues, and exempt them from certain social obligations. Those of our ancestors who kissed up to talented individuals advanced their own interests, making them more likely to survive and reproduce. Evolution thus favored sycophants.

This can backfire in the modern world. Now we don't just judge the prestige of people we encounter directly but also those we only know vicariously. To do this, we follow our natural tendency to watch others and conform. If certain people are routinely fawned over, we assume that they are skilled and prestigious individuals who we would be wise to kiss up to ourselves. Hence we show deference to the queen and any number of celebrities who are famous for being famous.

Prestige exerts such a strong pull on the human mind that the construction and perpetuation of hierarchies is hard to resist. In lab experiments, people find it easier to understand social situations where there is a clear pecking order, and they express preferences for hierarchies, even if they are at the wrong end of them. But we can at least be more discerning about whom we place at the top. If we base prestige on skill and genuine achievement, then those we kiss up to won't be the only ones to benefit. Yes ma'am.

Conservatism

Deep Down, We're All Status Quo Fans

If you've ever talked politics in the pub near closing time, chances are it wasn't an especially enlightened or right-on discussion. When researchers in the United States loitered outside a bar in New England and asked customers about their political views, they found that the drunker the punter, the more right wing their leanings. That wasn't because right-wing people drink more or get pissed more easily. Wherever people stood on the political spectrum when sober, alcohol shifted their views to the right.

Why might that be? The researchers, led by Scott Eidelmanat the University of Arkansas in Fayetteville, point out that alcohol strips away complex reasoning to reveal the default state of the mind. And that is why they were chatting to drunks: they were using drunkenness to test the hypothesis that low-effort, automatic thought promotes political conservatism.

The team also found that they could push people to the right by distracting them, putting them under time pressure or simply telling them not to think too hard. Participants who were asked to deliberate more deeply, in contrast, shifted their political thinking to the left. Similar effects have been seen with the three core components of conservative ideology: preference for the status quo, acceptance of hierarchy, and belief in personal responsibility. All three, the researchers say, come naturally to the human mind. We think that way without trying, without even noticing. More liberal views, in contrast, require effortful deliberation.

Lots of research points in the same direction. Our political views are shaped by many factors, including personality, upbringing, and education. However, as early as the 1950s, psychologists probing the appeal of fascism found that right-wing ideology was associated with dislike of ambiguity and cognitive complexity. That's not to say that conservatives are less intelligent. The relationship between IQ and political leanings is complex. Broadly speaking, people with lower-than-average IQs tend to be lefties, probably out of economic self-interest. People of moderately above-average intelligence lean right for the same reason. And the top 20 percent swing left again—although highly intelligent people are also overrepresented in the libertarian camp, which defies simple left–right categorization.

Nonetheless, dislike of—or lack of training in—analytical thinking is strongly associated with preference for the status quo. Conversely, people who are politically liberal tend to think more analytically than their conservative peers, and having studied science is strongly associated with progressive views. This has led to the suggestion that left-wing political ideas are more complex and counterintuitive than right-wing ones. Of course, not everyone agrees. "In some areas they are, in some they aren't," says Noah Carl, a sociologist at the University of Oxford. "Market allocation of resources is less intuitive than having somebody do it from the top, for example."

Whether you think our intuitive conservatism is good or bad probably depends on your personal politics. With around 85 percent of the world population largely untrained in critical thinking, preference for the status quo is the clear winner. Nevertheless, progressive change does usually happen eventually.

Tribalism

Everybody Wants to Be in the Gang

Desmond Morris was 45 when he went to his first ever football match—a club game in Malta, where he lived at the time. He had no interest in football but had been pestered into it by his young son. For the elder Morris, it was an awesome experience. Fighting between rival fans caused the match to be abandoned before half time. Most people would have been put off for life, but Morris—the author of the bestselling books *Manwatching* and *The Naked Ape*—was captivated. What had caused people to behave so passionately over something as meaningless as a football game?

On his return to England in 1977, Morris became a director of Oxford United FC so he could closely observe the culture of football—the players, directors, and, above all, the fans. Four years later, he published his conclusions in *The Soccer Tribe*, which argued that football is essentially tribal. Each club is a tribe, with territory, elders, doctors, heroes, foot soldiers, modes of dress, allies, and mortal enemies.

Morris saw this as a modern expression of a deep-rooted evolutionary instinct. For thousands of years, our ancestors lived in small nomadic bands of mostly related individuals in frequent conflict—and occasional alliance—with neighbors over scarce resources. Tribes made up of individuals prepared to fight for a common good had a competitive edge over those that weren't, so tribalism was selected for by evolution. We are one species, but we instinctively and effortlessly identify with smaller groups.

Tribalism and the hostility it engenders are frighteningly easy to induce. More than 60 years ago, Muzafer Sharif at the University of Oklahoma took 22 adolescent boys to Robbers Cave State Park in Oklahoma. The trip had all the trappings of a traditional summer camp, but in truth, it was a psychology experiment. Sharif had divided the boys into two groups, each unaware of the other's existence. They were given cooperative tasks to perform, and quickly bonded, developing hierarchies and cultural norms. Then, toward the end of the week, the experimenters engineered a fleeting encounter between the groups. Hostility flared, despite the boys having been chosen for their similarities. Soon the camp descended into a sort of tribal warfare, with derogatory insults, land grabs, nocturnal raids, flag burning and, eventually, a mass brawl. Hostilities only ended when the experimenters introduced a common enemy in the form of fictitious vandals.

Since then, numerous experiments have revealed how the flimsiest and most transient badges of cultural identity can trigger people to divide themselves into "us" and "them"—even the color of randomly assigned T-shirts can do it.

Tribalism can be a useful motivating force in the modern world: rivalry between scientific teams working on the same problem, for example. It also underpins some deeply unedifying behaviors including racism, xenophobia, and homophobia. But there's hope that we can reduce these negative repercussions. Our saving grace is that the boundaries between "us" and "them" are fluid. Fans of rival football clubs can forge an alliance as supporters of the national team. If we can extend our definition of the tribe in football, why not in other, more meaningful, areas of life?

Religion

The God-shaped Hole Inside Us

If God designed the human brain, he (or she) did a lousy job. Dogged by glitches and biases, requiring routine shutdown for maintenance for eight hours a day, and highly susceptible to serious malfunction, a product recall would seem to be in order. But in one respect at least, God played a blinder: our brains are almost perfectly designed to believe in him or her.

Almost everybody who has ever lived has believed in some kind of deity. Even in today's enlightened and materialistic times, atheism remains a minority pursuit requiring hard intellectual graft. Even committed atheists easily fall prey to supernatural ideas. Religious belief, in contrast, appears to be intuitive.

Cognitive scientists talk about us being born with a "god-shaped hole" in our heads. As a result, when children encounter religious claims, they instinctively find them plausible and attractive, and the hole is rapidly filled by the details of whatever religious culture they happen to be born into. When told that there is an invisible entity that watches over them, intervenes in their lives and passes moral judgment on them, most unthinkingly accept it. Ditto the idea that the same entity is directing events and that everything that happens, happens for a reason.

This is not brainwashing. The "cognitive byproduct theory" argues that religious belief is a side effect of cognitive skills that evolved for other reasons. It pays, for example, to assume that all events are caused by agents. The rustle in the dark could be the wind, but it could also be a predator. Running away from the wind has no existential consequences but not running away from a predator does. Humans who ran lived to pass on their genes; those who did not became carrion.

Then there's "theory of mind," which evolved so that we could infer the mental states and intentions of others, even when they aren't physically present. This is very useful for group living. However, it makes the idea of invisible entities with minds capable of seeing into yours, quite plausible. Religion also piggybacks on feelings of existential insecurity, which must have been common for our ancestors. Randomness, loss of control, and knowledge of death are soothed by the idea that somebody is watching over you and that death is not the end of existence.

This helps explain why religious ideas were widely accepted and disseminated once they got started. It has even been argued that religion was the key to civilization because it was the social glue that held large groups of strangers together as societies expanded. No doubt it still has much of its original appeal. But these days, religion's downsides are more apparent. Conflict, misogyny, prejudice, and terrorism all happen in the name of religion. However, as the rise of atheism attests, it is possible to override our deep-seated religious tendencies with rational deliberation—it just takes some mental effort.

Revenge

We All Want to Get Our Own Back

It is, according to popular wisdom, a dish best served cold. However you like yours, there's no denying that revenge is tasty. We get a hunger for it and feel satisfied once we've had our fill.

You can see why if you look at what's going on in your head. Brain scanning reveals the neural pathway of the revenge process, according to criminologist Manuel Eisner of the University of Cambridge. The initial humiliation fires up the brain's emotional centers, the amygdalae and hypothalamus. They inform the anterior insular cortex, which evaluates whether you have been treated unfairly. If so, the prefrontal cortex steps in to plan and execute retaliation. Finally, the brain's pleasure center, the nucleus accumbens, swings into action to judge whether the revenge is satisfactory.

Revenge appears to be a universal human trait. A study of 10 hunter-gatherer groups found that all of them had a culture of vengeance. The list of wrongs that need to be avenged is also common across all societies. It includes homicide, physical injury, theft, sexual aggression, adultery, and reputational damage to oneself, loved ones or members of your tribe. The concept of "an eye for an eye" also runs deep, with punishment usually being roughly proportional to the crime.

For many years, scientists viewed revenge as pathological and tried to find ways to promote its more cool-headed mirror image, forgiveness. Now, however, they are more likely to see it as an instinctive cognitive trait that evolved to lubricate our often-fraught social interactions. From this point of view, the desire to inflict punishment on somebody who has harmed you makes sense. The original wrong cannot be righted, but the revenge is a social signal that makes others think twice about wronging you again.

Even so, it's easy to get revenge wrong. Undercook it and you reveal that you are worth exploiting. Overcook it and you risk starting a tit-for-tat cycle of revenge, which is in nobody's interest. The fact that we often make such misjudgments might help explain why we have evolved an instinct for forgiveness, too. Evolutionary psychologists see this as part of the same cognitive tool, to minimize any fallout from revenge. Once it is enacted, mutual forgiveness follows, and the relationship is reset—until the next time.

In modern societies, revenge is normally delegated to the state, which can exact the ultimate punishment of locking people up or even putting them to death. Still, many people prefer to take it into their own hands. Revenge can spill over into vigilante violence. It is a major motivation for terrorists. And it is a causal factor in up to 20 percent of homicides worldwide. All of which suggests that revenge might in fact be a dish best avoided.

"The list of wrongs that need to be avenged is common across all societies."

Confabulation

We're All Fantasists

Everyone loves a good story. So much so that our brains make them up all the time, and most of the time we don't even notice. This is confabulation—and it can make fools of us all.

Confabulation is common in dementia, when people fabricate stories to fill in gaps in memory. In Capgras delusion, where a person insists that a loved one has been abducted and replaced by a doppelgänger, confabulation explains away the sensation of disconnection they feel in the company of someone they know they should love. More generally, we confabulate when the information we are getting from the outside world doesn't fit with our internal knowledge and feelings. This seems to be a basic feature of our brains.

Imagine, for example, that someone asked you to pick your favorite of two images, and then surreptitiously swapped it for the other one before asking you to explain why you like it best. You might assume that you would point out their mistake, but when researchers did this in the lab they found that people often launched into a justification of why they chose the image they had actually spurned.

Michael Gazzaniga at the University of California, Santa Barbara, who pioneered confabulation research in the 1960s has dubbed the part of the brain that creates such narratives "the interpreter." And he argues that it is behind our unified sense of self. The interpreter integrates information from different parts of the brain. It rationalizes decisions we make based on subconscious processing that is not accessible to our conscious mind. And it fills in the gaps when the information coming from the outside world doesn't fit with our expectations. In other words, the interpreter creates narratives that help us make sense of our world.

We seem compelled to do this. A new idea suggests we have evolved a "drive for sensemaking," akin to our drives for food, drink, and sex. We derive pleasure from joining the dots between disparate information to create simple stories that explain our complex world. This urge helps explain characteristic human attributes such as curiosity, science, and art. But also, why we find it so difficult to accept information that doesn't fit our world view. It can lead to fantastical confabulations too: religion, for example, may be the result of trying to make sense of a bunch of cognitive glitches. No wonder we are so susceptible to conspiracy theories and fake news.

Even though we can't resist concocting stories, we can try to make them less fanciful. Research on combating delusional thinking offers some tips: don't jump to conclusions, question your initial thoughts, and consider different explanations. In other words, avoid sloppy thinking. As you now know, it can get you into a lot of trouble.

Critical Thinking

1. How did "zero-sum bias" develop and why is it inadequate as an adaptation in the modern world?
2. Why is education so important for overcoming folk theories?
3. Why are humans "snap-judgment specialists" and how has it become maladaptive in the modern world?
4. Why did evolution favor sycophants?

5. How do conservatives and liberals differ in the way they think?
6. Why was tribalism selected for by evolution and what are its drawbacks in the modern world?
7. Why is it that our brains almost perfectly designed to believe in a god?
8. What is the evolutionary function of revenge?

Internet References

Folk Psychology
https://en.wikipedia.org/wiki/Folk_psychology

International Cognition and Culture Institute
http://cognitionandculture.net/

Snopes
https://www.snopes.com/

Article

Prepared by: Elvio Angeloni

The Adaptive Value of Religious Ritual

Rituals promote group cohesion by requiring members to engage in behavior that is too costly to fake.

RICHARD SOSIS

Learning Outcomes

After reading this article, you will be able to:

- Explain how beliefs about the supernatural contribute to a sense of personal security, individual responsibility, and social harmony.
- Discuss the relationship between the demands upon members of a religious group and the levels of devotion and commitment achieved.

I was 15 years old the first time I went to Jerusalem's Old City and visited the 2,000-year-old remains of the Second Temple, known as the Western Wall. It may have foreshadowed my future life as an anthropologist, but on my first glimpse of the ancient stones I was more taken by the people standing at the foot of the structure than by the wall itself. Women stood in the open sun, facing the Wall in solemn worship, wearing long-sleeved shirts, head coverings and heavy skirts that scraped the ground. Men in their thick beards, long black coats and fur hats also seemed oblivious to the summer heat as they swayed fervently and sang praises to God. I turned to a friend, "Why would anyone in their right mind dress for a New England winter only to spend the afternoon praying in the desert heat?" At the time I thought there was no rational explanation and decided that my fellow religious brethren might well be mad.

Of course, "strange" behavior is not unique to ultraorthodox Jews. Many religious acts appear peculiar to the outsider. Pious adherents the world over physically differentiate themselves from others: Moonies shave their heads, Jain monks of India wear contraptions on their heads and feet to avoid killing insects, and clergy almost everywhere dress in outfits that distinguish them from the rest of society. Many peoples also engage in some form of surgical alteration. Australian aborigines perform a ritual operation on adolescent boys in which a bone or a stone is inserted into the penis through an incision in the urethra. Jews and Muslims submit their sons to circumcision, and in some Muslim societies daughters are also subject to circumcision or other forms of genital mutilation. Groups as diverse as the Nuer of Sudan and the latmul of New Guinea force their adolescents to undergo ritual scarification. Initiation ceremonies, otherwise known as rites of passage, are often brutal. Among Native Americans, Apache boys were forced to bathe in icy water, Luiseno initiates were required to lie motionless while being bitten by hordes of ants, and Tukuna girls had their hair plucked out.

How can we begin to understand such behavior? If human beings are rational creatures, then why do we spend so much time, energy and resources on acts that can be so painful or, at the very least, uncomfortable? Archaeologists tell us that our species has engaged in ritual behavior for at least 100,000 years, and every known culture practices some form of religion. It even survives covertly in those cultures where governments have attempted to eliminate spiritual practices. And, despite the unparalleled triumph of scientific rationalism in the 20th century, religion continued to flourish. In the United States a steady 40 percent of the population attended church regularly throughout the century. A belief in God (about 96 percent), the afterlife (about 72 percent), heaven (about 72 percent) and hell (about 58 percent) remained substantial and remarkably constant. Why do religious beliefs, practices and institutions continue to be an essential component of human social life?

Such questions have intrigued me for years. Initially my training in anthropology did not provide an answer. Indeed, my studies only increased my bewilderment. I received my training in a subfield known as human behavioral ecology, which studies the adaptive design of behavior with attention to its ecological setting. Behavioral ecologists assume that natural selection has shaped the human nervous system to respond successfully to varying ecological circumstances. All organisms must balance trade-offs: Time spent doing one thing prevents them from pursuing other activities that can enhance their survival or reproductive success. Animals that maximize the rate at which they acquire resources, such as food and mates, can maximize the number of descendants, which is exactly what the game of natural selection is all about.

Behavioral ecologists assume that natural selection has designed our decision-making mechanisms to optimize the rate at which human beings accrue resources under diverse ecological conditions—a basic prediction of *optimal foraging theory.* Optimality models offer predictions of the "perfectly adapted" behavioral response, given a set of environmental constraints. Of course, a perfect fit with the environment is almost never achieved because organisms rarely have perfect information and because environments are always changing. Nevertheless, this assumption has provided a powerful framework to analyze a variety of decisions, and most research (largely conducted among foraging populations) has shown that our species broadly conforms to these expectations.

If our species is designed to optimize the rate at which we extract energy from the environment, why would we engage in religious behavior that seems so counterproductive? Indeed, some religious practices, such as ritual sacrifices, are a conspicuous display of wasted resources. Anthropologists can explain why foragers regularly share their food with others in the group, but why would anyone share their food with a dead ancestor by burning it to ashes on an altar? A common response to this question is that people believe in the efficacy of the rituals and the tenets of the faith that give meaning to the ceremonies. But this response merely begs the question. We must really ask why natural selection has favored a psychology that believes in the supernatural and engages in the costly manifestations of those beliefs.

Ritual Sacrifice

Behavioral ecologists have only recently begun to consider the curiosities of religious activities, so at first I had to search other disciplines to understand these practices. The scholarly literature suggested that I wasn't the only one who believed that intense religious behavior was a sign of madness. Some of the greatest minds of the past two centuries, such as Marx and Freud, supported my thesis. And the early anthropological theorists also held that spiritual beliefs were indicative of a primitive and simple mind. In the 19th century, Edward B. Tylor, often noted as one of the founding fathers of anthropology, maintained that religion arose out of a misunderstanding among "primitives" that dreams are real. He argued that dreams about deceased ancestors might have led the primitives to believe that spirits can survive death.

Eventually the discipline of anthropology matured, and its practitioners moved beyond the equation that "primitive equals irrational." Instead, they began to seek functional explanations of religion. Most prominent among these early 20th-century theorists was the Polish-born anthropologist Bronislaw Malinowski. He argued that religion arose out of "the real tragedies of human life, out of the conflict between human plans and realities." Although religion may serve to allay our fears of death, and provide comfort from our incessant search for answers, Malinowski's thesis did not seem to explain the origin of rituals. Standing in the midday desert sun in several layers of black clothing seems more like a recipe for increasing anxiety than treating it. The classical anthropologists didn't have the right answers to my questions. I needed to look elsewhere.

Fortunately, a new generation of anthropologists has begun to provide some explanations. It turns out that the strangeness of religious practices and their inherent costs are actually the critical features that contribute to the success of religion as a universal cultural strategy and why natural selection has favored such behavior in the human lineage. To understand this unexpected benefit we need to recognize the adaptive problem that ritual behavior solves. William Irons, a behavioral ecologist at Northwestern University, has suggested that the universal dilemma is the promotion of cooperation within a community. Irons argues that the primary adaptive benefit of religion is its ability to facilitate cooperation within a group—while hunting, sharing food, defending against attacks and waging war—all critical activities in our evolutionary history. But, as Irons points out, although everyone is better off if everybody cooperates, this ideal is often very difficult to coordinate and achieve. The problem is that an individual is even better off if everyone else does the cooperating, while he or she remains at home enjoying an afternoon siesta. Cooperation requires social mechanisms that prevent individuals from free riding on the efforts of others. Irons argues that religion is such a mechanism.

The key is that religious rituals are a form of communication, which anthropologists have long maintained. They borrowed this insight from ethologists who observed that many species engage in patterned behavior, which they referred to as "ritual." Ethologists recognized that ritualistic behaviors served as a form of communication between members of the same species, and often between members of different species. For example, the males of many avian species engage in courtship rituals—such as bowing, head wagging, wing waving and hopping (among many other gestures)—to signal their amorous

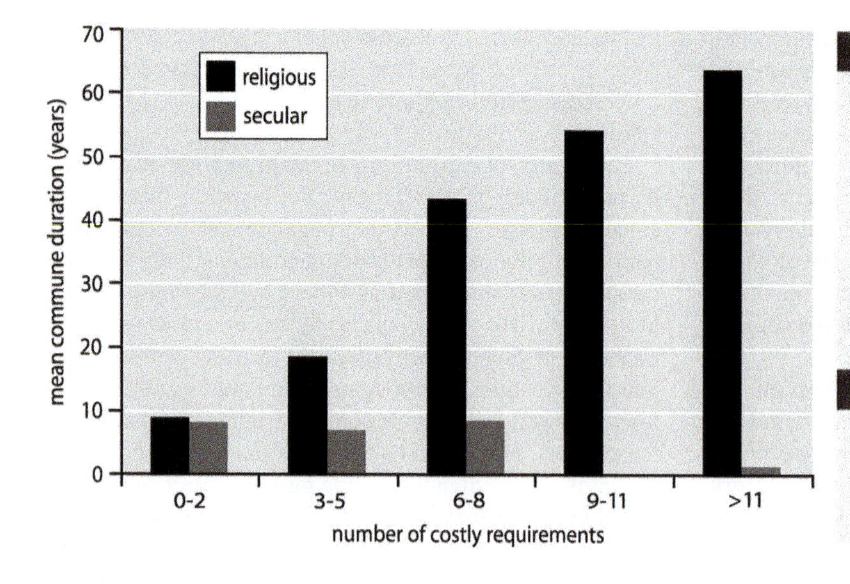

behaviors that are constrained

consumption of:
coffee, alcohol, tobacco, meat, other foods or beverages

use and ownership of:
photographs, jewelry, certain technology, other material items

activities:
monogamous marriage, gambling, communication with the outside, living as a nuclear family, maintaining rights to biological children

behaviors that are required

trial period for membership, surrender of material belongings, learn a body of knowledge, endure public sessions of criticism, certain clothing styles, certain hairstyles, fasting

intents before a prospective mate. And, of course, the vibration of a rattlesnake's tail is a powerful threat display to other species that enter its personal space.

Irons's insight is that religious activities signal commitment to other members of the group. By engaging in the ritual, the member effectively says, "I identify with the group and I believe in what the group stands for." Through its ability to signal commitment, religious behavior can overcome the problem of free riders and promote cooperation within the group. It does so because trust lies at the heart of the problem: A member must assure everyone that he or she will participate in acquiring food or in defending the group. Of course, hunters and warriors may make promises—"you have my word, I'll show up tomorrow"—but unless the trust is already established such statements are not believable.

It turns out that there is a robust way to secure trust. Israeli biologist Amotz Zahavi observes that it is often in the best interest of an animal to send a dishonest signal—perhaps to fake its size, speed, strength, health or beauty. The only signal that can be believed is one that is too costly to fake, which he referred to as a "handicap." Zahavi argues that natural selection has favored the evolution of handicaps. For example, when a springbok antelope spots a predator it often *stots*—it jumps up and down. This extraordinary behavior puzzled biologists for years: Why would an antelope waste precious energy that could be used to escape the predator? And why would the animal make itself more visible to something that wants to eat it? The reason is that the springbok is displaying its quality to the predator—its ability to escape, effectively saying, "Don't bother chasing me. Look how strong my legs are, you won't be able to catch me." The only reason a predator believes the springbok is because the signal is too costly to fake. An antelope that is not quick enough to escape cannot imitate the signal because it is not strong enough to repeatedly jump to a certain height. Thus, a display can provide honest information if the signals are so costly to perform that lower quality organisms cannot benefit by imitating the signal.

In much the same way, religious behavior is also a costly signal. By donning several layers of clothing and standing out in the midday sun, ultraorthodox Jewish men are signaling to others: "Hey! Look, I'm a *haredi* Jew. If you are also a member of this group you can trust me because why else would I be dressed like this? No one would do this *unless* they believed in the teachings of ultraorthodox Judaism and were fully committed to its ideals and goals." The quality that these men are signaling is their level of commitment to a specific religious group.

Adherence to a set of religious beliefs entails a host of ritual obligations and expected behaviors. Although there may be physical or psychological benefits associated with some ritual practices, the significant time, energy and financial costs involved serve as effective deterrents for anyone who does not believe in the teachings of a particular religion. There is no incentive for nonbelievers to join or remain in a religious group, because the costs of maintaining membership—such as praying three times a day, eating only kosher food, donating a certain part of your income to charity and so on—are simply too high.

Those who engage in the suite of ritual requirements imposed by a religious group can be trusted to believe sincerely in the doctrines of their respective religious communities. As a result of increased levels of trust and commitment among group members, religious groups minimize costly monitoring mechanisms that are otherwise necessary to overcome free-rider problems that typically plague communal pursuits. Hence, the adaptive

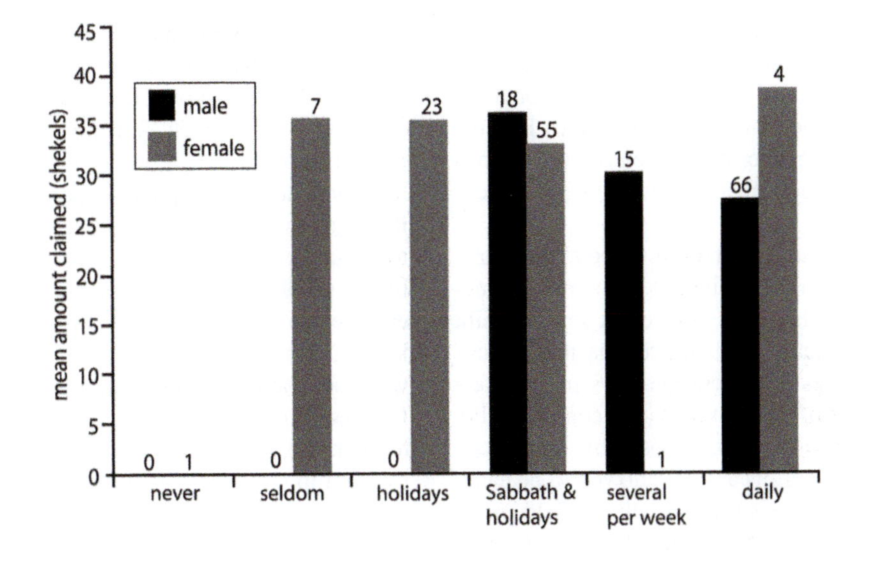

benefit of ritual behavior is its ability to promote and maintain cooperation, a challenge that our ancestors presumably faced throughout our evolutionary history.

Benefits of Membership

One prediction of the "costly signaling theory of ritual" is that groups that impose the greatest demands on their members will elicit the highest levels of devotion and commitment. Only committed members will be willing to dress and behave in ways that differ from the rest of society. Groups that maintain more-committed members can also offer more because it's easier for them to attain their collective goals than groups whose members are less committed. This may explain a paradox in the religious marketplace: Churches that require the most of their adherents are experiencing rapid rates of growth. For example, the Church of Jesus Christ of Latter-day Saints (Mormons), Seventh-day Adventists and Jehovah's Witnesses, who respectively abstain from caffeine, meat and blood transfusions (among other things), have been growing at exceptional rates. In contrast, liberal Protestant denominations such as the Episcopalians, Methodists and Presbyterians have been steadily losing members.

Economist Lawrence Iannaccone, of George Mason University, has also noted that the most demanding groups also have the greatest number of committed members. He found that the more distinct a religious group was—how much the group's lifestyle differed from mainstream America—the higher its attendance rates at services. Sociologists Roger Finke and Rodney Stark, of Penn State and the University of Washington, respectively, have argued that when the Second Vatican Council in 1962 repealed many of the Catholic Church's prohibitions and reduced the level of strictness in the church, it initiated a decline in church attendance among American Catholics and reduced the enrollments in seminaries. Indeed, in the late 1950s almost 75 percent of American Catholics were attending Mass weekly, but since the Vatican's actions there has been a steady decline to the current rate of about 45 percent.

The costly signaling theory of ritual also predicts that greater commitment will translate into greater cooperation within groups. My colleague Eric Bressler, a graduate student at McMaster University, and I addressed this question by looking at data from the records of 19th-century communes. All communes face an inherent problem of promoting and sustaining cooperation because individuals can free ride on the efforts of others. Because cooperation is key to a commune's survival, we employed commune longevity as a measure of cooperation. Compared to their secular counterparts, the religious communes did indeed demand more of their members, including such behavior as celibacy, the surrender of all material possessions and vegetarianism. Communes that demanded more of their members survived longer, overcoming the fundamental challenges of cooperation. By placing greater demands on their members, they were presumably able to elicit greater belief in and commitment toward the community's common ideology and goals.

I also wanted to evaluate the costly signaling theory of ritual within modern communal societies. The kibbutzim I had visited in Israel as a teenager provided an ideal opportunity to examine these hypotheses. For most of their 100-year history, these communal societies have lived by the dictum, "From each according to his abilities, to each according to his needs." The majority of the more than 270 kibbutzim are secular (and often ideologically antireligious); fewer than 20 are religiously oriented. Because of a massive economic failure—a collective debt of more than $4 billion—the kibbutzim are now moving in the direction of increased privatization and reduced communality. When news of the extraordinary debt surfaced in the late 1980s, it went largely unnoticed that the religious kibbutzim were financially stable. In the words of the Religious Kibbutz Movement Federation, "the economic position of the religious kibbutzim is sound, and they remain uninvolved in the economic crisis."

The success of the religious kibbutzim is especially remarkable given that many of their rituals inhibit economic productivity. For example, Jewish law does not permit Jews to milk cows on the Sabbath. Although rabbinic rulings now permit milking by kibbutz members to prevent the cows from suffering, in the early years none of this milk was used commercially. There are also significant constraints imposed by Jewish law on agricultural productivity. Fruits are not allowed to be eaten for the first few years of the tree's life, agricultural fields must lie fallow every seven years, and the corners of fields can never be harvested—they must be left for society's poor. Although these constraints appear detrimental to productivity, the costly signaling theory of ritual suggests that they may actually be the key to the economic success of the religious kibbutzim.

I decided to study this issue with economist Bradley Ruffle of Israel's Ben Gurion University. We developed a game to determine whether there were differences in how the members of secular and religious kibbutzim cooperated with each other. The game involves two members from the same kibbutz who remain anonymous to each other. Each member is told there are 100 shekels in an envelope to which both members have access. Each participant decides how many shekels to withdraw and keep. If the sum of both requests exceeds 100 shekels, both members receive no money and the game is over. However, if the requests are less than or equal to 100 shekels, the money remaining in the envelope is increased by 50 percent and divided evenly among the participants. Each member also keeps the original amount he or she requested. The game is an example of a common-pool resource dilemma in which publicly accessible goods are no longer available once they are consumed. Since the goods are available to more than one person, the maintenance of the resources requires individual self-restraint; in other words, cooperation.

After we controlled for a number of variables, including the age and size of the kibbutz and the amount of privatization, we found not only that religious kibbutzniks were more cooperative with each other than secular kibbutzniks, but that male religious kibbutz members were also significantly more cooperative than female members. Among secular kibbutzniks we found no sex differences at all. This result is understandable if we appreciate the types of rituals and demands imposed on religious Jews. Although there are a variety of requirements that are imposed equally on males and females, such as keeping kosher and refraining from work on the Sabbath, male rituals are largely performed in public, whereas female rituals are generally pursued privately. Indeed, none of the three major requirements imposed exclusively on women—attending a ritual bath, separating a portion of dough when baking bread and lighting Shabbat and holiday candles—are publicly performed. They are not rituals that signal commitment to a wider group; instead they appear to signal commitment to the family. Men, however, engage in highly visible rituals, most notably public prayer, which they are expected to perform three times a day. Among male religious kibbutz members, synagogue attendance is positively correlated with cooperative behavior. There is no similar correlation among females. This is not surprising given that women are not required to attend services, and so their presence does not signal commitment to the group. Here the costly signaling theory of ritual provides a unique explanation of these findings. We expect that further work will provide even more insight into the ability of ritual to promote trust, commitment and cooperation.

We know that many other species engage in ritual behaviors that appear to enhance trust and cooperation. For example, anthropologists John Watanabe of Dartmouth University and Barbara Smuts at the University of Michigan have shown that greetings between male olive baboons serve to signal trust and commitment between former rivals. So why are human rituals often cloaked in mystery and the supernatural? Cognitive anthropologists Scott Atran of the University of Michigan and Pascal Boyer at Washington University in St. Louis have pointed out that the counterintuitive nature of supernatural concepts are more easily remembered than mundane ideas, which facilitates their cultural transmission. Belief in supernatural agents such as gods, spirits and ghosts also appears to be critical to religion's ability to promote long-term cooperation. In our study of 19th-century communes, Eric Bressler and I found that the strong positive relationship between the number of costly requirements imposed on members and commune longevity only held for religious communes, not secular ones. We were surprised by this result because secular groups such as militaries and fraternities appear to successfully employ costly rituals to maintain cooperation. Cultural ecologist Roy Rappaport explained, however, that although religious and secular rituals can both promote cooperation, religious rituals ironically generate greater belief and commitment because they sanctify unfalsifiable statements that are beyond the possibility of examination. Since statements containing supernatural elements, such as "Jesus is the son of God," cannot be proved or disproved, believers verify them "emotionally." In contrast to religious propositions, the kibbutz's guiding dictum, taken from Karl Marx, is not beyond question; it can be evaluated by living according to its directives by distributing labor and resources appropriately. Indeed, as the economic situation on the kibbutzim has worsened, this fundamental proposition of kibbutz life has been challenged and is now disregarded by many who are pushing their communities to accept differential pay scales. The ability of religious rituals to evoke emotional experiences that can be associated with enduring supernatural concepts and symbols differentiates them from both animal and secular rituals and lies at the heart of their efficiency in promoting and maintaining long-term group cooperation and commitment.

Evolutionary research on religious behavior is in its infancy, and many questions remain to be addressed. The costly signaling theory of ritual appears to provide some answers, and, of course, it has given me a better understanding of the questions I asked as a teenager. The real value of the costly signaling theory of ritual will be determined by its ability to explain religious phenomena across societies. Most of us, including ultraorthodox Jews, are not living in communes. Nevertheless, contemporary religious congregations that demand much of their members are able to achieve a close-knit social community—an impressive accomplishment in today's individualistic world.

Religion has probably always served to enhance the union of its practitioners; unfortunately, there is also a dark side to this unity. If the intragroup solidarity that religion promotes is one of its significant adaptive benefits, then from its beginning religion has probably always played a role in intergroup conflicts. In other words, one of the benefits for individuals of intragroup solidarity is the ability of unified groups to defend and compete against other groups. This seems to be as true today as it ever was, and is nowhere more apparent than the region I visited as a 15-year-old boy—which is where I am as I write these words. As I conduct my fieldwork in the center of this war zone, I hope that by appreciating the depth of the religious need in the human psyche, and by understanding this powerful adaptation, we can learn how to promote cooperation rather than conflict.

References

Atran, S. 2002. *In Gods We Trust.* New York: Oxford University Press.

Iannaccone, L. 1992. Sacrifice and stigma: Reducing free-riding in cults, communes, and other collectives. *Journal of Political Economy* 100:271–291.

Iannaccone, L. 1994. Why strict churches are strong. *American Journal of Sociology* 99:1180–1211.

Irons, W. 2001. Religion as a hard-to-fake sign of commitment. In *Evolution and the Capacity for Commitment,* ed. R. Nesse, pp. 292–309. New York: Russell Sage Foundation.

Rappaport, R. 1999. *Ritual and Religion in the Making of Humanity.* Cambridge: Cambridge University Press.

Sosis, R. 2003. Why aren't we all Hutterites? Costly signaling theory and religious behavior. *Human Nature* 14:91–127.

Sosis, R., and C. Alcorta. 2003. Signaling, solidarity, and the sacred: The evolution of religious behavior. *Evolutionary Anthropology* 12:264–274.

Sosis, R., and E. Bressler. 2003. Cooperation and commune longevity: A test of the costly signaling theory of religion. *Cross-Cultural Research* 37:211–239.

Sosis, R., and B. Ruffle. 2003. Religious ritual and cooperation: Testing for a relationship on Israeli religious and secular kibbutzim. *Current Anthropology* 44:713–722.

Zahavi, A., and A. Zahavi. 1997. *The Handicap Principle.* New York: Oxford University Press.

Critical Thinking

1. What is the universal dilemma with regard to cooperation in a community, according to William Irons?
2. In what sense is religious ritual a form of communication?
3. What is the only kind of signal that can be believed? How does the example of the springbok antelope illustrate the point?
4. Why is there no incentive for nonbelievers to join or remain in a religious group? Are there costly monitoring mechanisms? Explain.
5. What is the relationship between demands upon members and levels of devotion and commitment? What paradox does this explain?
6. What groups have the most committed members?
7. What was observed among American Catholics once the Vatican Council reduced the level of strictness in the church?
8. Which 19th-century communes survived long and why?
9. Which kibbutzim survived better and why? What constraints existed among the religious kibbutzim and what effect did they have?
10. Describe the overall results of the game experiment with regard to religious versus secular kibbutzim and men versus women.
11. Why are religious rituals more successful at promoting belief than are secular rituals?
12. What is the "dark side" to the unity provided by religious intragroup solidarity?

Internet References

Apologetics Index
www.apologeticsindex.org/site/index-c

Journal of Anthropology of Religion
www.mehtapress.com/social-science-a-humanities/journal-of-anthropology-of-religion.html

Richard Sosis is an assistant professor of anthropology at the University of Connecticut. His research interests include the evolution of cooperation, utopian societies and the behavioral ecology of religion. Address: Department of Anthropology, U-2176, University of Connecticut, Storrs, CT 06269–2176. Internet: richard.sosis@uconn.edu

Article

Prepared by: Elvio Angeloni

Understanding Islam

KENNETH JOST

Learning Outcomes

After reading this article, you will be able to:

- Describe the basic tenets of Islam.
- Discuss whether Islam really clashes with Western values.

Is Islam Compatible with Western Values?

With more than 1 billion adherents, Islam is the world's second-largest religion after Christianity. Within its mainstream traditions, Islam teaches piety, virtue and tolerance. Ever since the Sept. 11, 2001, terrorist attacks in the United States, however, many Americans have associated Islam with the fundamentalist groups that preach violence against the West and regard "moderate" Muslims as heretics. Mainstream Muslims and religious scholars say Islam is wrongly blamed for the violence and intolerance of a few. But some critics say Muslims have not done enough to oppose terrorism and violence. They also contend that Islam's emphasis on a strong relationship between religion and the state is at odds with Western views of secularism and pluralism. Some Muslims are calling for a more progressive form of Islam. But radical Islamist views are attracting a growing number of young Muslims in the Islamic world and in Europe.

Overview

Aishah Azmi was dressed all in black, her face veiled by a *niqab* that revealed only her brown eyes through a narrow slit.

"Muslim women who wear the veil are not aliens," the 24-year-old suspended bilingual teaching assistant told reporters in Leeds, England, on Oct. 19. "Integration [of Muslims into British society] requires people like me to be in the workplace so that people can see that we are not to be feared or mistrusted."

But school officials defended their decision to suspend Azmi for refusing to remove her veil in class with a male teacher, saying it interfered with her ability to communicate with her students—most of them Muslims and, like Azmi, British Asians.

"The school and the local authority had to balance the rights of the children to receive the best quality education possible and Mrs. Azmi's desire to express her cultural beliefs," said local Education Minister Jim Dodds.

Although an employment tribunal rejected Azmi's discrimination and harassment claims, it said the school council had handled her complaint poorly and awarded her 1,100 British pounds—about $2,300.

Azmi's widely discussed case has become part of a wrenching debate in predominantly Christian England over relations with the country's growing Muslim population.

In September, a little more than a year after subway and bus bombings in London claimed 55 lives, a government minister called on Muslim parents to do more to steer their children away from violence and terrorism. Then, in October, a leaked report being prepared by the interfaith adviser of the Church of England complained that what he called the government's policy of "privileged attention" toward Muslims had backfired and was creating increased "disaffection and separation."

The simmering controversy grew even hotter after Jack Straw, leader of the House of Commons and former foreign secretary under Prime Minister Tony Blair, called full-face veils "a visible statement of separation and difference" that promotes separatism between Muslims and non-Muslims. Straw, whose constituency in northwestern England includes an estimated 25 percent Muslim population aired the comments in a local newspaper column.

Hamid Qureshi, chairman of the Lancashire Council of Mosques, called Straw's remarks "blatant Muslim-bashing."

"Muslims feel they are on center stage, and everybody is Muslim-bashing," says Anjum Anwar, the council's director of education. "They feel very sensitive."

Britain's estimated 1.5 million Muslims—comprising mostly Pakistani or Indian immigrants and their British-born children—are only a tiny fraction of Islam's estimated 1.2 billion adherents worldwide. But the tensions surfacing in the face-veil debate exemplify the increasingly strained relations between the predominantly Christian West and the Muslim world.

The world's two largest religions—Christianity has some 2 billion adherents—have had a difficult relationship at least since the time of the European Crusades against Muslim rulers, or caliphs, almost 1,000 years ago. Mutual suspicion and hostility have intensified since recent terrorist attacks around the world by militant Islamic groups and President George W. Bush proclaimed a worldwide "war on terror" in response to the Sept. 11, 2001, attacks in the United States.

Bush, who stumbled early on by referring to a "crusade" against terrorism, has tried many times since then to dispel perceptions of any official hostility toward Islam or Muslims generally. In Britain, Blair's government has carried on a 40-year-old policy of "multiculturalism" aimed at promoting cohesion among the country's various communities, Muslims in particular.

Despite those efforts, widespread distrust of Islam and Muslims prevails on both sides of the Atlantic. In a recent poll in the United States, 45 percent of those surveyed said they had an unfavorable view of Islam—a higher percentage than registered in a similar poll four years earlier.

British Muslim leaders also say they feel increasingly hostile anti-Muslim sentiments from the general public and government officials. "Muslims are very fearful, frustrated, upset, angry," says Asghar Bukhari, a spokesman for the Muslim Public Affairs Committee in London. "It's been almost like a mental assault on the Muslim psyche here."

As the face-veil debate illustrates, the distrust stems in part from an array of differences between today's Christianity and Islam as variously practiced in the so-called Muslim world, including the growing Muslim diaspora in Europe and North America.

In broad terms, Islam generally regards religion as a more pervasive presence in daily life and a more important source for civil law than contemporary Christianity, according to the British author Paul Grieve, who wrote a comprehensive guide to Islam after studying Islamic history and thought for more than three years. "Islam is a system of rules for all aspects of life," Grieve writes, while Western liberalism limits regulation of personal behavior. In contrast to the secular nation-states of the West, he explains, Islam views the ideal Muslim society as a universal community—such as the *ummah* established by the Prophet Muhammed in the seventh century.

Those theological and cultural differences are reflected, Grieve says, in Westerners' widespread view of Muslims as narrow-minded and extremist. Many Muslims correspondingly view Westerners as decadent and immoral.

The differences also can be seen in the debates over the role Islam plays in motivating terrorist violence by Islamic extremist groups such as al Qaeda and the objections raised by Muslims to what they consider unflattering and unfair descriptions of Islam in the West.

Muslim leaders generally deny responsibility for the violence committed by Islamic terrorists, including the 9/11 terrorist attacks in the United States and subsequent attacks in Indonesia, Spain and England. "Muslim organizations have done more than ever before in trying to advance community cohesion," Anwar says. They also deny any intention to deny freedom of expression, even though Muslims worldwide denounced a Danish cartoonist's satirical portrayal of Muhammad and Pope Benedict XVI's citation of a medieval Christian emperor's description of Islam as a violent religion.

For many Westerners, however, Islam is associated with radical Muslims—known as Islamists—who either advocate or appear to condone violence and who take to the streets to protest unfavorable depictions of Islam. "A lot of traditional or moderate Islam is inert," says Paul Marshall, a senior fellow at Freedom House's Center for Religious Freedom in Washington. "Many of the people who disagree with radicals don't have a developed position. They keep their heads down."

Meanwhile, many Muslims and non-Muslims alike despair at Islam's sometimes fratricidal intrafaith disputes. Islam split within the first decades of its founding in the seventh century into the Sunni and Shiite (Shia) branches. The Sunni-Shiite conflict helps drive the escalating insurgency in Iraq three years after the U.S.-led invasion ousted Saddam Hussein, a Sunni who pursued generally secularist policies. "A real geopolitical fracturing has taken place in the Muslim world since the end of the colonial era," says Reza Aslan, an Iranian-born Shiite Muslim now a U.S. citizen and author of the book *No god but God.*

The tensions between Islam and the West are on the rise as Islam is surging around the world, growing at an annual rate of about 7 percent. John Voll associate director of the Prince Alwaleed bin Talal Centre for Christian-Muslim Understanding at Georgetown University, notes that the growth is due largely to conversions, not the high birth rates that are driving Hinduism's faster growth.

Moreover, Voll says, Muslims are growing more assertive. "There has been an increase in intensity and an increase in strength in the way Muslims view their place in the world and their place in society," he says.

Teaching assistant Azmi's insistence on wearing the *niqab* exemplifies the new face of Islam in parts of the West. But her choice is not shared by all, or even, most of her fellow Muslim women. "I don't see why she needs to wear it," says Anwar.

"She's teaching young children under 11." (Azmi says she wears it because she works with a male classroom teacher.)

Muslim experts generally agree the Koran does not require veils, only modest dress. Observant Muslim women generally comply with the admonition with a head scarf and loose-fitting attire. In particularly conservative cultures, such as Afghanistan under Taliban rule, women cover their entire bodies, including their eyes.

Still, despite the varying practices, many Muslim groups see a disconnect between the West's self-proclaimed tolerance and its pressure on Muslims to conform. "It's a Muslim woman's right to dress as she feels appropriate, given her religious views," says Ibrahim Hooper, director of communications for the Council on American-Islamic Relations in Washington. "But then when somebody actually makes a choice, they're asked not to do that."

Indeed, in Hamtramck, Mich., a judge recently came under fire for throwing out a small-claims case because the Muslim plaintiff refused to remove her full-face veil.

As the debates continue, here are some of the questions being considered:

Is Islam a Religion That Promotes Violence?

Within hours of the London subway and bus bombings on July 7, 2005, the head of the Muslim World League condemned the attacks as un-Islamic. "The heavenly religions, notably Islam, advocate peace and security," said Abdallah al-Turki, secretary-general of the Saudi-funded organization based in Mecca.

The league's statement echoed any number of similar denunciations of Islamist-motivated terrorist attacks issued since 9/11 by Muslims in the United States and around the world. Yet many non-Muslim public officials, commentators, experts and others say Muslims have not done enough to speak out against terrorism committed in the name of their religion.

"Mainstream Muslims have not stepped up to the plate, by and large," says Angel Rabasa, a senior fellow at the Rand Corp., a California think tank, and lead author of a U.S. Air Force-sponsored study, *The Muslim World after 9/11.*

Muslim organizations voice indignant frustration in disputing the accusation. "We can always do more," says Hooper. "The problem is that it never seems to be enough. But that doesn't keep us from trying."

Many Americans, in fact, believe Islam actually encourages violence among its adherents. A CBS poll in April 2006 found that 46 percent of those surveyed believe Islam encourages violence more than other religions. A comparable poll four years earlier registered a lower figure: 32 percent.

Those perceptions are sometimes inflamed by U.S. evangelical leaders. Harsh comments about Islam have come from religious leaders like Franklin Graham, Jerry Falwell, Pat Robertson and Jerry Vines, the former president of the Southern Baptist Convention. Graham called Islam "a very evil and wicked religion," and Vines called Muhammad, Islam's founder and prophet, a "demon-possessed pedophile." Falwell, on the CBS news magazine "60 Minutes" in October 2002, declared, "I think Muhammad was a terrorist."

Mainstream Muslims insist Islam is a peaceful religion and that terrorist organizations distort its tenets and teachings in justifying attacks against the West or other Muslims. But Islamic doctrine and history sometimes seem to justify the use of violence in propagating or defending the faith. The dispute revolves around the meaning of *jihad,* an Arabic word used in the Koran and derived from a root meaning "to strive" or "to make an effort for." Muslim scholars can point to verses in the Koran that depict *jihad* merely as a personal, spiritual struggle and to others that describe *jihad* as encompassing either self-defense or conquest against non-believers.

Georgetown historian Voll notes that, in contrast to Christianity, Islam achieved military success during Muhammad's life and expanded into a major world empire within decades afterward. That history "reinforces the idea that militancy and violence can, in fact, be part of the theologically legitimate plan of the Muslim believer," says Voll.

"Islam, like all religions, has its historical share of violence," acknowledges Stephen Schwartz, an adult convert to Islam and executive director of the Center for Islamic Pluralism in Washington. "But there's no reason to single out Islam."

Modern-day jihadists pack their public manifestos with Koranic citations and writings of Islamic theologians to portray themselves as warriors for Allah and defenders of true Islam. But Voll and others stress that the vast majority of Muslims do not subscribe to their views. "You have a highly visible minority that represents a theologically extreme position in the Muslim world," Voll says.

In particular, writes Seyyed Hossein Nasr, a professor of Islamic studies at George Washington University, Islamic law prohibits the use of force against women, children or civilians—even during war. "Inflicting injuries outside of this context," he writes, "is completely forbidden by Islamic law."

Rabasa says, however, that Muslims who disapprove of terrorism have not said enough or done enough to mobilize opposition to terrorist attacks. "Muslims see themselves as part of a community and are reluctant to criticize radical Muslims," he says.

In addition, many Muslims are simply intimidated from speaking out, he explains. "Radicals are not reluctant to use violence and the threat of violence," he says. Liberal and moderate Muslims are known to receive death threats on their cell phones, even in relatively peaceful Muslim countries such as Indonesia.

Voll also notes that Islamic radicals have simply out-organized the moderates. "There is no moderate organization that even begins to resemble some of the radical organizations that have developed," he says.

In Britain, Bukhari of the Muslim Public Affairs Committee criticizes Muslim leaders themselves for failing to channel young people opposed to Britain's pro-U.S. foreign policy into non-violent political action. "Children who could have been peaceful react to that foreign policy in a way that they themselves become criminals," he says.

The Council on American-Islamic Relations' Hooper details several anti-terrorism pronouncements and drives issued following the London bombings by various Muslim groups and leaders in Britain and in the United States, including *fatwas,* or legal opinions, rejecting terrorism and extremism.

For his part, Omid Safi, an associate professor of Islamic studies at the University of North Carolina in Chapel Hill, points out that virtually every Muslim organization in the United States issued condemnations of violence almost immediately after the 9/11 terrorist attacks.

"How long must we keep answering this question?" Safi asks in exasperation. But he concedes a few moments later that the issue is more than perception. "Muslims must come to terms with our demons," he says, "and one of those demons is violence."

Basic Tenets of Islam

Islam is the youngest of the world's three major monotheistic religions. Like the other two, Judaism and Christianity, Islam (the word means both "peace" and "submission") holds there is but one God (Allah). Muslims believe God sent a number of prophets to teach mankind how to live according to His law. Muslims consider Jesus, Moses and Abraham as prophets of God and hold the Prophet Muhammad as his final and most sacred messenger. Many accounts found in Islam's sacred book, the Koran (Qur'an), are also found in sacred writings of Jews and Christians.

There are five basic pillars of Islam:

- Creed—Belief in God and Muhammad as his Prophet.
- Almsgiving—Giving money to charity is considered a sacred duty.
- Fasting—From dawn to dusk during the month of Ramadan.
- Prayer—Five daily prayers must be given facing Mecca, Islam's holiest city.
- Pilgrimage—All Muslims must make a baff to Mecca at least once during their lifetime, if they are physically able.

Is Islam Compatible with Secular, Pluralistic Societies?

In 2003, Germany's famed Deutsche Oper staged an avant-garde remake of Mozart's opera "Idomeneo," which dramatizes the composer's criticism of organized religion, with a scene depicting the severed heads of Muhammad, Jesus, Buddha and Poseidon. That production was mounted without incident, but the company dropped plans to restage it in November 2006 after police warned of a possible violent backlash from Muslim fundamentalists.

The cancellation prompted protests from German officials and artistic-freedom advocates in Europe and in the United States, who saw the move as appeasement toward terrorists. Wolfgang Bornsen, a spokesman for conservative Chancellor Angela Merkel, said the cancellation was "a signal" to other artistic companies to avoid any works critical of Islam.

The debate continued even after plans were discussed to mount the production after all—with enhanced security and the blessing of German Muslim leaders. "We live in Europe, where democracy was based on criticizing religion," remarked Philippe Val, editor of the French satirical magazine *Charlie Hebdo.* "If we lose the right to criticize or attack religions in our free countries . . . we are doomed."

As with the issue of violence, Islam's doctrines and history can be viewed as pointing both ways on questions of pluralism and tolerance. "There are a great many passages [in the Koran] that support a pluralistic interpretation of Islam," says the Rand Corp.'s Rabasa. "But you also find a great many that would support an intolerant interpretation."

"Intellectual pluralism is traditional Islam," says Schwartz at the Center for Islamic Pluralism. An oft-quoted verse from the Koran specifically prohibits compulsion in religion, he says. Voll and other historians agree that Muslim countries generally tolerated Christians and Jews, though they were often subject to special taxes or other restrictions.

"Islam is the only major religious system that has built-in protections for minorities," says Hooper at the Council on American-Islamic Relations. "You don't see the kind of persecutions of minorities that we often saw in Europe for hundreds of years. Many members of the Jewish community fled to find safety within the Muslim world."

Even so, Islam's view of religion and politics as inseparable creates difficult issues. Outside the Arab world, most Muslims live in practicing democracies with fair to good human-rights records. But some Muslim countries—Arab and non-Arab—have either adopted or been urged to adopt provisions of Islamic law—*sharia*—that are antithetical to modern ideas of human rights, such as limiting women's rights and prescribing stoning or amputations as criminal penalties.

Muslims participating in a society as a minority population face different issues, according to author Grieve. "Islam is difficult to accommodate in a determinedly secular Western society where almost all views are equally respected, and none is seen as either right or wrong," he writes.

The tensions played out in a number of controversies in recent years were provoked by unflattering depictions of Islam in Europe. A Danish cartoonist's satirical view of Muhammad provoked worldwide protests from Muslim leaders and groups after they were publicized in early 2006. Scattered violence resulted in property damage and more than 30 deaths.

Somewhat similarly, Pope Benedict XVI drew sharp criticism after a Sept. 12, 2006, lecture quoting a medieval Christian emperor's description of Islam as "evil and inhuman." Along with verbal denunciations, protesters in Basra, Iraq, burned an effigy of the pope. Within a week, he disclaimed the remarks and apologized.

Freedom House's Marshall says such controversies, as well as the cancellation of the opera in Berlin, strengthens radical Muslim elements. "Bending to more radical demands marginalizes the voices of moderate Muslims and hands over leadership to the radicals," he says.

Many Muslims in European countries, however, view the controversies—including the current debate over the veil in England—as evidence of pervasive hostility from the non-Muslim majorities. "There is a growing hatred of Muslims in Britain, and anybody who bashes Muslims can only get brownie points," says Bukhari of the Muslim Public Affairs Committee.

"These are not friendly times for Western Muslims," says Safi, at the University of North Carolina. "Whenever people find themselves under assault, opening their arms and opening their hearts is difficult."

Does Islam Need a "Reformation"?

If Pakistan's Punjab University expected a chorus of approval when it decided to launch a master's program in musicology in fall 2006, it was in for a surprise. At the Lahore campus, the conservative Islamic Assembly of Students, known as I.J.T., rose up in protest.

Handbills accused school authorities of forsaking Islamic ideological teachings in favor of "the so-called enlightened moderation" dictated by "foreign masters." Undeterred, administrators opened the program for enrollment in September. When fewer students applied than expected, they blamed the poor response in part on the I.J.T. campaign.

The episode reflects how Islam today is evolving differently in the West and in some parts of the Muslim world. Many Muslim writers and scholars in the United States and Europe are calling for Islam to adapt to modern times by, for example, embracing pluralism and gender equality. Introducing a collection of essays by "progressive" Muslims, the University of North Carolina's Safi says the movement seeks to "start swimming through the rising waters of Islam and modernity, to strive for justice in the midst of society."

In much of the Muslim world, however, Islam is growing—in numbers and intensity—on the strength of literal interpretations of the Koran and exclusivist attitudes toward the non-Muslim world. "In the Muslim world in general, more extreme or reactionary forms of Islam are getting stronger—in Africa, Asia and the Middle East," says Freedom House's Marshall, who has previously worked on issues pertaining to persecution of Christians around the world.

Islamist groups such as I.J.T. talk about "reforming" or "purifying" Islam and adopting Islamic law as the primary or exclusive source of civil law. In fact, one version of reformed Islam—Wahhabism[1] or the currently preferred term Salafism—espouses a literalistic reading of the Koran and a puritanical stance toward such modern practices as listening to music or watching television. It has been instituted in Saudi Arabia and has advanced worldwide because of financial backing from the oil-rich kingdom and its appeal to new generations of Muslims.

"The Salafi movement is a fringe," says the Rand Corp.'s Rabasa. "But it's growing because it's dynamic and revolutionary, whereas traditional Islam tends to be conservative. It has this appeal to young people looking for identity."

But the Center for Islamic Pluralism's Schwartz, an outspoken critic of Salafism, says many Muslims are rejecting it because of its tendency to view other branches of Islam as apostasy. "People are getting sick of this," he says. "They're tired of the social conflict and upheaval."

Voll at the Center for Christian-Muslim Understanding also says some Muslim legal scholars are disputing literalistic readings of *sharia* by contending that the Islamic law cited as divinely ordained is actually "a human construct subject to revision."

Some Western commentators refer to a "reformation" in calling for a more liberal form of Islam. Nicholas D. Kristof, a *New York Times* columnist who focuses on global human-rights issues, sees "hopeful rumblings . . . of steps toward a Muslim Reformation," especially on issues of gender equality. He notes that feminist Muslim scholars are reinterpreting passages in the Koran that other Muslims cite in justifying restrictions on women, such as the Saudi ban on women driving.

Safi says he avoids the term reformation because it has been adopted by Salafists and also because it suggests a need to break from traditional Islam. He says "progressive" Muslims return to the Prophet's vision of the common humanity of all human beings and seek "to hold Muslim societies accountable for justice and pluralism."

Rabasa also says reformation is historically inappropriate as a goal for liberal or progressive Muslims. "What is needed is not an Islamic reformation but an Islamic enlightenment," says Rabasa. The West's liberal tradition, he notes, was produced not by the Reformation but by the Enlightenment—the 18th-century movement that used reason to search for objective truth.

Whatever terms are used, the clash between different visions of Islam will be less susceptible to resolution than analogous disputes within most branches of Christianity because Islam lacks any recognized hierarchical structure. Islam has no pope or governing council. Instead, each believer is regarded as having a direct relationship with God, or Allah, with no ecclesiastical intermediary.

"In the face of contemporary Islam, there is absolutely the sense of an authority vacuum," says Safi. Islam's future, he adds, "is a question that can only be answered by Muslims."

Note

1. Wahhabism originated in the Arabian peninsula in the late 1700s from the teachings of Arabian theologian Muhammand ibn Abd al Wahhab (1703–1792).

Critical Thinking

1. What are the main points of contention regarding the strained relationship between the Christian West and Muslim world?
2. Does Islam encourage violence? Explain.
3. Is Islam compatible with secular, pluralistic societies? Explain.
4. Does Islam need a "Reformation"? Explain.

Internet References

Journal of Anthropology of Religion
www.mehtapress.com/social-science-a-humanities/journal-of-anthropology-of-religion.html

Journal of Islamic Studies
http://jis.oxfordjournals.org

Article

Prepared by: Elvio Angeloni

We Were Different

Why nativism persists among U.S. Catholics?

JULIA G. YOUNG

Learning Outcomes

After reading this article, you will be able to:

- Discuss the discrimination that has existed within the Catholic Church since 1910.
- Explain the impact of suburbanization on immigrant sentiments.

On A few years ago, I taught an undergraduate course on migration at the Catholic University of America. During one lecture, I compared nineteenth-century Italian migration and contemporary Mexican migration to the United States. A hand shot up, and a student—one of several with an Italian surname—objected. "They're not the same," he protested. "My great-grandmother came here legally and learned English—Mexicans don't do that."

As a historian who studies Mexican immigration to the United States, I'm used to hearing statements like this. Concerns about new immigrants' legal status and failure to assimilate are widespread, and nativism has reemerged in recent decades. Still, I wondered why this proud young Italian-American Catholic was so unwilling to compare his ancestors to the Mexican Catholic immigrants of today. Why did he not feel a sense of sympathy and solidarity for contemporary immigrants who share so much with the great waves of Irish, Italians, Poles, and other immigrants of the late nineteenth century?

At the time, I didn't quite grasp how many U.S. Catholics feel the widespread American discontent over immigration. After all, the Catholic hierarchy is vocally proimmigrant, and the U.S. Catholic population is entirely composed of immigrants and descendants of immigrants. Catholics have a proud tradition of social justice, and numerous Catholic organizations have done immensely valuable work to protect immigrants. Nevertheless, in our new Trumpian era of border walls and travel bans, it has become more apparent to me (and others, such as Paul Moses in a recent piece for *Commonweal*, "White Catholics & Nativism," September 1, 2017) that White Catholics have a nativism problem of their own.

Given the history of Catholic immigration to the United States, perhaps I shouldn't have been surprised. Catholic nativism toward other Catholic immigrants is a recurring sentiment that dates to at least the second half of the nineteenth century, when the influx of Catholics changed the religious landscape of the United States. From then until today, Irish, Italian, Polish, Mexican, and other Catholics have fought over power, identity, religious practice, and shared spaces.

This tense history is something that Catholics don't always acknowledge. Instead, it's far more common to hear Catholics describe their ancestors as victims of nativism—especially when those ancestors were Irish and Italian Catholics in the late nineteenth and early twentieth centuries. (Certainly, that's the narrative I heard growing up—and I have found that most of my Catholic students are well aware of the "Know Nothing" movement and other instances of historical antipathy toward Irish and Italian Catholics.) And while nativism was certainly directed at Catholics by non-Catholics, that's not the whole story.

Catholics were only a tiny minority in the United States until after the 1840s, when Irish immigrants began to arrive in the wake of the famine. Relatively quickly, Irish Catholics began to compete with German Americans (who had arrived somewhat earlier) in the clergy and hierarchy, and soon the Irish dominated Catholic leadership on the East Coast (less so in the Midwest, where Germans still maintained majorities). In 1880s Boston, nearly 80 percent of priests were Irish or Irish American; in New York, 70 percent. These clergymen ascended to the hierarchy, and by the turn of the century, it has been said, the U.S. Catholic Church was "one, holy, apostolic, and Irish Church."

Nevertheless, this Irish-led church soon began to face challenges from new immigrants arriving from Italy, Poland, and other Southern and Eastern European countries. Each ethnic group brought their own tradition, language, and clergy. Conflict between (and within) Catholic ethnic groups was quite common. It is no wonder that most new Catholic immigrants preferred to worship with their compatriots—and Catholic bishops responded by creating separate "national" parishes for each group.

Yet the national parish model may have also hindered interethnic solidarity. In and around New York, Chicago, Boston, and other Catholic cities and neighborhoods, the Irish and Italians in particular shared a mutual antipathy and often outright hostility (see Paul Moses's *An Unlikely Union: The Love-Hate Story of New York's Irish and Italians*). The Irish were nonplussed by Italian anticlericalism, as well as by their unfamiliar religious practices (such as local street festivals), which they perceived as mere superstition. The Italians, in turn, were less than impressed by the seemingly cold and austere faith of the Irish and even more rankled by their dominance of the hierarchy. Street fights between Italians and Irish were quite common: at one Irish parish (St. Francis in Flatbush, Brooklyn), Italian adults were excluded from church services and Italian children were harassed at the parochial grade school.

The Poles and the Irish did not get along much better. According to Anthony M. Stevens-Arroyo, Cardinal John McCloskey (the second archbishop of New York) famously told Polish Catholics who requested a church that they didn't need a parish, but rather a pig shanty. At the turn of the twentieth century, some Polish Catholics were so aggrieved by such treatment—and by their lack of representation within the U.S. Catholic hierarchy—that they defected, founding the Polish National Catholic Church in Scranton, PA, in 1897. Subsequently, Lithuanians founded a Lithuanian National Church (they later joined the PNCC), and the PNCC attracted other immigrants, such as Slovaks, as well. (This story is told in detail in a fascinating 2003 master's thesis by Margaret Rencewicz, titled "The Polish National Catholic Church: The Founding of an American Schism.")

Of course, religion was not the only issue dividing these ethnic groups. The widely held belief in eugenics, which cast Italians and Eastern Europeans as inferior races, certainly didn't help matters. Nor did the fact that the new immigrants of the late nineteenth century competed with more established Irish Americans for jobs (and were often willing to work for lower pay). Yet the divisions on the streets and in neighborhoods were reinforced by the "separate but equal" model of the national churches.

Eventually—and in part to cope with dissension between ethnic groups—Catholic bishops abolished the national parish, in an effort to promote "Americanization." This meant that immigrants arriving after the 1920s would no longer be granted their own parish churches but rather that churches would be allocated by population and neighborhood.

In practice, however, new immigrants still found themselves excluded or marginalized from the parishes of groups that arrived earlier. This was certainly true for Mexicans who began migrating to the United States in increasing numbers during the 1910s and 1920s. A 1929 report by the National Catholic Welfare Conference on Mexican immigration noted that discrimination against Mexicans was rampant within White Catholic communities in the Southwest, describing churches with signs stating that Mexicans were prohibited, or limiting Mexicans to the last pew in the church. "There are many towns," the report continued, "where [the Mexican] is not served an ice cream cone over the counter and where he is not admitted to moving picture houses which others attend. Many congregations do not welcome him and in places where there is no Spanish-speaking priest the Mexican stays away."

After 1930, immigration decreased sharply, as the Great Depression and new restrictive laws put a temporary brake on arrivals. But internal migration had been ongoing since World War I, when thousands of African Americans began leaving the South for Northern cities in what became known as the Great Migration. Some were Catholics, especially those coming from Louisiana and the Gulf region. As they arrived and settled in the urban North, they faced rejection, discrimination, and hatred from Whites—including many White Catholics who resisted their integration into White parishes.

Many of these Catholics were the children of Irish and Polish immigrants who had only recently begun to feel like Americans. Some scholars, such as Noel Ignatiev and Matthew Frye Jacobson, have speculated that their disdain for Black Americans prompted these former rivals to overcome their ethnic differences and mutual hostilities and "become White." Certainly, the racial tensions wrought by White resistance to Black migration after World War II spurred White Catholics to move to the suburbs; this suburbanization intensified after school desegregation and would continue well into the 1970s. As a consequence, the old urban national parishes, once thriving centers of Catholic life, emptied out. As White Catholics fled the cities, the rate of intermarriage increased, and the old ethnic tensions faded. (Paul Moses tells this story in his book; so does the 2015 movie *Brooklyn*.)

European immigration slowed significantly between 1940 and 1970. Nevertheless, new waves of Latino Catholic immigrants arrived during that period, and, like other groups before them, they found that the native-born Catholic population was not always welcoming. Without the possibility of the national parish, these new populations found themselves shoehorned into existing parishes. In New York and Philadelphia, arriving Puerto Ricans often felt that they were treated as second-class citizens within their new churches; and Catholic Cubans coming to South Florida after 1960 also clashed with the Irish Catholic population there. Mexican *braceros* likewise struggled for recognition and representation in churches across Texas and the rest of the Southwest during the 1940s, 1950s, and 1960s.

Nevertheless, with the strong support of prominent prelates (including Archbishop Robert E. Lucey in San Antonio, Archbishop Coleman Carroll in Miami, and Cardinal Francis Spellman in New York), these groups eventually received resources and attention from the hierarchy, if not representation within it. Carroll, for example, was supportive of Cuban migrants, welcomed them to South Florida, and tried to portray them positively to the non-Cuban Catholic community. Eventually Cubans, at least, were able to achieve success, prominence, and a Cuban Catholic shrine—Our Lady of Charity—of their own.

Today, we are living through another great wave of immigration. After 1965, when laws were reformed, the immigrant population began to grow and has not stopped since. Currently, the foreign-born population in the United States is around 14 percent—a proportion not seen since the 1920s. Many of these new immigrants—from Latin America, Asia (especially Vietnam and the Philippines), and Africa—are Catholic. According to a 2017 survey by the Center for Migration Studies, the foreign born make up about 15.1 million of the 67.7 million Catholics in America. Nevertheless, tensions between native-born Catholics and immigrants—especially Latinos—persist. One respondent to the CMS survey characterized the work of educating the native-born community as "the most challenging part of our job and mission" and reported that "sadly enough some of our priests are not comfortable supporting our immigrant population."

According to the Center for Applied Research in the Apostolate, about 14.1 million of these Catholic immigrants are from Latin America (another 16.4 million Latino Catholics are native-born). As the largest single immigrant group, Latinos are a particularly common target for discrimination within Catholic parishes, reports University of Notre Dame sociologist Timothy Matovina. These tensions often surface as different groups try to share parish spaces, and it is not uncommon for "established" parishioners to resist Latino efforts to schedule Spanish masses or to express the opinion that "our ancestors built this church" or "we were here first." Many Catholics of European origin—forgetting, perhaps, their own ancestors' experiences—"presume that newcomers who do not adopt U.S. customs and speak English in public are ungrateful or even not qualified to remain in the United States." According to Matovina, one parishioner in Tulsa became so angry about hearing services in Spanish that he "offered to 'drive a bus' to evict undocumented immigrants from the country."

This last comment encapsulates the views of many native-born Catholics: that this new generation of Catholic immigrants, particularly Latinos, are fundamentally different from previous generations of Catholic immigrants because they are undocumented. And it is true that the number of undocumented immigrants—the majority of whom come from Latin America, particularly Mexico—has risen dramatically since the 1970s. Undoubtedly, undocumented immigration presents significant challenges for governments, law enforcement officials, and immigrants themselves, which is why the U.S. Conference of Catholic Bishops has continuously promoted just and humane immigration reform through their Migration Policy Office.

Yet undocumented immigration is not actually a new problem. The great wave of 1840–1920 immigration, which brought so many Catholics to the United States, was largely "undocumented" as well; immigrants were not required to have visas until 1924, and the majority, according to the American Immigration Council, arrived without any paperwork at all. Although there were laws barring certain categories of immigrants from entering the country, many of these excluded groups found that it was quite easy to enter without inspection, and frequently did so. (Until the turn of the last century, there were almost no officials at the U.S.–Mexico border, and it was easy to walk across that frontier.) After a series of restrictive new immigration laws was enacted in the 1920s, many of these undocumented immigrants were granted legal status through amnesty. Thus, the differences between the old and new immigrants may be less stark than they appear.

Over the coming years, it will be imperative to resolve these tensions among the laity. After all, immigration is the future of the church: Hispanics and Latinos constitute about 50 percent of all Catholics under the age of 29. Yet, as Timothy Matovina has pointed out, Latino Catholics, like the Italians and Poles a century ago, face a lack of representation in the United States. Catholic clergy and hierarchy. Furthermore, recent studies by the Pew Research Center indicate that despite the fact that the church is becoming more Latino, Latinos are leaving the church in alarming numbers.

Yet there are also bright spots. According to the CARA survey mentioned above, the most active Catholics (in terms of church attendance and participation) are also the most enthusiastic about the ethnic mix that has resulted from the latest wave of immigration. And while the process of welcoming new Catholic immigrants to established parishes can be painful (the 2009 documentary *Scenes From a Parish* captures some of that pain), Catholics across the country are not fighting over neighborhoods and territory in the same way they did at the turn of the last century.

In the course of researching this article, I asked Fr. Tom Gaunt, the head of CARA, to compare the two eras. He was relatively sanguine. "There are a lot of headaches and challenges, but no huge conflicts," he said. "There's no breakaway or schism" like that of the Polish National Catholic Church. Instead, Catholics are responding to the challenge and bridging ethnic divides. Many parishes in urban areas with large immigrant populations—such as St. Camillus Church in Silver Spring, Maryland, where Haitians, Latinos, White Catholics, and others worship together—celebrate multiculturalism and navigate the new church landscape with aplomb.

Indeed, it is possible that, over time, the new immigrants of today will follow the same patterns as the Irish, Poles, and Italians: intermarrying with other Catholics, assimilating and adapting to life in the United States, while continuing to incorporate their own religious practices into the rich fabric of American Catholic life.

It remains troubling, however, that Latinos and other recent Catholic immigrants continue to face discrimination and rejection from some Catholics, including those who—like that student in my class—are the descendants of earlier Catholic immigrants. There is still much work to be done, and Catholic immigration advocates from the hierarchy on down will have to grapple with the long and cyclical legacy of nativism within the American Catholic laity.

Critical Thinking

1. How could tensions between immigrant groups be reduced? Make three suggestions.
2. Are the immigrants of today similar to immigrants of the past? How do they differ?

Internet References

Catholic Social Teaching on Immigration and the Movement of Peoples

http://www.usccb.org/issues-and-action/human-life-and-dignity/immigration/catholic-teaching-on-immigration-and-the-movement-of-peoples.cfmn

The Facts on Immigration Today: 2017 Edition

https://www.americanprogress.org/issues/immigration/reports/2017/04/20/430736/facts-immigration-today-2017-edition/

We're All 'Nations of Immigrants' Now but Our Immigration Problems Are Different

https://www.fairobserver.com/region/north_america/were-all-nations-immigrants-now-our-immigration-problems-are-different/

Will Immigrants Today Assimilate Like Those of 100 Years Ago?

https://www.theatlantic.com/business/archive/2016/08/will-immigrants-today-assimilate-like-those-of-100-years-ago/495746/

Julia G. Young is an associate professor of history at the Catholic University of America, and the author of Mexican Exodus: Emigrants, Exiles, and Refugees of the Cristero War (Oxford).

Article

Prepared by: Elvio Angeloni

Reputation Is Everything: Unearthing Honour Culture in America

High murder and suicide rates among whites in the US south may have the same root cause as honour killings in Pakistan and India, says a Southern researcher.

EMMA YOUNG

Learning Outcomes

After reading this article, you will be able to:

- Contrast "dignity cultures" and "honor cultures" with respect their differing value systems.
- Discuss the differences between dignity cultures and honor cultures with respect to gender expectations, felony homicides, gun laws, rape rates, and mental health problems.
- Discuss the historical and socioeconomic circumstances that help to explain the existence of honor cultures.

MUBEEN RAJHU pleaded with his sister, Tasleem, to end her relationship with a Christian man because it brought shame on the family. Then he put a bullet in her head. "I had to do it," Rajhu told a reporter earlier this year. "There was no choice." Many of his neighbours in Lahore, Pakistan, agreed: Rajhu deserved praise for doing the right thing, they insisted.

Most of us cannot fathom the kind of thinking that condones "honour" killings, when fathers and brothers murder loved ones, typically women, in the name of reputation. We tend to associate this strict code of honour with countries like Pakistan, Afghanistan and Somalia, and with extreme religious beliefs. But Ryan Brown thinks it is more familiar than you might think.

Brown, a social psychologist at the University of Oklahoma in Norman, studies "honour cultures"—ones characterized by a deep concern for reputation and a sense of being duty-bound to retaliate against anything perceived as a slight. His research in the US south shows that it is alive and well among millions of people there, and potentially in other Western countries too. He also argues that honour culture is an important cause of all kinds of problems, from elevated murder rates to a reluctance to address mental health issues. Can he be right?

Insult to Injury

Anthropologists and social scientists distinguish between what are sometimes called dignity cultures and honour cultures. Dignity cultures value people simply by dint of being human. Here, people seldom turn violent at the first hint of a challenge to their reputation, instead ignoring it or perhaps seeking redress in the courts.

In honour cultures, on the other hand, your value rests on your reputation, the impulse to defend it is heightened and individuals are expected to avenge insults themselves. There are plenty of historical precedents: think of the dueling tradition in the Old West or in Europe, from the chivalrous knights of medieval times right up until the 18th century.

Honour cultures are also characterized by contrasting gender expectations. For women, the key requirements are to be faithful and protect one's virtue. Men should be strong, self-reliant and intolerant of disrespect. They must earn this reputation, and then defend it—even if that requires violence.

One of the clearest signs of an honour culture, then, is that people are likely to react violently to insults. A landmark social psychology study carried out two decades ago revealed this as an intriguing point of difference between the north of the United States and the south—defined by the US Census Bureau as the 16 states from Texas to Delaware, including the eastern seaboard, below the Mason-Dixon line. When Richard Nisbett at the University of Michigan and Dov Cohen at the University of Illinois at Urbana-Champaign assessed how male college students responded to annoyances and insults, such as being bumped into and called an "asshole," they found that those born in the south reacted more aggressively than northerners.

Nisbett also found that "felony" homicides—killings committed during another crime—are equally common in the north and south, whereas "argument-based" homicides—killings that follow a disagreement or insult—are significantly more common in the south. In both cases, this clear geographical difference held only for white people.

Brown, who was himself born and raised in Alabama, had suspected that these attitudes might be rooted in religious fervour. The south is known as the "Bible Belt," after all, and countries with much stricter honour cultures, such as Pakistan, are highly religious. However, repeated studies both in the United States and elsewhere have found no link between a person's religiosity and how much they endorse honour-culture attitudes.

Instead, honour cultures seem to develop wherever there is severe economic insecurity and a degree of lawlessness. "When these factors come together, we believe honour culture is a sort of natural byproduct, because reputation is a way you protect yourself when no one else is coming to your aid," says Brown.

So why is honour culture more prevalent in the US south, and particularly among whites? In his new book, Honor Bound, Brown argues that the underlying ideology arrived in the early to mid-16th century, brought by Scots migrating via Northern Ireland. Many of these Ulster Scots were herders, and having first settled the Appalachians, they then moved south and west, where the ecology is more suitable for herding than farming. Here, the argument goes, the chronic threat of livestock theft meant that a culture of honour-based violence conferred an economic advantage. Over the centuries, the attitudes these migrants brought have been diluted, but still they persist—and for Brown, at least, they have a big impact on people's behaviour.

Brown has led several studies of how honour ideology manifests itself, in each case attempting to strip out the effects of poverty and other factors that could skew the results. In one, he and his team looked at US school shootings and found roughly twice as many per capita in "honour states"—defined by researchers as those ranking in the top half for endorsement of honour-based values (see "League of honour," page 35)—than non-honour states. Honour states generally have laxer gun control laws, but the researchers adjusted for this. Besides, says Brown, those laws reflect honour ideology, which considers that individuals have a right—even a duty—to defend themselves and their reputation.

Given the gender divide in honour cultures, you might expect higher levels of violence against women in them than in other societies. Sure enough, rapes are significantly more common in honour states—but, again, only for white perpetrators. Likewise, the rates of domestic homicide among whites are 62 per cent higher in honour states than elsewhere, Brown and his colleagues have found in research they hope to publish soon. There's no study yet linking a man's level of endorsement of honour-related values to his likelihood of committing rape or murdering his wife. But men who score higher on ratings of honour ideology than other men are more prone to sexually objectify women and display stronger beliefs that men should have power over women.

Show No Weakness

There has also been precious little work on the persistence of honour culture in modern Western societies outside the US south. We know it is found in gang cultures everywhere, for example, and it may exist beyond gangs in parts of Europe. But it has yet to be studied extensively in such places.

In the United States, honour ideology is strong in the growing Latino population too, and their particular take on it may prove to be influential over the next 50 years, Brown predicts. But, for now, he argues that his work reveals what many might see as a surprising influence on life today in white communities across the south.

Brown has recently investigated the connection between honour culture and mental health. A 2014 study showed that people who strongly endorse honour-related values are especially concerned that seeking help for mental health problems would indicate weakness and harm their reputations. This makes a skewed sort of sense. In an honour culture, "if you need help, that suggests you are mentally fragile and weak," says Brown. "But going to get help would be a second blow: 'Not only do I have a need, but I can't handle that need on my own.'" Such results chime with another of Brown's findings: that honour states not only have higher levels of depression and lower use of antidepressants than other states, but also have higher suicide rates, even after controlling for other relevant factors.

So far, so bleak. But the influence of honour culture isn't entirely negative. The premium placed on loyalty might explain why soldiers from southern states fighting in the second world war were more likely than those from the north to win the Congressional Medal of Honour, typically given to those who died trying to save their comrades. "That's not just saying: 'We care about loyalty'," says Brown. "It's demonstrating it in the ultimate way."

For Cohen and Nisbett, honour culture also helps to account for the famous politeness of southerners. After all, it pays to be well mannered in a society where an insult could cost you a beating. But that only holds up to a point. In one study, Cohen and colleagues brought northerners and southerners together for a simulated art therapy session, during which they were constantly pestered by someone they thought was another volunteer but was actually a researcher. "The northerners consistently showed their annoyance and then plateaued in their anger," says Cohen. "Southerners, on the other hand, were polite, polite, polite – and then you got a big explosion."

He thinks this style of interaction contributes to violence in honour cultures because it prevents people from openly telling others that they are crossing the line. Children grow up learning to behave like this, which might explain the persistence of higher rates of adult violence centuries after the arrival of the Ulster Scots, according to Cohen. Another explanation for the persistence of honour cultures could be the way that honour ideals are built into gender definitions. "What it means to be masculine or feminine has real staying power and persists long after the conditions that might have produced those ideals and values have dissipated," says Brown.

Today, the United States is far from lawless, but economic uncertainty lingers for many. Brown thinks this could help explain support for Donald Trump, whose presidential campaign rhetoric played heavily on the idea that the nation's reputation has crashed. Brown's research indicates that honour-oriented people tend to be more sensitive than others to the idea that they might be "taken advantage of" by immigrants.

What's more, in unpublished work, he and colleagues looked for evidence of honour ideology in the language used by candidates in recent presidential elections, and found it to be prevalent in the rhetoric of several Republican hopefuls. "Some sell it better than others, and I think Trump sold it pretty well," says Brown. "He talks a lot about respect." Take his comment, made in June 2015 when he announced his candidacy, about Mexicans "laughing at us," says Brown. "To somebody who is steeped in the ideology of honour, very few things are more repugnant than being laughed at, whether that's personally or as a family, community or nation."

Of course, no one thinks honour culture is the only factor that can explain differences between the US north and south, least of all Brown. But if it has a big influence on behaviour, should we be looking to shape it to alleviate some of the problems it has been linked to? Collin Barnes, a psychologist at Hillsdale College in Michigan, thinks not. "The alteration of a culture on social scientific grounds is not an activity I'd wish to associate with," he says.

Although he has worked with Brown in the past, Barnes now has reservations about this research. It is difficult to support claims of cultural causation, he says, because even when researchers control for confounding factors, attributing behavioural differences to one construct requires a heavy burden of evidence. In this case, Barnes is not convinced that burden has been met. Take Cohen and Nisbett's landmark study. "It is not too much to ask that the result of this experiment and others like it be replicated," says Barnes. "To my knowledge, no such attempt has been made, and this makes me hesitant."

Barnes also thinks that the methods of social psychology tend to oversimplify reality. In that sense, his reservations don't apply exclusively to research into honour culture.

For his part, Brown is well aware of the pitfalls of attempting to reduce the workings of human societies, in all their glorious messiness, to simple answers. Even so, he and Barnes agree that allying such research with lessons from history and experience can improve our understanding of how culture influences thinking and behaviour.

And although he does try to teach his sons to avoid taking offence too readily, Brown seeks only to understand this aspect of southern culture, not to change it. "These are my people. It's part of my cultural heritage," he says. "I'm an insider saying: 'Let's be honest about our culture. Let's turn over the rock and see what's on the underside.'"

This Means War!

We all care about what other people think of us, but some societies take reputation more seriously than others. If "honour culture" exerts a particular sway over the southern states of the United States, as some researchers suggest (see main story), there may be global repercussions whenever this ideology spills over into US foreign policy.

Dov Cohen, a psychologist at the University of Illinois at Urbana-Champaign, has found that members of Congress from the south argue for greater military spending, and were more likely to have supported the first Gulf war after Iraq invaded Kuwait in 1990. Likewise, a study of 36 US presidents between 1816 and 2001 suggests a relationship between the endorsement of honour-based ideology and war: Allan Dafoe at Yale University and Devin Caughey at the Massachusetts Institute of Technology found that southern presidents were twice as likely to use military force in international disputes as their peers from elsewhere.

When force was used, they found, it tended to be exerted for twice as long with a southern president in charge. And the United States was three times more likely to win a conflict under a southern leader.

Ryan Brown at the University of Oklahoma, who studies honour culture in the US south, argues that this is not down to some general level of aggression in the south. Instead, he says, it happens partly because an honour-oriented leader believes that if you make a threat, you have to follow through. Not doing so will damage your reputation even more than failing to make a threat in the first place.

"If you don't threaten an honour-oriented person—don't threaten their sense of honour, don't insult them—they are, in fact, more likely to be polite," says Brown.

League of Honour

Where in the United States do people care most deeply about their reputation? Social psychologists have compiled a league table based on surveys designed to tell them which states most strongly endorse the values of "honour culture."

Top 5
South Carolina
North Carolina
Alabama
Georgia
Arkansas

Bottom 5
Hawaii
Rhode Island
Wisconsin
Minnesota
North Dakota

Critical Thinking

1. How and why do "dignity cultures" and "honor cultures" differ from each other?
2. How is "honor ideology" distributed within the United States and how is it to be explained?

Internet References

International Association for the Psychology of Religion—Links
psychology-of-religion.com/links/

Society for the Psychology of Religion and Spirituality
www.apadivisions.org/division-36

Article

Prepared by: Elvio Angeloni

Losing Our Religion

Graham Lawton

Learning Outcomes

After reading this article, you will be able to:

- Discuss the worldwide trend towards secularization in the modern world and the reasons for it.
- Describe the human mind's receptivity to religious ideas and what it means for a secular society.
- Describe the various kinds of atheism and the reasons for them.

On an unseasonably warm Sunday morning in London, I do something I haven't done for more than 30 years: get up and go to church. For an hour and a half, I sing, listen to readings, enjoy moments of quiet contemplation and throw a few coins into a collection. At the end there is tea and cake, and a warm feeling in what I guess must be my soul.

This is like hundreds of congregations taking place across the city this morning, but with one notable exception: there is no god.

Welcome to the Sunday Assembly, a "godless congregation" held every other week in Conway Hall, home of the world's oldest free-thought organisation. On the day I went there were at least 200 people in the hall; sometimes as many as 600 turn up.

Founded by comedians Sanderson Jones and Pippa Evans in 2013, the Sunday Assembly aims to supply some of the uplifting features of a religious service without any of the supernatural stuff. Atheism is also off the agenda: the Assembly is simply about celebrating being alive. "Our mission is to help people live this one life as fully as possible," says Jones.

The Assembly's wider goal is "a godless congregation in every town, city and village that wants one". And many do: from a humble start in a deconsecrated church in London, there are now 28 active assemblies in the UK, Ireland, US and Australia. Jones now works full-time to fulfil the demand for more; he expects to have 100 by the end of this year.

The people I joined on that sunny Sunday are a small part of the world's fastest-growing religious identity—the "nones". Comprising non-believers of all stripes, from convinced atheists like me to people who simply don't care about religion, they now number more than some major world religions.

In London, admittedly, they are nothing special. The UK is one of the least religious countries in the world, with around half of the population saying they don't belong to any religion.

But elsewhere, their rise is both rapid and remarkable. A decade ago, more than three-quarters of the world's population identified themselves as religious. Today, less than 60 percent do, and in about a quarter of countries the nones are now a majority. Some of the biggest declines have been seen in countries where religion once seemed part of the furniture, such as Ireland. In 2005, 69 percent of people there said they were religious; now only 47 percent do.

"We have a powerful secularisation trend worldwide," says Ara Norenzayan, a psychologist at the University of British Columbia in Vancouver, Canada. "There are places where secularisation is making huge inroads: western and northern Europe, Canada, Australia, New Zealand, Japan and China."

Even in the US—a deeply Christian country—the number of people expressing "no religious affiliation" has risen from 5 percent in 1972 to 20 percent today; among people under 30, that number is closer to a third.

That's not to say that they have all explicitly rejected religion; only 13 percent of people around the world say they are "committed" atheists. Even so, it means there are almost a billion atheists globally. Only Christianity and Islam can claim more adherents. And alongside them are another billion and a half who, for whatever reason, don't see themselves as religious.

A century ago, these trends would have seemed inevitable. The founders of sociology, Émile Durkheim and Max Weber, expected scientific thinking to lead to the gradual erosion and eventual demise of religion. They saw the rise of humanist, rationalist and free thought organisations in western Europe as the start of a secular revolution.

Born to Believe

It didn't quite work out that way. Although parts of western Europe, Australia, Canada and New Zealand did secularise after the second world war, the rest of the world remained resolutely god-fearing. Even the official atheism of the communist bloc didn't really take hold at grass-roots level.

If anything, at the end of the twentieth century, religion seemed to be resurgent. Fundamentalist movements were gaining ground around the world; Islam was becoming a powerful political force; the US remained stubbornly religious. Increasingly, secular Europe looked like an outlier.

Now, though, secularisation is back in business. "The past 20 years has seen a precipitous decline in religiosity in all societies," says Phil Zuckerman, a sociologist at Pitzer College in Claremont, California. "We are seeing religion withering across the board. Yes, there are pockets of increased fundamentalism, but overall we are seeing rising rates of secularism in societies where we have never seen it before—places like Brazil, Ireland, even in Africa."

So is the nineteenth century prediction of a godless world finally coming true? Is it possible that one day the majority of people will see themselves as non-religious? And if that happens, will the world be a better place?

To answer these questions, we need to know why people believe in god in the first place.

For many, the answer is obvious: because god exists. Whether or not that is the case, it illustrates something very interesting about the nature of religious belief. To most people, probably the vast majority who have ever lived, belief in god is effortless. Like being able to breathe or learning one's native language, faith in god is one of those things that comes naturally.

Why is that? In recent years, cognitive scientists have produced a comprehensive account of the human mind's receptivity to religious ideas. Called cognitive by-product theory, it holds that certain features of human psychology that evolved for non-religious reasons also create fertile ground for god. As a result, when people encounter religious stories and claims, they find them intuitively appealing and plausible.

For example, our early ancestors were regularly on the dinner menu of predators, and so evolved a "hypersensitive agency detection device"—a fancy name for an assumption that events in the environment are caused by sentient beings, or agents. That makes evolutionary sense: when any rustle in the bushes might be a prowling predator it is better to err on the side of caution. But it also primes us to assume agency where there is none. That, of course, is a central claim of most religions: that an unseen agent is responsible for doing and creating things in the world.

Existential Comfort

Humans have evolved other quirks that encourage the spread of religious beliefs. Notions of a benevolent personal god, higher purpose and an afterlife, for example, help people to manage the existential dread and uncertainty that are part of being human.

We also have a tendency to imitate high status individuals—think of modern celebrity culture—and to conform to social norms, both of which promote the spread and maintenance of belief. We are especially impressed by what social scientists call CREDs or "credibility-enhancing displays"—costly and extravagant acts of faith such as fasting, self-flagellation or martyrdom.

Finally, people who think they are being watched tend to behave themselves and cooperate more. Societies that chanced on the idea of supernatural surveillance were likely to have been more successful than those that didn't, further spreading religious ideas.

Taken together, the way our minds work makes us naturally receptive to religious ideas and extremely likely to acquire them when we encounter them. Once humans stumbled on the idea of god, it spread like wildfire.

Cognitive by-product theory is a very successful account of why humans gravitate towards religious ideas. However, it has also been turned on the opposite problem: if belief in god comes so easily, why are there atheists?

Until quite recently, it was widely assumed that people had to reason their way to atheism: they analysed the claims of religion and rejected them on the grounds of implausibility. This explained why atheism was a minority pursuit largely practised by more educated people, and why religion was so prevalent and durable. Overcoming all of those evolved biases, and continuing to do so, requires hard cognitive work.

This "analytical atheism" is clearly an important route to irreligion and might explain some of the recent increase in secularity. It certainly flourishes in places where people are exposed to science and other analytical systems of thought. But it is by no means the only flavour of irreligion. In the US, for example, among the 20 percent of people who say they have no religious affiliation, only about 1 in 10 say they are atheists; the vast majority, 71 percent, are "nothing in particular".

"There are many pathways and motivations for becoming atheist," says Norenzayan. "Disbelief does not always require hard cognitive effort."

So if people aren't explicitly rejecting religious claims, what is causing them to abandon god? To Norenzayan, the answer lies in some of the other psychological biases that make religious ideas so easy to digest.

One of the main motivations for abandoning god is that people increasingly don't need the comfort that belief in god brings. Religion thrives on existential angst: where people feel insecure and uncertain, religion provides succour. But as societies become more prosperous and stable, this security blanket becomes less important.

By this reckoning it is no coincidence that the world's least religious countries also tend to be the most secure. Denmark, Sweden and Norway, for example, are consistently rated as among the most irreligious. They are also among the most prosperous, stable and safe, with universal healthcare and generous social security.

Conversely, the world's most religious countries are among its poorest. And within countries, poorer segments of society tend to be more religious, according to the Global Index of Religion and Atheism.

The link is supported by laboratory studies showing that making people aware of existential threats such as pain, randomness and death temporarily strengthens their belief in god. It seems to hold in the real world too: after the 2011 Christchurch earthquake in New Zealand—normally a stable and safe country with corresponding low levels of religiosity—religious commitment in the area increased.

Norenzayan refers to the kind of atheism that exists in these places as "apatheism". "This is not so much doubting or being sceptical, but more about not caring," he says. "They simply don't think about religion."

Counter-intuitively, he adds, apatheism could also explain the strength of religion in the US. In comparison to other rich nations, the US has high levels of existential angst. A lack of universal healthcare, widespread job insecurity and a feeble social safety net create fertile conditions for religion to flourish.

Another important source of irreligion is "inCREDulous atheism". That doesn't mean incredulous as in unbelieving, but as in not being exposed to CREDs, those dramatic displays of faith. "These have a powerful effect on how religion is transmitted," says Norenzayan. "Where people are willing to die for their beliefs, for example, those beliefs become more contagious. When people don't see extravagant displays, even if they are surrounded by people who claim to believe, then there is some evidence that this leads to decline of religion."

Norenzayan has yet to work out the relative importance of these different routes to atheism, partly because they are mutually reinforcing. But he says his hunch is that apatheism is the most important. "That is probably surprising to a lot of people who think you get atheism by analytical thinking. But I see striking evidence that as societies become more equal and there are social safety nets, secularisation follows," he says.

To some religious proponents, this is evidence that most of the "nones" aren't really atheists at all—a claim that is backed by a recent survey from UK-based Christian think tank Theos. It found that even as formal religion is waning in the UK, spiritual beliefs are not. Almost 60 percent of adults questioned said they believed in some form of higher power or spiritual being; a mere 13 percent agreed with the line "humans are purely material beings with no spiritual element".

Some scientists—notably Pascal Boyer at Washington University in St Louis—have even claimed that atheism is psychologically impossible because of the way humans think. They point to studies showing, for example, that even people who claim to be committed atheists tacitly hold religious beliefs, such as the existence of an immortal soul.

To Norenzayan, this is all semantics. "Labels don't concern me as much as psychology and behaviour. Do people say they believe in god? Do they go to a church or synagogue or mosque? Do they pray? Do they find meaning in religion? These are the variables that should interest us." By these measures, most of the nones really are irreligious, meaning atheism is much more durable and widespread than would be the case if the only route to atheism was actively rejecting religious ideas.

Nones on the Run

Will the trend continue? On the face of it, it looks unlikely. If godlessness flourishes where there is stability and prosperity, then climate change and environmental degradation could seriously slow the spread of atheism. "If there was a massive natural disaster I would expect a resurgence of religion, even in societies that are secularised," says Norenzayan. The Christchurch earthquake is a case in point.

It is also not clear that European secularisation will be replicated elsewhere. "The path that countries take is historically contingent and there are exceptions," says Stephen Bullivant, a theologian at St Mary's University in the UK and co-editor of *The Oxford Handbook of Atheism.*

Nonetheless, he says, there is widespread agreement that if prosperity, security and democracy continue to advance, secularisation will probably follow. Ireland's shift towards irreligion coincided with its economic boom, says Michael Nugent, chairperson of Atheist Ireland. Interestingly, Ireland is showing no signs of a religious revival despite its recent economic woes, suggesting that once secularisation gets going it is hard to stop.

Ireland's experience also suggests that the most unlikely of places can begin to turn their back on long-held beliefs. "Ireland was always one of Europe's exceptions. If it can happen there it can happen elsewhere—Poland, or even the Philippines," says Bullivant.

And then there's the fact that the US seems to be moving away from god. The "nones" have been the fastest growing religious group there for the past 20 years, especially among young adults. One explanation for this is one of those historical contingencies: the cold war. For decades, Americans defined themselves in opposition to godless communists and atheism was seen as unpatriotic. The generation that grew up after the fall of the Berlin Wall in 1989 are the most irreligious since records began.

Interestingly, after the cold war Russia rebounded in the other direction. In 1991, 61 percent of Russians identified as nones; by 2008, that had dropped to just 18 percent. But even the Russians now seem to have joined the recent secularisation trend: according to the Global Index of Religion and Atheism, only 55 percent of people polled there in 2012 regard themselves as religious.

Bullivant thinks the secularisation trend will continue for another reason: the way religion is passed down the generations. "The strongest predictor of whether a person grows up to be religious is whether their parents are," he says. A child whose parents are actively religious has about a 50 percent chance of following them. A child whose parents are not has only about a 3 percent chance of becoming religious.

"In terms of keeping people, the nonreligious are doing very well indeed," says Bullivant. "It is extremely unusual for somebody brought up in a non-religious household to join a religion, but it is not at all unusual for somebody brought up with a religious affiliation to end up as nonreligious." In the UK, for every 10 people who leave the Catholic church, only one joins—usually from another Christian denomination.

Bullivant also points out that religiosity tends to be fixed by the time people reach their mid-20s. So the 30 percent or so of young people in the US who don't identify with any religion are unlikely to change their minds as they get older, and are likely to pass their irreligion on to their own children. "The very fact that there is such a group, that it is quite big and that there wasn't such a group before is an indicator of secularisation," says Bullivant.

So can the world really give up on god? "I think it is possible," says Norenzayan, "because we are seeing it happen already."

What would a world without god actually look like? One oft-voiced concern is that religion is the moral glue that holds society together, and that if you get rid of it, everything collapses. "That position is constantly articulated in the US—even secular people buy into it," says Zuckerman.

The evidence, however, suggests otherwise. In 2009, Zuckerman ran a global analysis comparing levels of religiosity in various countries with measures of societal health: wealth, equality, women's rights, educational attainment, life expectancy, infant mortality, teenage pregnancy, STI rates, crime rates, suicide rates and murder rates. "On just about every measure of societal health, the more secular a country or a state, the better it does." The same holds for the 50 US states.

That, of course, doesn't necessarily mean that secularism creates a healthy society: perhaps the rise of apatheists is a consequence rather than a cause. "But it allows us to debunk the notion that religion is necessary for a healthy society," says Zuckerman.

He goes further, however, arguing that secularisation can lead to social improvements. "I now believe there are aspects of the secular world view that contribute to healthy societies," he says. "First, if you believe that this is the only world and there is no afterlife, that's going to motivate you to make it as good a place as possible. Number two is the emphasis on science, education and rational problem-solving that seems to come with the secular orientation—for example, are we going to pray to end crime in our city or are we going to look at the root causes?"

It is also hard to discuss mass atheism without invoking the spectre of the Soviet Union, the Khmer Rouge, North Korea and many other regimes that suppressed or banned religion. Is there a risk that a majority secular world will be more like Stalingrad than Stockholm?

To Zuckerman, there is a very good reason to think not. "I distinguish between coercive atheism that is imposed from above by a dictatorial regime, and organic atheism that emerges in free societies. It is in the latter that we see positive societal health outcomes."

Perhaps a more credible worry is what would happen to our physical and mental health. The past 20 years have seen a great deal of research into the benefits of being religious, and most studies claim to find a small association between religiosity, health and happiness. This is usually explained by religious people leading healthier lifestyles and having strong social support networks.

Some researchers have therefore jumped to the conclusion that if religion brings health and happiness, then atheism must come at a corresponding cost. Yet the link between religion and health is nowhere near as well established as is often claimed. A meta-analysis of 226 such studies, for example, found a litany of methodological problems and erroneous conclusions. What's more, the little research that has been done on atheists' physical and psychological health found no difference between them and religious people. And at a societal level, of course, a greater proportion of atheism is associated with better public health.

But if you think an atheist world would be a paradise of rationality and reason, think again. "When people no longer believe in god, it doesn't mean they don't have intuitions that are powerfully connected to the supernatural," says Norenzayan. "Even in societies that are majority atheist, you find a lot of paranormal belief—astrology, karma, extraterrestrial life, things that don't have any scientific evidence but are intuitively obvious to people."

That, however, isn't necessarily a bad thing. "It is important to appreciate that there are powerful psychological reasons why we have religion," says Norenzayan. "We can't just say 'it is a superstition, we need to get rid of it'. We need to find alternative solutions to the deep and perennial problems of life that religion tries to solve. If societies can do that I think atheism is a viable alternative."

Godless congregations like the Sunday Assembly can help, by serving the needs of nones who yearn for a sense of community and a common moral vision. They also articulate secular values and get the message across that godless societies can be healthy ones. If that means accepting a certain level of new-agey irrationality, then so be it.

All of which adds up to a vision of an atheist future rather different from the coldly rational one that Weber and Durkheim—and more recently Richard Dawkins and the other New Atheists—envisaged. A bit happy-clappy, a bit spiritual, driven more by indifference to religion rather than hostility to it—but a good society nonetheless. In fact, a society not unlike modern Britain. And as I walk back to my car on a sunny Sunday morning, I can't help feeling that wouldn't be so bad.

Critical Thinking

1. Why is atheism on the rise in today's world?
2. What kinds of atheism are there and why?
3. What seems to be the relationship between secularism and social and economic health?
4. What do you think is the future of religion and why?

Internet References

Anthropology of Religion-Indiana University
http://www.indiana.edu/~wanthro/religion.htm

Journal of Anthropology of Religion
http://www.publicationhosting.org/mehtapress/Journals/Journal-of-Anthropology-of-Religion/

Society for the Anthropology of Religion
http://www.aaanet.org/sections/sar/

The Journal for the Study of Religion, Nature & Culture
http://www.religionandnature.com/journal/editorial-board.htm

Article

Prepared by: Elvio Angeloni

Body Ritual among the Nacirema

HORACE MINER

Learning Outcomes

After reading this article, you will be able to:

- Discuss the role of rituals and taboos in our modern industrial society.
- Discuss the ways in which this article serves as a cautionary note in interpreting other people's customs.

The anthropologist has become so familiar with the diversity of ways in which different peoples behave in similar situations that he is not apt to be surprised by even the most exotic customs. In fact, if all of the logically possible combinations of behavior have not been found somewhere in the world, he is apt to suspect that they must be present in some yet undescribed tribe. This point has, in fact, been expressed with respect to clan organization by Murdock (1949: 71). In this light, the magical beliefs and practices of the Nacirema present such unusual aspects that it seems desirable to describe them as an example of the extremes to which human behavior can go.

Professor Linton first brought the ritual of the Nacirema to the attention of anthropologists twenty years ago (1936: 326), but the culture of this people is still very poorly understood. They are a North American group living in the territory between the Canadian Cree, the Yaqui and Tarahumare of Mexico, and the Carib and Arawak of the Antilles. Little is known of their origin, though tradition states that they came from the east. According to Nacirema mythology, their nation was originated by a culture hero, Notgnishaw, who is otherwise known for two great feats of strength—the throwing of a piece of wampum across the river Pa-To-Mac and the chopping down of a cherry tree in which the Spirit of Truth resided.

Nacirema culture is characterized by a highly developed market economy which has evolved in a rich natural habitat. While much of the people's time is devoted to economic pursuits, a large part of the fruits of these labors and a considerable portion of the day are spent in ritual activity. The focus of this activity is the human body, the appearance and health of which loom as a dominant concern in the ethos of the people. While such a concern is certainly not unusual, its ceremonial aspects and associated philosophy are unique.

The fundamental belief underlying the whole system appears to be that the human body is ugly and that its natural tendency is to debility and disease. Incarcerated in such a body, man's only hope is to avert these characteristics through the use of the powerful influences of ritual and ceremony. Every household has one or more shrines devoted to this purpose. The more powerful individuals in the society have several shrines in their houses and, in fact, the opulence of a house is often referred to in terms of the number of such ritual centers it possesses. Most houses are of wattle and daub construction, but the shrine rooms of the more wealthy are walled with stone. Poorer families imitate the rich by applying pottery plaques to their shrine walls.

While each family has at least one such shrine, the rituals associated with it are not family ceremonies but are private and secret. The rites are normally only discussed with children, and then only during the period when they are being initiated into these mysteries. I was able, however, to establish sufficient rapport with the natives to examine these shrines and to have the rituals described to me.

The focal point of the shrine is a box or chest which is built into the wall. In this chest are kept the many charms and magical potions without which no native believes he could live. These preparations are secured from a variety of specialized practitioners. The most powerful of these are the medicine men, whose assistance must be rewarded with substantial gifts. However, the medicine men do not provide the curative potions for their clients, but decide what the ingredients should be and then write them down in an ancient and secret language. This writing is understood only by the medicine men and by the herbalists who, for another gift, provide the required charm.

The charm is not disposed of after it has served its purpose, but is placed in the charm-box of the household shrine. As these magical materials are specific for certain ills, and the real or imagined maladies of the people are many, the charm-box is usually full to overflowing. The magical packets are so numerous that people forget what their purposes were and fear to use them again. While the natives are very vague on this point, we can only assume that the idea in retaining all the old magical materials is that their presence in the charm-box, before which the body rituals are conducted, will in some way protect the worshipper.

Beneath the charm-box is a small font. Each day every member of the family, in succession, enters the shrine room, bows his head before the charm-box, mingles different sorts of holy water in the font, and proceeds with a brief rite of ablution. The holy waters are secured from the Water Temple of the community, where the priests conduct elaborate ceremonies to make the liquid ritually pure.

In the hierarchy of magical practitioners, and below the medicine men in prestige, are specialists whose designation is best translated "holy-mouth-men." The Nacirema have an almost pathological horror and fascination with the mouth, the condition of which is believed to have a supernatural influence on all social relationships. Were it not for the rituals of the mouth, they believe that their teeth would fall out, their gums bleed, their jaws shrink, their friends desert them, and their lovers reject them. (They also believe that a strong relationship exists between oral and moral characteristics. For example, there is a ritual ablution of the mouth for children which is supposed to improve their moral fiber.)

The daily body ritual performed by everyone includes a mouth-rite. Despite the fact that these people are so punctilious about care of the mouth, this rite involves a practice which strikes the uninitiated stranger as revolting. It was reported to me that the ritual consists of inserting a small bundle of hog hairs into the mouth, along with certain magical powders, and then moving the bundle in a highly formalized series of gestures.

In addition to the private mouth-rite, the people seek out a holy-mouth-man once or twice a year. These practitioners have an impressive set of paraphernalia, consisting of a variety of augers, awls, probes, and prods. The use of these objects in the exorcism of the evils of the mouth involves almost unbelievable ritual torture of the client. The holy-mouth-man opens the client's mouth and, using the above mentioned tools, enlarges any holes which decay may have created in the teeth. Magical materials are put into these holes. If there are no naturally occurring holes in the teeth, large sections of one or more teeth are gouged out so that the supernatural substance can be applied. In the client's view, the purpose of these ministrations is to arrest decay and to draw friends. The extremely sacred and traditional character of the rite is evident in the fact that the natives return to the holy-mouth-men year after year, despite the fact that their teeth continue to decay.

It is to be hoped that, when a thorough study of the Nacirema is made, there will be a careful inquiry into the personality structure of these people. One has but to watch the gleam in the eye of a holy-mouth-man, as he jabs an awl into an exposed nerve, to suspect that a certain amount of sadism is involved. If this can be established, a very interesting pattern emerges, for most of the population shows definite masochistic tendencies. It was to these that Professor Linton referred in discussing a distinctive part of the daily body ritual which is performed only by men. This part of the rite involves scraping and lacerating the surface of the face with a sharp instrument. Special women's rites are performed only four times during each lunar month, but what they lack in frequency is made up in barbarity. As part of this ceremony, women bake their heads in small ovens for about an hour. The theoretically interesting point is that what seems to be a preponderantly masochistic people have developed sadistic specialists.

The medicine men have an imposing temple, or *latipso,* in every community of any size. The more elaborate ceremonies required to treat very sick patients can only be performed at this temple. These ceremonies involve not only the thaumaturge but a permanent group of vestal maidens who move sedately about the temple chambers in distinctive costume and headdress.

The *latipso* ceremonies are so harsh that it is phenomenal that a fair proportion of the really sick natives who enter the temple ever recover. Small children whose indoctrination is still incomplete have been known to resist attempts to take them to the temple because "that is where you go to die." Despite this fact, sick adults are not only willing but eager to undergo the protracted ritual purification, if they can afford to do so. No matter how ill the supplicant or how grave the emergency, the guardians of many temples will not admit a client if he cannot give a rich gift to the custodian. Even after one has gained admission and survived the ceremonies, the guardians will not permit the neophyte to leave until he makes still another gift.

The supplicant entering the temple is first stripped of all his or her clothes. In every-day life the Nacirema avoids exposure of his body and its natural functions. Bathing and excretory acts are performed only in the secrecy of the household shrine, where they are ritualized as part of the body-rites. Psychological shock results from the fact that body secrecy is suddenly lost upon entry into the *latipso.* A man, whose own wife has never seen him in an excretory act, suddenly finds himself naked and assisted by a vestal maiden while he performs his natural functions into a sacred vessel. This sort of ceremonial treatment is necessitated by the fact that the excreta are used by a diviner to ascertain the course and nature of the client's sickness. Female clients, on the other hand, find their naked bodies are subjected to the scrutiny, manipulation, and prodding of the medicine men.

Few supplicants in the temple are well enough to do anything but lie on their hard beds. The daily ceremonies, like the rites of the holy-mouth-men, involve discomfort and torture. With ritual precision, the vestals awaken their miserable charges each dawn and roll them about on their beds of pain while performing ablutions, in the formal movements of which the maidens are highly trained. At other times they insert magic wands in the supplicant's mouth or force him to eat substances which are supposed to be healing. From time to time the medicine men come to their clients and jab magically treated needles into their flesh. The fact that these temple ceremonies may not cure, and may even kill the neophyte, in no way decreases the people's faith in the medicine men.

There remains one other kind of practitioner, known as a "listener." This witch-doctor has the power to exorcise the devils that lodge in the heads of people who have been bewitched. The Nacirema believe that parents bewitch their own children. Mothers are particularly suspected of putting a curse on children while teaching them the secret body rituals. The countermagic of the witch-doctor is unusual in its lack of ritual. The patient simply tells the "listener" all his troubles and fears, beginning with the earliest difficulties he can remember. The memory displayed by the Nacirema in these exorcism sessions is truly remarkable. It is not uncommon for the patient to bemoan the rejection he felt upon being weaned as a babe, and a few individuals even see their troubles going back to the traumatic effects of their own birth.

In conclusion, mention must be made of certain practices which have their base in native esthetics but which depend upon the pervasive aversion to the natural body and its functions. There are ritual fasts to make fat people thin and ceremonial feasts to make thin people fat. Still other rites are used to make women's breasts large if they are small, and smaller if they are large. General dissatisfaction with breast shape is symbolized in the fact that the ideal form is virtually outside the range of human variation. A few women afflicted with almost inhuman hypermammary development are so idolized that they make a handsome living by simply going from village to village and permitting the natives to stare at them for a fee.

Reference has already been made to the fact that excretory functions are ritualized, routinized, and relegated to secrecy. Natural reproductive functions are similarly distorted. Intercourse is taboo as a topic and scheduled as an act. Efforts are made to avoid pregnancy by the use of magical materials or by limiting intercourse to certain phases of the moon. Conception is actually very infrequent. When pregnant, women dress so as to hide their condition. Parturition takes place in secret, without friends or relatives to assist, and the majority of women do not nurse their infants.

Our review of the ritual life of the Nacirema has certainly shown them to be a magic-ridden people. It is hard to understand how they have managed to exist so long under the burdens which they have imposed upon themselves. But even such exotic customs as these take on real meaning when they are viewed with the insight provided by Malinowski when he wrote (1948:70):

> Looking from far and above, from our high places of safety in the developed civilization, it is easy to see all the crudity and irrelevance of magic. But without its power and guidance early man could not have mastered his practical difficulties as he has done, nor could man have advanced to the higher stages of civilization.

References

Linton, Ralph. 1936. *The Study of Man.* New York, D. Appleton-Century Co.

Malinowski, Bronislaw. 1948. *Magic, Science, and Religion.* Glencoe, The Free Press.

Murdock, George P. 1949. *Social Structure.* New York, The Macmillan Co.

Critical Thinking

1. What is "Nacirema" spelled backwards? Where are they actually located on a map? Who are they, really?
2. Why do the customs of the Nacirema seem so bizarre when they are written about in anthropological style?
3. Having read the article, do you view American culture any differently than you did before? If so, how?
4. Has this article helped you to view other cultures differently? If so, how?
5. If this article has distorted the picture of American culture, how difficult is it for all of us, anthropologists included, to render objective descriptions of other cultures?

Internet References

Apologetics Index
www.apologeticsindex.org/site/index-c

Journal of Anthropology of Religion
www.mehtapress.com/social-science-a-humanities/journal-of-anthropology-of-religion.html

Magic and Religion
http://anthro.palomar.edu/religion/default.htm

Miner, Horace. "Body Ritual among the Nacirema," *American Anthropologist*, June 1956.

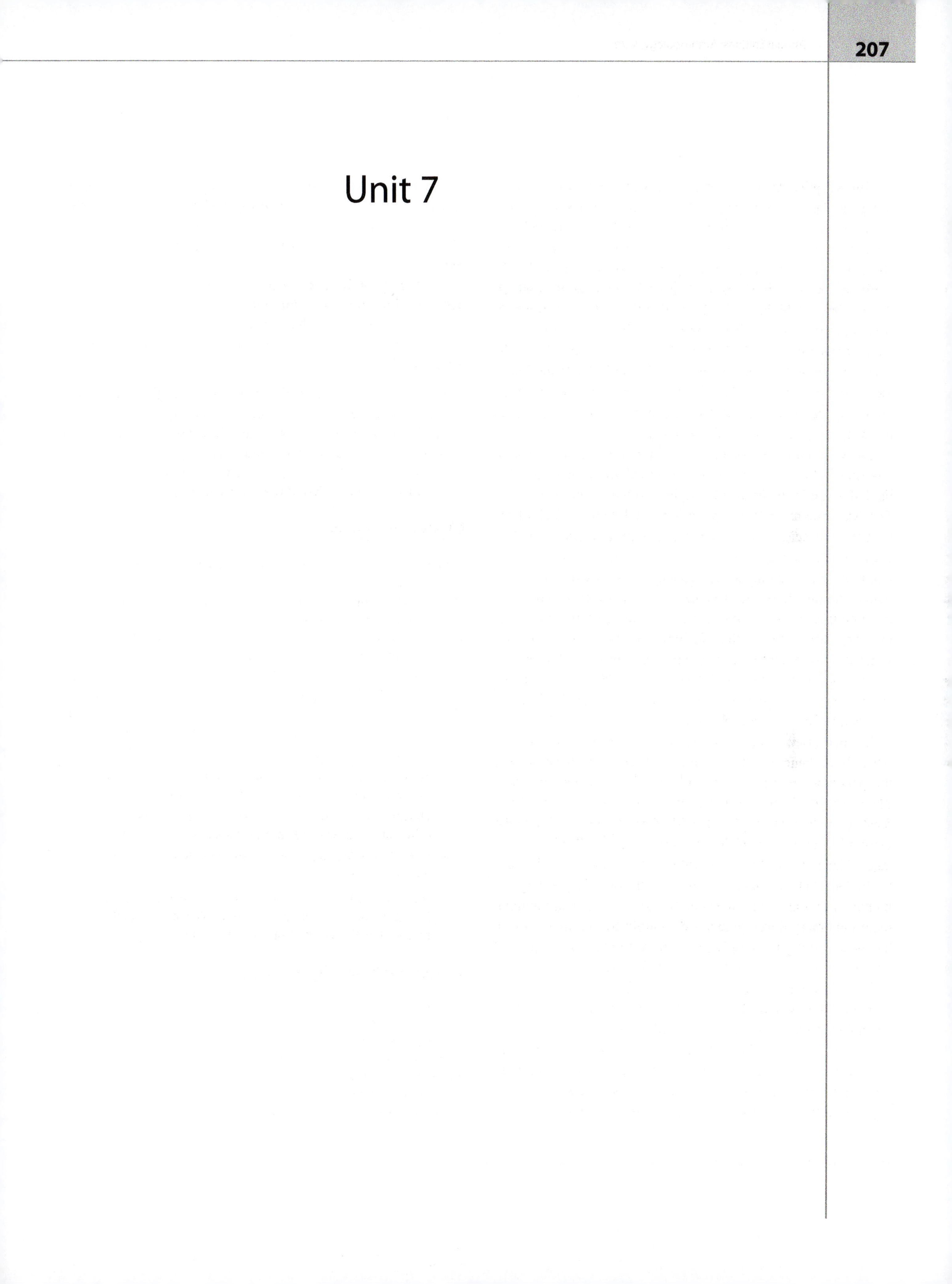

Unit 7

UNIT
Prepared by: Elvio Angeloni

Sociocultural Change

The origins of academic anthropology lie in the colonial and imperial ventures of the past five hundred years. During this period, many people of the world were brought into a relationship with Europe and the United States that was usually exploitative and often socially and culturally disruptive. For over a century, anthropologists have witnessed this process and the transformations that have taken place in those social and cultural systems brought under the umbrella of a world economic order. Early anthropological studies—even those widely regarded as pure research—directly or indirectly served colonial interests. Many anthropologists certainly believed that they were extending the benefits of Western technology and society, while preserving the cultural rights of those people whom they studied. But representatives of poor nations challenge this view and are far less generous in describing the past role of the anthropologist. Most contemporary anthropologists, however, have a deep moral commitment to defending the legal, political, and economic rights of the people with whom they work.

When anthropologists discuss social change, they usually mean the change brought about in pre-industrial societies through longstanding interaction with the nation-states of the industrialized world. In early anthropology, contact between the West and the remainder of the world was characterized by the terms *acculturation* and *culture contact.* These terms were used to describe the diffusion of cultural traits between the developed and the less-developed countries. Often this was analyzed as a one-way process, in which cultures of the less-developed world were seen, for better or worse, as receptacles for Western cultural traits. Nowadays, many anthropologists believe that the diffusion of cultural traits across social, political, and economic boundaries was emphasized at the expense of the real issues of dominance, subordination, and dependence that characterized the colonial experience. Just as important, many anthropologists recognize that the present-day forms of cultural, economic, and political interaction between the developed and the so-called underdeveloped world are best characterized as neocolonial. They take the perspective that anthropology should be critical as well as descriptive and they raise questions about cultural contact and subsequent economic and social disruption.

None of this is to say that indigenous peoples can or even should be left entirely alone to live in isolation from the rest of the world. A much more sensible, as well as more practical, approach would involve some degree of self-determination and considerably more respect for their cultures.

Of course, traditional peoples are not the only losers in the process of technological "progress" and cultural destruction. The very same climate change that now seems to be flooding some of the low-lying Pacific islands may also be causing the most highly destructive hurricanes ever to hit the American coasts such as Katrina and Sandy and should be taken as a warning to the rest of us. The more we deprive the traditional stewards (the Indigenous peoples) of their land, the greater the loss in overall biodiversity.

Finally, all of humanity stands to suffer as resources dwindle and as a vast store of human knowledge—embodied in tribal subsistence practices, language, medicine, and folklore—is obliterated, in a manner not unlike the burning of the library of Alexandria 1,600 years ago. We can only hope that it is not too late to save what is left.

Article

Prepared by: Elvio Angeloni

Quiet Revolutions

Bob Holmes

Learning Outcomes

After reading this article, you will be able to:

- Discuss the various circumstances in which farming first developed.
- In the light of new evidence discuss the various theories as to why crop domestication originally occurred.
- Explain how, in some cases, there was a long overlap between the use of wild foods and the domestication of crops.

In February 1910, British botanist Lilian Gibbs walked across North Borneo and climbed Mount Kinabalu, a lone white woman among 400 locals. She later wrote: "The 'untrodden jungle' of fiction seems to be nonexistent in this country. Everywhere the forest is well worked and has been so for generations."

What Gibbs saw was a seemingly curated tropical forest, regularly set alight by local tribes and with space carefully cleared around selected wild fruit trees, to give them room to flourish. The forest appeared to be partitioned and managed to get the most rattan canes, fibre for basketry, medicinal plants and other products. Generation after generation of people had cared for the trees, gradually shaping the forest they lived in. This wasn't agriculture in the way we know it today but a more ancient form of cultivation, stretching back more than 10,000 years. Half a world away from the Fertile Crescent, Gibbs was witnessing a living relic of the earliest days of human farming. In recent years, archaeologists have found signs of this "proto-farming" on nearly every continent, transforming our picture of the dawn of agriculture. Gone is the simple story of a sudden revolution in what is now the Middle East with benefits so great that it rapidly spread around the world. It turns out farming was invented many times, in many places and was rarely an instant success. In short, there was no agricultural revolution. "We're going to have to start thinking about things in a different way," says Tim Denham, an archaeologist at the Australian National University in Canberra.

Farming is seen as a pivotal invention in the history of humanity. Before, our ancestors roamed the landscape gathering edible fruits, seeds, and plants and hunting whatever game they could find. They lived in small mobile groups that usually set up temporary homes according to the movement of the prey they hunted. Then one fine day in the Fertile Crescent, around 8000 to 10,000 years ago—or so the story goes—someone noticed sprouts growing out of seeds they had accidentally left on the ground. Over time, people learned how to grow and care for plants in order to get the most out of them. Doing this for generations gradually transformed the wild plants into rich domestic varieties, most of which we still eat today.

This accidental revolution is credited with irreversibly shaping the course of humanity. As fields began to appear on the landscape, more people could be fed. Human populations—already on the rise and stretching the resources available to hunter-gatherers—exploded. At the same time, our ancestors traded their migratory habits for sedentary settlements: these were the first villages, with adjoining fields and pastures. A steadier food supply freed up time for new tasks. Craftspeople were born: the first specialised toolmakers, farmers, carers. Complex societies began to develop, as did trade networks between villages. The rest, as they say, is history.

The enormous impact of farming is widely accepted, but in recent decades the story of how it all began has been completely turned on its head. For starters, while the inhabitants of the Fertile Crescent were undoubtedly some of the earliest farmers, they weren't the only ones. Archaeologists now agree farming was independently "invented" in at least 11 regions, from Central America all the way to China. Decades of digging have kicked up numerous instances of ancient proto-farming, similar to what Gibbs saw in Borneo.

Another point archaeologists are rethinking is the notion that our ancestors were forced into farming when their populations outgrew what the land could provide naturally. If humans had turned to crops out of hunger and desperation, you would expect their efforts to have intensified when the climate took a turn for the worse. In fact, archaeological sites in Asia and the Americas show that most early cultivation happened during periods of relatively stable, warm climates when wild foods would have been plentiful, says Dorian Fuller of University College London.

Nor is there much evidence that early farming coincided with overpopulation. When crops first appeared in eastern North America, for example, people were living in small, scattered settlements. "The sites are less than 10 houses and they're not very numerous," says Bruce Smith, an archaeologist at the Smithsonian Institution in Washington DC. "There's no real evidence that population increase was the prime mover causing them to shift over to domesticated crops." The earliest South American farmers also lived in the very best habitats, where resource shortages would have been least likely. Similarly, in China and the Middle East, domesticated crops appear well before dense human populations would have made foraging impractical.

Instead, Smith suggests, the first farmers appear to have been pulled into experimenting with cultivation, presumably out of curiosity rather than necessity. "These are additional food supply sources, but otherwise the subsistence system based on wild species pretty much remains unchanged," he says. That lack of pressure would explain why so many societies kept crops as a low-intensity sideline—a hobby, almost—for so many generations. Only much later in the process would densely populated settlements have forced people to abandon wild foods in favour of near-exclusive reliance on farming.

Those first experiments most likely happened when bands of hunter-gatherers started tweaking the landscape to encourage the most productive habitats. On the islands of South-East Asia, people were burning patches of tropical forest way back during the last ice age. This created clearings where plants with edible tubers could flourish. In Borneo, evidence of this stretches back 53,000 years; in New Guinea, 20,000 years. We know the burns were deliberate because the charcoal they left behind peaks during wet periods, when natural fires would be less common and people would be fighting forest encroachment, says Christopher Hunt of Liverpool John Moores University, UK, who has worked in Borneo for many years.

Burnt Riches

Burning forest would have paid off for hunters too, as game is easier to spot at forest edges. At Niah Cave on the northern coast of Borneo, Hunt's colleagues have found hundreds of orangutan bones among the remains of early hunters, suggesting forest regrowth after a burn brought the apes low enough to catch, even before the invention of blowpipes. Burning probably intensified as the last ice age gave way to the warmer, wetter Holocene beginning about 13,000 years ago. Rainfall in Borneo doubled, producing a denser forest that would have been much harder to forage without fire.

This wasn't only happening in South-East Asia. Changing climates also pushed hunter-gatherers into landscape management in Central and South America. At the end of the last ice age, the perfect open hunting grounds of the savannahs began to give way to closed forest. By 13,000 years ago, people were burning forests during the dry season when fires would carry, says Dolores Piperno, also at the Smithsonian Institution. Researchers are now turning up evidence of similar management activities in Africa, Brazil and North America.

From burning, it is just a short step to actively nurturing favoured wild species, something that also happened soon after the end of the ice age in some places. Weeds that thrive in cultivated fields appear in the Fertile Crescent at least 13,000 years ago, for example, and New Guinea highlanders were building mounds on swampy ground to grow bananas, yams, and taro about 7000 years ago. In parts of South America, traces of cultivated crops such as gourds, squash, arrowroot, and avocado appear as early as 11,000 years ago, says Piperno. Evidence suggests that these people lived in small groups, often sheltering under rock overhangs or in shallow caves, and they tended small plots along the banks of seasonal streams in addition to foraging for wild plants.

Their early efforts wouldn't have looked much like farming is today. "It's better to see it as small gardens," says Fuller. "Small, intensively managed plots on riverbanks and alluvial fans—possibly not all that important in terms of the overall calories." Instead, Fuller thinks these gardens may have provided high-value foods, such as rice, for special occasions. "It's like growing something for Christmas dinner instead of year-round meals," he says.

As Gibbs discovered in Borneo, and others have seen elsewhere since, this kind of proto-farming is still practised by some hunter-gatherer tribes today. They often move every few years as local game populations are depleted, leaving behind fruit trees that their descendants may return to decades later. Hunt recalls meeting a man gathering fruit in the forest near Niah who told him he was harvesting the trees "that my grandfather planted for me". (Sadly, as younger people abandon their traditional lifestyles, this multi-generational knowledge is rapidly being lost, says Hunt.)

Archaeologists have long assumed that this proto-farming was a shortlived predecessor to fully domesticated crops. They believed that the first farmers quickly transformed the plants' genetic make-up by selecting traits like larger seeds and easier harvesting to produce modern domestic varieties. After all, similar selection has produced great changes in dogs within just the past few hundred years.

We'll Farm Maybe

But new archaeological sites and better techniques for recognising ancient plant remains have made it clear that crop domestication was often very slow. Through much of the Middle East, Asia, and New Guinea, at least a thousand—and often several thousand—years of proto-farming preceded the first genetic hints of domestication.

In China, for example, people began cultivating wild forms of rice on a small scale about 10,000 years ago. But physical traits associated with domesticated rice, such as larger grains that stay in the seed head instead of falling off to seed the next generation, didn't appear until about two-and-a-half millennia later. Fully domesticated rice didn't appear until 6000 years ago, says Fuller.

Even after crops were domesticated, there was often a lag, sometimes of thousands of years, before people began to rely on them for most of their calories. During this prolonged transition period, people often act as though they haven't made up their mind how much to trust the newfangled agricultural technology.

The inhabitants of China's Yangtze delta about 6900 years ago, for example, lived primarily on wild foods like acorns and water chestnuts. They also grew a small amount of partially domesticated rice, often in small depressions just a metre or two across. But Fuller has found that rice makes up only 8 per cent of plant remains in archaeological sites in the region. Three hundred years later, the use of rice had tripled, and yet wild foods still made up the bulk of the diet. "They're keeping their options open," says Fuller.

The record also shows a long period of overlap in other regions, with cultures using both wild foods and domesticated crops. We know from the type of starch grains found on their teeth that people living in southern Mexico 8700 years ago were eating domesticated maize, yet large-scale slash-and-burn agriculture did not begin until nearly a millennium later. In several cases—Scandinavia, for example—societies began to rely on domesticated crops, then switched back to wild foods when they couldn't make a go of farming. And in eastern North America, Native Americans had domesticated squash, sunflowers and several other plants by about 3800 years ago, but only truly committed to agriculture about AD 900, says Smith.

Indeed, some cultures didn't commit to domesticated crops until modern times. The highlanders of Borneo, for example, only began growing domestic rice after the second world war. Many of the indigenous crops grown by traditional New Guineans, like sago palm and some tubers, are even now only semi-domesticated at best, says Denham. One reason may be that traditional gardening hunter-gatherers use so many plants—often a different mix for each month of the year—that their crops experience very little evolutionary pressure toward domestication.

The story of agriculture, in short, is not the sudden agricultural revolution of textbooks, but rather an agricultural evolution. "The evidence is showing a much more patchwork-quilt mosaic, with different sorts of practices and different plants being used in different ways," says Denham. "In those conditions, when agriculture emerges over time, it's a long, drawn-out process. It's a much more diffuse event, both in time and in space."

That means people's motivations for making the switch were equally complex, as crops become gradually more dominant in their lives. "If people are cultivating plots, their life is going to be oriented to those areas," says Denham. "That would require a shift in their way of engaging with the landscape, and with each other as well. That's really why we're interested in it—because it's a story about us."

Where Did All the Potatoes Come From?

Our picture of the dawn of farming is being redrawn. Gone is the simple story of a sudden agricultural revolution in the Fertile Crescent at the end of the last ice age that spread around the world. Archaeologists now agree that farming was "invented" at least 11 times in 11 different places

The ingredients you cook with were once separated by oceans. We now know that most went through long periods of "proto-farming" before being grown in recognisable fields and turned into the crops we still eat today. Proto-farmers would tend to wild plants, perhaps planting some in small gardens

Cuscus to Slaughter

Domestic food animals, traditionally viewed as a later add-on in the development of agriculture, may have been part of the picture from the very beginning. In fact, the roots of animal husbandry probably stretch back into the last ice age.

There is some evidence that the common cuscus, a small marsupial native to New Guinea, appeared on remote islands such as New Ireland 20,000 and 10,000 years ago, at the same time as the first humans arrived. The cuscus is a favoured prey for modern hunter-gatherers, so the suspicious timing may mean early Pacific islanders brought the animals with them to seed their new home with prey.

In the Fertile Crescent of south-west Asia, skeletal remains of sheep and goats suggest that by 10,500 years ago, humans living in what is now Turkey were preferentially killing young male animals, says Melinda Zeder, an archaeologist at the Smithsonian Institution. This implies that they were not just hunting the animals, but deliberately managing herds to maintain fertile females. She is now looking at 11,700-year-old sites for evidence that the practice began even earlier. If she is successful, it would imply people began domesticating animals in the region at the same time as they began domesticating crops like wheat and barley.

So why have historians assumed that animal domestication came second? Further south in the Levant, the most common prey animal back then was a species of gazelle whose behaviour made it unsuitable for domestication.

Since most archaeologists working in the region have tended to study the Levant, which is more accessible, this may have led them to the erroneous conclusion that animal domestication lagged behind that of plants, says Zeder.

Critical Thinking

1. What were the apparent reasons for crop domestication—in contrast to previous theories?
2. Why was crop domestication a very slow process and not quite the revolution that was once thought?
3. Why was there often a long overlap between the use of wild foods and the domestication of crops?

Internet References

Ancient World History
http://earlyworldhistory.blogspot.com/2012/02/neolithic-age.html

Neolithic Revolution
http://www.regentsprep.org/regents/global/themes/change/neo.cfm

Bob Holmes is a consultant for New Scientist based in Edmonton, Canada.

Article

Prepared by: Elvio Angeloni

Ruined

MICHAEL MARSHALL

Learning Outcomes

After reading this article, you will be able to:

- Discuss the relationship between climate change and the decline of civilizations in the past.
- Discuss the prospects of societal collapse as a result of climate change in the modern world.

The most beautiful woman in the world, Helen, is abducted by Paris of Troy. A Greek fleet of more than a thousand ships sets off in pursuit. After a long war, heroes like Achilles lead the Greeks to victory over Troy.

At least, this is the story told by the poet Homer around four centuries later. Yet Homer was not only writing about events long before his time, he was also describing a long-lost civilization. Achilles and his compatriots were part of the first great Greek civilization, a warlike culture centered on the city of Mycenae that thrived from around 1600 BC.

By 1100 BC, not long after the Trojan War, many of its cities and settlements had been destroyed or abandoned. The survivors reverted to a simpler rural lifestyle. Trade ground to a halt, and skills such as writing were lost. The script the Mycenaeans had used, Linear B, was not read again until 1952.

The region slowly recovered after around 800 BC. The Greeks adopted the Phoenician script, and the great city states of Athens and Sparta rose to power. "The collapse was one of the most important events in history, because it gave birth to two major cultures," says anthropologist Brandon Drake. "It's like the phoenix from the ashes." Classical Greece, as this second period of civilization is known, far outshone its predecessor. Its glory days lasted only a couple of centuries, but the ideas of its citizens were immensely influential. Their legacy is still all around us, from the math we learn in school to the idea of democracy.

But what caused the collapse of Mycenaean Greece, and thus had a huge impact on the course of world history? A change in the climate, according to the latest evidence. What's more, Mycenaean Greece is just one of a growing list of civilizations whose fate is being linked to the vagaries of climate. It seems big swings in the climate, handled badly, brought down whole societies, while smaller changes led to unrest and wars.

The notion that climate change toppled entire civilizations has been around for more than a century, but it was only in the 1990s that it gained a firm footing as researchers began to work out exactly how the climate had changed, using clues buried in lake beds or petrified in stalactites. Harvey Weiss of Yale University set the ball rolling with his studies of the collapse of one of the earliest empires: that of the Akkadians.

It began in the Fertile Crescent of the Middle East, a belt of rich farmland where an advanced regional culture had developed over many centuries. In 2334 BC, Sargon was born in the city state of Akkad. He started out as a gardener, was put in charge of clearing irrigation canals, and went on to seize power. Not content with that, he conquered many neighboring city states, too. The empire Sargon founded thrived for nearly a century after his death before it collapsed.

Excavating in what is now Syria, Weiss found dust deposits suggesting that the region's climate suddenly became drier around 2200 BC. The drought would have led to famine, he argued, explaining why major cities were abandoned at this time (*Science,* vol 261, p. 995). A piece of contemporary writing, called *The Curse of Akkad,* does describe a great famine (see end of article).

Weiss's work was influential, but there wasn't much evidence. In 2000, climatologist Peter deMenocal of Columbia University in New York found more. His team showed, based on modern records going back to 1700, that the flow of the region's two great rivers, the Tigris and the Euphrates, is linked to conditions in the north Atlantic: cooler waters reduce rainfall by altering the paths of weather systems. Next, they discovered that the north Atlantic cooled just before the Akkadian empire fell apart (*Science,* vol 288, p 2198). "To our surprise we got this big whopping signal at the time of the Akkadian collapse."

It soon became clear that major changes in the climate coincided with the untimely ends of several other civilizations. Of these, the Maya became the poster child for climate-induced decline. Mayan society arose in Mexico and Central America around 2000 BC. Its farmers grew maize, squashes and beans, and it was the only American civilization to produce a written language. The Maya endured for millennia, reaching a peak between AD 250 and 800, when they built cities and huge stepped pyramids.

Then the Maya civilization collapsed. Many of its incredible structures were swallowed up by the jungle after being abandoned. Not all was lost, though—Mayan people and elements of their culture survive to the present day.

Numerous studies have shown that there were several prolonged droughts around the time of the civilisation's decline. In 2003, Gerald Haug of the Swiss Federal Institute of Technology in Zurich found it was worse than that. His year-by-year reconstruction based on lake sediments shows that rainfall was abundant from 550 to 750, perhaps leading to a rise in population and thus to the peak of monument-building around 721. But over the next century there were not only periods of particularly severe drought, each lasting years, but also less rain than normal in the intervening years (*Science,* vol 299, p 1731). Monument construction ended during this prolonged dry period, around 830, although a few cities continued on for many centuries.

Even as the evidence grew, there was something of a backlash against the idea that changing climates shaped the fate of civilizations. "Many in the archaeological community are really reticent to accept a role of climate in human history," says deMenocal.

Much of this reluctance is for historical reasons. In the 18th and 19th centuries, anthropologists argued that a society's environment shaped its character, an idea known as environmental determinism. They claimed that the warm, predictable climates of the tropics bred indolence, while cold European climates produced intelligence and a strong work ethic. These ideas were often used to justify racism and exploitation.

Understandably, modern anthropologists resist anything resembling environmental determinism. "It's a very delicate issue," says Ulf Büntgen, also at the Swiss Federal Institute of Technology, whose work suggests the decline of the Western Roman Empire was linked to a period of highly variable weather. "The field is evolving really slowly, because people are afraid to make bold statements."

Yet this resistance is not really warranted, deMenocal says. No one today is claiming that climate determines people's characters, only that it sets limits on what is feasible. When the climate becomes less favorable, less food can be grown. Such changes can also cause plagues of locusts or other pests, and epidemics among people weakened by starvation. When it is no longer feasible to maintain a certain population level and way of life, the result can be collapse. "Climate isn't a determinant, but it is an important factor," says Drake, who is at the University of New Mexico in Albuquerque. "It enables or disables."

Some view even this notion as too simplistic. Karl Butzer of the University of Texas at Austin, who has studied the collapse of civilizations, thinks the role of climate has been exaggerated. It is the way societies handle crises that decides their fate, he says. "Things break through institutional failure." When it comes to the Akkadians, for instance, Butzer says not all records support the idea of a megadrought.

In the case of the Maya, though, the evidence is strong. Earlier this year, Eelco Rohling of the University of Southampton, UK, used lake sediments and isotope ratios in stalactites to work out how rainfall had changed. He concluded that annual rainfall fell 40 per cent over the prolonged dry period, drying up open water sources (*Science,* vol 335, p 956). This would have seriously affected the Maya, he says, because the water table lay far underground and was effectively out of reach.

So after a century of plentiful rain, the Maya were suddenly confronted with a century of low rainfall. It is not clear how they could have avoided famine and population decline in these circumstances. Even today, our ability to defy hostile climes is limited. Saudi Arabia managed to become self-sufficient in wheat by tapping water reservoirs deep beneath its deserts and subsidising farmers, but is now discouraging farming to preserve what is left of the water. In dry regions where plenty of water is available for irrigation, the build-up of salts in the soil is a serious problem, just as it was for some ancient civilisations. And if modern farmers are still at the mercy of the climate despite all our knowledge and technology, what chance did ancient farmers have?

Greek Dark Ages

While many archaeologists remain unconvinced, the list of possible examples continues to grow. The Mycenaeans are the latest addition. The reason for their downfall has been the subject of much debate, with one of the most popular explanations being a series of invasions and attacks by the mysterious "Sea Peoples." In 2010, though, a study of river deposits in Syria suggested there was a prolonged dry period between 1200 and 850 BC—right at the time of the so-called Greek Dark Ages. Earlier this year, Drake analysed several climate records and concluded that there was a cooling of the Mediterranean at this time, reducing evaporation and rainfall over a huge area.

What's more, several other cultures around the Mediterranean, including the Hittite Empire and the "New Kingdom" of Egypt, collapsed around the same time as the Mycenaeans—a phenomenon known as the late Bronze Age collapse. Were all these civilisations unable to cope with the changing climate? Or were the invading Sea Peoples the real problem? The story could be complex: civilisations weakened by hunger may have become much more vulnerable to invaders, who may themselves have been driven to migrate by the changing climate. Or the collapse of one civilisation could have had knock-on effects on its trading partners.

Climate change on an even greater scale might be behind another striking coincidence. Around 900, as the Mayan civilisation was declining in South America, the Tang dynasty began losing its grip on China. At its height, the Tang ruled over 50 million subjects. Woodblock printing meant that written words, particularly poetry, were widely accessible. But the dynasty fell after local governors usurped its authority.

Since the two civilisations were not trading partners, there was clearly no knock-on effect. A study of lake sediments in China by Haug suggests that this region experienced a prolonged dry period at the same time as that in Central America. He thinks a shift in the tropical rain belt was to blame, causing civilisations to fall apart on either side of the Pacific (*Nature,* vol 445, p 74).

Critics, however, point to examples of climate change that did not lead to collapse. "There was a documented drought and even famines during the period of the Aztec Empire," says archaeologist Gary Feinman of the Field Museum in Chicago. "These episodes caused hardships and possibly even famines, but no overall collapse."

Realizing that case studies of collapses were not enough to settle the debate, in 2005 David Zhang of Hong Kong University began to look for larger patterns. He began with the history of the Chinese dynasties. From 2500 BC until the 20th century, a series of powerful empires like the Tang controlled China. All were eventually toppled by civil unrest or invasions.

When Zhang compared climate records for the last 1200 years to the timeline of China's dynastic wars, the match was striking. Most of the dynastic transitions and periods of social unrest took place when temperatures were a few tenths of a degree colder. Warmer periods were more stable and peaceful (*Chinese Science Bulletin,* vol 50, p 137).

The Thirty Years War

Zhang gradually built up a more detailed picture showing that harvests fell when the climate was cold, as did population levels, while wars were more common. Of 15 bouts of warfare he studied, 12 took place in cooler times. He then looked at records of war across Europe, Asia and North Africa between 1400 and 1900. Once again, there were more wars when the temperatures were lower. Cooler periods also saw more deaths and declines in the population.

These studies suggest that the effects of climate on societies can be profound. The problem is proving it. So what if wars and collapses often coincide with shifts in the climate? It doesn't prove one caused the other. "That's always been the beef," says deMenocal. "It's a completely valid point."

Trying to move beyond mere correlations, Zhang began studying the history of Europe from 1500 to 1800 AD. In the mid-1600s, Europe was plunged into the General Crisis, which coincided with a cooler period called the Little Ice Age. The Thirty Years War was fought then, and many other wars. Zhang analysed detailed records covering everything from population and migration to agricultural yields, wars, famines and epidemics in a bid to identify causal relationships. So, for instance, did climate change affect agricultural production and thus food prices? That in turn might lead to famine—revealed by a reduction in the average height of people—epidemics and a decline in population. High food prices might also lead to migration and social unrest, and even wars.

He then did a statistical analysis known as a Granger causality test, which showed that the proposed causes consistently occurred before the proposed effects, and that each cause was followed by the same effect. The Granger test isn't conclusive proof of causality, but short of rerunning history under different climes, it is about the best evidence there can be (*Proceedings of the National Academy of Sciences,* vol 108, p 17296).

The paper hasn't bowled over the critics. Butzer, for instance, claims it is based on unreliable demographic data. Yet others are impressed. "It's a really remarkable study," deMenocal says. "It does seem like they did their homework." He adds that such a detailed breakdown is only possible for recent history, because older civilizations left fewer records.

So while further studies should reveal much more about how the climate changed in the past, the debate about how great an effect these changes had on societies is going to rumble on for many more decades. Let's assume, though, that changing climates did play a major role. What does that mean for us? On the face of it, things don't look so bad. It was often cooling that hurt past civilizations. What's more, studies of the past century have found little or no link between conflict and climate change. "Industrialized societies have been more robust against changing climatic conditions," says Jürgen Scheffran of the University of Hamburg, who studies the effects of climate change.

On the other hand, we are triggering the most extreme change for millions of years, and what seems to matter is food production rather than temperature. Production is expected to increase at first as the planet warms, but then begin to decline as warming exceeds 3°C. This point may not be that far away—it is possible that global average temperature will rise by 4°C as early as 2060. We've already seen regional food production hit by extreme heat waves like the one in Russia in 2010. Such extreme heat was not expected until much later this century.

And our society's interconnectedness is not always a strength. It can transmit shocks—the 2010 heat wave sent food prices soaring worldwide, and the drought in the US this year is having a similar effect. The growing complexity of modern society may make us more vulnerable to collapse rather than less.

We do have one enormous advantage, though—unlike the Mycenaeans and the Mayas, we know what's coming. We can prepare for what is to come and also slow the rate of change if we act soon. So far, though, we are doing neither.

The Curse of Akkad

'Look on my works, ye mighty, and despair!' All empires fall, but why?

A great drought did occur at the time this tablet was inscribed

For the first time since cities were built and founded,

The great agricultural tracts produced no grain,

The inundated tracts produced no fish,

The irrigated orchards produced neither syrup nor wine,

The gathered clouds did not rain, the masgurum did not grow.

At that time, one shekel's worth of oil was only one-half quart, One shekel's worth of grain was only one-half quart. . . .

These sold at such prices in the markets of all the cities!

He who slept on the roof, died on the roof,

He who slept in the house, had no burial,

People were flailing at themselves from hunger.

Critical Thinking

1. Discuss the causes of the decline of civilizations such as those of the Akkadian Empire and the Maya.
2. Why was there initially a backlash against the idea that changing climates shaped the fate of civilizations? Why is such resistance not warranted?
3. What are some of the specific consequences when the climate becomes less favorable?
4. Why does Karl Butzer view the notion of climate change's impact on civilizations as exaggerated?
5. What is the specific evidence for the impact of climate change on the Maya?
6. What evidence is there that our ability to defy hostile climes is limited even today?
7. Discuss the possible factors for Bronze Age collapse, i.e., the decline of the civilizations of the Mycenaeans (the Greek Dark Ages), the Hittite Empire, and the "New Kingdom" of Egypt.
8. What is the significance of the "striking coincidence" of the simultaneous collapse of the Tang dynasty in China and the Mayan civilization?
9. In what respect are the Aztecs an exception?
10. What do the climate records say about China's dynastic wars and transitions? About wars in Europe, Asia, and North Africa?
11. How was David Zhang able to "move beyond mere correlations" by using the "Granger causality test" with respect to the effects of climate change in Europe?
12. Why does there seem to have been little or no link between conflict and climate change over the past century?
13. Why might we become more vulnerable to collapse rather than less?
14. What is the one "enormous advantage" that we have today?

Internet References

Murray Research Center
www.radcliffe.edu/murray_redirect/index.php

Small Planet Institute
www.smallplanet.org/food

Michael Marshall is an environment reporter for *New Scientist.*

Article

Prepared by: Elvio Angeloni

The Traders Are Kidnapping Our People

ADAM HOCHSCHILD

Learning Outcomes

After reading this article, you will be able to:

- Compare and contrast the nature of African slavery with that which Europeans established in the New World.
- Explain how the African trade in human beings would turn out to be catastrophic for Africa.
- Discuss both the African motivation and the European motivation for participating in the international slave trade.

WHEN EUROPEANS began imagining Africa beyond the Sahara, the continent they pictured was a dreamscape, a site for fantasies of the fearsome and the supernatural. Ranulf Higden, a Benedictine monk who mapped the world about 1350, claimed that Africa contained one-eyed people who used their feet to cover their heads. A geographer in the next century announced that the continent held people with one leg, three faces, and the heads of lions. In 1459, an Italian monk, Fra Mauro, declared Africa the home of the roc, a bird so large that it could carry an elephant through the air.

In the Middle Ages, almost no one in Europe was in a position to know whether Africa contained giant birds, one-eyed people, or anything else. Hostile Moors lived on Africa's Mediterranean coast, and few Europeans dared set foot there, much less head south across the Sahara. And as for trying to sail down the west African coast, everyone knew that as soon as you passed the Canary Islands you would be in the Mare Tenebroso, the Sea of Darkness.

> In the medieval imagination [writes Peter Forbath], this was a region of uttermost dread . . . where the heavens fling down liquid sheets of flame and the waters boil . . . where serpent rocks and ogre islands lie in wait for the mariner, where the giant hand of Satan reaches up from the fathomless depths to seize him, where he will turn black in face and body as a mark of Gods vengeance for the insolence of his prying into this forbidden mystery. And even if he should be able to survive all these ghastly perils and sail on through, he would then arrive in the Sea of Obscurity and be lost forever in the vapors and slime at the edge of the world.

It was not until the fifteenth century, the dawn of the age of ocean navigation, that Europeans systematically began to venture south, the Portuguese in the lead. In the 1440s, Lisbon's shipbuilders developed the caravel, a compact vessel particularly good at sailing into the wind. Although rarely more than a hundred feet long, this sturdy ship carried explorers far down the west coast of Africa, where no one knew what gold, spices, and precious stones might lie. But it was not only lust for riches that drove the explorers. Somewhere in Africa, they knew, was the source of the Nile, a mystery that had fascinated Europeans since antiquity. They were also driven by one of the most enduring of medieval myths, the legend of Prester John, a Christian king who was said to rule a vast empire in the interior of Africa, where, from a palace of translucent crystal and precious stones, he reigned over 42 lesser kings, in addition to assorted centaurs and giants. No traveler was ever turned away from his dinner table of solid emerald, which seated thousands. Surely Prester John would be eager to share his riches with his fellow Christians and to help them find their way onward, to the fabled wealth of India.

Successive Portuguese expeditions probed ever farther southward. In 1482, an experienced naval captain named Diogo Cão set off on the most ambitious voyage yet. As he sailed close to the west African coast, he saw the North Star disappear from the sky once his caravel crossed the equator, and he found himself much farther south than anyone from Europe had ever been.

One day, Cão came upon something that astounded him. Around his ship, the sea turned a dark, slate-tinged yellow, and brownish-yellow waves were breaking on the nearby beaches.

Sailing toward the mouth of an inlet many miles wide, his caravel had to fight a current of eight to nine knots. Furthermore, a taste of the water surrounding the ship revealed that it was fresh, not salt. Cão had stumbled on the mouth of an enormous silt-filled river, larger than any a European had ever seen. The impression its vastness made on him and his men is reflected in a contemporary account:

> For the space of 20 leagues [the river] preserves its fresh water unbroken by the briny billows which encompass it on every side; as if this noble river had determined to try its strength in pitched battle with the ocean itself, and alone deny it the tribute which all other rivers in the world pay without resistance.

Modern oceanographers have discovered more evidence of the great river's strength in its "pitched battle with the ocean": a hundred-mile-long canyon, in places four thousand feet deep, that the river has carved out of the sea floor.

Cão went ashore at the river's mouth and erected a limestone pillar topped with an iron cross and inscribed with the royal coat of arms and the words: "in the year 6681 of the World and in that of 1482 since the birth of our Lord Jesus Christ, the most serene, the most excellent and potent prince, King João II of Portugal did order this land to be discovered and this pillar of stone to be erected by Diogo Cão, an esquire in his household."

The river where he had landed would be known by Europeans for most of the next 500 years as the Congo. It flowed into the sea at the northern end of a thriving African kingdom, an imperial federation of 2–3 million people. Ever since then, geographers have usually spelled the name of the river and the eventual European colony on its banks one way, and that of the people living around its mouth and their indigenous kingdom another.

The Kingdom of the Kongo was roughly 300 miles square, comprising territory that today lies in several countries. Its capital was the town of Mbanza Kongo—mbanza means "court"—on a commanding hilltop some 10 days' walk inland from the coast and today just on the Angolan side of the Angola–Congo border. In 1491, nine years and several voyages after Diogo Cão's landfall, an expedition of awed Portuguese priests and emissaries made this 10-day trek and set up housekeeping as permanent representatives of their country in the court of the Kongo king. Their arrival marked the beginning of the first sustained encounter between Europeans and a black African nation.

The Kingdom of the Kongo had been in place for at least a 100 years before the Portuguese arrived. Its monarch, the ManiKongo, was chosen by an assembly of clan leaders. Like his European counterparts, he sat on a throne, in his case made of wood inlaid with ivory. As symbols of royal authority, the ManiKongo carried a zebra-tail whip, had the skins and heads of baby animals suspended from his belt, and wore a small cap.

In the capital, the king dispensed justice, received homage, and reviewed his troops under a fig tree in a large public square. Whoever approached him had to do so on all fours. On pain of death, no one was allowed to watch him eat or drink. Before he did either, an attendant struck two iron poles together, and anyone in sight had to lie face down on the ground.

The ManiKongo who was then on the throne greeted the Portuguese warmly. His enthusiasm was probably due less to the Savior his unexpected guests told him about than to the help their magical fire-spouting weapons promised in suppressing a troublesome provincial rebellion. The Portuguese were glad to oblige.

The newcomers built churches and mission schools. Like many white evangelists who followed them, they were horrified by polygamy; they thought it was the spices in the African food that provoked the dreadful practice. But despite their contempt for Kongo culture, the Portuguese grudgingly recognized in the kingdom a sophisticated and well-developed state—the leading one on the west coast of central Africa. The ManiKongo appointed governors for each of some half-dozen provinces, and his rule was carried out by an elaborate civil service that included such specialized positions as mani vangu vangu or first judge in cases of adultery. Although they were without writing or the wheel, the inhabitants forged copper into jewelry and iron into weapons, and wove clothing out of fibers stripped from the leaves of the raffia palm tree. According to myth, the founder of the Kongo state was a blacksmith king, so ironwork was an occupation of the nobility. People cultivated yams, bananas, and other fruits and vegetables, and raised pigs, cattle, and goats. They measured distance by marching days and marked time by the lunar month and by a four-day week, the first day of which was a holiday. The king collected taxes from his subjects and, like many a ruler, controlled the currency supply: cowrie shells found on a coastal island under royal authority.

As in much of Africa, the kingdom had slavery. The nature of African slavery varied from one area to another and changed over time, but most slaves were people captured in warfare. Others had been criminals or debtors or were given away by their families as part of a dowry settlement. Like any system that gives some human beings total power over others, slavery in Africa could be vicious. Some Congo basin peoples sacrificed slaves on special occasions, such as the ratification of a treaty between chiefdoms; the slow death of an abandoned slave, his bones broken, symbolized the fate of anyone who violated the treaty. Some slaves might also be sacrificed to give a dead chief's soul some company on its journey into the next world.

In other ways, African slavery was more flexible and benign than the system Europeans would soon establish in the New World. Over a generation or two, slaves could often earn or be granted their freedom, and free people and slaves sometimes intermarried. Nonetheless, the fact that trading in human beings existed in any form turned out to be catastrophic for Africa, for when Europeans showed up, ready to buy endless shiploads of slaves, they found African chiefs willing to sell.

Soon enough, the slave-buyers came. They arrived in small numbers at first, but then in a flood unleashed by events across the Atlantic. In 1500, only nine years after the first Europeans arrived at Mbanza Kongo, a Portuguese expedition was blown off course and came upon Brazil. Within a few decades, the Western Hemisphere became a huge, lucrative, nearly insatiable market for African slaves. They were put to work by the millions in Brazil's mines and on its coffee plantations as well as on the Caribbean islands where other European powers quickly began using the lush, fertile land to grow sugar.

In the Kingdom of the Kongo, the Portuguese forgot the search for Prester John. Slaving fever seized them. Men sent out from Lisbon to be masons or teachers at Mbanza Kongo soon made far more money by herding convoys of chained Africans to the coast and selling them to the captains of slave-carrying caravels.

The lust for slave profits engulfed even some of the priests, who abandoned their preaching, took black women as concubines, kept slaves themselves, and sold their students and converts into slavery. The priests who strayed from the fold stuck to their faith in one way; however, after the Reformation, they tried to ensure that none of their human goods ended up in Protestant hands. It was surely not right, said one, "for persons baptized in the Catholic church to be sold to peoples who are enemies of their faith."

A village near Diogo Cão's stone pillar on the south shore of the Congo River estuary became a slave port, from which more than 5,000 slaves a year were being shipped across the Atlantic by the 1530s. By the next century, 15,000 slaves a year were exported from the Kingdom of the Kongo as a whole. Traders kept careful records of their booty. One surviving inventory from this region lists "68 head" of slaves by name, physical defects, and cash value, starting with the men, who were worth the most money, and ending with: "child, name unknown as she is dying and cannot speak, male without value, and a small girl Callenbo, no value because she is dying; one small girl Cantunbe, no value because she is dying."

Many of the slaves shipped to the Americas from the great river's mouth came from the Kingdom of the Kongo itself; many others were captured by African slave-dealers who ranged more than 700 miles into the interior, buying slaves from local chiefs and headmen. Forced-marched to the coast, their necks locked into wooden yokes, the slaves were rarely given enough food, and because caravans usually traveled in the dry season, they often drank stagnant water. The trails to the slave ports were soon strewn with bleaching bones.

Once they were properly baptized, clothed in leftover burlap cargo wrappings, and chained together in ships' holds, most slaves from this region were sent to Brazil, the nearest part of the New World. Starting in the 1,600s, however, a growing demand tempted many ship captains to make the longer voyage to the British colonies in North America. Roughly one of every four slaves imported to work the cotton and tobacco plantations of the American South began his or her journey across the Atlantic from equatorial Africa, including the Kongo kingdom. The KiKongo language, spoken around the Congo River's mouth, is one of the African tongues whose traces linguists have found in the Gullah dialect spoken by black Americans today on the coastal islands of South Carolina and Georgia.

...

When the Atlantic slave trade began decimating the Kongo, that nation was under the reign of a ManiKongo named Nzinga Mbemba Affonso who had gained the throne in 1506 and ruled as Affonso I for nearly 40 years. Affonso's life spanned a crucial period. When he was born, no one in the kingdom knew that Europeans existed. When he died, his entire realm was threatened by the slave-selling fever they had caused. He was a man of tragic self-awareness, and he left his mark. Some 300 years later, a missionary said, "A native of the Kongo knows the name of three kings: that of the present one, that of his predecessor, and that of Affonso."

He was a provincial chief in his early 30s when the Portuguese first arrived at Mbanza Kongo, in 1491. A convert to Christianity, he took on the name Affonso and some Portuguese advisers and studied for 10 years with the priests at Mbanza Kongo. One wrote to the king of Portugal that Affonso "knows better than us the prophets, the Gospel of our Savior Jesus Christ, all the lives of the saints and all that has to do with our holy mother Church. If Your Highness saw him, You would be astonished. He speaks so well and with such assurance that it always seems to me that the Holy Spirit speaks through his mouth. My Lord, he does nothing but study; many times he falls asleep over his books and many times he forgets to eat or drink because he is speaking of our Savior." It is hard to tell how much of this glowing portrait was inspired by the priest's attempt to impress the Portuguese king and how much by Affonso's attempt to impress the priest.

In the language of a later age, King Affonso I was a modernizer. He urgently tried to acquire European learning, weapons, and goods in order to strengthen his rule and fortify it against the destabilizing force of the white arrival. Having noticed the Portuguese appetite for copper, for example, he traded it for European products that would help him buy the submission of outlying provinces. Clearly a man of unusual intelligence, Affonso tried to do something as difficult in his time as in ours: to be a selective modernizer. He was an enthusiast for the church, for the written word, for European medicine, and for woodworking, masonry, and other skills to be learned from Portuguese craftsmen. But when his fellow king in Lisbon sent an envoy to urge the adoption of Portugal's legal code and court protocol, Affonso wasn't interested. And he tried hard to keep out prospectors, fearing total takeover of his land if Europeans found the gold and silver they coveted.

Because virtually everything we know about this part of Africa for the next several hundred years comes to us from its white conquerors, King Affonso I provides something rare and valuable: an African voice. Indeed, his has one of the very few central African voices that we can hear at all before the twentieth century. He used his fluency in Portuguese to dictate a remarkable series of letters to two successive Portuguese kings, the first known documents composed by a black African in any European language. Several dozen of the letters survive, above his signature, with its regal flourish of double underlings. Their tone is the formal one of monarch to monarch, usually beginning "Most high and powerful prince and king my brother. . . ." But we can hear not just a king speaking; we hear a human being, one who is aghast to see his people taken away in ever greater numbers on slave ships.

Affonso was no abolitionist. Like most African rulers of his time and later, he owned slaves, and at least once he sent some as a present to his "brother" king in Lisbon, along with leopard skins, parrots, and copper anklets. But this traditional exchange of gifts among kings seemed greatly different to Affonso from having tens of thousands of his previously free subjects taken across the sea in chains. Listen to him as he writes King João III of Portugal in 1526:

> Each day the traders are kidnapping our people—children of this country, sons of our nobles and vassals, even people of our own family. . . . This corruption and depravity are so widespread that our land is entirely depopulated. . . . We need in this kingdom only priests and schoolteachers, and no merchandise, unless it is wine and flour for Mass. . . . It is our wish that this kingdom not be a place for the trade or transport of slaves.

Later the same year:

> Many of our subjects eagerly lust after Portuguese merchandise that your subjects have brought into our domains. To satisfy this inordinate appetite, they seize many of our black free subjects. . . . They sell them . . . after having taken these prisoners [to the coast] secretly or at night. . . . As soon as the captives are in the hands of white men they are branded with a red-hot iron.

Again and again Affonso speaks about the twin themes of the slave trade and the alluring array of cloth, tools, jewelry, and other knickknacks that the Portuguese traders used to buy their human cargoes:

> These goods exert such a great attraction over simple and ignorant people that they believe in them and forget their belief in God. . . . My Lord, a monstrous greed pushes our subjects, even Christians, to seize members of their own families, and of ours, to do business by selling them as captives.

While begging the Portuguese king to send him teachers, pharmacists, and doctors instead of traders, Affonso admits that the flood of material goods threatened his authority. His people "can now procure, in much greater quantity than we can, the things we formerly used to keep them obedient to us and content." Affonso's lament was prescient; this was not the last time that lust for Europe's great cornucopia of goods undermined traditional ways of life elsewhere.

The Portuguese kings showed no sympathy. King João III replied: "You . . . tell me that you want no slave-trading in your domains, because this trade is depopulating your country. . . . The Portuguese there, on the contrary, tell me how vast the Congo is, and how it is so thickly populated that it seems as if no slave has ever left."

Affonso pleaded with his fellow sovereigns as one Christian with another, complete with the prejudices of the day. Of the priests turned slave-traders, he wrote:

> In this kingdom, faith is as fragile as glass because of the bad examples of the men who come to teach here, because the lusts of the world and lure of wealth have turned them away from the truth. Just as the Jews crucified the Son of God because of covetousness, my brother, so today He is again crucified.

Several times Affonso sent his appeals for an end to the slave trade directly to the Pope in Rome, but the Portuguese detained his emissaries to the Vatican as they stepped off the boat in Lisbon.

Affonso's despair reached its depth in 1539, near the end of his life, when he heard that 10 of his young nephews, grandsons, and other relatives who had been sent to Portugal for a religious education had disappeared en route. "We don't know whether they are dead or alive," he wrote in desperation, "nor how they might have died, nor what news we can give of them to their fathers and mothers." We can imagine the king's horror at being unable to guarantee the safety even of his own family.

Portuguese traders and sea captains along the long route back to Europe sidetracked many a cargo between the Kongo kingdom and Lisbon; these youngsters, it turned out, ended up in Brazil as slaves.

His hatred for the overseas slave trade and his vigilance against its erosion of his authority won Affonso the enmity of some of the Portuguese merchants living in his capital. A group of eight made an attempt on his life as he was attending Mass on Easter Sunday in 1540. He escaped with only a bullet hole in the fringe of his royal robe, but one of his nobles was killed and two others wounded.

After Affonso's death, the power of the Kongo state gradually diminished as provincial and village chiefs, themselves growing rich on slave sales, no longer gave much allegiance to the court at Mbanza Kongo. By the end of the 1500s, other European countries had joined in the slave trade; British, French, and Dutch vessels roamed the African coast, looking for human cargo. In 1665, the army of the weakened Kingdom of the Kongo fought a battle with the Portuguese. It was defeated, and the ManiKongo was beheaded. Internal strife further depleted the kingdom, whose territory was all taken over by European colonies by the late 1800s.

...

Except for Affonso's letters, the written record of these times still shows them entirely through white men's eyes. How did the Europeans, beginning with Diogo Cão and his three ships with faded red crosses on their sails, appear to the people living at the great river's mouth? To see with their eyes, we must turn to the myths and legends that have filtered down over the centuries. At first, Africans apparently saw the white sailors not as men but as vumbi—ancestral ghosts—since the Kongo people believed that a person's skin changed to the color of chalk when he passed into the land of the dead. And it was obvious that this was where these menacing white vumbi had come from, for people on the shore saw first the tips of an approaching ship's masts, then its superstructure, then its hull. Clearly the ship had carried its passengers up from their homes beneath the surface of the earth. Here is how the Portuguese arrival was recounted by Mukunzo Kioko, a twentieth-century oral historian of the Pende people:

> Our fathers were living comfortably. . . . They had cattle and crops; they had salt marshes and banana trees.
>
> Suddenly they saw a big boat rising out of the great ocean. This boat had wings all of white, sparkling like knives.
>
> White men came out of the water and spoke words which no one understood.
>
> Our ancestors took fright; they said that these were vumbi, spirits returned from the dead.
>
> They pushed them back into the ocean with volleys of arrows. But the vumbi spat fire with a noise of thunder. Many men were killed. Our ancestors fled.
>
> The chiefs and wise men said that these vumbi were the former possessors of the land. . . .
>
> From that time to our days now, the whites have brought us nothing but wars and miseries.

The trans-Atlantic slave trade seemed further confirmation that Europeans had come from the land of the dead, for after they took their shiploads of slaves out to sea, the captives never returned. Just as Europeans would be long obsessed with African cannibalism, so Africans imagined Europeans practicing the same thing. The whites were thought to turn their captives' flesh into salt meat, their brains into cheese, and their blood into the red wine Europeans drank. African bones were burned, and the gray ash became gunpowder. The huge, smoking copper cooking kettles that could be seen on sailing vessels were, it was believed, where all these deadly transformations began. The death tolls on the packed slave ships that sailed west from the Congo coast rose higher still when some slaves refused to eat the food they were given, believing that they would be eating those who had sailed before them.

As the years passed, new myths arose to explain the mysterious objects the strangers brought from the land of the dead. A nineteenth-century missionary recorded, for example, an African explanation of what happened when captains descended into the holds of their ships to fetch trading goods like cloth. The Africans believed that these goods came not from the ship itself but from a hole that led into the ocean. Sea sprites weave this cloth in an "oceanic factory, and, whenever we need cloth, the captain . . . goes to this hole and rings a bell." The sea sprites hand him up their cloth, and the captain "then throws in, as payment, a few dead bodies of black people he has bought from those bad native traders who have bewitched their people and sold them to the white men." The myth was not so far from reality. For what was slavery in the American South, after all, but a system for transforming the labor of black bodies, via cotton plantations, into cloth?

Critical Thinking

1. How was African slavery similar but also different from that of the Europeans?
2. Why was the preexisting African form of slavery ultimately catastrophic for Africa?
3. How was the African myth about European slavery not so far from the truth?

Internet References

Atlantic Slave Trade

https://en.wikipedia.org/wiki/Atlantic_slave_trade

Atrocities in the Congo Free State

https://en.wikipedia.org/wiki/Atrocities_in_the_Congo_Free_State

International Slavery Museum

http://www.liverpoolmuseums.org.uk/ism/slavery/

Article

Prepared by: Elvio Angeloni

The Price of Progress

JOHN BODLEY

Learning Outcomes

After reading this article, you will be able to:

- Discuss "economic development" as an ethnocentric Western concept.
- Determine if wealth and power are distributed fairly across the world.

In aiming at progress . . . you must let no one suffer by too drastic a measure, nor pay too high a price in upheaval and devastation, for your innovation.

Maunier, 1949: 725

Until recently, government planners have always considered economic development and progress beneficial goals that all societies should want to strive toward. The social advantage of progress—as defined in terms of increased incomes, higher standards of living, greater security, and better health—are thought to be positive, *universal* goods, to be obtained at any price. Although one may argue that tribal peoples must sacrifice their traditional cultures to obtain these benefits, government planners generally feel that this is a small price to pay for such obvious advantages.

In earlier chapters [in *Victims of Progress,* 3rd ed.], evidence was presented to demonstrate that autonomous tribal peoples have not *chosen* progress to enjoy its advantages, but that governments have *pushed* progress upon them to obtain tribal resources, not primarily to share with the tribal peoples the benefits of progress. It has also been shown that the price of forcing progress on unwilling recipients has involved the deaths of millions of tribal people, as well as their loss of land, political sovereignty, and the right to follow their own life style. This chapter does not attempt to further summarize that aspect of the cost of progress, but instead analyzes the specific effects of the participation of tribal peoples in the world-market economy. In direct opposition to the usual interpretation, it is argued here that the benefits of progress are often both illusory and detrimental to tribal peoples when they have not been allowed to control their own resources and define their relationship to the market economy.

Progress and the Quality of Life

One of the primary difficulties in assessing the benefits of progress and economic development for any culture is that of establishing a meaningful measure of both benefit and detriment. It is widely recognized that *standard of living,* which is the most frequently used measure of progress, is an intrinsically ethnocentric concept relying heavily upon indicators that lack universal cultural relevance. Such factors as GNP, per capita income, capital formation, employment rates, literacy, formal education, consumption of manufactured goods, number of doctors and hospital beds per thousand persons, and the amount of money spent on government welfare and health programs may be irrelevant measures of actual *quality* of life for autonomous or even semiautonomous tribal cultures. In its 1954 report, the Trust Territory government indicated that since the Micronesian population was still largely satisfying its own needs within a cashless subsistence economy, "Money income is not a significant measure of living standards, production, or well-being in this area" (TTR, 1953: 44). Unfortunately, within a short time the government began to rely on an enumeration of certain imported consumer goods as indicators of a higher standard of living in the islands, even though many tradition-oriented islanders felt that these new goods symbolized a lowering of the quality of life.

A more useful measure of the benefits of progress might be based on a formula for evaluating cultures devised by Goldschmidt (1952: 135). According to these less ethnocentric criteria, the important question to ask is: Does progress or economic development increase or decrease a given culture's ability to satisfy the physical and psychological needs of its population, or its stability? This question is a far more direct measure of quality of life than are the standard economic correlates of development, and it is universally relevant. Specific indication of this *standard* of living could be found for any society in the nutritional status and general physical and mental health of its population, the incidence of crime and delinquency, the demographic structure, family stability, and the society's relationship to its natural resource base. A society with high rates of malnutrition and crime, and one degrading its natural environment to the extent of threatening its continued existence, might be described as at a lower standard of living than is another society where these problems did not exist.

Careful examination of the data, which compare, on these specific points, the former condition of self-sufficient tribal peoples with their condition following their incorporation into the world-market economy, leads to the conclusion that their standard of living is *lowered,* not raised, by economic progress—and often to a dramatic degree. This is perhaps the most outstanding and inescapable fact to emerge from the years of research that anthropologists have devoted to the study of culture change and modernization. Despite the best intentions of those who have promoted change and improvement, all too often the results have been poverty, longer working hours, and much greater physical exertion, poor health, social disorder, discontent, discrimination, overpopulation, and environmental deterioration—combined with the destruction of the traditional culture.

Diseases of Development

> *Perhaps it would be useful for public health specialists to start talking about a new category of diseases. . . . Such diseases could be called the "diseases of development" and would consist of those pathological conditions which are based on the usually unanticipated consequences of the implementation of developmental schemes.*
>
> Hughes & Hunter, 1972: 93

Economic development increases the disease rate of affected peoples in at least three ways. First, to the extent that development is successful, it makes developed populations suddenly become vulnerable to all of the diseases suffered almost exclusively by "advanced" peoples. Among these are diabetes, obesity, hypertension, and a variety of circulatory problems. Second, development disturbs traditional environmental balances and may dramatically increase certain bacterial and parasite diseases. Finally, when development goals prove unattainable, an assortment of poverty diseases may appear in association with the crowded conditions of urban slums and the general breakdown in traditional socioeconomic systems.

Outstanding examples of the first situation can be seen in the Pacific, where some of the most successfully developed native peoples are found. In Micronesia, where development has progressed more rapidly than perhaps anywhere else, between 1958 and 1972 the population doubled, but the number of patients treated for heart disease in the local hospitals nearly tripled, mental disorder increased eightfold, and by 1972 hypertension and nutritional deficiencies began to make significant appearances for the first time (TTR, 1959, 1973, statistical tables).

Although some critics argue that the Micronesian figures simply represent better health monitoring due to economic progress, rigorously controlled data from Polynesia show a similar trend. The progressive acquisition of modern degenerative diseases was documented by an eight-member team of New Zealand medical specialists, anthropologists, and nutritionists, whose research was funded by the Medical Research Council of New Zealand and the World Health Organization. These researchers investigated the health status of a genetically related population at various points along a continuum of increasing cash income, modernizing diet, and urbanization. The extremes on this acculturation continuum were represented by the relatively traditional Pukapukans of the Cook Islands and the essentially Europeanized New Zealand Maori, while the busily developing Rarotongans, also of the Cook Islands, occupied the intermediate position. In 1971, after eight years of work, the team's preliminary findings were summarized by Dr. Ian Prior, cardiologist and leader of the research, as follows:

> *We are beginning to observe that the more an islander takes on the ways of the West, the more prone he is to succumb to our degenerative diseases. In fact, it does not seem too much to say our evidence now shows that the farther the Pacific natives move from the quiet, carefree life of their ancestors, the closer they come to gout, diabetes, atherosclerosis, obesity, and hypertension.*
>
> Prior, 1971: 2

In Pukapuka, where progress was limited by the island's small size and its isolated location some 480 kilometers from the nearest port, the annual per capita income was only about thirty-six dollars and the economy remained essentially at a subsistence level. Resources were limited and the area was visited by trading ships only three or four times a year; thus, there was little opportunity for intensive economic development. Predictably, the population of Pukapuka was characterized by relatively low levels of imported sugar and salt intake, and a presumably related low level of heart disease, high blood pressure, and diabetes. In Rarotonga, where economic success was introducing town life, imported food, and motorcycles, sugar and salt intakes nearly tripled, high blood pressure increased approximately ninefold, diabetes two- to threefold, and heart disease doubled for men and more than quadrupled for women, while the number of grossly obese women increased more than tenfold. Among the New Zealand Maori, sugar intake was nearly eight times that of the Pukapukans, gout in men was nearly double its rate on Pukapuka, and diabetes in men was more than fivefold higher, while heart disease in women had increased more than sixfold. The Maori were, in fact, dying of "European" diseases at a greater rate than was the average New Zealand European.

Government development policies designed to bring about changes in local hydrology, vegetation, and settlement patterns and to increase population mobility, and even programs aimed at reducing certain diseases, have frequently led to dramatic increases in disease rates because of the unforeseen effects of disturbing the preexisting order. Hughes and Hunter (1972) published an excellent survey of cases in which development led directly to increased disease rates in Africa. They concluded that hasty development intervention in relatively balanced local cultures and environments resulted in "a drastic deterioration in the social and economic conditions of life."

Traditional populations in general have presumably learned to live with the endemic pathogens of their environments, and in some cases they have evolved genetic adaptations to specific diseases, such as the sickle-cell trait, which provided an immunity to malaria. Unfortunately, however, outside intervention has entirely changed this picture. In the late 1960s, sleeping sickness suddenly increased in many areas of Africa and even spread to areas where it did not formerly occur, due to the building of new roads and migratory labor, both of which caused increased population movement. Large-scale relocation schemes, such as the Zande Scheme, had disastrous results when natives were moved from their traditional disease-free refuges into infected areas. Dams and irrigation developments inadvertently created ideal conditions for the rapid proliferation of snails carrying schistosomiasis (a liver fluke disease), and major epidemics suddenly occurred in areas where this disease had never before been a problem. DDT spraying programs have been temporarily successful in controlling malaria, but there is often a rebound effect that increases the problem when spraying is discontinued, and the malarial mosquitoes are continually evolving resistant strains.

Urbanization is one of the prime measures of development, but it is a mixed blessing for most former tribal peoples. Urban health standards are abysmally poor and generally worse than in rural areas for the detribalized individuals who have crowded into the towns and cities throughout Africa, Asia, and Latin America seeking wage employment out of new economic necessity. Infectious diseases related to crowding and poor sanitation are rampant in urban centers, while greatly increased stress and poor nutrition aggravate a variety of other health problems. Malnutrition and other diet-related conditions are, in fact, one of the characteristic hazards of progress faced by tribal peoples and are discussed in the following sections.

The Hazards of Dietary Change

The traditional diets of tribal peoples are admirably adapted to their nutritional needs and available food resources. Even though these diets may seem bizarre, absurd, and unpalatable to outsiders, they are unlikely to be improved by drastic modifications. Given the delicate balances and complexities involved in any subsistence system, change always involves risks, but for tribal people the effects of dietary change have been catastrophic.

Under normal conditions, food habits are remarkably resistant to change, and indeed people are unlikely to abandon their traditional diets voluntarily in favor of dependence on difficult-to-obtain exotic imports. In some cases it is true that imported foods may be identified with powerful outsiders and are therefore sought as symbols of greater prestige. This may lead to such absurdities as Amazonian Indians choosing to consume imported canned tunafish when abundant high-quality fish is available in their own rivers. Another example of this situation occurs in tribes where mothers prefer to feed their infants expensive nutritionally inadequate canned milk from unsanitary, but *high status,* baby bottles. The high status of these items is often promoted by clever traders and clever advertising campaigns.

Aside from these apparently voluntary changes, it appears that more often dietary changes are forced upon unwilling tribal peoples by circumstances beyond their control. In some areas, new food crops have been introduced by government decree, or as a consequence of forced relocation or other policies designed to end hunting, pastoralism, or shifting cultivation. Food habits have also been modified by massive disruption of the natural environment by outsiders—as when sheepherders transformed the Australian Aborigines' foraging territory or when European invaders destroyed the bison herds that were the primary element in the Plains Indians' subsistence patterns. Perhaps the most frequent cause of diet change occurs when formerly self-sufficient peoples find that wage labor, cash cropping, and other economic development activities that feed tribal resources into the world-market economy must inevitably divert time and energy away from the production of subsistence foods. Many developing peoples suddenly discover that, like it or not, they are unable to secure traditional foods and must spend their newly acquired cash on costly, and often nutritionally inferior, manufactured foods.

Overall, the available data seem to indicate that the dietary changes that are linked to involvement in the world-market economy have tended to *lower* rather than raise the nutritional levels of the affected tribal peoples. Specifically, the vitamin, mineral, and protein components of their diets are often drastically reduced and replaced by enormous increases in starch and carbohydrates, often in the form of white flour and refined sugar.

Any deterioration in the quality of a given population's diet is almost certain to be reflected in an increase in deficiency diseases and a general decline in health status. Indeed, as tribal peoples have shifted to a diet based on imported manufactured or processed foods, there has been a dramatic rise in malnutrition, a massive increase in dental problems, and a variety of other nutritional-related disorders. Nutritional physiology is so complex that even well-meaning dietary changes have had tragic consequences. In many areas of Southeast Asia, government-sponsored protein supplementation programs supplying milk to protein-deficient populations caused unexpected health problems and increased mortality. Officials failed to anticipate that in cultures where adults do not normally drink milk, the enzymes needed to digest it are no longer produced and milk *intolerance* results (Davis & Bolin, 1972). In Brazil, a similar milk distribution program caused an epidemic of permanent blindness by aggravating a preexisting vitamin A deficiency (Bunce, 1972).

Teeth and Progress

> *There is nothing new in the observation that savages, or peoples living under primitive conditions, have, in general, excellent teeth. . . . Nor is it news that most civilized populations possess wretched teeth which begin to decay almost before they have erupted completely, and that dental caries is likely to be accompanied by periodontal disease with further reaching complications.*
>
> Hooton, 1945: xviii

Anthropologists have long recognized that undisturbed tribal peoples are often in excellent physical condition. And it has often been noted specifically that dental caries and the other dental abnormalities that plague industrialized societies are absent or rare among tribal peoples who have retained their traditional diets. The fact that tribal food habits may contribute to the development of sound teeth, whereas modernized diets may do just the opposite, was illustrated as long ago as 1894 in an article in the *Journal of the Royal Anthropological Institute* that described the results of a comparison between the teeth of ten Sioux Indians who were examined when they came to London as members of Buffalo Bill's Wild West Show and were found to be completely free of caries and in possession of all their teeth, even though half of the group were over thirty-nine years of age. Londoners' teeth were conspicuous for both their caries and their steady reduction in number with advancing age. The difference was attributed primarily to the wear and polishing caused by the traditional Indian diet of coarse food and the fact that they chewed their food longer, encouraged by the absence of tableware.

One of the most remarkable studies of the dental conditions of tribal peoples and the impact of dietary change was conducted in the 1930s by Weston Price (1945), an American dentist who was interested in determining what caused normal, healthy teeth. Between 1931 and 1936, Price systematically explored tribal areas throughout the world to locate and examine the most isolated peoples who were still living on traditional foods. His fieldwork covered Alaska, the Canadian Yukon, Hudson Bay, Vancouver Island, Florida, the Andes, the Amazon, Samoa, Tahiti, New Zealand, Australia, New Caledonia, Fiji, the Torres Strait, East Africa, and the Nile. The study demonstrated both the superior quality of aboriginal dentition and the devastation that occurs as modern diets are adopted. In nearly every area where traditional foods were still being eaten, Price found perfect teeth with normal dental arches and virtually no decay, whereas caries and abnormalities increased steadily as new diets were adopted. In many cases the change was sudden and striking. Among Eskimo groups subsisting entirely on traditional food he found caries totally absent, whereas in groups eating a considerable quantity of store-bought food approximately 20 percent of their teeth were decayed. This figure rose to more than 30 percent with Eskimo groups subsisting almost exclusively on purchased or government-supplied food, and reached an incredible 48 percent among the Vancouver Island Indians. Unfortunately for many of these people, modern dental treatment did not accompany the new food, and their suffering was appalling. The loss of teeth was, of course, bad enough in itself, and it certainly undermined the population's resistance to many new diseases, including tuberculosis. But new foods were also accompanied by crowded, misplaced teeth, gum diseases, distortion of the face, and pinching of the nasal cavity. Abnormalities in the dental arch appeared in the new generation following the change in diet, while caries appeared almost immediately even in adults.

Price reported that in many areas the affected peoples were conscious of their own physical deterioration. At a mission school in Africa, the principal asked him to explain to the native schoolchildren why they were not physically as strong as children who had had no contact with schools. On an island in the Torres Strait the natives knew exactly what was causing their problems and resisted—almost to the point of bloodshed—government efforts to establish a store that would make imported food available. The government prevailed, however, and Price was able to establish a relationship between the length of time the government store had been established and the increasing incidence of caries among a population that showed an almost 100 percent immunity to them before the store had been opened.

In New Zealand, the Maori, who in their aboriginal state are often considered to have been among the healthiest, most perfectly developed of people, were found to have "advanced" the furthest. According to Price:

> *Their modernization was demonstrated not only by the high incidence of dental caries but also by the fact that 90 percent of the adults and 100 percent of the children had abnormalities of the dental arches.*
>
> Price, 1945: 206

Malnutrition

Malnutrition, particularly in the form of protein deficiency, has become a critical problem for tribal peoples who must adopt new economic patterns. Population pressures, cash cropping, and government programs all have tended to encourage the replacement of traditional crops and other food sources that were rich in protein with substitutes, high in calories but low in protein. In Africa, for example, protein-rich staples such as millet and sorghum are being replaced systematically by high-yielding manioc and plantains, which have insignificant amounts of protein. The problem is increased for cash croppers and wage laborers whose earnings are too low and unpredictable to allow purchase of adequate amounts of protein. In some rural areas, agricultural laborers have been forced systematically to deprive nonproductive members (principally children) of their households of their minimal nutritional requirements to satisfy the need of the productive members. This process has been documented in northeastern Brazil following the introduction of large-scale sisal plantations (Gross & Underwood, 1971). In urban centers the difficulties of obtaining nutritionally adequate diets are even more serious for tribal immigrants, because costs are higher and poor quality foods are more tempting.

One of the most tragic, and largely overlooked, aspects of chronic malnutrition is that it can lead to abnormally undersized brain development and apparently irreversible brain damage; it has been associated with various forms of mental impairment or retardation. Malnutrition has been linked clinically with mental retardation in both Africa and Latin America (see, for example, Mönckeberg, 1968), and this appears to be a worldwide phenomenon with serious implications (Montagu, 1972).

Optimistic supporters of progress will surely say that all of these new health problems are being overstressed and that the introduction of hospitals, clinics, and the other modern health institutions will overcome or at least compensate for all of these difficulties. However, it appears that uncontrolled population growth and economic impoverishment probably will keep most of these benefits out of reach for many tribal peoples, and the intervention of modern medicine has at least partly contributed to the problem in the first place.

The generalization that civilization frequently has a broad negative impact on tribal health has found broad empirical support (see especially Kroeger & Barbira-Freedman [1982] on Amazonia; Reinhard [1976] on the Arctic; and Wirsing [1985] globally), but these conclusions have not gone unchallenged. Some critics argue that tribal health was often poor before modernization, and they point specifically to tribals' low life expectancy and high infant mortality rates. Demographic statistics on tribal populations are often problematic because precise data are scarce, but they do show a less favorable profile than that enjoyed by many industrial societies. However, it should be remembered that our present life expectancy is a recent phenomenon that has been very costly in terms of medical research and technological advances. Furthermore, the benefits of our health system are not enjoyed equally by all members of our society. High infant mortality could be viewed as a relatively inexpensive and egalitarian tribal public health program that offered the reasonable expectation of a healthy and productive life for those surviving to age fifteen.

Some critics also suggest that certain tribal populations, such as the New Guinea highlanders, were "stunted" by nutritional deficiencies created by tribal culture and are "improved" by "acculturation" and cash cropping (Dennett & Connell, 1988). Although this argument does suggest that the health question requires careful evaluation, it does not invalidate the empirical generalizations already established. Nutritional deficiencies undoubtedly occurred in densely populated zones in the central New Guinea highlands. However, the specific case cited above may not be widely representative of other tribal groups even in New Guinea, and it does not address the facts of outside intrusion or the inequities inherent in the contemporary development process.

Ecocide

> *"How is it," asked a herdsman . . . "how is it that these hills can no longer give pasture to my cattle? In my father's day they were green and cattle thrived there; today there is no grass and my cattle starve." As one looked one saw that what had once been a green hill had become a raw red rock.*
>
> Jones, 1934

Progress not only brings new threats to the health of tribal peoples, but it also imposes new strains on the ecosystems upon which they must depend for their ultimate survival. The introduction of new technology, increased consumption, lowered mortality, and the eradication of all traditional controls have combined to replace what for most tribal peoples was a relatively stable balance between population and natural resources, with a new system that is imbalanced. Economic development is forcing *ecocide* on peoples who were once careful stewards of their resources. There is already a trend toward widespread environmental deterioration in tribal areas, involving resource depletion, erosion, plant and animal extinction, and a disturbing series of other previously unforeseen changes.

After the initial depopulation suffered by most tribal peoples during their engulfment by frontiers of national expansion, most tribal populations began to experience rapid growth. Authorities generally attribute this growth to the introduction of modern medicine and new health measures and the termination of intertribal warfare, which lowered morality rates, as well as to new technology, which increased food production. Certainly all of these factors played a part, but merely lowering mortality rates would not have produced the rapid population growth that most tribal areas have experienced if traditional birth-spacing mechanisms had not been eliminated at the same time. Regardless of which factors were most important, it is clear that all of the natural and cultural checks on population growth have suddenly been pushed aside by culture change, while tribal lands have been steadily reduced and consumption levels have risen. In many tribal areas, environmental deterioration due to overuse of resources has set in, and in other areas such deterioration is imminent as resources continue to dwindle relative to the expanding population and increased use. Of course, population expansion by tribal peoples may have positive political consequences, because where tribals can retain or regain their status as local majorities they may be in a more favorable position to defend their resources against intruders.

Swidden systems and pastoralism, both highly successful economic systems under traditional conditions, have proved particularly vulnerable to increased population pressures and outside efforts to raise productivity beyond its natural limits. Research in Amazonia demonstrates that population pressures and related resource depletion can be created indirectly by official policies that restrict swidden peoples to smaller territories. Resource depletion itself can then become a powerful means of forcing tribal people into participating in the world-market economy—thus leading to further resource depletion. For example, Bodley and Benson (1979) showed how the Shipibo Indians in Peru were forced to further deplete their forest resources by cash cropping in the forest area to replace the resources that had been destroyed earlier by the intensive cash cropping necessitated by the narrow confines of their reserve. In this case, certain species of palm trees that had provided critical housing materials were destroyed by forest clearing and had to be replaced by costly purchased materials. Research by Gross (1979) and others showed similar processes at work among four tribal groups in central Brazil and demonstrated that the degree of market involvement increases directly with increases in resource depletion.

The settling of nomadic herders and the removal of prior controls on herd size have often led to serious overgrazing and erosion problems where these had not previously occurred. There are indications that the desertification problem in the Sahel region of Africa was aggravated by programs designed to settle nomads. The first sign of imbalance in a swidden system appears when the planting cycles are shortened to the point that garden plots are reused before sufficient forest regrowth can occur. If reclearing and planting continue in the same area, the natural patterns of forest succession may be disturbed irreversibly and the soil can be impaired permanently. An extensive tract of tropical rainforest in the lower Amazon of Brazil was reduced to a semiarid desert in just fifty years through such a process (Ackermann, 1964). The soils in the Azande area are also now seriously threatened with laterization and other problems as a result of the government-promoted cotton development scheme (McNeil, 1972).

The dangers of overdevelopment and the vulnerability of local resource systems have long been recognized by both anthropologists and tribal peoples themselves. But the pressures for change have been overwhelming. In 1948 the Maya villagers of Chan Kom complained to Redfield (1962) about the shortening of their swidden cycles, which they correctly attributed to increasing population pressures. Redfield told them, however, that they had no choice but to go "forward with technology" (Redfield, 1962: 178). In Assam, swidden cycles were shortened from an average of twelve years to only two or three within just twenty years, and anthropologists warned that the limits of swiddening would soon be reached (Burling, 1963: 311–312). In the Pacific, anthropologists warned of population pressures on limited resources as early as the 1930s (Keesing, 1941: 64–65). These warnings seemed fully justified, considering the fact that the crowded Tikopians were prompted by population pressures on their tiny island to suggest that infanticide be legalized. The warnings have been dramatically reinforced since then by the doubling of Micronesia's population in just the fourteen years between 1958 and 1972, from 70,600 to 114,645, while consumption levels have soared. By 1985 Micronesia's population had reached 162,321.

The environmental hazards of economic development and rapid population growth have become generally recognized only since worldwide concerns over environmental issues began in the early 1970s. Unfortunately, there is as yet little indication that the leaders of the new developing nations are sufficiently concerned with environmental limitations. On the contrary, governments are forcing tribal peoples into a self-reinforcing spiral of population growth and intensified resource exploitation, which may be stopped only by environmental disaster or the total impoverishment of the tribals.

The reality of ecocide certainly focuses attention on the fundamental contrasts between tribal and industrial systems in their use of natural resources, who controls them, and how they are managed. Tribal peoples are victimized because they control resources that outsiders demand. The resources exist because tribals managed them conservatively. However, as with the issue of the health consequences of detribalization, some anthropologists minimize the adaptive achievements of tribal groups and seem unwilling to concede that ecocide might be a consequence of cultural change. Critics attack an exaggerated "noble savage" image of tribals living in perfect harmony with nature and having no visible impact on their surroundings. They then show that tribals do in fact modify the environment, and they conclude that there is no significant difference between how tribals and industrial societies treat their environments. For example, Charles Wagley declared that Brazilian Indians such as the Tapirape

> *are not "natural men." They have human vices just as we do. . . . They do not live "in tune" with nature any more than I do; in fact, they can often be as destructive of their environment, within their limitations, as some civilized men. The Tapirape are not innocent or childlike in any way.*
>
> Wagley, 1977: 302

Anthropologist Terry Rambo demonstrated that the Semang of the Malaysian rain forests have a measurable impact on their environment. In his monograph *Primitive Polluters,* Rambo (1985) reported that the Semang live in smoke-filled houses. They sneeze and spread germs, breathe, and thus emit carbon dioxide. They clear small gardens, contributing "particulate matter" to the air and disturbing the local climate because cleared areas proved measurably warmer and drier than the shady forest. Rambo concluded that his research "demonstrates the essential functional similarity of the environmental interactions of primitive and civilized societies" (1985: 78) in contrast to a "noble savage" view (Bodley, 1983) which, according to Rambo (1985: 2), mistakenly "claims that traditional peoples almost always live in essential harmony with their environment."

This is surely a false issue. To stress, as I do, that tribals tend to manage their resources for sustained yield within relatively self-sufficient subsistence economies is not to make them either innocent children or natural men. Nor is it to deny that tribals "disrupt" their environment and may never be in absolute "balance" with nature.

The ecocide issue is perhaps most dramatically illustrated by two sets of satellite photos taken over the Brazilian rain forests of Rôndonia (Allard & McIntyre, 1988: 780–781). Photos taken in 1973, when Rôndonia was still a tribal domain, show virtually unbroken rain forest. The 1987 satellite photos, taken after just fifteen years of highway construction and "development" by outsiders, show more than 20 percent of the forest destroyed. The surviving Indians were being concentrated by FUNAI (Brazil's national Indian foundation) into what would soon become mere islands of forest in a ravaged landscape. It is irrelevant to quibble about whether tribals are noble, childlike, or innocent, or about the precise meaning of balance with nature, carrying capacity, or adaptation, to recognize that for the past 200 years rapid environmental deterioration on an unprecedented global scale has followed the wresting of control of vast areas of the world from tribal groups by resource-hungry industrial societies.

Deprivation and Discrimination

> *Contact with European culture has given them a knowledge of great wealth, opportunity and privilege, but only very limited avenues by which to acquire these things.*
>
> Crocombe, 1968

Unwittingly, tribal peoples have had the burden of perpetual relative deprivation thrust upon them by acceptance—either by themselves or by the governments administering them—of the standards of socioeconomic progress set for them by industrial civilizations. By comparison with the material wealth of industrial societies, tribal societies become, by definition, impoverished. They are then forced to transform their cultures and work to achieve what many economists now acknowledge to be unattainable goals. Even though in many cases the modest GNP goals set by development planners for the developing nations during the "development decade" of the 1960s were often met, the results were hardly noticeable for most of the tribal people involved. Population growth, environmental limitations, inequitable distribution of wealth, and the continued rapid growth of the industrialized nations have all meant that both the absolute and the relative gap between the rich and poor in the world is steadily widening. The prospect that tribal peoples will actually be able to attain the levels of resource consumption to which they are being encouraged to aspire is remote indeed except for those few groups who have retained effective control over strategic mineral resources.

Tribal peoples feel deprivation not only when the economic goals they have been encouraged to seek fail to materialize, but also when they discover that they are powerless, second-class citizens who are discriminated against and exploited by the dominant society. At the same time, they are denied the satisfactions of their traditional cultures, because these have been sacrificed in the process of modernization. Under the impact of major economic change family life is disrupted, traditional social controls are often lost, and many indicators of social anomie such as alcoholism, crime, delinquency, suicide, emotional disorders, and despair may increase. The inevitable frustration resulting from this continual deprivation finds expression in the cargo cults, revitalization movements, and a variety of other political and religious movements that have been widespread among tribal peoples following their disruption by industrial civilization.

References

Ackermann, F. L. 1964. *Geologia e Fisiografia da Região Bragantina, Estado do Pará.* Manaus, Brazil: Conselho Nacional de Pesquisas, Instituto Nacional de Pesquisas da Amazonia.

Allard, William Albert, and Loren McIntyre. 1988. Rondônia's settlers invade Brazil's imperiled rain forest. *National Geographic* 174(6):772–799.

Bodley, John H. 1970. *Campa Socio-Economic Adaptation.* Ann Arbor: University Microfilms.

———. 1983. *Der Weg der Zerstörung: Stammesvölker und die industrielle Zivilization.* Munich: Trickster-Verlag. (Translation of *Victims of Progress.*)

Bodley, John H., and Foley C. Benson. 1979. Cultural ecology of Amazonian palms. *Reports of Investigations,* no. 56. Pullman: Laboratory of Anthropology, Washington State University.

Bunce, George E. 1972. Aggravation of vitamin A deficiency following distribution of non-fortified skim milk: An example of nutrient interaction. In *The Careless Technology: Ecology and International Development,* ed. M. T. Farvar and John P. Milton, pp. 53–60. Garden City, N.Y.: Natural History Press.

Burling, Robbins. 1963. *Rengsanggri: Family and Kinship in a Garo Village.* Philadelphia: University of Pennsylvania Press.

Davis, A. E., and T. D. Bolin. 1972. Lactose intolerance in Southeast Asia. In *The Careless Technology: Ecology and International Development,* ed. M. T. Farvar and John P. Milton, pp. 61–68. Garden City, N.Y.: Natural History Press.

Dennett, Glenn, and John Connell. 1988. Acculturation and health in the highlands of Papua New Guinea. *Current Anthropology* 29(2):273–299.

Goldschmidt, Walter R. 1972. The interrelations between cultural factors and the acquisition of new technical skills. In *The Progress of Underdeveloped Areas,* ed. Bert F. Hoselitz, pp. 135–151. Chicago: University of Chicago Press.

Gross, Daniel R., et al. 1979. Ecology and acculturation among native peoples of Central Brazil. *Science* 206(4422):1043–1050.

Hughes, Charles C., and John M. Hunter. 1972. The role of technological development in promoting disease in Africa. In *The Careless Technology: Ecology and International Development,* ed. M. T. Farvar and John P. Milton, pp. 69–101. Garden City, N.Y.: Natural History Press.

Keesing, Felix M. 1941. *The South Seas in the Modern World.* Institute of Pacific Relations International Research Series. New York: John Day.

Kroeger, Axel, and François Barbira-Freedman. 1982. *Culture Change and Health: The Case of South American Rainforest Indians.* Frankfurt am Main: Verlag Peter Lang. (Reprinted in Bodley, 1988a:221–236.)

McNeil, Mary. 1972. Lateritic soils in distinct tropical environments: Southern Sudan and Brazil. In *The Careless Technology: Ecology and International Development,* ed. M. T. Farvar and John P. Milton, pp. 591–608. Garden City, N.Y.: Natural History Press.

Mönckeberg, F. 1968. Mental retardation from malnutrition. *Journal of the American Medical Association* 206:30–31.

Montagu, Ashley. 1972. Sociogenic brain damage. *American Anthropologist* 74(5):1045–1061.

Rambo, A. Terry. 1985. *Primitive Polluters: Semang Impact on the Malaysian Tropical Rain Forest Ecosystem.* Anthropological Papers no. 76, Museum of Anthropology, University of Michigan.

Redfield, Robert. 1953. *The Primitive World and Its Transformations.* Ithaca, N.Y.: Cornell University Press.

———. 1962. *A Village That Chose Progress: Chan Kom Revisited.* Chicago: University of Chicago Press, Phoenix Books.

Smith, Wilberforce. 1894. The teeth of ten Sioux Indians. *Journal of the Royal Anthropological Institute* 24:109–116.

TTR: *See under* United States.

United States, Department of the Interior, Office of Territories. 1953. *Report on the Administration of the Trust Territory of the Pacific Islands* (by the United States to the United Nations) for the Period July 1, 1951 to June 30, 1952.

———. 1954. *Annual Report, High Commissioner of the Trust Territory of the Pacific Islands to the Secretary of the Interior* (for 1953).

United States, Department of State. 1955. *Seventh Annual Report to the United Nations on the Administration of the Trust Territory of the Pacific Islands* (July 1, 1953 to June 30, 1954).

———. 1959. *Eleventh Annual Report to the United Nations on the Administration of the Trust Territory of the Pacific Islands* (July 1, 1957 to June 30, 1958).

———. 1964. *Sixteenth Annual Report to the United Nations on the Administration of the Trust Territory of the Pacific Islands* (July 1, 1962 to June 30, 1963).

———. 1973. *Twenty-Fifth Annual Report to the United Nations on the Administration of the Trust Territory of the Pacific Islands* (July 1, 1971 to June 30, 1972).

Critical Thinking

1. Why is "standard of living" an intrinsically ethnocentric concept as a measure of progress? What is a more useful measure and why? What does a careful examination based upon the specific points show?
2. In what ways does economic development increase the disease rate of affected peoples?
3. How does the author answer critics who argue that such figures simply represent better health monitoring? List the examples cited.
4. Explain the effects of government policy on peoples' adaptations to local environmental conditions.
5. Describe the circumstances under which peoples' dietary habits have been changed as a result of outside influences. What has happened to nutritional levels and why?
6. To what was attributed the differences in dental health between the Sioux Indians of Buffalo Bill's Wild West Show and Londoners?
7. What did Weston Price find in his studies?
8. Describe the chain of events that goes from the adoption of new economic patterns to changes in the kinds of crops grown to low wages to nutritional deprivation (principally of children).
9. What is one of the most tragic, and largely overlooked, aspects of chronic malnutrition?
10. What are the prospects that modern health institutions will overcome these problems?
11. How does the author respond to critics who charge that tribal peoples have always had low life expectancies, high infant mortality rates, and nutritional deficiencies?
12. What factors have contributed to population growth?
13. What are the consequences for each of the following:
    - Official policy restricting swidden people to smaller territories?
    - Resource depletion forcing people to participate in the world-market economy?
    - The settling of nomadic herders and the removal of prior controls on herd size?
    - Shortening the planting cycles?
14. How does the reality of ecocide focus attention on the fundamental contrasts between tribal and industrial systems in their use of natural resources? Who controls such resources and how they are managed?
15. What do the critics of the "noble savage" image claim? How does the author respond?
16. In what respects do tribal peoples feel deprivation as a result of "modernization"?

Internet References

Association for Political and Legal Anthropology
www.aaanet.org/apla/index.htm

Human Rights and Humanitarian Assistance
www.etown.edu/vl/humrts.html

The Indigenous Rights Movement in the Pacific
www.inmotionmagazine.com/pacific.html

Murray Research Center
www.radcliffe.edu/murray_redirect/index.php

WWW Virtual Library: Indigenous Studies
www.cwis.org

Article

Prepared by: Elvio Angeloni

We Walk on Our Ancestors: The Sacredness of the Black Hills

LEONARD LITTLE FINGER

Learning Outcomes

After reading this article, you will be able to:

- Discuss the importance of the Black Hills to the Lakota.
- Describe the treaties and how and why they were broken.
- Understand the legal struggles over the Black Hills and their outcomes.
- Describe the ways in which the Black Hills have been desecrated in the eyes of the Lakota.

In 1883, my grandfather, Saste, was a child of seven years. With his parents, he traveled in a group into the Black Hills in South Dakota for a sacred prayer journey to Washun Niye, a site from which Mother Earth breathes. They were following a path that had been a journey for his people for thousands of years. In preparation for the ceremony, the women dried the hide of apte, or tatanka (buffalo), which was carried to this site for the sacred ceremony. The cannupa (sacred pipe) acknowledged apte by returning the hide to the world; upon completion of the prayers, the hide would be dropped into the hole. As my grandfather watched, Washun Niye carried the hide downward in a spiraling motion, soon to be enveloped into the darkness. The power of the sacred circle which has no ending was affirmed.

I heard this story in 1947, in Lakota, at the age of eight, seven years before he was to make his spirit journey—from which we all come as a spirit or soul. It took me many years to understand the importance of his story, because we must revisit anything of importance many times before we can fully understand its significance. When one finally understands, then begins the process of interpretation. The spiritual quest of truth, especially for Indigenous people, is in this process.

My grandfather and I are from a sub-band of the Teton, a member of the Nation of the Seven Council Fires. We are called the Mniconjou, or People Who Plant Near the Water. In the 1500s, one of our villages was the location of present day Rapid City along the streams of Mniluzahan Creek, or Rapid Creek, which is today's northern gateway to the Black Hills of South Dakota. Our family has had a spiritual relationship with this special land for over 500 years.

The Black Hills were recognized as the Black Hills because of the darkness from the distance. The term also referred to a container of meat; in those days people used a box made out of dried buffalo hide to carry spiritual tools, like the sacred pipe, or the various things that were used in prayers or to carry food. That's the term that was used for the Black Hills: they were a container for our spiritual need as well as our needs of food and water, whatever it is that allows survival.

A Legacy of Threats

The story of the Black Hills is an age-old conflict between imperialism and the understanding of their spiritual significance as a sacred site. The threats to our sacred lands began when the first two treaties were drawn up with the federal government. The first was in 1851 recognizing several tribes, including the People of the Seven Council Fires, and identified the territories of each tribe. In 1868 the Fort Laramie treaty designated an area that included the entire western half of South Dakota, with the eastern line marked by the Missouri River and a portion of North Dakota and Wyoming. We would not, as a nation, be recognized.

When gold was discovered in Montana, the trails leading to it came into the territory of the Sioux. In 1872, General Custer led a contingent of gold mining experts, theologists, and botanists into the Black Hills. Although just traces of gold were found in the streams, it was an indication that there was probably gold, veins of gold in the hills, so the US government sent two commissions to renegotiate the treaty. One of the articles stated that three-fourths of the male population had to agree to any amendments. Both commissions failed to achieve an agreement, so in 1874 Congress declared that treaties would no longer be used. Following this action (which nullified Article 6 of the US Constitution), more than 25,000 gold seekers came into the Black Hills over a very short period of time, essentially claiming that land. It's been estimated that during that time up until 2005, when the last gold mine was shut down, approximately 500 billion ounces, or $9 trillion worth, of gold were extracted.

Problems continued in 1888 when North and South Dakota were admitted into the union and the Sioux were forced onto reservations to become US citizens. In 1876 the Sioux had wiped out General Custer and the entire 7th Cavalry in Montana, becoming the only nation to ever defeat the United States in battle. That really marked us for violation, leading to the massacre at Wounded Knee in 1890. All of these things led to the people moving away from the Black Hills, away from the sacred sites for their spiritual journeys; we could no longer go back without the threat of being jailed or killed.

In the early 1920s the Sioux filed a complaint with the Indian Claims Commission alleging that the United States had illegally taken the land that had been designated to us by the treaties of 1851 and 1868. The claim entered the Supreme Court in 1962 and took nearly 20 years to settle, enduring as the longest court case in US history. On June 30,1980 the Supreme Court determined that the United States had indeed violated the treaty of the People of the Seven Council Fires: not just the Sioux, but the original title that we were known by. However, the federal government argued that it could not give back the land since it is occupied and includes the national monument of Mount Rushmore, a sculpture on a sacred site. The government offered compensation—for the value of the land in 1876, prior to its occupation and the gold that was extracted, including interest—of $350 million. Of course the People of the Seven Council Fires rejected that offer. The Black Hills is a sacred grandmother to us, filled with sacred power sites. How can one sell a sacred grandmother?

Now we have an opportunity to sit down in a unified way to discuss the Black Hills and the threat that is coming from ourselves as a people, as we have begun to travel the road of assimilation. Less and less people speak our native language, Lakota. Less and less adhere to the spiritual significance because of the introduction of Christianity to the reservations. One of my fears is that there is a day coming that the Bureau of Indian Affairs will sit down at a table with the offer and our people will accept the money. At that point, thousands and thousands of years of spiritual significance of the Black Hills will be left to the wayside because the new culture of the new people that have come onto the reservation will see the same meaning in the value of the money.

Our Place in History

Recently we were asked as elders to look at some aerial photos of the southern Black Hills. We looked at them as sacred circles, and in an aerial photo we saw the image of the big dipper. This is an image of what we are, the journey of the Black Hills, the sacred journey known as "seeking sacred goodness" and the pipe that is used, the cannupa. Today the UN Declaration on the Rights of Indigenous Peoples gives us the modern tools to stand up and declare our rights. We have come back to the table on the basis of what is recognized for Indigenous Peoples' rights and on the basis of what sacredness is. Our beliefs are substantiated by the image of the aerial rock formations in the sacred circle that were left by our ancestors thousands of years ago.

The desecration of the Black Hills is indicative of the violation of the sacredness of who we are as a people. The insides of Grandmother Earth are being taken; the atmosphere, the area that's there to protect us and all things is being destroyed. Earth is our grandmother, as animate as we all are, because she provides us with all of our needs to live. From the time of birth until now I look at that relationship as sacred. When our life ends here on Grandmother Earth, we become as one. This sacredness means that we walk on our ancestors. As Indigenous Peoples we are guided by the spiritualism of greater powers than we humans. We don't seek equality, we seek justice. This is who we are, and this is where we come from.

Critical Thinking

1. Why are the Black Hills sacred to the Lakota?
2. How have the Black Hills been desecrated, according to the Lakota?
3. What have been the legal claims set forth by the Lakota with respect to the Black Hills and what have been the results?

Internet References

Association for Political and Legal Anthropology
www.aaanet.org/apla/index.htm

Human Rights and Humanitarian Assistance
www.etown.edu/vl/humrts.html

Sioux Treaty of 1868—The U.S. National Archives and Records Administration
https://www.archives.gov/education/lessons/sioux-treaty/

LEONARD LITTLE FINGER is a respected Lakota elder and the founder-director of Sacred Hoop School, a Lakota language school in Ogalala, South Dakata.

Article

Prepared by: Elvio Angeloni

Green Grab, Red Light

Global intervention in tropical forests to fight climate change could sideline their most effective guardians.

FRED PEARCE

Learning Outcomes

After reading this article, you will be able to:

- Provide examples from around the world in which indigenous peoples are more protective of forests than are governments.
- Explain why deforestation rates in community-owned forests have been generally lower than in regions dominated by government-protected areas.

Satellite images of the Amazon rainforest are startling. Islands of green are surrounded by brown areas of land cleared for farming. In places, the brown advances, year by year. But in others, the forest holds firm. Why the difference? Mostly, the surviving green areas belong to local tribes.

Brazil's Kayapo, for instance, control 10.6 million hectares along the Xingu river in the south-eastern Amazon, an area often called the "arc of deforestation." They held back the invasion that engulfed areas close by, often violently repelling loggers, gold miners, cattle ranchers and soya farmers. The Kayapo have kept deforestation rates "close to zero," according to Daniel Nepstad, a long-time Amazon researcher now at the Earth Innovation Institute in San Francisco.

In these critical frontier zones, the assumption was that government protection could best halt the onslaught. But there is growing evidence that indigenous peoples often provide a stronger bulwark than state decree. The 300 or so indigenous territories created in the Brazilian Amazon since 1980 are now widely held to have played a key role in a dramatic decline in rates of deforestation there.

Similar effects have been documented in many other parts of the world. Forest dwellers are typically seen as forest destroyers. But the opposite is often the case, says David Bray of Florida International University.

Bray has spent a lifetime studying Mexico, where rural communities have long-standing ownership of 60 per cent of the country's forests, and have logged them for timber to sell. This may sound like a recipe for disaster, yet he says that deforestation rates in community-owned forests have been "generally lower than in regions dominated by protected areas."

One example is in the Yucatan region, where communities outperformed the local Calakmul Biosphere Reserve 200-fold.

Why? Because, Bray says, "communities with rights to resources conserve those resources; communities without rights have no reason to conserve and deforestation will ensue." Andrew Steer, the head of the Washington DC-based environment group the World Resources Institute, agrees: "If you want to stop deforestation, give legal rights to communities."

Some environmentalists pay lip service to this new conservation narrative. But too often, forest communities face growing efforts by outsiders to grab their land in the name of conservation.

The latest threat will probably be a global agreement on climate change in Paris later this year, which is expected to formalise a mechanism called Reducing Emissions from Deforestation and Forest Degradation (REDD), already being piloted.

Under REDD, large areas of forests are to be protected as "carbon sinks." It works by allowing those claiming to protect REDD forests to gain carbon "credits," representing the carbon locked up in the forest that would otherwise have been lost to the atmosphere as trees are chopped down or burned. The credits can then be sold to offset industrial emissions elsewhere.

Large areas deemed at risk of deforestation are earmarked for REDD protection in tropical countries as diverse as Indonesia, Cambodia, Colombia, the Democratic Republic of the Congo and the Solomon Islands. It is becoming clearer that forest communities are best placed to do conservation—especially in frontier zones next to heavily degraded forest, where the biggest carbon savings can be made. So you might expect communities to be in the forefront for owning, managing and profiting from REDD schemes. But so far it hasn't turned out that way.

For most, the legal, logistical and scientific barriers are too high. And their governments, sniffing revenues, are not generally supportive of community proposals.

Instead, most pilot REDD projects have been set up by governments with international environment groups and corporations, often in countries with a poor record on land rights for forest communities. Such projects amount to "green grab."

A prime example, one of the largest of a series of planned World Bank pilot REDD projects, is in the Democratic Republic of the Congo. Here, according to forest researcher Aili Pyhala of the University of Helsinki, Finland, forest cover is strongly correlated with community control, and the main threat is from government-backed logging and mining. The REDD project is intended to cover 120,000 square kilometres of forest spanning the entire province of Mai-Ndombe—an area almost the size of England.

The World Bank is due to approve the scheme later this year. But most of the 1.8 million local inhabitants haven't heard about it yet, says Simon Counsell of the Rainforest Foundation UK—even though it threatens their traditional livelihoods of hunting, gathering and forest farming, and ignores their history of successfully managing the forest.

Grabbing such land in the name of conservation risks triggering conflicts that destroy forests. "By conferring new value on forest lands, REDD could create incentives for government and commercial interests to actively deny or passively ignore the rights of indigenous and other forest-dependent communities to access and control forest resources," warns Frances Seymour, former director of the Center for International Forestry Research.

We are used to thinking of the rights of forest communities and the need to conserve forests as competing imperatives. But the good news is that conservation and human rights can and do go together. To deny forest communities territorial rights is bad for them, but also bad for maintaining the forests.

The benefits of a more people-based approach to conservation could be huge.

Critical Thinking

1. Who is better at preventing deforestation, indigenous peoples or their governments?
2. When it comes to dealing with forest protection, how do indigenous peoples and their governments contrast in their motivations?

Internet References

Amazon Watch
http://amazonwatch.org/

Cultural Survival Quarterly
https://www.culturalsurvival.org/node/1

World Wildlife Fund
https://www.worldwildlife.org/places/amazon

Article

Prepared by: Elvio Angeloni

Being Indigenous in the 21st Century

With a shared sense of history and a growing set of tools, the world's Indigenous Peoples are moving into a future of their own making without losing sight of who they are and where they come from.

WILMA MANKILLER

Learning Outcomes

After reading this article, you will be able to:

- Discuss the values Indigenous People share about the natural world.
- Explain why we should care about the loss of human cultures.

There are more than 300 million Indigenous People, in virtually every region of the world, including the Sámi peoples of Scandinavia, the Maya of Guatemala, numerous tribal groups in the Amazonian rainforest, the Dalits in the mountains of Southern India, the San and Kwei of Southern Africa, Aboriginal people in Australia, and, of course the hundreds of Indigenous Peoples in Mexico, Central and South America, as well as here in what is now known as North America.

There is enormous diversity among communities of Indigenous Peoples, each of which has its own distinct culture, language, history, and unique way of life. Despite these differences, Indigenous Peoples across the globe share some common values derived in part from an understanding that their lives are part of and inseparable from the natural world.

Onondaga Faith Keeper Oren Lyons once said, "Our knowledge is profound and comes from living in one place for untold generations. It comes from watching the sun rise in the east and set in the west from the same place over great sections of time. We are as familiar with the lands, rivers, and great seas that surround us as we are with the faces of our mothers. Indeed, we call the earth Etenoha, our mother from whence all life springs."

Indigenous people are not the only people who understand the interconnectedness of all living things. There are many thousands of people from different ethnic groups who care deeply about the environment and fight every day to protect the earth. The difference is that Indigenous People have the benefit of being regularly reminded of their responsibilities to the land by stories and ceremonies. They remain close to the land, not only in the way they live, but in their hearts and in the way they view the world. Protecting the environment is not an intellectual exercise; it is a sacred duty. When women like Pauline Whitesinger, an elder at Big Mountain, and Carrie Dann, a Western Shoshone land rights activist, speak of preserving the land for future generations, they are not just talking about future generations of humans. They are talking about future generations of plants, animals, water, and all living things. Pauline and Carrie understand the relative insignificance of human beings in the totality of the planet.

Aside from a different view of their relationship to the natural world, many of the world's Indigenous Peoples also share a fragmented but still-present sense of responsibility for one another. Cooperation always has been necessary for the survival of tribal people, and even today cooperation takes precedence over competition in more traditional communities. It is really quite miraculous that a sense of sharing and reciprocity continues into the 21st century given the staggering amount of adversity Indigenous Peoples have faced. In many communities, the most respected people are not those who have amassed great material wealth or achieved great personal success. The greatest respect is reserved for those who help other people, those who understand that their lives play themselves out within a set of reciprocal relationships.

There is evidence of this sense of reciprocity in Cherokee communities. My husband, Charlie Soap, leads a widespread self-help movement among the Cherokee in which low-income volunteers work together to build walking trails, community centers, sports complexes, water lines, and houses. The self-help movement taps into the traditional Cherokee value of cooperation for the sake of the common good. The projects also build a sense of self-efficacy among the people.

Besides values, the world's Indigenous Peoples are also bound by the common experience of being "discovered" and subjected to colonial expansion into their territories that has led to the loss of an incalculable number of lives and millions and millions of acres of land and resources. The most basic rights of Indigenous Peoples were disregarded, and they were subjected to a series of policies that were designed to dispossess them of their land and resources and assimilate them into colonial society and culture. Too often the policies resulted in poverty, high infant mortality, rampant unemployment, and substance abuse, with all its attendant problems.

The stories are shockingly similar all over the world. When I read Chinua Achebe's *Things Fall Apart,* which chronicled the systematic destruction of an African tribe's social, cultural, and economic structure, it sounded all too familiar: take the land, discredit the leaders, ridicule the traditional healers, and send the children off to distant boarding schools.

And I was sickened by the Stolen Generation report about Aboriginal children in Australia who were forcibly removed from their families and placed in boarding schools far away from their families and communities. My own father and my Aunt Sally were taken from my grandfather by the U.S. government and placed in a government boarding school when they were very young. There is a connection between us. Indigenous Peoples everywhere are connected both by our values and by our oppression.

When contemplating the contemporary challenges and problems faced by Indigenous Peoples worldwide, it is important to remember that the roots of many social, economic, and political problems can be found in colonial policies. And these policies continue today across the globe.

Several years ago Charlie and I visited an indigenous community along the Rio Negro in the Brazilian rainforest. Some of the leaders expressed concern that some environmentalists, who should be natural allies, focus almost exclusively on the land and appear not to see or hear the people at all. One leader pointed out that a few years ago it was popular for famous musicians to wear T-shirts emblazoned with the slogan "Save the Rainforests," but no one ever wore a T-shirt with the slogan "Save the People of the Rainforest," though the people of the forest possess the best knowledge about how to live with and sustain the forests.

With so little accurate information about Indigenous Peoples available in educational institutions, in literature, films, or popular culture, it is not surprising that many people are not even conscious of Indigenous Peoples.

The battle to protect the human and land rights of Indigenous Peoples is made immeasurably more difficult by the fact that so few people know much about either the history or contemporary lives of our people. And without any kind of history or cultural context, it is almost impossible for outsiders to understand the issues and challenges faced by Indigenous Peoples.

This lack of accurate information leaves a void that is often filled with nonsensical stereotypes, which either vilify Indigenous Peoples as troubled descendants of savage peoples, or romanticize them as innocent children of nature, spiritual but incapable of higher thought.

Public perceptions will change in the future as indigenous leaders more fully understand that there is a direct link between public perception and public policies. Indigenous Peoples must frame their own issues, because if they don't frame the issues for themselves, their opponents most certainly will. In the future, as more indigenous people become filmmakers, writers, historians, museum curators, and journalists, they will be able to use a dazzling array of technological tools to tell their own stories, in their own voice, in their own way.

Once, a journalist asked me whether people in the United States had trouble accepting the government of the Cherokee Nation during my tenure as principal chief. I was a little surprised by the question. The government of the Cherokee Nation predated the government of the United States and had treaties with other countries before it executed a treaty with one of the first U.S. colonies.

Cherokee and other tribal leaders sent delegations to meet with the English, Spanish, and French in an effort to protect their lands and people. Traveling to foreign lands with a trusted interpreter, tribal ambassadors took maps that had been painstakingly drawn by hand to show their lands to heads of other governments. They also took along gifts, letters, and proclamations. Though tribal leaders thought they were being dealt with as heads of state and as equals, historical records indicate they were often objects of curiosity, and that there was a great deal of disdain and ridicule of these earnest delegates.

Tribal governments in the United States today exercise a range of sovereign rights. Many tribal governments have their own judicial systems, operate their own police force, run their own schools, administer their own clinics and hospitals, and operate a wide range of business enterprises. There are now more than two dozen tribally controlled community colleges. All these advancements benefit everyone in the community, not just tribal people. The history, contemporary lives, and future of tribal governments is intertwined with that of their neighbors.

One of the most common misperceptions about Indigenous Peoples is that they are all the same. There is not only great diversity among Indigenous Peoples, there is great diversity within each tribal community, just as there is in the larger society. Members of the Cherokee Nation are socially, economically, and culturally stratified. Several thousand Cherokee continue to speak the Cherokee language and live in Cherokee communities in rural northeastern Oklahoma. At the other end of the spectrum, there are enrolled tribal members who have never been to even visit the Cherokee Nation. Intermarriage has created an enrolled Cherokee membership that includes people with Hispanic, Asian, Caucasian, and African American heritage.

So what does the future hold for Indigenous Peoples across the globe? What challenges will they face moving further into the 21st century?

To see the future, one needs only to look at the past. If, as peoples, we have been able to survive a staggering loss of land, of rights, of resources, of lives, and we are still standing in the early 21st century, how can I not be optimistic that we will survive whatever challenges lie ahead, that 100 or 500 years from now we will still have viable indigenous communities? Without question, the combined efforts of government and various religious groups to eradicate traditional knowledge systems has had a profoundly negative impact on the culture as well as the social and economic systems of Indigenous Peoples. But if we have been able to hold onto our sense of community, our languages, culture, and ceremonies, despite everything, how can I not be optimistic about the future?

And though some of our original languages, medicines, and ceremonies have been irretrievably lost, the ceremonial fires of many Indigenous Peoples across the globe have survived all the upheaval. Sometimes indigenous communities have almost had to reinvent themselves as a people but they have never given up their sense of responsibility to one another and to the land. It is this sense of interdependence that has sustained tribal people thus far and I believe it will help sustain them well into the future.

Indigenous Peoples know about change and have proven time and time again they can adapt to change. No matter where they go in the world, they hold onto a strong sense of tribal identity while fully interacting with and participating in the larger society around them. In my state of Oklahoma alone, we have produced an indigenous astronaut, two United States congressmen, a Pulitzer Prize-winning novelist, and countless others who have made great contributions to their people, the state, and the world.

One of the great challenges for Indigenous Peoples in the 21st century will be to develop practical models to capture, maintain, and pass on traditional knowledge systems and values to future generations. Nothing can replace the sense of continuity that a genuine understanding of traditional tribal knowledge brings. Many communities are working on discrete aspects of culture, such as language or medicine, but it is the entire system of knowledge that needs to be maintained, not just for Indigenous Peoples but for the world at large.

Regrettably, in the future the battle for human and land rights will continue. But the future does look somewhat better for tribal people. Last year, after 30 years of advocacy by Indigenous Peoples, the United Nations finally passed a declaration supporting their distinct human rights. The challenge will be to make sure the provisions of the declaration are honored and that the rights of Indigenous Peoples all over the world are protected.

Indigenous Peoples simply do better when they have control of their own lives. In the case of my own people, after we were forcibly removed by the United States military from the southeastern part of the United States to Indian Territory, now Oklahoma, we picked ourselves up and rebuilt our nation, despite the fact that approximately 4,000 Cherokee lives were lost during the forced removal. We started some of the first schools west of the Mississippi, Indian or non-Indian, and built schools for the higher education of women. We printed our own newspapers in Cherokee and English and were more literate than our neighbors in adjoining states. Then, in the early 20th century, the federal government almost abolished the Cherokee Nation, and within two decades, our educational attainment levels dropped dramatically and many of our people were living without the most basic amenities. But our people never gave up the dream of rebuilding the Cherokee Nation. In my grandfather's time, Cherokee men rode horses from house to house to collect dimes in a mason jar so they could send representatives to Washington to remind the government to honor its treaties with the Cherokee people.

Over the past 35 years, we have revitalized the Cherokee Nation and once again run our own school, and we have an extensive array of successful education programs. The youth at our Sequoyah High School recently won the state trigonometry contest, and several are Gates Millennium Scholars. We simply do better when we have control over our own destiny.

Critical Thinking

1. What do the 300 million Indigenous People of the world have in common? Where does such knowledge come from?
2. In what ways do Indigenous People differ from others who care about the environment?
3. In what respects is there a "shared sense of responsibility for one another" among Indigenous People?
4. Describe the Indigenous People's common experience of "being discovered" and "being subjected to colonial expansion."

5. Why is it important to not just "save the rainforests," but also to "save the people"?
6. How is the battle to protect the human and land rights of Indigenous Peoples made immeasurably more difficult? How does the author suggest that such public perceptions be changed?
7. In what respects were tribal groups, such as the Cherokee, independent entities at one time?
8. In what respects do tribal governments in the United States still exercise a range of sovereign rights?
9. Why is the author optimistic about the future survival of indigenous communities?
10. What challenges lie ahead for Indigenous Peoples and how does the author suggest that they are meeting these challenges?
11. How have the Cherokee shown that "Indigenous Peoples simply do better when they have control over their own lives"?

Internet References

Association for Political and Legal Anthropology
www.aaanet.org/apla/index.htm

Human Rights and Humanitarian Assistance
www.etown.edu/vl/humrts.html

The Indigenous Rights Movement in the Pacific
www.inmotionmagazine.com/pacific.html

Murray Research Center
www.radcliffe.edu/murray_redirect/index.php

Small Planet Institute
www.smallplanet.org/food

WWW Virtual Library: Indigenous Studies
www.cwis.org

Article

Prepared by: Elvio Angeloni

On the Road Again

From origins in Africa we've conquered the world. Can modern migration really be a crisis?

DEBORA MACKENZIE

Learning Outcomes

After reading this article, you will be able to:

- Discuss the facts as well as the myths regarding global migration.
- Discuss the benefits to those countries to which people are migrating.
- Discuss the costs as well as the benefits to those countries that receive asylum seekers.
- Assess the pros and cons of the increased cultural diversity that results from international migration.

HUMANS migrate. It is a characteristic of our species. Yet now a migration crisis is headline news. More than a million desperate people fled to Europe in 2015, and nearly 4000 died trying. The influx is increasing and about to swell more as the weather improves. The United Nations says Europe faces "an imminent humanitarian crisis, largely of its own making." And it is not alone. The UN has also censured Australia for sending boatloads of refugees to squalid camps in other countries. And US politicians talk of building a wall while tens of thousands of lone children flee violence in Latin America across the US-Mexican border.

In January the World Economic Forum ranked large-scale refugee flows as its global risk of highest concern. When the US Council on Foreign Relations drew up its top ten priorities for conflict prevention in 2016, it included political instability in the EU due to the influx of migrants. Concerns about refugees and economic migrants are grist to the mill for those who want Britain to vote to leave the EU in June. And there's no doubt migration will increase as the world's economy becomes more global, and as demographic and environmental pressures bite.

Should we be alarmed? What is the truth about migration? It is an emotive issue. But the scientific study of what happens when humans move is starting to supply some non-emotive answers. It's showing that many widespread beliefs don't hold up to scrutiny. "Concern about immigrants falls sharply when people are given even the most basic facts," notes Peter Sutherland the UN Special Representative for migration. One analyst even says removing all barriers to migration would be like finding trillion dollar bills on the sidewalk.

The millions fleeing Syria have shone a spotlight on refugees, but that tragedy is just a small part of a bigger picture. More than 240 million people worldwide are international migrants. Refugees account for fewer than 10 per cent of the total and, in theory, they are the least contentious group, as many countries have signed international commitments to admit them. The rest are moving to work, or joining family members who have. When such people travel with refugees they are often derided as "just" economic migrants. This is unfair, says Alex Betts head of the Refugee Studies Centre at the University of Oxford. Whether or not they meet the official definition of a refugee, many are fleeing dire conditions that still pose a threat to their survival. Although globalisation of the world's economy has lifted millions out of poverty, it has not been able to create enough jobs where there are people in need of work. Aid funds are starting to address this problem—but for the most part people must go where there are jobs.

The Origins of Xenophobia

All the evidence suggests migrants boost economic growth. So why don't we just fly people who want to work to countries where there are jobs and welcome them with open arms? Prejudices rooted in humanity's evolutionary past may be partly to blame.

"Perceptions of competition drive a lot of our thinking and are difficult to avoid," says Victoria Esses at the University of Western Ontario in London, Canada. Humans think of their support systems as a zero-sum game. Such perceptions were accurate during our evolutionary history as hunter-gatherers when the appearance of others on our patch really meant fewer mastodons or mushrooms for us. If they were close relatives they might share—or at least our common genes would benefit from their success. But anyone displaying different cultural markers was likely to be a competitor. A modern capitalist economy is not a zero-sum game—if you add more workers, it grows (see main story). Regardless of this, our evolutionary hangups make it difficult to accept the economic sense in welcoming immigrants.

That's not all. We are instinctively wary of close contact with different groups because in our evolutionary past this helped us guard against infectious disease, according to Mark Schaller at the University of British Columbia in Canada. Separate groups of people often have different histories of exposure and acquired immunity to pathogens. A disease carried innocuously by one might devastate another, as happened to the native Americans after Europeans arrived.

Steven Neuberg at Arizona State University at Tempe notes that groups also evolve different survival-enhancing behavioural rules. "Foreigners with different rules might interfere with the social coordination you need to do important tasks, or might get members of your group to follow their rules instead," he says. "Chaos could emerge if your group makes decisions by consensus but theirs is authoritarian."

Schaller and Neuberg believe that for both these reasons, human cultures evolved to be wary of close interaction with people who were different from their group.

This xenophobia persists, says Neuberg, who has found that people feel threatened by groups with different values of many kinds. Ethnic groups in modern cities often form enclaves rather than mixing randomly—which can foster strong local communities but also engenders wider mistrust. Our evolved tendencies to avoid outgroups could be making it hard to live in multicultural societies.

That's why some see migration as a crisis. The 2008 financial crash spawned insecurity about jobs, increasing concerns about economic migrants. Several populist parties took the opportunity to warn of a flood of freeloaders at the gates, increasing the issue's political visibility and hardening the policies of some mainstream parties, including in the United Kingdom. The US government decided not to bail out firms that hired too many immigrants. Spain paid migrants to leave—even after they had stopped coming as jobs disappeared. And feelings of insecurity remain.

"The logic driving this is the idea that migrant workers present additional competition for scarce jobs," says Ian Goldin at the University of Oxford. That appears reasonable. Indeed, it's probably part of our evolved human nature to see our support system as a zero-sum game—more for you means less for me (see "The Origins of xenophobia," above). But that's not how modern economies work.

If an economy really were zero-sum, wages would go down as labour supply increased and natives might well lose jobs to immigrants. But no modern economic system is that simple, says Jacques Poot at the University of Waikato, New Zealand. The knock-on of economic migration is that increased labour also brings an increase in profit, which business owners can invest in more production. They can also diversify, creating opportunities for a broader range of workers. In addition, migration means workers can be more efficiently matched to demand, and make the economy more resilient by doing jobs natives won't or can't do.

"More people expand the economy," says Goldin, because people are moving from places where they cannot work productively to places where they can. In a survey of 15 European countries, the UN's International Labour Organisation (ILO) found that for every 1 per cent increase in a country's population caused by immigration, its GDP grew between 1.25 and 1.5 per cent. The World Bank estimates that if immigrants increased the workforces of wealthy countries by 3 per cent, that would boost world GDP by $356 billion by 2025. And removing all barriers to migration could have a massive effect. A meta-analysis of several independent mathematical models suggests it would increase world GDP by 50 to 150 per cent. "There appear to be trillion-dollar bills on the sidewalk" if we lift restrictions on emigration, says Michael Clemens at the Center for Global Development, a think-tank in Washington DC, who did the research.

The Reluctant Migrant

Humans have always migrated. Our species started as African apes and now covers the planet. Tales of migration are central to our religions, our literature and our family histories. And migration is at the heart of modern life. I am a migrant. You may be too. Some 38 per cent of scientists working in the United States and 33 per cent in the United Kingdom are foreign-born. Yet they may be exceptions to an ancient rule. In fact, few people migrate. And when we do, often it's because we feel we have no other option.

Take our ancient ancestors who left Africa between 55,000 and 65,000 years ago. At the time, humans had evolved 35 different lineages of mitochondrial DNA, a stretch of genes that changes very slowly. The migrants were carrying just two of these, which with other DNA data suggests that they could have numbered as few as 1000. The vast majority of human diversity outside Africa stems from this single migration, suggesting this small band of pioneers may not have gone far, occupying the first lands they came to in the Middle East and discouraging followers. Their descendants would then have expanded into further territories when those hunting grounds got crowded. In this way, over tens of thousands of years, humans occupied the world, moving first to Asia and Australia, then to Europe, and finally colonising the Americas.

The biggest emigration the world has ever seen is much more recent. A mass movement of people from Europe to the New World occurred between 1850 and 1910. At its peak, over 2 million people a year were relocating. Nevertheless, the vast majority chose to stay put. On average, only 5 per cent of the population of Britain—among the biggest sources of migrants—left each decade.

Today, just 3.3 per cent of the world's people are migrants, little more than in 1990. Even within the European Union, where citizens are free to live wherever they choose, only 2.8 per cent, 14 million people, now reside outside their native country. "The idea that without controls, everyone moves, is contradicted by the evidence," says Philippe Legrain at the London School of Economics. "Niger is next to Nigeria, Nigeria is six times richer and there are no border controls, but Niger is not depopulated. Sweden is six times richer than Romania, the EU permits free movement, but Romania is not depopulated." Even strong economic incentives are often not enough to tempt us to leave home.

But who gets those billions? Most of the extra wealth goes to migrants and to their home countries. In 2015, migrants sent home $440 billion, two and a half times the amount those countries received in foreign aid—promoting development and jobs at home. But what do natives of countries that attract migrants get out of it?

In the EU, it has been difficult to tease out the effect of free movement of workers from other economic results of membership. However, a study of non-EU member, Switzerland, is illuminating. Different parts of Switzerland allowed free access to EU workers at different times, enabling Giovanni Peri of the University of California at Davis to isolate the effects. He found that while the workforce grew by 4 per cent, there was no change in wages and employment for natives overall. Wages increased a little for more educated Swiss people, who got jobs supervising newcomers, while some less educated Swiss people were displaced into different jobs.

Peri has also looked at the situation in the United States. "Data show that immigrants expand the US economy's productive capacity, stimulate investment, and promote specialisation, which in the long run boosts productivity," he says. "There is no evidence that immigrants crowd out US-born workers in either the short or the long run." Natives instead capitalise on language and other skills by moving from manual jobs to better-paid positions. Peri calculates that immigration to the US between 1990 and 2007 boosted the average wage by $5100—a quarter of the total wage rise during that period.

Further evidence comes from a meta-analysis Poot did in 2010, which collated all the research done to that point. It reveals that rises in a country's workforce due to foreign-born workers has only a small effect on wages, which could be positive or negative. At worst, a 1 per cent rise caused wages to fall by 0.2 per cent, mostly for earlier generations of immigrants. The impact on the availability of jobs for natives is "basically zero," he says. Any tendency for wages to fall with an increase in immigration can be counteracted by enforcing minimum wage.

Britain's Migration Advisory Committee came to a similar conclusion in 2012. "Both EU and non-EU migrants who have been in the UK for over five years are not associated with the displacement of British-born workers," it reported. Very recent migrants do have a small impact, but mainly on previous migrants. What's more, the ILO notes that low-skilled migrants do "dirty, dangerous and difficult" jobs, which locals do not want—crop picking, care work, cleaning and the like. Meanwhile, high-skilled migrants plug chronic labour shortages in sectors such as healthcare, education and IT. Nearly a third of UK doctors and 13 per cent of nurses are foreign born.

Another presumption made about migrants is that they put a strain on benefit systems. This is also not borne out by the evidence. "It is widely assumed that economic migrants are mainly poor people out to live off the tax money of the relatively rich," observes human rights expert Ian Buruma. "Most of them are not spongers. They want to work." Indeed, a lot do not go to countries offering generous benefits, but wherever there are jobs. Some 82 million people, 36 per cent of the world's migrants, have moved from one developing country to another, especially from Haiti to the Dominican Republic, Burkina Faso to Ivory Coast, Egypt to Jordan and Indonesia to Malaysia.

Those that do end up in developed countries are not the burden people sometimes assume. The Organization for Economic Co-operation and Development, which represents 34 of the world's most wealthy nations, calculates that its immigrants on average pay as much in taxes as they take in benefits. Recent research shows that EU workers in the UK take less from the benefits system than native Brits do, mostly because they are younger on average. Moreover, they bring in education paid for by their native countries, and many return to their homeland before they need social security. Based on recent numbers, Britain should conservatively expect 140,000 net immigrants a year for the next 50 years. The Office for Budget Responsibility, the UK's fiscal watchdog, calculates that if that number doubled it would cut UK government debt by almost a third—while stopping immigration would up the debt by almost 50 per cent.

Illegal migrants make a surprising extra contribution, says Goldin. While many work "informally" without declaring income for taxes, those in formal work often have taxes automatically deducted from their pay cheques, but rarely claim benefits for fear of discovery. Social security paid by employers on behalf of such migrants but never claimed by them netted the US $20 billion between 1990 and 1998, says Goldin. That, plus social security contributions by young legal migrants who will not need benefits for decades, is now keeping US social security afloat, he says.

"One of the dominant, but empirically unjustified images is of masses of people flowing in...taking away jobs, pushing up housing prices and overloading social services," writes Stephen Castles at the University of Sydney, Australia, and two colleagues in their book, *The Age of Migration*. They argue that an increase in migration is often the result rather than the cause of economic changes that harm natives—such as neo-liberal economic policies. "The overwhelming majority of research finds small to no effects of migration on employment and wages," says Douglas Nelson of Tulane University in New Orleans. "On purely economic grounds, immigration is good for everyone."

That may come as a welcome surprise to many. But economics is not the whole story. If perceptions about jobs and wages

Passport to Success?

Governments only started to control who entered their country relatively recently. Other than in wartime, premodern authorities worried more about people getting out. Roman and medieval laws kept peasants bound to their farms. In the 1600s, English labourers needed locally issued passes to travel for work, partly to stop them "benefits shopping" for parish poor relief. But controls were largely internal. External passports were mere requests for safe conduct, rather than restrictive documents determining where you could go, says John Torpey at the City University of New York. This was partly because technology to identify individuals, such as photography, was not widely available until the late 19th century.

But the main reason was that an individual's nationality had little political meaning before the late 1700s. The passport as an instrument of state regulation was born of the French revolution of 1789. At first, ordinary people were issued passes to control internal movement, especially to Paris. But after the king tried to escape, and foreign aristocrats attacked the revolution, the authorities started requiring such papers for exit and entry to the country. The revolution created one of the world's first "nation-states," defined by the "national" identity of its people rather than its monarchs' claims. "This novel importance of the people and their nationality made identity papers integral to creating the modern state," says Torpey.

As the idea of the nation-state spread, so did passports. But as the industrial revolution snowballed in the 19th century, there was pressure to allow free movement of all the factors of production—money, trade and labour. Passport requirements were widely relaxed across Europe—in 1872, the British foreign secretary, Earl Granville, even wrote: "all foreigners have the unrestricted right of entrance into and residence in this country." The situation was similar in North America.

In the early 20th century, European legal experts were divided over whether states even had the right to control people's international movements. But the nationalism that was propelling Europe towards war changed that. Among other things, it meant foreigners might be spies. Passport controls were re-applied, and never lifted again.

were the only problem, you would expect anti-immigrant views to run high where jobs are scarce. Yet a 2013 study of 24 European countries found that people living in areas of high unemployment tended not to have negative views of migrants. So, what else are we worried about?

One major issue is a perceived threat to social cohesion. In particular, immigrants are often associated with crime. But here again the evidence doesn't stack up. In 2013, Brian Bell and colleagues at the London School of Economics found no change in violent crime in Britain linked either to a wave of asylum seekers in the 1990s, or eastern EU migrants after 2004. The asylum seekers were associated with a small increases in property crime such as theft—boosting existing local crime rates some 2 per cent—perhaps because they were not allowed to work, suggest the authors. But areas where eastern Europeans settled had significantly less of any crime. Another study found that immigrants had no impact on crime in Italy. And immigrants in the United States are much less likely to commit crimes and are imprisoned less often than nativeborn Americans. Tim Wadsworth of the University of Colorado has even suggested a rise in immigration in the 1990s may have driven an overall drop in US crime rates since then.

Nevertheless, immigrants can put pressure on local communities. High rates of arrival can temporarily strain schools, housing and other services. "That is what people tend to see," says Goldin. He says investment is required to mitigate these problems.

"Governments need to manage the costs, which tend to be short-term and local," he says. That's a challenge, but it can be done. Bryan Caplan of George Mason University in Fairfax, Virginia, points out that since the 1990s, 155 million Chinese have moved from the countryside to cities for work. "This shows it's entirely possible to build new homes for hundreds of millions of migrants given a couple of decades."

China may be managing the biggest mass migration in history, but there's one problem it mostly doesn't face. Perceived threats to national identity often top natives' list of concerns about immigrants. It can even be an issue when such identities are relatively recent constructs. But countries with a clear ethnic identity and no recent history of significant immigration face the biggest problem, says Nelson. "It's tricky for Sweden, which went from essentially no immigrants to 16 percent in half a generation," he says. And Denmark is another nation where anxiety over the loss of cultural homogeneity has been blamed for a backlash against immigrants.

Elsewhere, there has been a hardening of attitudes. Ellie Vasta of MacQuarie University in Sydney, Australia, is trying to understand why Europe, which embraced multiculturalism in the 1970s, today calls for cohesion and nationalism, demanding that immigrants conform and testing them for "Britishness" or "Dutchness." She blames an increasing loss of cohesion in society due to "individualising" forces from mass media to the structure of work. As people rely more on their own resources, they have a longing for community. The presence of foreigners appears to disrupt this, creating a "desire to control differences," she says.

Research by Robert Putnam at Harvard University suggests this move away from multiculturalism could be problematic.

Age Concerns

As birth rates plummet in the developed world, migrants are keeping our economies afloat. They account for half of the increase in the US workforce since 2005, and 70 per cent in Europe. Even so, the number of people of working age supporting each retiree over 65 is falling. In 2000, this "dependency ratio" was 4 across the European Union. Today it is 3.5. And even with current levels of migration it's set to fall to 2 by 2050.

In 2000, the UN Department of Economic and Social Affairs ran a detailed simulation to see how many immigrants would be needed to support the population over 65 in developed countries. They found that with no migration, Europe's population is set to fall 17 per cent by 2050—with a 30 per cent decrease in working-age people. To maintain overall numbers, the EU needs 850,000 immigrants per year—for comparison, the net migrant number from outside the EU in 2013 was 540,000. However, to keep the working age population from falling it needs nearly double that: 1.5 million a year. That would mean recent migrants and their children would account for 14 per cent of the UK population and over a third of Germany's and Japan's. Even then, the dependency ratio would be just over two. The US fares better—current and expected migration kept its dependency ratio at three.

"Migration might be the most relevant force to have an impact on the age distribution in Europe to 2050," says demographer Pablo Lattes, an author of the study. Germany, which has a shortfall of 1.8 million skilled workers, is keenly aware of this. Officials have been saying quietly at international meetings that this is why they have accepted so many of Europe's current wave of refugees. In 2000, the government tried to bring in 20,000 foreign high-tech workers, but this was met with strong opposition from the public. Germany may hope refugees will be harder for people to object to.

He finds that increased diversity lowers "social capital" such as trust, cooperation and altruism. However, this can be overcome in societies that accommodate, rather than erase, diversity by creating "a new, broader sense of 'we'." In other words, success lies not in assimilation, but in adaptation on both sides. Canada has tried to achieve this by basing its national identity on immigration. Canadian prime minister Justin Trudeau told the World Economic Forum in Davos, Switzerland, this year that "diversity is the engine of investment. It generates creativity that enriches the world."

This view is shared by complex systems analyst Scott Page at the University of Michigan, Ann Arbor. He argues that culturally diverse groups, from cities to research teams, consistently out-perform less diverse groups due to "cognitive diversity" — exposure to disagreement and alternative ways of thinking.

"Immigration provides a steady inflow of new ways of seeing and thinking—hence the great success of immigrants in business start-ups, science and the arts," he says. But more diversity means more complexity, and complex systems need more energy to maintain—investment in management, for example. The fact that immigrants have settled more successfully in some places than others suggests specific efforts are required to get this right. Achieving broad agreement on core goals and principles is one, says Page.

We had better learn how to manage diversity soon because it's about to skyrocket in wealthy countries. As birth rates fall, there's a growing realisation that workers from abroad will be required to take up the slack (see "Age concerns," left). In addition, the fertility of incomers remains higher than that of natives for several generations. In 2011, for the first time since mass European migration in the 19th century, more non-white than white babies were born in the United States, mainly to recent Asian and Hispanic immigrants and their children. By 2050, white Americans will be a minority, says Bill Frey of the Brookings Institution in Washington DC. That's good news for the United States, he adds, as it gives the country a younger workforce, and outlook, than its competitors in Europe and Japan.

Even if we finesse multiculturalism, there is a potential game changer looming on the horizon. Massive automation and use of robotics could make production less dependent on human labour. This "fourth industrial revolution" may see governments paying their citizens a guaranteed minimum wage independent of work. There has been little discussion of how this might affect a mobile global workforce. However, some warn that cheap, automated production in wealthy countries could destroy export markets for poor countries. This would worsen unemployment and political instability, leading to massive migration pressure.

One way to prepare for this would be to take a more coordinated and strategic approach to the global workforce. As it is, it's hard to track migration amidst a mess of nonstandardised data and incompatible rules. Countries do not agree on who is a migrant. Even the EU has no common policy or information for matching people to jobs. Migrants are usually managed by foreign ministries, not labour ministries that understand the job market. "What could be of real value would be for governments, companies and trade unions to get together and look at where the labour shortages are, and how they could be filled, with natives or migrants," says Michelle Leighton head of migration at the ILO.

Amazingly, says Goldin, there is no body to oversee the global movement of people. Governments belong to the International Organisation for Migration but it is not an official UN agency so it cannot set common policy. Instead, each country jealously guards its borders while competing for workers. Goldin and others think there should be a UN agency managing migration in the global interest, rather than leaving it to nations with differing interests and powers. This, combined with real empirical understanding of the impacts of migration, might finally allow humanity to capitalise on the huge positive potential of its ancient penchant for moving.

Critical Thinking

1. What have been the benefits of international migration to local economies?
2. What is the case to be made for asylum seekers?
3. In what ways have immigrants expanded the US economy? The UK economy?
4. What effect have immigrants generally had on crime rates and why?
5. In what sense might automation become a "game changer" with regard to the world economy?

Internet References

Globalization—Global Policy Forum
https://www.globalpolicy.org/globalization.html

International Forum on Globalization
Ifg.org/

Migration Advisory Committee—GOV.UK
https://www.gov.uk/government/organizations/migration-advisory-committee

Debora MacKenzie is a consultant for New Scientist based in Brussels. See online version for links to research.

Article

Prepared by: Elvio Angeloni

Coming to America

Beyond the Border Battles, Immigrants Continue to Take the Oath of Citizenship and Contribute to American Life.

ANN MORSE

Learning Outcomes

After reading this article, you will be able to:

- Discuss immigration to America in terms of what is drive people to come here and the economic impact of their presence.
- Discuss migration reform with respect to the perceived problems and the proposed solutions.

Given the persistent focus on illegal immigration in the public dialogue, it may be surprising to learn that most immigrants come to the United States legally. They come to marry, to rejoin family, and to work. Some come to seek haven from persecution or natural disasters.

As the baby boomer generation retires at a rate of 10,000 workers a day, immigrants are also filling niches within the U.S. economy in both high- and low-wage jobs.

They create small businesses for their families in the restaurant and hospitality industries and fill seasonal shortages in agriculture and meatpacking, returning year after year. Some help address the growing demands in areas such as health care.

And throughout U.S. history, politicians and citizens debate whether immigrants take jobs away from Americans, lower wages, and fail to adopt American values.

Who is coming to America currently? What role do they play in our economy and communities? How are state lawmakers responding?

Who Are America's Immigrants?

Each year, about a million immigrants arrive here legally. In 2015, 679,000 of them were relatives of U.S. citizens, 144,000 gained permanent work visas, 70,000 were refugees, and 47,000 received "diversity" visas because they were from countries with low emigration rates to the United States.

The 44.2 million foreign-born residents living in the United States in fiscal year 2017 comprise 13.7 percent of the total population. About half, or 20 million, have become naturalized citizens and make up 6 percent of the population. One-fourth, or 13.1 million, are legal noncitizens (4 percent of total population).

About 11.1 million U.S. residents (down from a high of 12.2 million in 2007) have come here illegally or have overstayed their visas, with an estimated 300,000–400,000 illegal immigrants arriving and leaving each year.

They make up 3 percent of the U.S. population. Most come from Mexico (56 percent), Guatemala (7 percent), El Salvador (4 percent), Honduras (3 percent), and China (2 percent).

In 2015, most of the immigrants who became permanent residents and received green cards were from Mexico, China, India, the Philippines, and Cuba, while a majority of the refugees accepted into the country were fleeing from Myanmar, Iraq, Somalia, Congo, and Bhutan.

Finally, a substantial number of foreigners enter the United States with temporary visas to study or work. About 3.7 million were admitted in 2015 to work in areas such as agricultural or seasonal work or specialty occupations such as high tech or health care. Another 2 million visas were issued to students.

Who's in Charge?

The federal government determines how many immigrants are permitted to enter the United States and the conditions for their stay. But, in general, immigration policy has evolved into a shared responsibility among local, state, and federal governments.

Since Congress passed the last major reform of legal and illegal immigration 30 years ago, it has been unsuccessful in bringing the system up to date. In recent years, states and localities have taken on additional responsibilities in both immigration enforcement and immigrant integration.

The Deferred Action for Childhood Arrivals, or DACA program, was established by the Obama administration in 2012. It has allowed around 800,000 young unauthorized immigrants (who had lived in the United States since 2007 and who had no criminal record) to apply for temporary legal status. This protected them from being deported for two years and was renewable. It neither granted permanent legal immigration status nor offered a pathway to citizenship.

Opponents criticize the program as an executive overreach into legislative authority since Obama implemented it without going through Congress. Earlier this year, 10 state attorneys general threatened to sue the Trump administration if the program was not terminated, which was countered by about 20 state attorneys general writing in support of it.

In September, the U.S. Department of Homeland Security rescinded the DACA program with a six-month phaseout to allow Congress to act to save it. U.S. Attorney General Jeff Sessions argued the program has encouraged illegal immigration, denied jobs to hundreds of thousands of Americans, and put our nation at risk for more crime.

David Bier, an immigration policy analyst at the Cato Institute, agrees that the program was implemented wrongly but argues in an article in *The Washington Post* that the administration's "correct response, however—for economic reasons and security reasons, but above all for moral reasons—would have been to actively push for Congress to enact the program." He debunks the arguments sessions gave as not based on the facts. "If we're going to debate the merits of DACA, we should know what we're talking about," he writes.

Bipartisan legislation, entitled the Dream Act of 2017, has been introduced in both houses of Congress to enact DACA into law.

States Respond with Action

After DACA's implementation, state legislatures debated what government services—in the areas of education, health, human services, and licensing—the program's young recipients, as well as unauthorized immigrants in general, should be eligible to receive.

All states now issue driver's licenses to DACA recipients. California, Colorado, Connecticut, Delaware, Hawaii, Illinois, Maryland, New Mexico, Nevada, Utah, Vermont, Washington, and the District of Columbia also issue licenses to unauthorized immigrants if they provide certain documentation.

Twenty states offer in-state tuition to unauthorized immigrant students, 16 by state legislative action and 4 by state university systems action. Seven states and the District of Columbia offer state-funded financial aid to unauthorized immigrant students.

Alabama and South Carolina allow DACA recipients to enroll in public colleges and universities but prohibit undocumented students from doing so, and some institutions in Alabama allow DACA recipients to receive in-state tuition rates.

Tennessee Representative Mark White (R) introduced a bill for the third year in a row this year to allow in-state tuition rates to students whose parents brought them to the country illegally. "It is a basic, Republican, conservative position to support a person who is willing to get up every morning, go to work, go to school, and better their lives. That is what we have been about as a party all my life," he says.

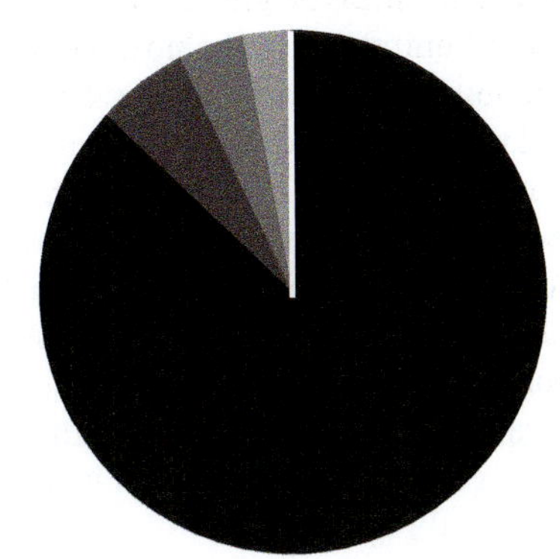

How Many?

Immigrants comprise 13 percent of the total U.S. population.

Native Born U.S. Citizens	**278.8 million**	**87%**
Naturalized Citizens	20 million	6%
Legal Noncitizens	13.1 million	4%
Unauthorized Immigrants	11.1 million	3%
U.S. Population	**323 million**	

Source: Migration Policy Institute, 2017

Others, like White's colleague Representative Judd Matheny (R), feel the country and the state of Tennessee have been "more than generous" in letting the students receive the same K–12 public education as native-born children.

"This [bill] will lead to an influx of noncitizen students into our education system," Matheny said before the bill was voted down in committee.

Another area states have addressed is professional licensing. Florida and Illinois allow eligible DACA recipients to receive law licenses. The New York Board of Regents allows eligible DACA recipients to receive professional licenses and some teacher certifications. Nebraska issues certain professional and commercial licenses to eligible recipients. California allows unauthorized immigrants to receive professional licenses if all other requirements are met.

Immigrants' Economic Impact

In the public debates over who should be admitted to the United States, some argue immigrants take jobs away from Americans and depress wages because they are willing to work for less. They question whether immigrants receive more in government services than they pay for in taxes.

Studies show, however, that immigrants pay their share of sales, property, and income taxes and have positive effects on economic growth and business development.

In 2016, the National Academies of Sciences, Engineering, and Medicine set out to examine the fiscal and economic consequences of immigrants at the national and state levels, using a snapshot of time from 2011 to 2013.

"In synthesizing hundreds of studies, in the long term, there is little negative impact of immigrants overall on wages or employment," says The Urban Institute's Kim Rueben, a participant in the NAS study.

But in the short term, "There is some compelling evidence of impact on some groups, like recent immigrants and those without a high school degree who are at the bottom of the wage scale," she says.

Other findings from the study include:

- First-generation immigrants cost more than native-born residents, mainly at the state and local levels, in part due to the costs of educating their children. When these second-generation children grow up, however, they are among the strongest economic and fiscal contributors in the U.S. population, contributing more in taxes than their parents or the native population.
- Immigrants have higher representation in certain occupations requiring high levels of education (science, technology, engineering, and health).
- The children of immigrants working in low-status jobs find substantially better paying jobs than their parents had.
- Undocumented workers, as a group, tend to get low-paying jobs that don't require certifications

"Immigrants arrive in their prime working years and help fill the jobs that Americans leave as they age out of the work force," writes Rueben. "Skilled foreign-born workers boost innovation and productivity, hold more patents, and are more likely to start new businesses than native-born Americans."

Rueben goes on to say that government spending and revenues related to immigrants are roughly the same as for the native-born. Children cost more for education, workers pay more in taxes, and older people receive retirement benefits.

Looking specifically at the refugee population, a new report from the National Bureau of Economic Research found that the longer refugees live in this country, the better their economic situation becomes. Refugees who arrived as adults (18–45 years old) contributed, on average, $21,000 more in taxes than they received in benefits after 20 years in the United States.

Do Immigrants Become Americans?

How well do immigrants successfully integrate into the nation's social, economic, and civic life? Do they learn English, become self-sufficient and adopt American values?

Another National Academies of Sciences study, completed in 2015, found that the level of educational attainment, English ability, and income improved the more immigrants were integrated into American life.

The study found that today's immigrants appear to be learning English as fast or faster than earlier waves of immigrants.

In general, immigrants' incomes improved the longer they lived in the United States, although more slowly for Hispanic immigrants than for others.

Researchers also discovered that when immigrants arrive, they are less likely to die from cardiovascular disease and cancer, and they have fewer chronic health conditions, lower infant mortality and obesity rates, and a longer life expectancy than native-born Americans. Over time, however, as they integrate into American life, these advantages decline.

And finally, the study found first-generation immigrant communities to have lower rates of crime and violence than comparable nonimmigrant neighborhoods. But in the second and third generations, crime rates increase and resemble those of the general population.

Steps to a Solution

While the federal government has been stalled on immigration reform, state legislatures across the country have continued to work on local immigration challenges and solutions.

"States are coming up with innovative ways to address immigration issues—in education, health care, and economic development—that the federal government seems to ignore," says Florida Senator René García (R).

Each year, over the last decade or so, state legislatures have considered an average of 1,300 bills and resolutions on immigration and have enacted an average of 200 of them.

This year, lawmakers in 47 states and the District of Columbia enacted 133 laws and 195 resolutions on immigration, almost twice as many as in 2016.

Many of the laws are budget related, but the rest address all kinds of areas. Examples range from requiring employers to use the federal E-Verify Internet-based system to validate new hires to authorizing a seal of biliteracy on high school diplomas.

State lawmakers are also assessing their role in immigration enforcement, debating sanctuary policies that limit cooperation with federal immigration authorities and detainer policies that help identify potentially deportable people.

"You're seeing this state legislation come up because the feds haven't fixed the issue, so states are taking the lead," says Nevada Senator Mo Denis (D).

Ultimately, however, immigration is a national responsibility that requires a national solution. It's time to align our economic and security needs for the 21st century.

The good news is there are plenty of lessons and best practices that can be drawn from state legislatures' experiences to build strong economies and safe communities.

Critical Thinking

1. Who's migrating to America and why?
2. Are immigrants good or bad for America? Explain.
3. What do you think should be done with respect to "immigration reform?"

Internet References

Legal Rights of Undocumented Immigrants
https://www.lawyers.com/legal-info/immigration/general-immigration/legal-rights-of-illegal-immigrants.html

The Meaning of "Natural Born Citizen" in Presidential Elections
https://www.thoughtco.com/presidents-not-born-in-the-us-3368103

The Most Popular Immigration Issues of 2018
https://www.isidewith.com/polls/immigration

The Rights of Immigrants
https://www.aclu.org/other/rights-immigrants-aclu-position-paper

What Is an American?
https://www.iwp.edu/news_publications/detail/what-is-an-american

ANN MORSE directs NCSL's Immigrant Policy Project.

Article

Prepared by: Elvio Angeloni

Population Seven Billion

By 2045 global population is projected to reach nine billion. Can the planet take the strain? As we reach the milestone of seven billion people this year, it's time to take stock. In the coming decades, despite falling birthrates, the population will continue to grow—mostly in poor countries. If the billions of people who want to boost themselves out of poverty follow the path blazed by those in wealthy countries, they too will step hard on the planet's resources. How big will the population actually grow? What will the planet look like in 2045? Throughout the year we'll offer an in-depth series exploring those questions. The answers will depend on the decisions each of us makes.

ROBERT KUNZIG

Learning Outcomes

After reading this article, you will be able to:

- Define what is meant by the *demographic transition* and discuss the role it has played in world population growth.
- Discuss whether we should be alarmed by population growth, the environment, or both.

One day in Delft in the fall of 1677, Antoni van Leeuwenhoek, a cloth merchant who is said to have been the long-haired model for two paintings by Johannes Vermeer—"The Astronomer" and "The Geographer"—abruptly stopped what he was doing with his wife and rushed to his worktable. Cloth was Leeuwenhoek's business but microscopy his passion. He'd had five children already by his first wife (though four had died in infancy), and fatherhood was not on his mind. "Before six beats of the pulse had intervened," as he later wrote to the Royal Society of London, Leeuwenhoek was examining his perishable sample through a tiny magnifying glass. Its lens, no bigger than a small raindrop, magnified objects hundreds of times. Leeuwenhoek had made it himself; nobody else had one so powerful. The learned men in London were still trying to verify Leeuwenhoek's earlier claims that unseen "animalcules" lived by the millions in a single drop of lake water and even in French wine. Now he had something more delicate to report: Human semen contained animalcules too. "Sometimes more than a thousand," he wrote, "in an amount of material the size of a grain of sand." Pressing the glass to his eye like a jeweler, Leeuwenhoek watched his own animalcules swim about, lashing their long tails. One imagines sunlight falling through leaded windows on a face lost in contemplation, as in the Vermeers. One feels for his wife.

Leeuwenhoek became a bit obsessed after that. Though his tiny peephole gave him privileged access to a never-before-seen microscopic universe, he spent an enormous amount of time looking at spermatozoa, as they're now called. Oddly enough, it was the milt he squeezed from a cod one day that inspired him to estimate, almost casually, just how many people might live on Earth.

Nobody then really had any idea; there were few censuses. Leeuwenhoek started with an estimate that around a million people lived in Holland. Using maps and a little spherical geometry, he calculated that the inhabited land area of the planet was 13,385 times as large as Holland. It was hard to imagine the whole planet being as densely peopled as Holland, which seemed crowded even then. Thus, Leeuwenhoek concluded triumphantly, there couldn't be more than 13.385 billion people on Earth—a small number indeed compared with the 150 billion sperm cells of a single codfish! This cheerful little calculation, writes population biologist Joel Cohen in his book *How Many People Can the Earth Support?*, may have been the first attempt to give a quantitative answer to a question that has become far more pressing now than it was in the 17th century. Most answers these days are far from cheerful.

Historians now estimate that in Leeuwenhoek's day there were only half a billion or so humans on Earth. After rising very slowly for millennia, the number was just starting to take off. A century and a half later, when another scientist reported the discovery of human egg cells, the world's population had doubled to more than a billion. A century after that, around 1930, it had doubled again to two billion. The acceleration since then has been astounding. Before the 20th century, no human had lived through a doubling of the human population, but there are people alive today who have seen it triple. Sometime in late 2011, according to the UN Population Division, there will be seven billion of us.

And the explosion, though it is slowing, is far from over. Not only are people living longer, but so many women across the world are now in their childbearing years—1.8 billion—that the global population will keep growing for another few decades at least, even though each woman is having fewer children than she would have had a generation ago. By 2050 the total number could reach 10.5 billion, or it could stop at eight billion—the difference is about one child per woman. UN demographers consider the middle road their best estimate: They now project that the population may reach nine billion before 2050—in 2045. The eventual tally will depend on the choices individual couples make when they engage in that most intimate of human acts, the one Leeuwenhoek interrupted so carelessly for the sake of science.

With the population still growing by about 80 million each year, it's hard not to be alarmed. Right now on Earth, water tables are falling, soil is eroding, glaciers are melting, and fish stocks are vanishing. Close to a billion people go hungry each day. Decades from now, there will likely be two billion more mouths to feed, mostly in poor countries. There will be billions more people wanting and deserving to boost themselves out of poverty. If they follow the path blazed by wealthy countries—clearing forests, burning coal and oil, freely scattering fertilizers and pesticides—they too will be stepping hard on the planet's natural resources. How exactly is this going to work?

There may be some comfort in knowing that people have long been alarmed about population. From the beginning, says French demographer Hervé Le Bras, demography has been steeped in talk of the apocalypse. Some of the field's founding papers were written just a few years after Leeuwenhoek's discovery by Sir William Petty, a founder of the Royal Society. He estimated that world population would double six times by the Last Judgment, which was expected in about 2,000 years. At that point it would exceed 20 billion people—more, Petty thought, than the planet could feed. "And then, according to the prediction of the Scriptures, there must be wars, and great slaughter, &c.," he wrote.

As religious forecasts of the world's end receded, Le Bras argues, population growth itself provided an ersatz mechanism of apocalypse. "It crystallized the ancient fear, and perhaps the ancient hope, of the end of days," he writes. In 1798 Thomas Malthus, an English priest and economist, enunciated his general law of population: that it necessarily grows faster than the food supply, until war, disease, and famine arrive to reduce the number of people. As it turned out, the last plagues great enough to put a dent in global population had already happened when Malthus wrote. World population hasn't fallen, historians think, since the Black Death of the 14th century.

In the two centuries after Malthus declared that population couldn't continue to soar, that's exactly what it did. The process started in what we now call the developed countries, which were then still developing. The spread of New World crops like corn and the potato, along with the discovery of chemical fertilizers, helped banish starvation in Europe. Growing cities remained cesspools of disease at first, but from the mid-19th century on, sewers began to channel human waste away from drinking water, which was then filtered and chlorinated; that dramatically reduced the spread of cholera and typhus.

Moreover in 1798, the same year that Malthus published his dyspeptic tract, his compatriot Edward Jenner described a vaccine for smallpox—the first and most important in a series of vaccines and antibiotics that, along with better nutrition and sanitation, would double life expectancy in the industrializing countries, from 35 years to 77 today. It would take a cranky person to see that trend as gloomy: "The development of medical science was the straw that broke the camel's back," wrote Stanford population biologist Paul Ehrlich in 1968.

Ehrlich's book, *The Population Bomb,* made him the most famous of modern Malthusians. In the 1970s, Ehrlich predicted, "hundreds of millions of people are going to starve to death," and it was too late to do anything about it. "The cancer of population growth . . . must be cut out," Ehrlich wrote, "by compulsion if voluntary methods fail." The very future of the United States was at risk. In spite or perhaps because of such language, the book was a best seller, as Malthus's had been. And this time too the bomb proved a dud. The green revolution—a combination of high-yield seeds, irrigation, pesticides, and fertilizers that enabled grain production to double—was already under way. Today many people are undernourished, but mass starvation is rare.

Ehrlich was right, though, that population would surge as medical science spared many lives. After World War II the developing countries got a sudden transfusion of preventive care, with the help of institutions like the World Health Organization and UNICEF. Penicillin, the smallpox vaccine, DDT (which, though later controversial, saved millions from dying of malaria)—all arrived at once. In India life expectancy went from 38 years in 1952 to 64 today; in China, from 41 to 73. Millions of people in developing countries who would have died in childhood survived to have children themselves. That's why the population explosion spread around the planet: because a great many people were saved from dying.

And because, for a time, women kept giving birth at a high rate. In 18th-century Europe or early 20th-century Asia, when the average woman had six children, she was doing what it took to replace herself and her mate, because most of those children never reached adulthood. When child mortality declines, couples eventually have fewer children—but that transition usually takes a generation at the very least. Today in developed countries, an average of 2.1 births per woman would maintain a steady population; in the developing world, "replacement fertility" is somewhat higher. In the time it takes for the birthrate to settle into that new balance with the death rate, population explodes.

When child mortality declines, couples eventually have fewer children—but that transition takes a generation.

Demographers call this evolution the demographic transition. All countries go through it in their own time. It's a hallmark of human progress: In a country that has completed the transition, people have wrested from nature at least some control over death and birth. The global population explosion is an inevitable side effect, a huge one that some people are not sure our civilization can survive. But the growth rate was actually at its peak just as Ehrlich was sounding his alarm. By the early 1970s, fertility rates around the world had begun dropping faster than anyone had anticipated. Since then, the population growth rate has fallen by more than 40 percent.

The fertility decline that is now sweeping the planet started at different times in different countries. France was one of the first. By the early 18th century, noblewomen at the French court were knowing carnal pleasures without bearing more than two children. They often relied on the same method Leeuwenhoek used for his studies: withdrawal, or coitus interruptus. Village parish records show the trend had spread to the peasantry by the late 18th century; by the end of the 19th, fertility in France had fallen to three children per woman—without the help of modern contraceptives. The key innovation was conceptual, not contraceptive, says Gilles Pison of the National Institute for Demographic Studies in Paris. Until the Enlightenment, "the number of children you had, it was God who decided. People couldn't fathom that it might be up to them."

Other countries in the West eventually followed France's lead. By the onset of World War II, fertility had fallen close to the replacement level in parts of Europe and the U.S. Then, after the surprising blip known as the baby boom, came the bust, again catching demographers off guard. They assumed some instinct would lead women to keep having enough children to ensure the survival of the species. Instead, in country after developed country, the fertility rate fell below replacement level. In the late 1990s in Europe it fell to 1.4. "The evidence I'm familiar with, which is anecdotal, is that women couldn't care less about replacing the species," Joel Cohen says.

The end of a baby boom can have two big economic effects on a country. The first is the "demographic dividend"—a blissful few decades when the boomers swell the labor force and the number of young and old dependents is relatively small, and there is thus a lot of money for other things. Then the second effect kicks in: The boomers start to retire. What had been considered the enduring demographic order is revealed to be a party that has to end. The sharpening American debate over Social Security and last year's strikes in France over increasing the retirement age are responses to a problem that exists throughout the developed world: how to support an aging population. "In 2050 will there be enough people working to pay for pensions?" asks Frans Willekens, director of the Netherlands Interdisciplinary Demographic Institute in The Hague. "The answer is no."

In industrialized countries it took generations for fertility to fall to the replacement level or below. As that same transition takes place in the rest of the world, what has astonished demographers is how much faster it is happening there. Though its population continues to grow, China, home to a fifth of the world's people, is already below replacement fertility and has been for nearly 20 years, thanks in part to the coercive one-child policy implemented in 1979; Chinese women, who were bearing an average of six children each as recently as 1965, are now having around 1.5. In Iran, with the support of the Islamic regime, fertility has fallen more than 70 percent since the early '80s. In Catholic and democratic Brazil, women have reduced their fertility rate by half over the same quarter century. "We still don't understand why fertility has gone down so fast in so many societies, so many cultures and religions. It's just mind-boggling," says Hania Zlotnik, director of the UN Population Division.

"At this moment, much as I want to say there's still a problem of high fertility rates, it's only about 16 percent of the world population, mostly in Africa," says Zlotnik. South of the Sahara, fertility is still five children per woman; in Niger it is seven. But then, 17 of the countries in the region still have life expectancies of 50 or less; they have just begun the demographic transition. In most of the world, however, family size has shrunk dramatically. The UN projects that the world will reach replacement fertility by 2030. "The population as a whole is on a path toward nonexplosion—which is good news," Zlotnik says.

The bad news is that 2030 is two decades away and that the largest generation of adolescents in history will then be entering their childbearing years. Even if each of those women has only two children, population will coast upward under its own momentum for another quarter century. Is a train wreck in the offing, or will people then be able to live humanely and in a way that doesn't destroy their environment? One thing is certain: Close to one in six of them will live in India.

> *I have understood the population explosion intellectually for a long time. I came to understand it emotionally one stinking hot night in Delhi a couple of years ago. . . . The temperature was well over 100, and the air was a haze of dust and smoke. The streets seemed alive with people. People eating, people washing, people sleeping. People visiting, arguing, and screaming. People thrusting their hands through the taxi window, begging. People defecating and urinating. People clinging to buses. People herding animals. People, people, people, people.*
>
> —Paul Ehrlich

In 1966, when Ehrlich took that taxi ride, there were around half a billion Indians. There are 1.2 billion now. Delhi's population has increased even faster, to around 22 million, as people have flooded in from small towns and villages and crowded into sprawling shantytowns. Early last June in the stinking hot city, the summer monsoon had not yet arrived to wash the dust from the innumerable construction sites, which only added to the dust that blows in from the deserts of Rajasthan. On the new divided highways that funnel people into the unplanned city, oxcarts were heading the wrong way in the fast lane. Families of four cruised on motorbikes, the women's scarves flapping like vivid pennants, toddlers dangling from their arms. Families of a dozen or more sardined themselves into buzzing, bumblebee-colored auto rickshaws designed for two passengers. In the stalled traffic, amputees and wasted little children cried for alms. Delhi today is boomingly different from the city Ehrlich visited, and it is also very much the same.

At Lok Nayak Hospital, on the edge of the chaotic and densely peopled nest of lanes that is Old Delhi, a human tide flows through the entrance gate every morning and crowds inside on the lobby floor. "Who could see this and not be worried about the population of India?" a surgeon named Chandan Bortamuly asked one afternoon as he made his way toward his vasectomy clinic. "Population is our biggest problem." Removing the padlock from the clinic door, Bortamuly stepped into a small operating room. Inside, two men lay stretched out on examination tables, their testicles poking up through holes in the green sheets. A ceiling fan pushed cool air from two window units around the room.

Bortamuly is on the front lines of a battle that has been going on in India for nearly 60 years. In 1952, just five years after it gained independence from Britain, India became the first country to establish a policy for population control. Since then the government has repeatedly set ambitious goals—and repeatedly missed them by a mile. A national policy adopted in 2000 called for the country to reach the replacement fertility of 2.1 by 2010. That won't happen for at least another decade. In the UN's medium projection, India's population will rise to just over 1.6 billion people by 2050. "What's inevitable is that India is going to exceed the population of China by 2030," says A. R. Nanda, former head of the Population Foundation of India, an advocacy group. "Nothing less than a huge catastrophe, nuclear or otherwise, can change that."

China is already below replacement fertility, thanks in part to its coercive one-child policy.

Sterilization is the dominant form of birth control in India today, and the vast majority of the procedures are performed on women. The government is trying to change that; a no-scalpel vasectomy costs far less and is easier on a man than a tubal ligation is on a woman. In the operating theater Bortamuly worked quickly. "They say the needle pricks like an ant bite," he explained, when the first patient flinched at the local anesthetic. "After that it's basically painless, bloodless surgery." Using the pointed tip of a forceps, Bortamuly made a tiny hole in the skin of the scrotum and pulled out an oxbow of white, stringy vas deferens—the sperm conduit from the patient's right testicle. He tied off both ends of the oxbow with fine black thread, snipped them, and pushed them back under the skin. In less than seven minutes—a nurse timed him—the patient was walking out without so much as a Band-Aid. The government will pay him an incentive fee of 1,100 rupees (around $25), a week's wages for a laborer.

The Indian government tried once before to push vasectomies, in the 1970s, when anxiety about the population bomb was at its height. Prime Minister Indira Gandhi and her son Sanjay used state-of-emergency powers to force a dramatic increase in sterilizations. From 1976 to 1977 the number of operations tripled, to more than eight million. Over six million of those were vasectomies. Family planning workers were pressured to meet quotas; in a few states, sterilization became a condition for receiving new housing or other government benefits.

In some cases the police simply rounded up poor people and hauled them to sterilization camps.

The excesses gave the whole concept of family planning a bad name. "Successive governments refused to touch the subject," says Shailaja Chandra, former head of the National Population Stabilisation Fund (NPSF). Yet fertility in India has dropped anyway, though not as fast as in China, where it was nose-diving even before the draconian one-child policy took effect. The national average in India is now 2.6 children per woman, less than half what it was when Ehrlich visited. The southern half of the country and a few states in the northern half are already at replacement fertility or below.

In Kerala, on the southwest coast, investments in health and education helped fertility fall to 1.7. The key, demographers there say, is the female literacy rate: At around 90 percent, it's easily the highest in India. Girls who go to school start having children later than ones who don't. They are more open to contraception and more likely to understand their options.

So far this approach, held up as a model internationally, has not caught on in the poor states of northern India—in the "Hindi belt" that stretches across the country just south of Delhi. Nearly half of India's population growth is occurring in Rajasthan, Madhya Pradesh, Bihar, and Uttar Pradesh, where fertility rates still hover between three and four children per woman. More than half the women in the Hindi belt are illiterate, and many marry well before reaching the legal age of 18. They gain social status by bearing children—and usually don't stop until they have at least one son.

As an alternative to the Kerala model, some point to the southern state of Andhra Pradesh, where sterilization "camps"—temporary operating rooms often set up in schools—were introduced during the '70s and where sterilization rates have remained high as improved hospitals have replaced the camps. In a single decade beginning in the early 1990s, the fertility rate fell from around three to less than two. Unlike in Kerala, half of all women in Andhra Pradesh remain illiterate.

Amarjit Singh, the current executive director of the NPSF, calculates that if the four biggest states of the Hindi belt had followed the Andhra Pradesh model, they would have avoided 40 million births—and considerable suffering. "Because 40 million were born, 2.5 million children died," Singh says. He thinks if all India were to adopt high-quality programs to encourage sterilizations, in hospitals rather than camps, it could have 1.4 billion people in 2050 instead of 1.6 billion.

Critics of the Andhra Pradesh model, such as the Population Foundation's Nanda, say Indians need better health care, particularly in rural areas. They are against numerical targets that pressure government workers to sterilize people or cash incentives that distort a couple's choice of family size. "It's a private decision," Nanda says.

In Indian cities today, many couples are making the same choice as their counterparts in Europe or America. Sonalde Desai, a senior fellow at New Delhi's National Council of Applied Economic Research, introduced me to five working women in Delhi who were spending most of their salaries on private-school fees and after-school tutors; each had one or two children and was not planning to have more. In a nationwide survey of 41,554 households, Desai's team identified a small but growing vanguard of urban one-child families. "We were totally blown away at the emphasis parents were placing on their children," she says. "It suddenly makes you understand—that is why fertility is going down." Indian children on average are much better educated than their parents.

That's less true in the countryside. With Desai's team I went to Palanpur, a village in Uttar Pradesh—a Hindi-belt state with as many people as Brazil. Walking into the village we passed a cell phone tower but also rivulets of raw sewage running along the lanes of small brick houses. Under a mango tree, the keeper of the grove said he saw no reason to educate his three daughters. Under a neem tree in the center of the village, I asked a dozen farmers what would improve their lives most. "If we could get a little money, that would be wonderful," one joked.

The goal in India should not be reducing fertility or population, Almas Ali of the Population Foundation told me when I spoke to him a few days later. "The goal should be to make the villages livable," he said. "Whenever we talk of population in India, even today, what comes to our mind is the increasing numbers. And the numbers are looked at with fright. This phobia has penetrated the mind-set so much that all the focus is on reducing the number. The focus on people has been pushed to the background."

It was a four-hour drive back to Delhi from Palanpur, through the gathering night of a Sunday. We sat in traffic in one market town after another, each one hopping with activity that sometimes engulfed the car. As we came down a viaduct into Moradabad, I saw a man pushing a cart up the steep hill, piled with a load so large it blocked his view. I thought of Ehrlich's epiphany on his cab ride all those decades ago. People, people, people, people—yes. But also an overwhelming sense of energy, of striving, of aspiration.

The annual meeting of the Population Association of America (PAA) is one of the premier gatherings of the world's demographers. Last April the global population explosion was not on the agenda. "The problem has become a bit passé," Hervé Le Bras says. Demographers are generally confident that by the second half of this century we will be ending one unique era in history—the population explosion—and entering another, in which population will level out or even fall.

But will there be too many of us? At the PAA meeting, in the Dallas Hyatt Regency, I learned that the current population of the planet could fit into the state of Texas, if Texas were settled as densely as New York City. The comparison made me start thinking like Leeuwenhoek. If in 2045 there are nine billion people living on the six habitable continents, the world population density will be a little more than half that of France today. France is not usually considered a hellish place. Will the world be hellish then?

Some parts of it may well be; some parts of it are hellish today. There are now 21 cities with populations larger than ten million, and by 2050 there will be many more. Delhi adds hundreds of thousands of migrants each year, and those people arrive to find that "no plans have been made for water, sewage, or habitation," says Shailaja Chandra. Dhaka in Bangladesh and Kinshasa in the Democratic Republic of the Congo are 40 times larger today than they were in 1950. Their slums are filled with desperately poor people who have fled worse poverty in the countryside.

Whole countries today face population pressures that seem as insurmountable to us as India's did to Ehrlich in 1966. Bangladesh is among the most densely populated countries in the world and one of the most immediately threatened by climate change; rising seas could displace tens of millions of Bangladeshis. Rwanda is an equally alarming case. In his book *Collapse,* Jared Diamond argued that the genocidal massacre of some 800,000 Rwandans in 1994 was the result of several factors, not only ethnic hatred but also overpopulation—too many farmers dividing the same amount of land into increasingly small pieces that became inadequate to support a farmer's family. "Malthus's worst-case scenario may sometimes be realized," Diamond concluded.

Many people are justifiably worried that Malthus will finally be proved right on a global scale—that the planet won't be able to feed nine billion people. Lester Brown, founder of Worldwatch Institute and now head of the Earth Policy Institute in Washington, believes food shortages could cause a collapse of global civilization. Human beings are living off natural capital, Brown argues, eroding soil and depleting groundwater faster than they can be replenished. All of that will soon be cramping food production. Brown's Plan B to save civilization would put the whole world on a wartime footing, like the U.S. after Pearl Harbor, to stabilize climate and repair the ecological damage. "Filling the family planning gap may be the most urgent item on the global agenda," he writes, so if we don't hold the world's population to eight billion by reducing fertility, the death rate may increase instead.

Eight billion corresponds to the UN's lowest projection for 2050. In that optimistic scenario, Bangladesh has a fertility rate of 1.35 in 2050, but it still has 25 million more people than it does today. Rwanda's fertility rate also falls below the replacement level, but its population still rises to well over twice what it was before the genocide. If that's the optimistic scenario, one might argue, the future is indeed bleak.

But one can also draw a different conclusion—that fixating on population numbers is not the best way to confront the future. People packed into slums need help, but the problem that needs solving is poverty and lack of infrastructure, not overpopulation. Giving every woman access to family planning services is a good idea—"the one strategy that can make the biggest difference to women's lives," Chandra calls it. But the most aggressive population control program imaginable will not save Bangladesh from sea level rise, Rwanda from another genocide, or all of us from our enormous environmental problems.

People packed into slums need help, but the problem that needs solving is poverty, not overpopulation.

Global warming is a good example. Carbon emissions from fossil fuels are growing fastest in China, thanks to its prolonged economic boom, but fertility there is already below replacement; not much more can be done to control population. Where population is growing fastest, in sub-Saharan Africa, emissions per person are only a few percent of what they are in the U.S.—so population control would have little effect on climate. Brian O'Neill of the National Center for Atmospheric Research has calculated that if the population were to reach 7.4 billion in 2050 instead of 8.9 billion, it would reduce emissions by 15 percent. "Those who say the whole problem is population are wrong," Joel Cohen says. "It's not even the dominant factor." To stop global warming we'll have to switch from fossil fuels to alternative energy—regardless of how big the population gets.

The number of people does matter, of course. But how people consume resources matters a lot more. Some of us leave much bigger footprints than others. The central challenge for the future of people and the planet is how to raise more of us out of poverty—the slum dwellers in Delhi, the subsistence farmers in Rwanda—while reducing the impact each of us has on the planet.

The World Bank has predicted that by 2030 more than a billion people in the developing world will belong to the "global middle class," up from just 400 million in 2005. That's a good thing. But it will be a hard thing for the planet if those people are eating meat and driving gasoline-powered cars at the same rate as Americans now do. It's too late to keep the new middle class of 2030 from being born; it's not too late to change how they and the rest of us will produce and consume food and energy. "Eating less meat seems more reasonable to me than saying, 'Have fewer children!' " Le Bras says.

It's too late to keep the new middle class of 2030 from being born. But it's not too late to change the ways we all consume.

How many people can the Earth support? Cohen spent years reviewing all the research, from Leeuwenhoek on. "I wrote the book thinking I would answer the question," he says. "I found out it's unanswerable in the present state of knowledge." What he found instead was an enormous range of "political numbers, intended to persuade people" one way or the other.

For centuries population pessimists have hurled apocalyptic warnings at the congenital optimists, who believe in their bones that humanity will find ways to cope and even improve its lot. History, on the whole, has so far favored the optimists, but history is no certain guide to the future. Neither is science. It cannot predict the outcome of *People* v. *Planet,* because all the facts of the case—how many of us there will be and how we will live—depend on choices we have yet to make and ideas we have yet to have. We may, for example, says Cohen, "see to it that all children are nourished well enough to learn in school and are educated well enough to solve the problems they will face as adults." That would change the future significantly.

The debate was present at the creation of population alarmism, in the person of Rev. Thomas Malthus himself. Toward the end of the book in which he formulated the iron law by which unchecked population growth leads to famine, he declared that law a good thing: It gets us off our duffs. It leads us to conquer the world. Man, Malthus wrote, and he must have meant woman too, is "inert, sluggish, and averse from labour, unless compelled by necessity." But necessity, he added, gives hope:

"The exertions that men find it necessary to make, in order to support themselves or families, frequently awaken faculties that might otherwise have lain for ever dormant, and it has been commonly remarked that new and extraordinary situations generally create minds adequate to grapple with the difficulties in which they are involved."

Seven billion of us soon, nine billion in 2045. Let's hope that Malthus was right about our ingenuity.

Critical Thinking

1. Why should we be alarmed about continued world population growth?
2. How did Thomas Malthus explain world growth?
3. Discuss the "demographic transition" as an explanation for population growth.
4. How has medical science aided population growth?
5. What is meant by "replacement fertility"? Why do populations continue to expand for a period after reaching replacement fertility?
6. In what parts of the world has fertility fallen significantly? What was the "demographic dividend" and what did it mean for the United States? Where do we still find high fertility rates?
7. What have been some of the key factors in reducing fertility in such places as China and India?
8. Why do critics say is it more important to focus on health, education, and the personal decisions people make regarding fertility rather than on "numerical targets"?
9. Why are many people justifiably worried that Malthus will finally be proved right on a global scale?
10. In what respects do some say the focus on population rather than the environment is wrong? What matters more than simply the number of people, according to the author?
11. In what sense did Malthus express hope?

Internet References

Murray Research Center
www.radcliffe.edu/murray_redirect/index.php

Small Planet Institute
www.smallplanet.org/food

Robert Kunzig is *National Geographic*'s senior editor for the environment.